The Demon Girl Next Door

03

story & art by Izumo Ito

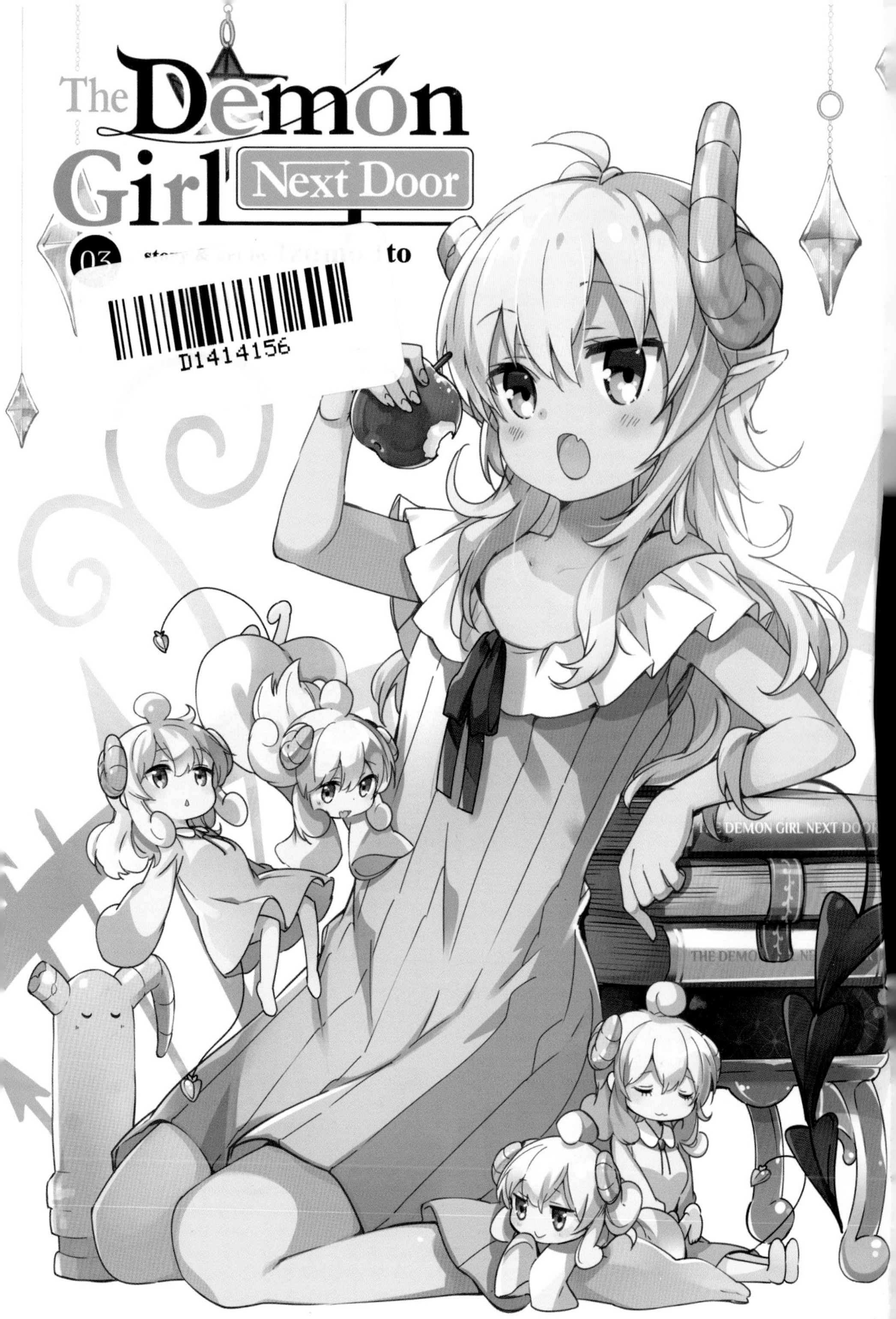

THE DEMON GIRL NEXT DOOR
THE DEMO   L NE

THE DEMON GIRL NEXT DOOR

CHARACTERS

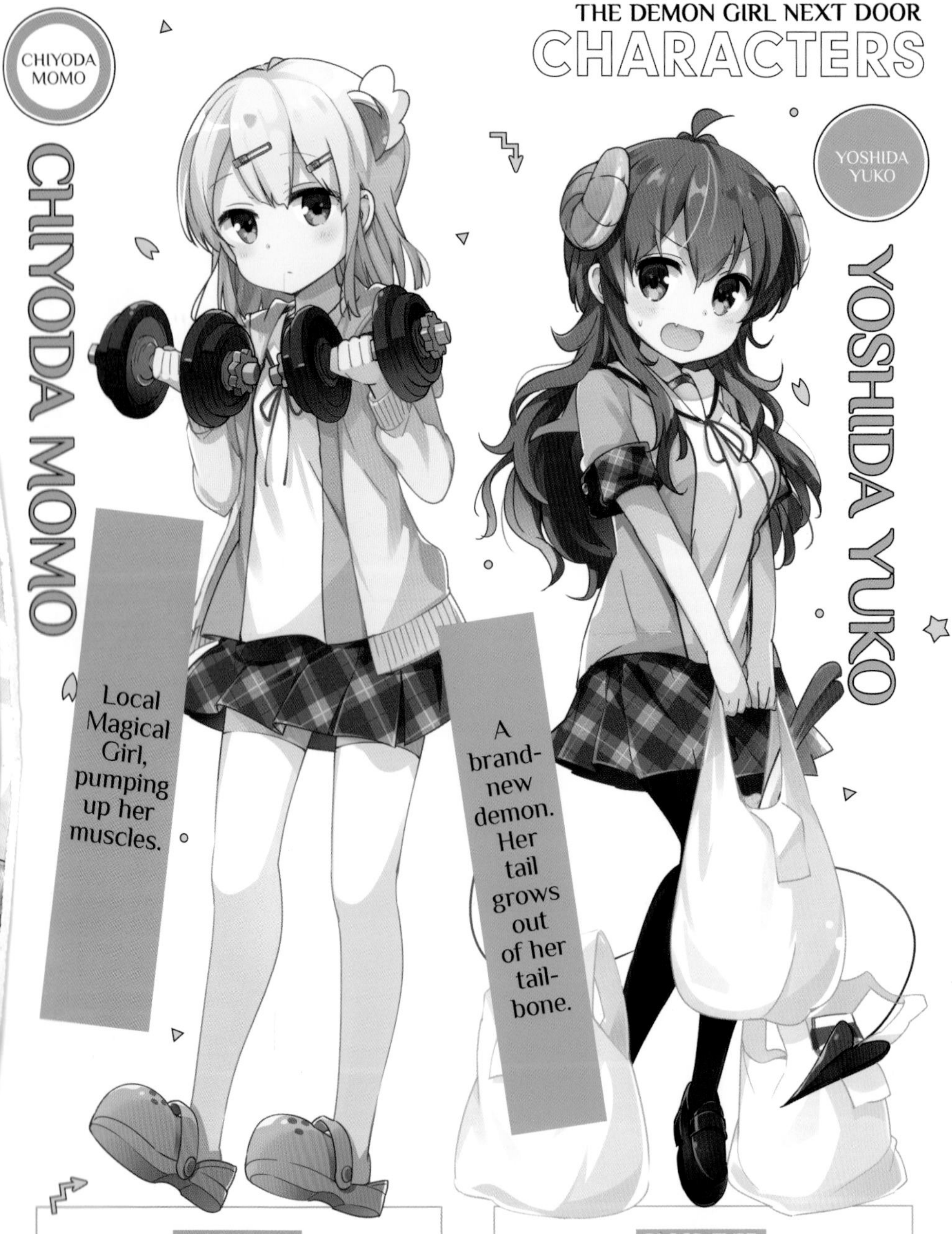
CHIYODA MOMO
CHIYODA MOMO
Local Magical Girl, pumping up her muscles.
YOSHIDA YUKO
YOSHIDA YUKO
A brand-new demon. Her tail grows out of her tail-bone.

BLOOD TYPE

It's A.

HOW I SPEND DAYS OFF

Weight training.

Also, watching videos online and stuff.

BLOOD TYPE

Mine is O.

HOW I SPEND DAYS OFF

Lately I haven't *had* any days off at all.

I have to defeat a Magical Girl!

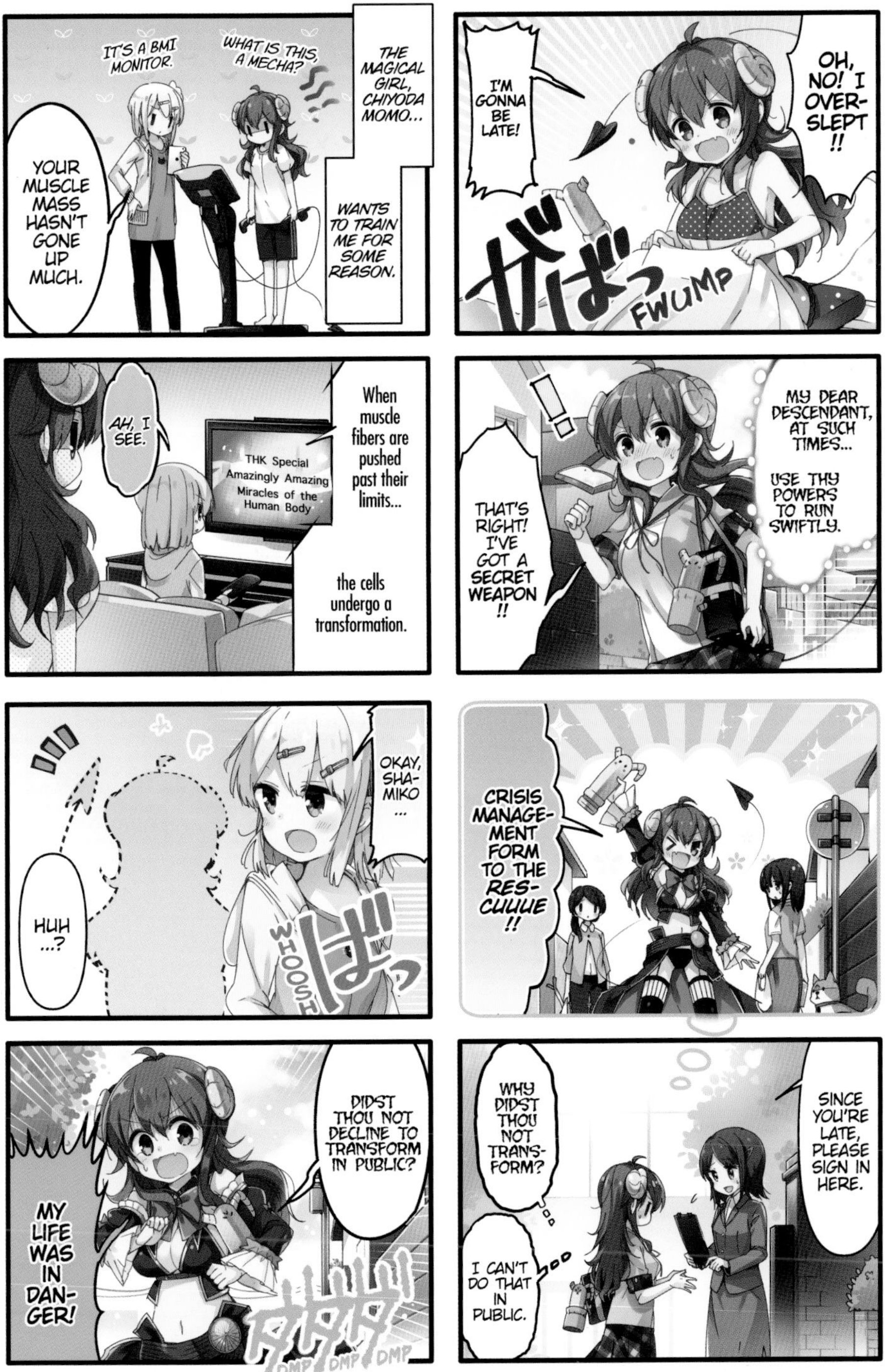
OH, NO! I OVERSLEPT!!
I'M GONNA BE LATE!
がばっ
FWUMP
MY DEAR DESCENDANT, AT SUCH TIMES...
USE THY POWERS TO RUN SWIFTLY.
THAT'S RIGHT! I'VE GOT A SECRET WEAPON!!
CRISIS MANAGEMENT FORM TO THE RESCUUUE!!
SINCE YOU'RE LATE, PLEASE SIGN IN HERE.
WHY DIDST THOU NOT TRANSFORM?
I CAN'T DO THAT IN PUBLIC.
THE MAGICAL GIRL, CHIYODA MOMO...
WANTS TO TRAIN ME FOR SOME REASON.
WHAT IS THIS, A MECHA?
IT'S A BMI MONITOR.
YOUR MUSCLE MASS HASN'T GONE UP MUCH.
When muscle fibers are pushed past their limits...
the cells undergo a transformation.
THK Special Amazingly Amazing Miracles of the Human Body
AH, I SEE.
OKAY, SHAMIKO...
ばっ
WHOOSH
HUH...?
DIDST THOU NOT DECLINE TO TRANSFORM IN PUBLIC?
MY LIFE WAS IN DANGER!
DMP DMP DMP

HINATSUKI MIKAN

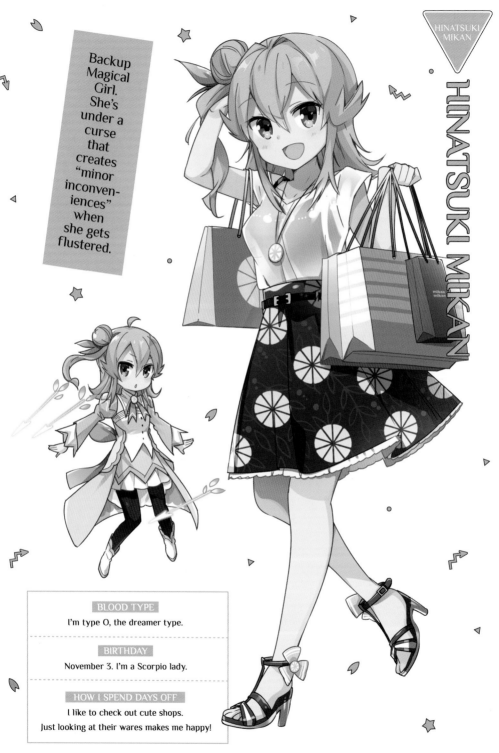

HINATSUKI MIKAN

Backup Magical Girl. She's under a curse that creates "minor inconveniences" when she gets flustered.

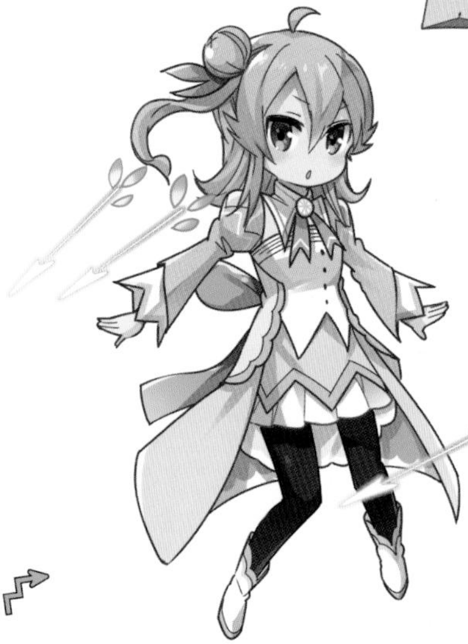

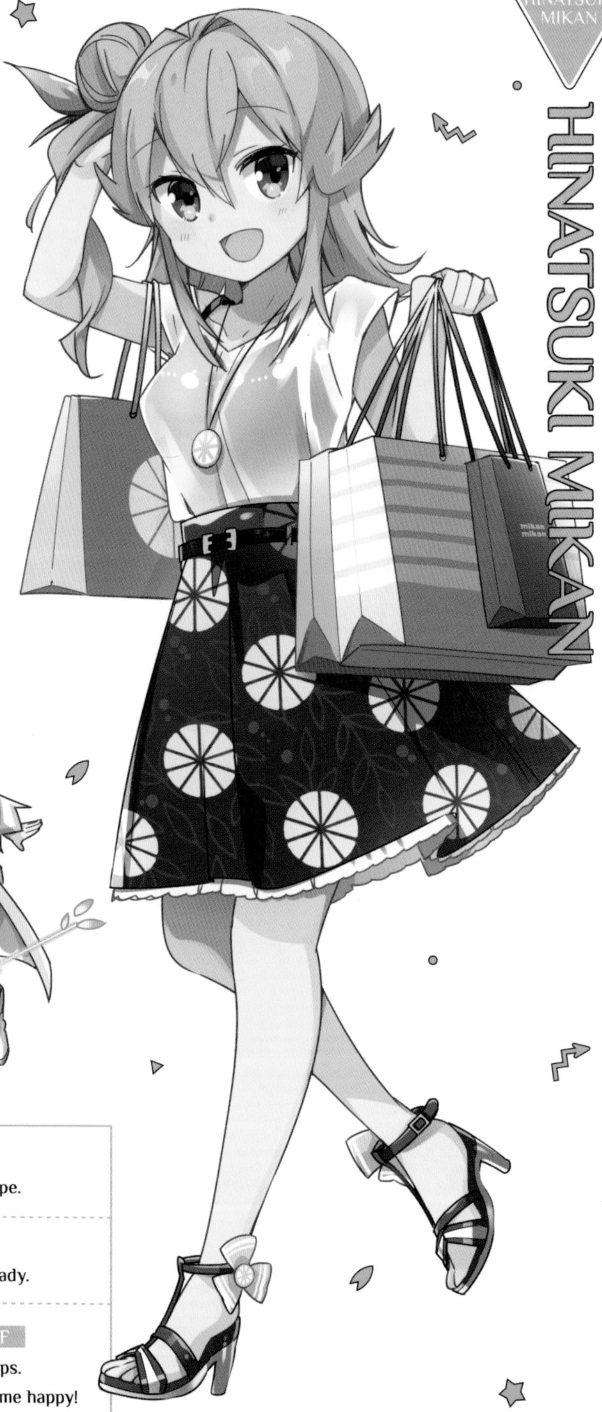
mikan mikan

BLOOD TYPE

I'm type O, the dreamer type.

BIRTHDAY

November 3. I'm a Scorpio lady.

HOW I SPEND DAYS OFF

I like to check out cute shops.
Just looking at their wares makes me happy!

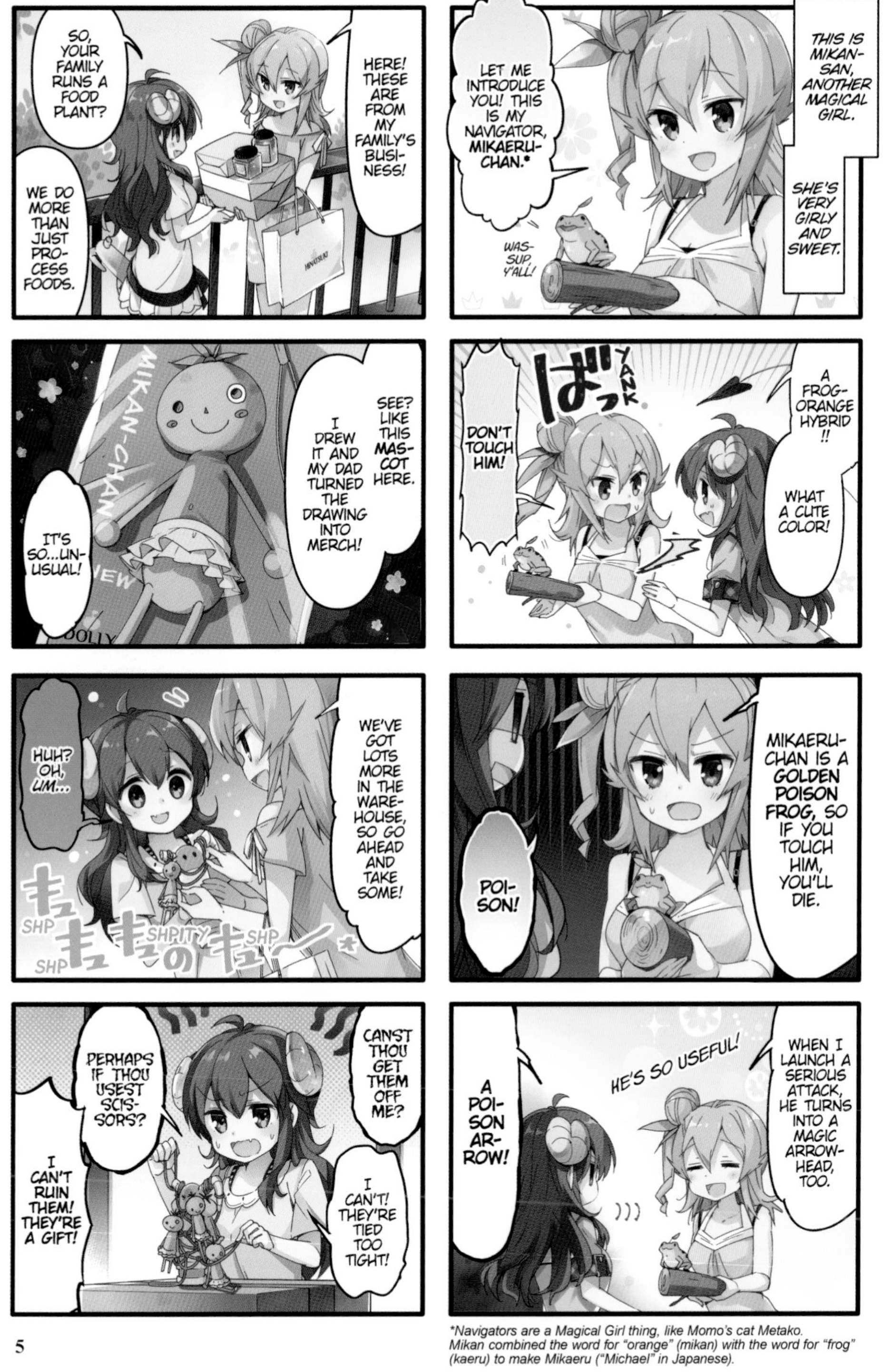

THIS IS MIKAN-SAN, ANOTHER MAGICAL GIRL.
SHE'S VERY GIRLY AND SWEET.
LET ME INTRODUCE YOU! THIS IS MY NAVIGATOR, MIKAERU-CHAN.*
WAS-SUP, Y'ALL!
A FROG-ORANGE HYBRID !!
WHAT A CUTE COLOR!
ぱっ YANK
DON'T TOUCH HIM!
MIKAERU-CHAN IS A GOLDEN POISON FROG, SO IF YOU TOUCH HIM, YOU'LL DIE.
POI-SON!
WHEN I LAUNCH A SERIOUS ATTACK, HE TURNS INTO A MAGIC ARROW-HEAD, TOO.
HE'S SO USEFUL!
A POI-SON AR-ROW!
HERE! THESE ARE FROM MY FAMILY'S BUSI-NESS!
SO, YOUR FAMILY RUNS A FOOD PLANT?
WE DO MORE THAN JUST PRO-CESS FOODS.
SEE? LIKE THIS MAS-COT HERE.
I DREW IT AND MY DAD TURNED THE DRAWING INTO MERCH!
MIKAN-CHAN
IT'S SO...UN-USUAL!
WE'VE GOT LOTS MORE IN THE WARE-HOUSE, SO GO AHEAD AND TAKE SOME!
HUH? OH, UM...
キュキュキュのキュ〜
SHP SHPITY SHP SHP SHP
CANST THOU GET THEM OFF ME?
I CAN'T! THEY'RE TIED TOO TIGHT!
PERHAPS IF THOU USEST SCIS-SORS?
I CAN'T RUIN THEM! THEY'RE A GIFT!

*Navigators are a Magical Girl thing, like Momo's cat Metako. Mikan combined the word for "orange" (mikan) with the word for "frog" (kaeru) to make Mikaeru ("Michael" in Japanese).

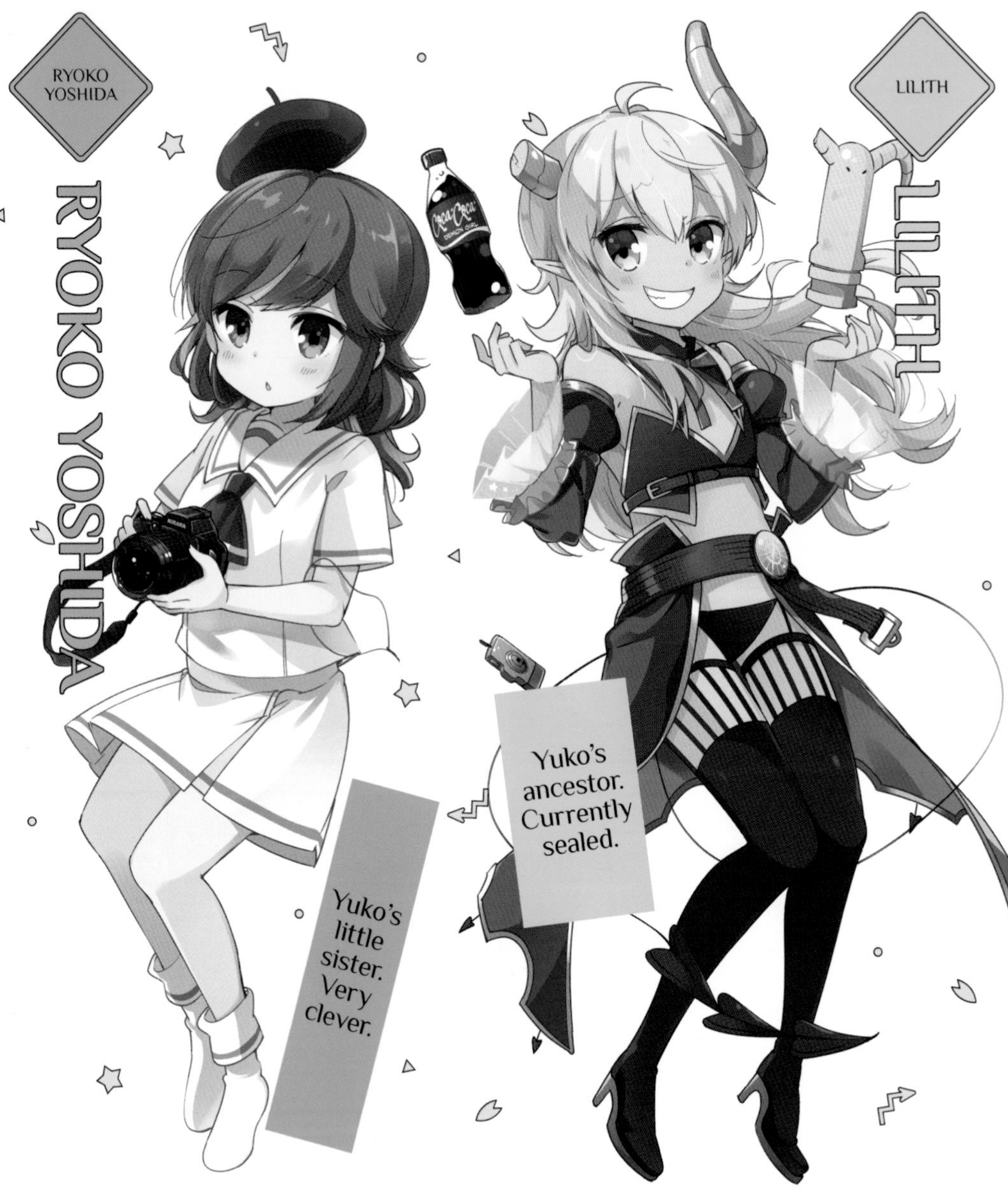
RYOKO YOSHIDA
RYOKO YOSHIDA
Yuko's little sister. Very clever.
LILITH
LILITH
Yuko's ancestor. Currently sealed.

BLOOD TYPE

A. I'm a little sad it's not the same as my sister's.

BIRTHDAY

I was born on January 7,
but I've never eaten seven-herb rice porridge.*

WHAT I DO ON DAYS OFF

I'd like to do a photoshoot of my big sis,
if she can ever spare the time.

BLOOD TYPE

There were no blood tests in ancient Mesopotamia.

BIRTHDAY

Ancient Mesopotamia did not use today's calendar.

WHAT I DO ON DAYS OFF

Every day is a holiday
in my seal space.

**There's a Japanese tradition of eating seven-herb rice porridge (nanakusa gayu) on the seventh day of the year for good health. The porridge contains seven wild spring herbs.*

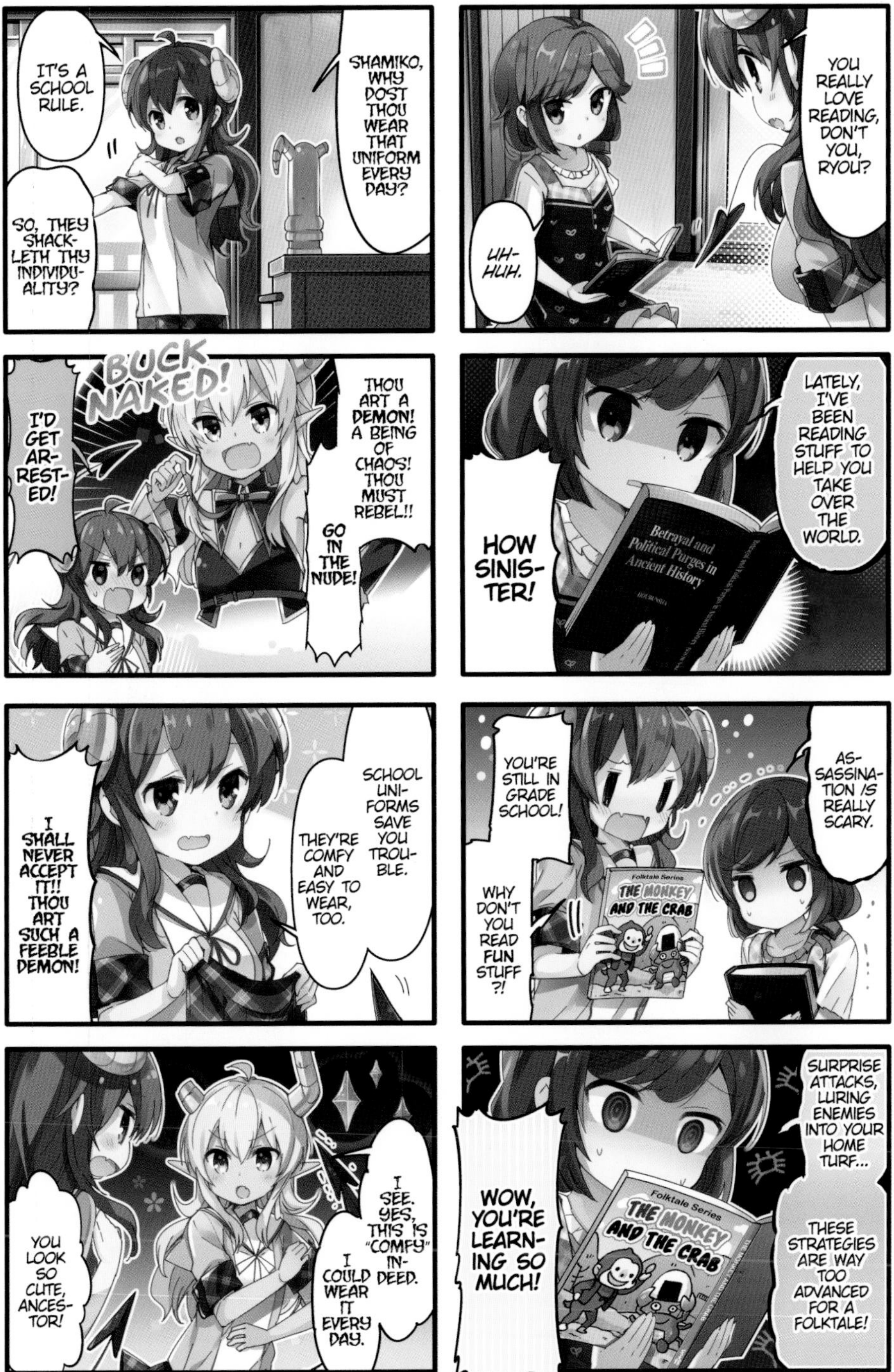
YOU REALLY LOVE READING, DON'T YOU, RYOU?
UH-HUH.
LATELY, I'VE BEEN READING STUFF TO HELP YOU TAKE OVER THE WORLD.
Betrayal and Political Purges in Ancient History
HOW SINISTER!
ASSASSINATION IS REALLY SCARY.
YOU'RE STILL IN GRADE SCHOOL!
WHY DON'T YOU READ FUN STUFF?!
Folktale Series
THE MONKEY AND THE CRAB
SURPRISE ATTACKS, LURING ENEMIES INTO YOUR HOME TURF...
THESE STRATEGIES ARE WAY TOO ADVANCED FOR A FOLKTALE!
WOW, YOU'RE LEARNING SO MUCH!
Folktale Series
THE MONKEY AND THE CRAB
SHAMIKO, WHY DOST THOU WEAR THAT UNIFORM EVERY DAY?
IT'S A SCHOOL RULE.
SO, THEY SHACKLETH THY INDIVIDUALITY?
THOU ART A DEMON! A BEING OF CHAOS! THOU MUST REBEL!!
GO IN THE NUDE!
BUCK NAKED!
I'D GET ARRESTED!
SCHOOL UNIFORMS SAVE YOU TROUBLE.
THEY'RE COMFY AND EASY TO WEAR, TOO.
I SHALL NEVER ACCEPT IT!! THOU ART SUCH A FEEBLE DEMON!
I SEE. YES, THIS IS "COMFY" INDEED.
I COULD WEAR IT EVERY DAY.
YOU LOOK SO CUTE, ANCESTOR!

SAKURAGAOKA SIGHTSEEING GUIDE

TAMA HEALTH SPA

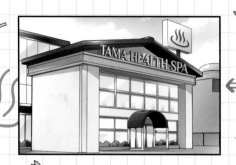

TAMA HEALTH SPA

THE BIGGEST BATHHOUSE IN TOWN, WITH A GYM, POOL, AND HOT SPRINGS. THEY SAY HITTING THE HOT SPRINGS AFTER A WORKOUT MAKES FOR A SATISFYING DAY!

TAMASAKURA SHOPPING DISTRICT

AN OLD SHOPPING DISTRICT NEAR THE TRAIN STATION'S EAST EXIT. THERE ARE MANY UNIQUE RETRO STORES. TOGETHER WITH THE NEW SHOPPING CENTER WEST OF THE STATION, THEY'VE BEEN LIVENING UP THE TOWN WITH A NEW MASCOT CHARACTER AND FUN EVENTS.

TAMASAKURA
ITOU

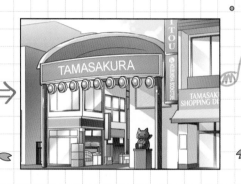

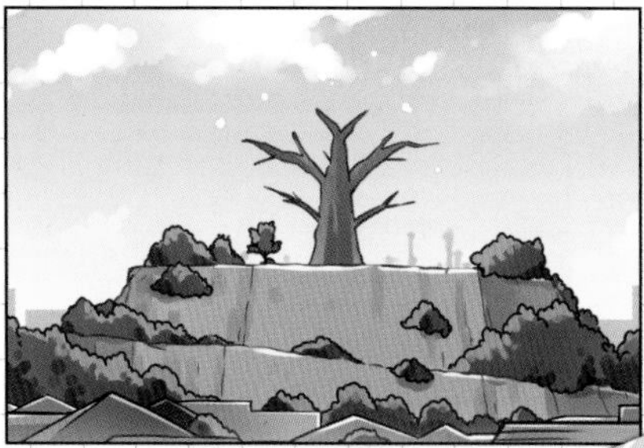

SAKURAGAOKA PARK

A HIGH-ELEVATION PARK THAT OVERLOOKS THE WHOLE TOWN.
ITS GREAT VIEWS MAKE IT THE PERFECT PICNIC SPOT.

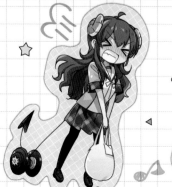

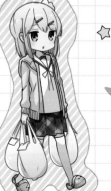

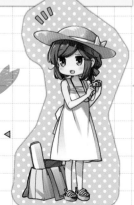

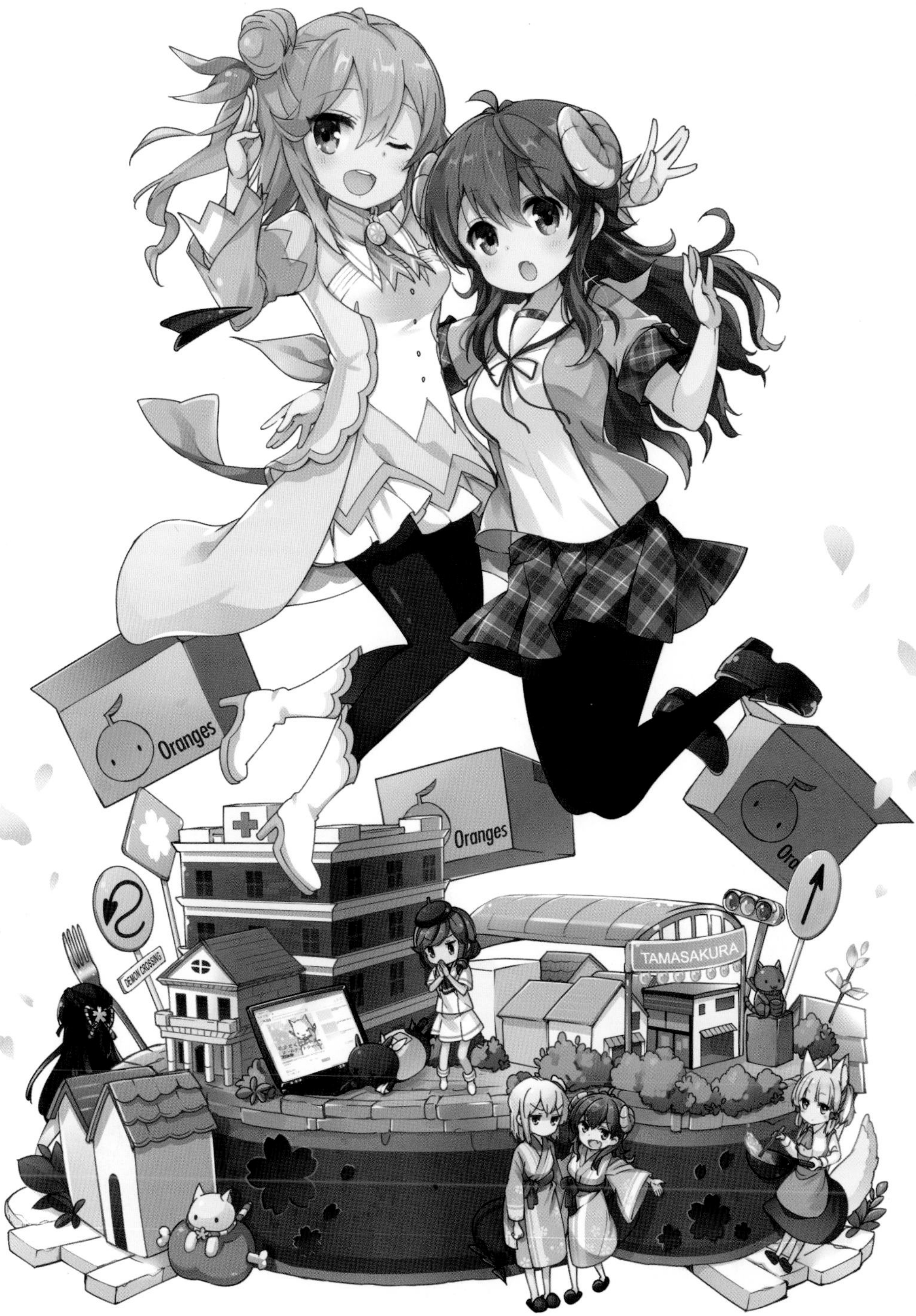
Oranges
Oranges
Ora
DEMON CROSSING
TAMASAKURA

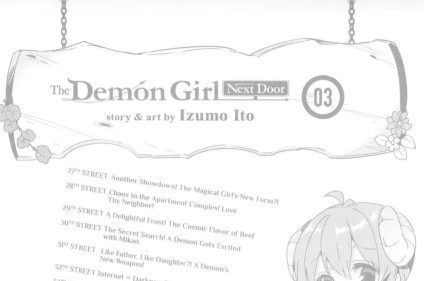

The Demon Girl Next Door 03

story & art by Izumo Ito

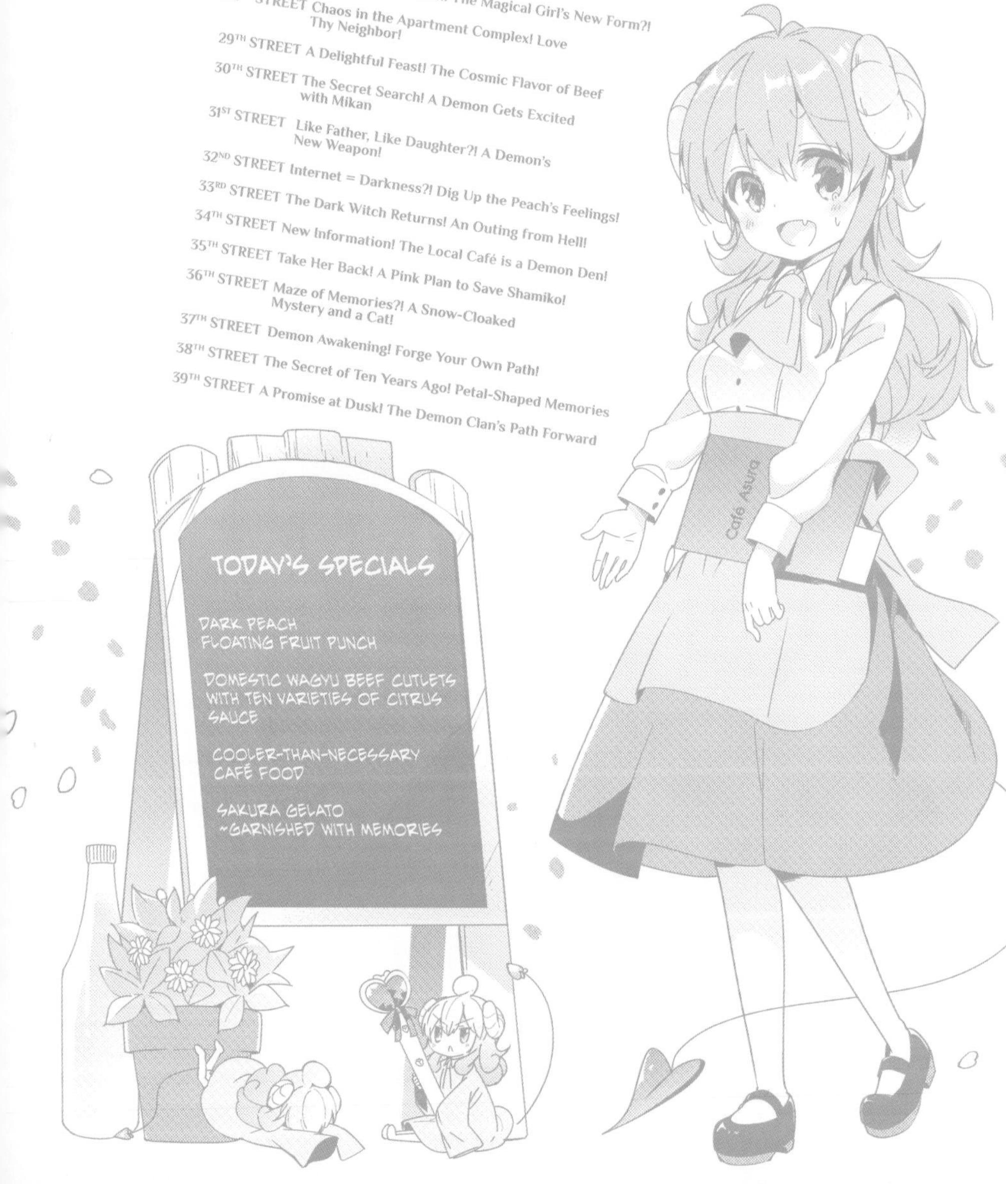
TODAY'S SPECIALS
DARK PEACH
FLOATING FRUIT PUNCH
DOMESTIC WAGYU BEEF CUTLETS
WITH TEN VARIETIES OF CITRUS
SAUCE
COOLER-THAN-NECESSARY
CAFÉ FOOD
SAKURA GELATO
~GARNISHED WITH MEMORIES
Café Asura

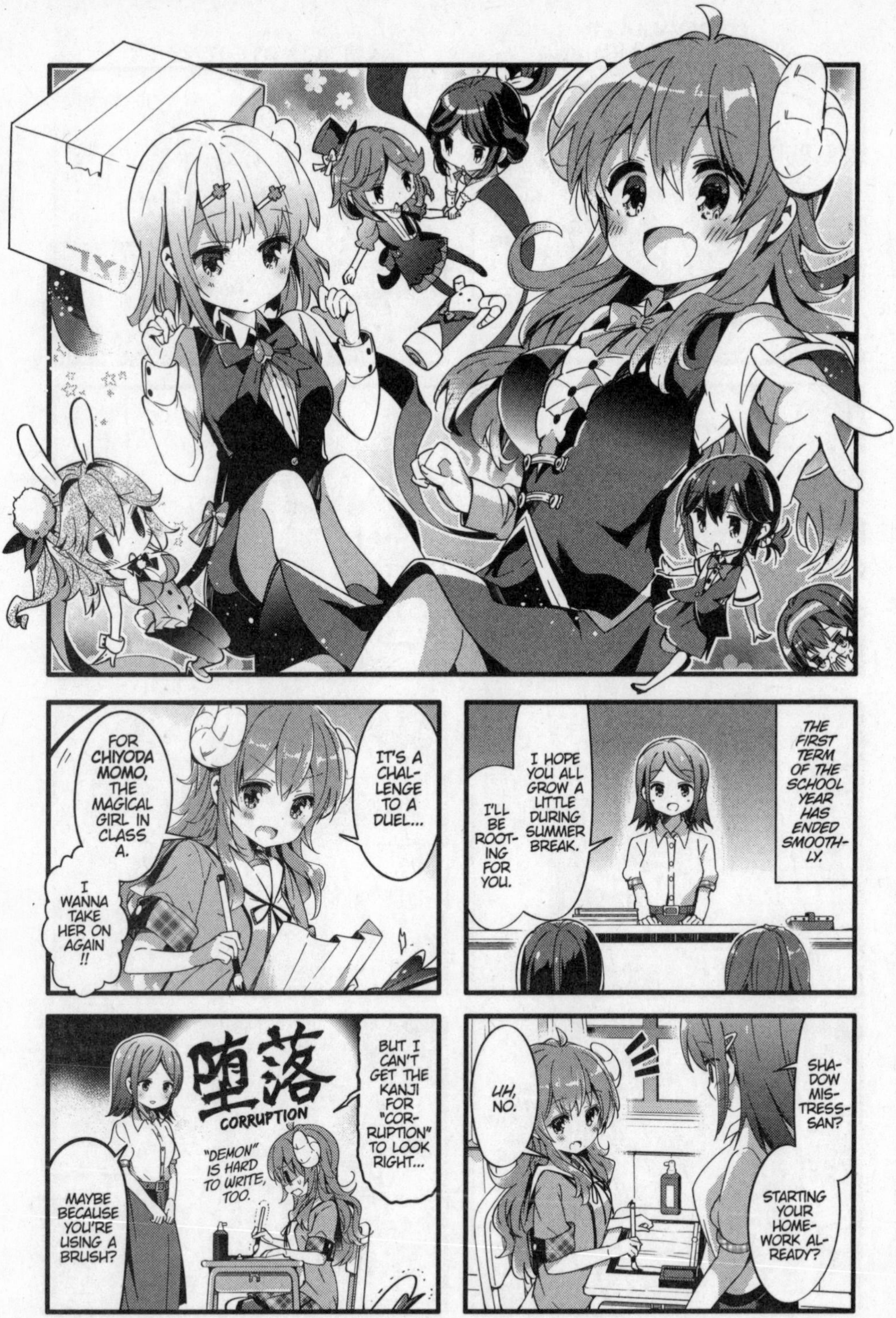
THE FIRST TERM OF THE SCHOOL YEAR HAS ENDED SMOOTHLY.
I HOPE YOU ALL GROW A LITTLE DURING SUMMER BREAK.
I'LL BE ROOTING FOR YOU.
IT'S A CHALLENGE TO A DUEL...
FOR CHIYODA MOMO, THE MAGICAL GIRL IN CLASS A.
I WANNA TAKE HER ON AGAIN!!
SHADOW MISTRESS-SAN?
UH, NO.
STARTING YOUR HOMEWORK ALREADY?
BUT I CAN'T GET THE KANJI FOR "CORRUPTION" TO LOOK RIGHT...
堕落
CORRUPTION
"DEMON" IS HARD TO WRITE, TOO.
MAYBE BECAUSE YOU'RE USING A BRUSH?

A PERCEPTIVE TEACHER

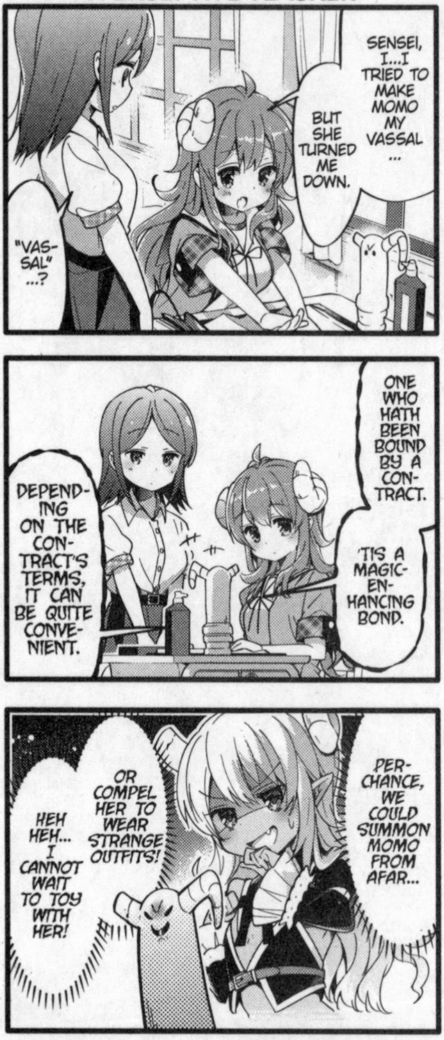
SENSEI, I...I TRIED TO MAKE MOMO MY VASSAL...
BUT SHE TURNED ME DOWN.
"VASSAL"...?
ONE WHO HATH BEEN BOUND BY A CONTRACT.
'TIS A MAGIC-ENHANCING BOND.
DEPENDING ON THE CONTRACT'S TERMS, IT CAN BE QUITE CONVENIENT.
PERCHANCE, WE COULD SUMMON MOMO FROM AFAR...
OR COMPEL HER TO WEAR STRANGE OUTFITS!
HEH HEH... I CANNOT WAIT TO TOY WITH HER!
LILITH-SAN SEEMS TO HAVE... MINOR ISSUES ABOUT BEING A GUARDIAN.
LET ME TAKE HER FOR A LITTLE CHAT.
WHAT'S THIS?
SHFF

ONLY VAGUELY AWARE OF THE MEANING

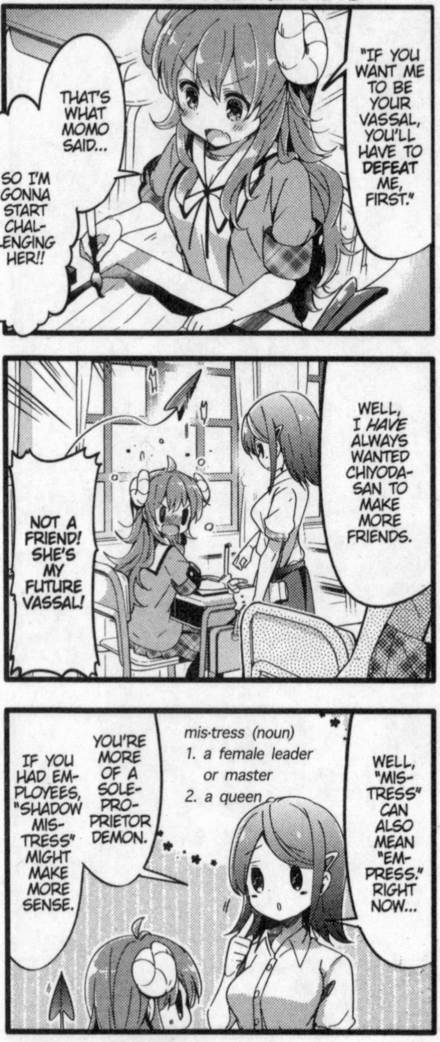
"IF YOU WANT ME TO BE YOUR VASSAL, YOU'LL HAVE TO DEFEAT ME, FIRST."
THAT'S WHAT MOMO SAID...
SO I'M GONNA START CHALLENGING HER!!
WELL, I *HAVE* ALWAYS WANTED CHIYODA-SAN TO MAKE MORE FRIENDS.
NOT A FRIEND! SHE'S MY FUTURE VASSAL!
WELL, "MISTRESS" CAN ALSO MEAN "EMPRESS." RIGHT NOW...
mis·tress (noun) 1. a female leader or master 2. a queen
YOU'RE MORE OF A SOLE-PROPRIETOR DEMON.
IF YOU HAD EMPLOYEES, "SHADOW MISTRESS" MIGHT MAKE MORE SENSE.
SO, "MISTRESS" CAN MEAN "BOSS," TOO?!
SILLY OL' ME!
WAIT, WHAT?!
YOU DIDN'T KNOW THAT?!

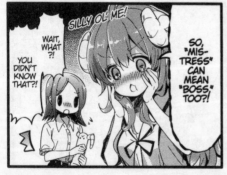

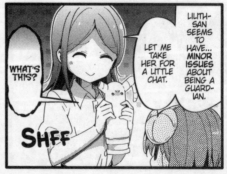

RE: DUELING

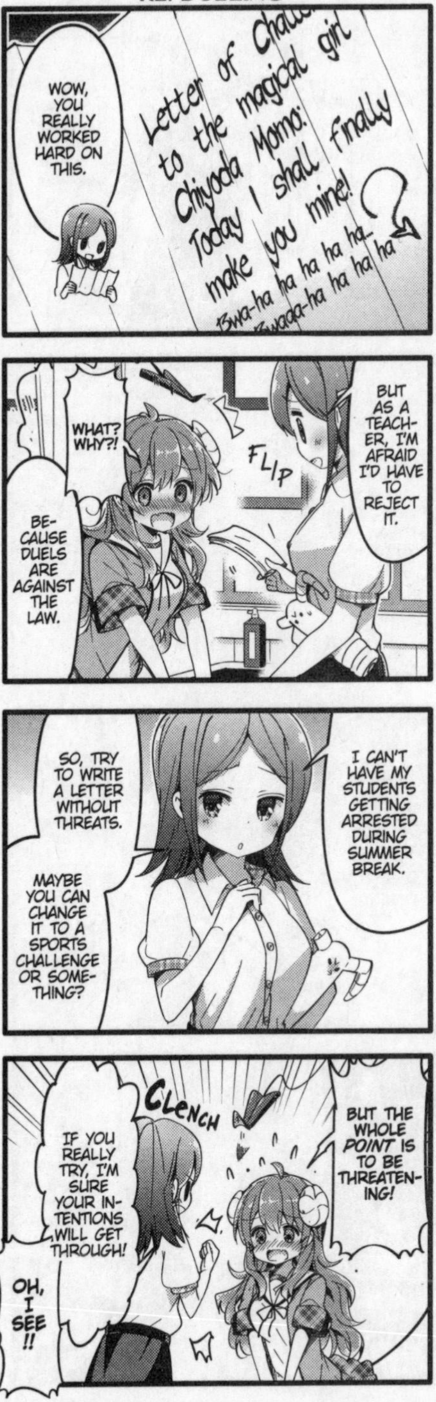
Letter of Chall
to the magical girl
Chiyoda Momo:
Today I shall finally
make you mine!
Bwa-ha ha ha ha...
Bwaaa-ha ha ha ha
WOW, YOU REALLY WORKED HARD ON THIS.
BUT AS A TEACHER, I'M AFRAID I'D HAVE TO REJECT IT.
FLIP
WHAT? WHY?!
BECAUSE DUELS ARE AGAINST THE LAW.
I CAN'T HAVE MY STUDENTS GETTING ARRESTED DURING SUMMER BREAK.
SO, TRY TO WRITE A LETTER WITHOUT THREATS.
MAYBE YOU CAN CHANGE IT TO A SPORTS CHALLENGE OR SOMETHING?
BUT THE WHOLE *POINT* IS TO BE THREATENING!
CLENCH
IF YOU REALLY TRY, I'M SURE YOUR INTENTIONS WILL GET THROUGH!
OH, I SEE!!

A CHALLENGING TOPIC

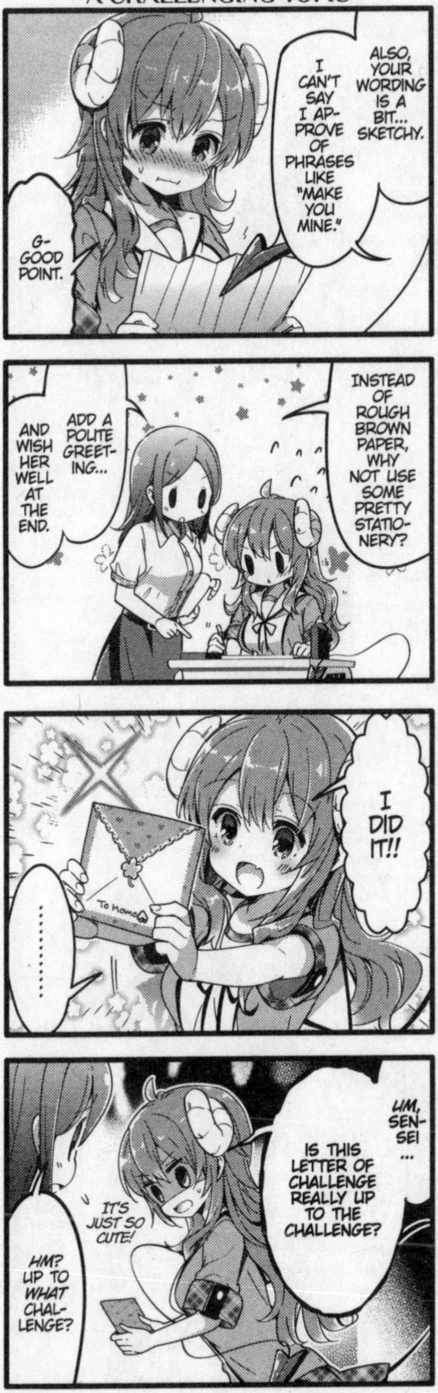
ALSO, YOUR WORDING IS A BIT... SKETCHY.
I CAN'T SAY I APPROVE OF PHRASES LIKE "MAKE YOU MINE."
G-GOOD POINT.
INSTEAD OF ROUGH BROWN PAPER, WHY NOT USE SOME PRETTY STATIONERY?
ADD A POLITE GREETING...
AND WISH HER WELL AT THE END.
I DID IT!!
To Momo
......
UM, SENSEI...
IS THIS LETTER OF CHALLENGE REALLY UP TO THE CHALLENGE?
IT'S JUST SO CUTE!
HM? UP TO *WHAT* CHALLENGE?

THE CHALLENGE OF READING OUT LOUD

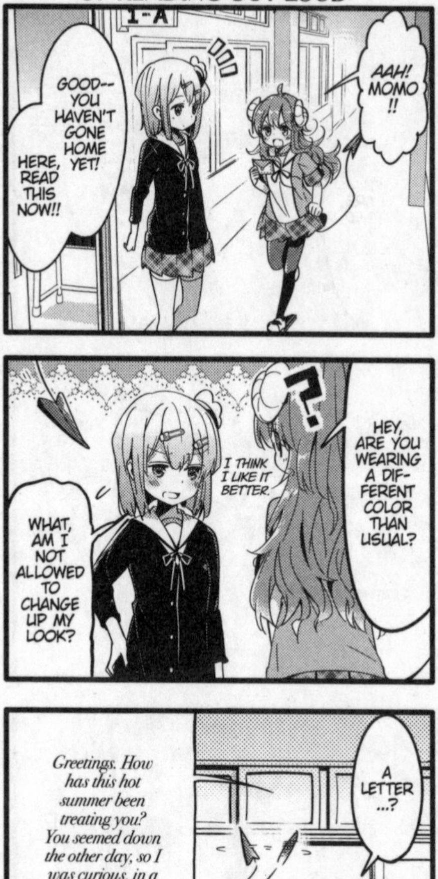
1-A
AAH! MOMO !!
GOOD-- YOU HAVEN'T GONE HOME YET!
HERE, READ THIS NOW!!
HEY, ARE YOU WEARING A DIF- FERENT COLOR THAN USUAL?
I THINK I LIKE IT BETTER.
WHAT, AM I NOT ALLOWED TO CHANGE UP MY LOOK?
A LETTER ...?
Greetings. How has this hot summer been treating you? You seemed down the other day, so I was curious, in a demonic way.
AWW, SHA- MIKO, YOU WERE WOR- RIED ABOUT ME?
NO... WAIT !!
ON SECOND THOUGHT, WAIT UNTIL I LEAVE TO READ IT!!
AND DON'T READ IT OUT LOUD!!
......?

ROUNDABOUT EXPRESSIONS

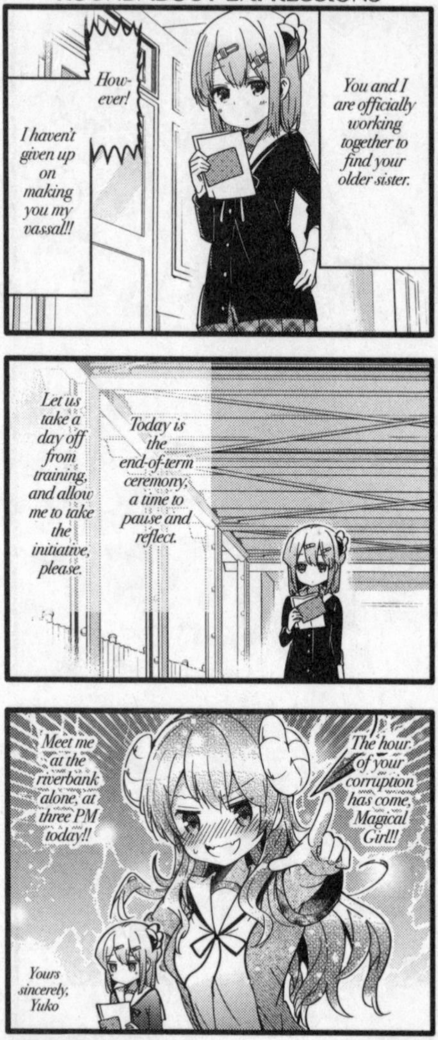
You and I are officially working together to find your older sister.
How- ever!
I haven't given up on making you my vassal!!
Today is the end-of-term ceremony, a time to pause and reflect.
Let us take a day off from training, and allow me to take the initiative, please.
The hour of your corruption has come, Magical Girl!!
Meet me at the riverbank alone, at three PM today!!
Yours sincerely, Yuko
P.S. It's still quite hot, so be sure to wear light, workout- ready clothing.
I HAVE NO IDEA WHAT SHE'S TRYING TO SAY.

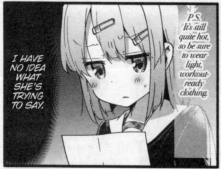

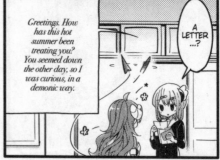

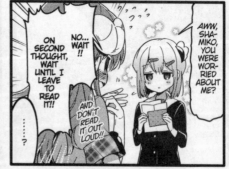

MOMO CAN'T READ BETWEEN THE LINES

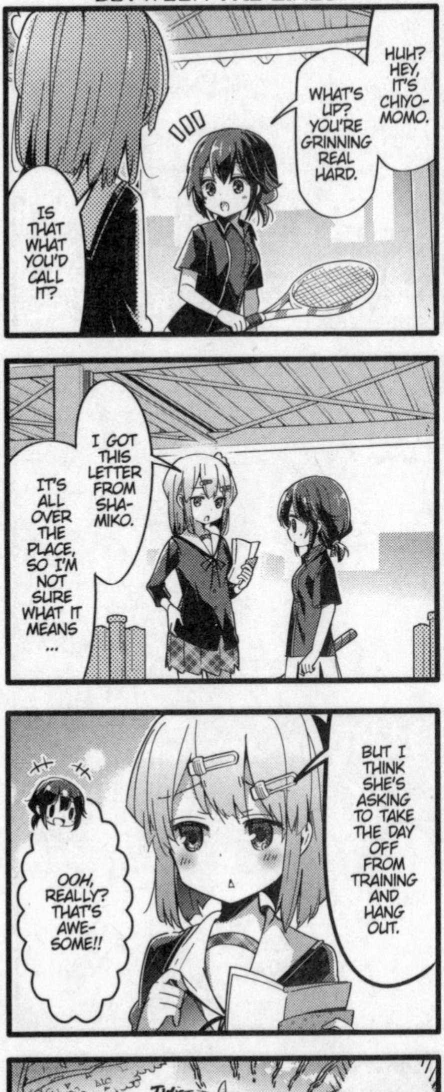
HUH? HEY, IT'S CHIYO-MOMO.
WHAT'S UP? YOU'RE GRINNING REAL HARD.
IS THAT WHAT YOU'D CALL IT?
I GOT THIS LETTER FROM SHA-MIKO.
IT'S ALL OVER THE PLACE, SO I'M NOT SURE WHAT IT MEANS...
BUT I THINK SHE'S ASKING TO TAKE THE DAY OFF FROM TRAINING AND HANG OUT.
OOH, REALLY? THAT'S AWESOME!!
MOMO MUST BE READING MY LETTER OF CHALLENGE RIGHT NOW!
TWIST...
TWIST...
JUST WAIT, MAGICAL GIRL...
TODAY WE WILL FORM A NEW KIND OF RELATIONSHIP!!
TWIST...
TWIST...

LET THE SUMMER WARS BEGIN!

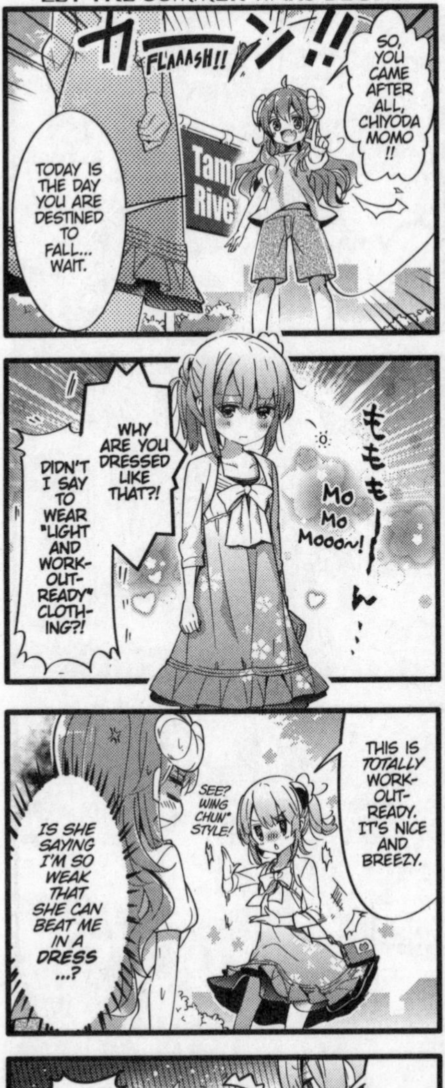
カーーン!!
FL'AAASH!!
SO, YOU CAME AFTER ALL, CHIYODA MOMO!!
TODAY IS THE DAY YOU ARE DESTINED TO FALL... WAIT.
ももも…
Mo Mo Mooon!
WHY ARE YOU DRESSED LIKE THAT?!
DIDN'T I SAY TO WEAR "LIGHT AND WORKOUT-READY" CLOTHING?!
THIS IS TOTALLY WORKOUT-READY. IT'S NICE AND BREEZY.
SEE? WING CHUN* STYLE!
IS SHE SAYING I'M SO WEAK THAT SHE CAN BEAT ME IN A DRESS...?
THANKS FOR THE INVITE, THOUGH.
WHY ARE YOU THANKING ME?!
STOP THAT! IT'S SCARY!

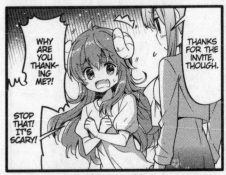

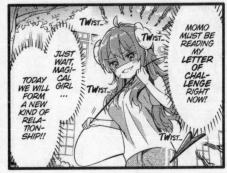

*Wing Chun is a form of Chinese martial arts.

BECOME A DEMON WHO CAN PLAN

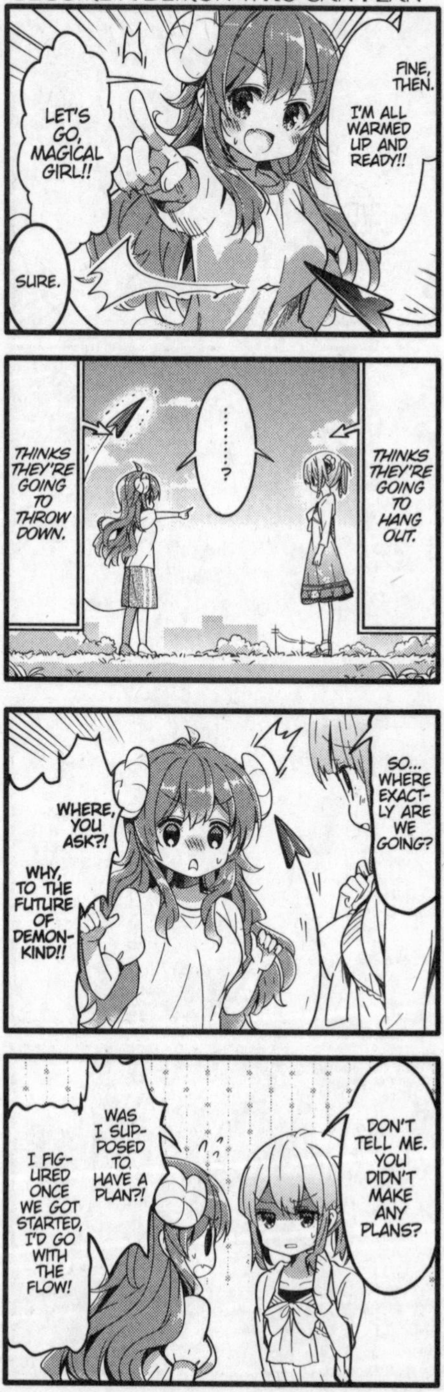
FINE, THEN.
I'M ALL WARMED UP AND READY!!
LET'S GO, MAGICAL GIRL!!
SURE.
THINKS THEY'RE GOING TO HANG OUT.
......?
THINKS THEY'RE GOING TO THROW DOWN.
SO... WHERE EXACTLY ARE WE GOING?
WHERE, YOU ASK?!
WHY, TO THE FUTURE OF DEMON-KIND!!
DON'T TELL ME. YOU DIDN'T MAKE ANY PLANS?
WAS I SUPPOSED TO HAVE A PLAN?!
I FIGURED ONCE WE GOT STARTED, I'D GO WITH THE FLOW!

MOMO PASSES THE TIME

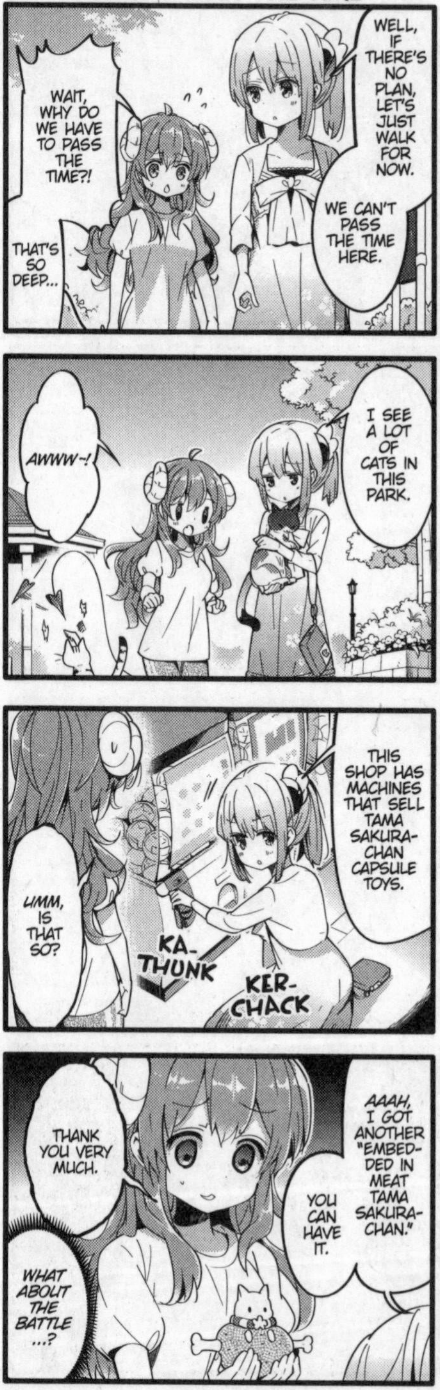
WELL, IF THERE'S NO PLAN, LET'S JUST WALK FOR NOW.
WE CAN'T PASS THE TIME HERE.
WAIT, WHY DO WE HAVE TO PASS THE TIME?!
THAT'S SO DEEP...
I SEE A LOT OF CATS IN THIS PARK.
AWWW~!
THIS SHOP HAS MACHINES THAT SELL TAMA SAKURA-CHAN CAPSULE TOYS.
KER-CHACK
KA-THUNK
UMM, IS THAT SO?
AAAH, I GOT ANOTHER "EMBEDDED IN MEAT TAMA SAKURA-CHAN."
YOU CAN HAVE IT.
THANK YOU VERY MUCH.
WHAT ABOUT THE BATTLE ...?

THE WRONG KIND OF DARKNESS

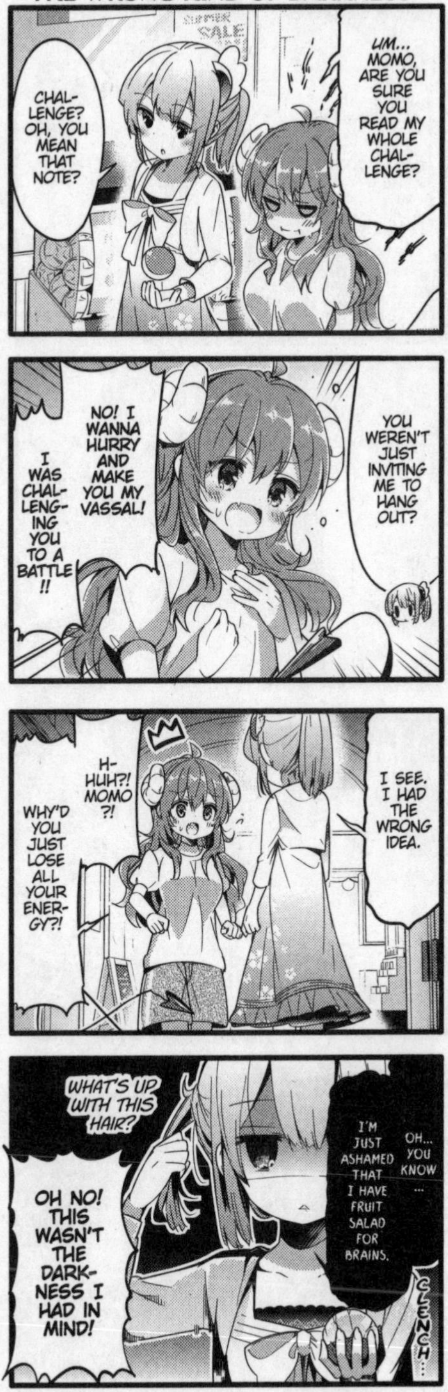

UM... MOMO, ARE YOU SURE YOU READ MY WHOLE CHALLENGE?
SUMMER SALE
CHALLENGE? OH, YOU MEAN THAT NOTE?
YOU WEREN'T JUST INVITING ME TO HANG OUT?
NO! I WANNA HURRY AND MAKE YOU MY VASSAL!
I WAS CHALLENGING YOU TO A BATTLE!!
I SEE. I HAD THE WRONG IDEA.
H-HUH?! MOMO?!
WHY'D YOU JUST LOSE ALL YOUR ENERGY?!
OH... YOU KNOW...
I'M JUST ASHAMED THAT I HAVE FRUIT SALAD FOR BRAINS.
WHAT'S UP WITH THIS HAIR?
OH NO! THIS WASN'T THE DARKNESS I HAD IN MIND!
CLENCH...

HEARTFUL PEACH MORPHING STICK

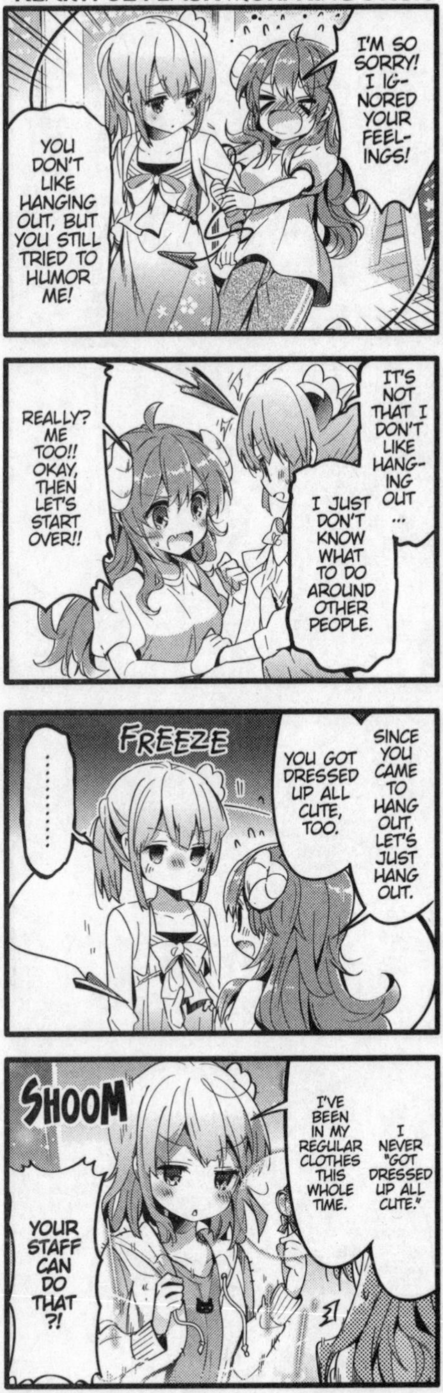

I'M SO SORRY! I IGNORED YOUR FEELINGS!
YOU DON'T LIKE HANGING OUT, BUT YOU STILL TRIED TO HUMOR ME!
IT'S NOT THAT I DON'T LIKE HANGING OUT...
I JUST DON'T KNOW WHAT TO DO AROUND OTHER PEOPLE.
REALLY? ME TOO!! OKAY, THEN LET'S START OVER!!
SINCE YOU CAME TO HANG OUT, LET'S JUST HANG OUT.
YOU GOT DRESSED UP ALL CUTE, TOO.
FREEZE
....
I NEVER "GOT DRESSED UP ALL CUTE."
I'VE BEEN IN MY REGULAR CLOTHES THIS WHOLE TIME.
SHOOM
YOUR STAFF CAN DO THAT?!

HAIR CLIPS OF PROMISE

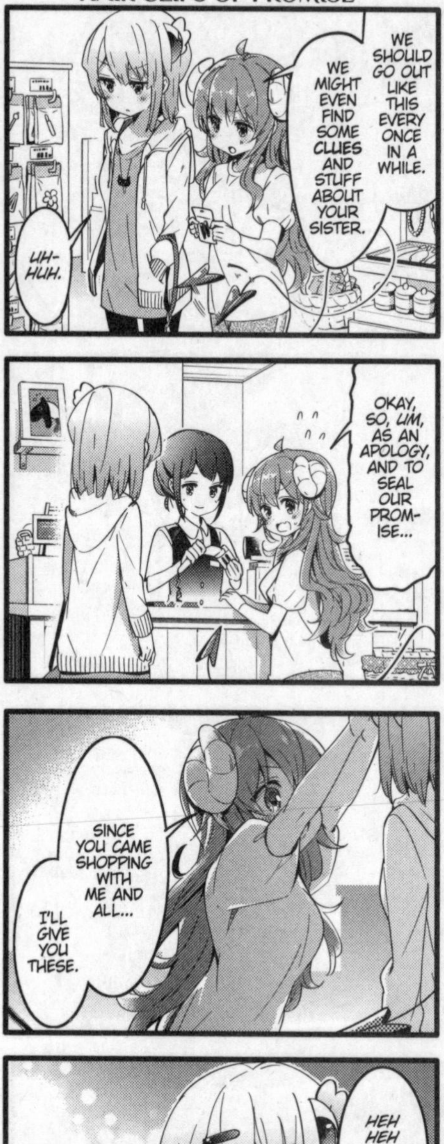
WE SHOULD GO OUT LIKE THIS EVERY ONCE IN A WHILE.
WE MIGHT EVEN FIND SOME CLUES AND STUFF ABOUT YOUR SISTER.
UH-HUH.
OKAY, SO, UM, AS AN APOLOGY, AND TO SEAL OUR PROMISE...
SINCE YOU CAME SHOPPING WITH ME AND ALL...
I'LL GIVE YOU THESE.
HEH HEH HEH! CHIYODA MOMO...
I MADE YOUR HAIR CLIPS FALL INTO DARKNESS, AT LEAST!!

ONE-ON-ONE INTERVIEW

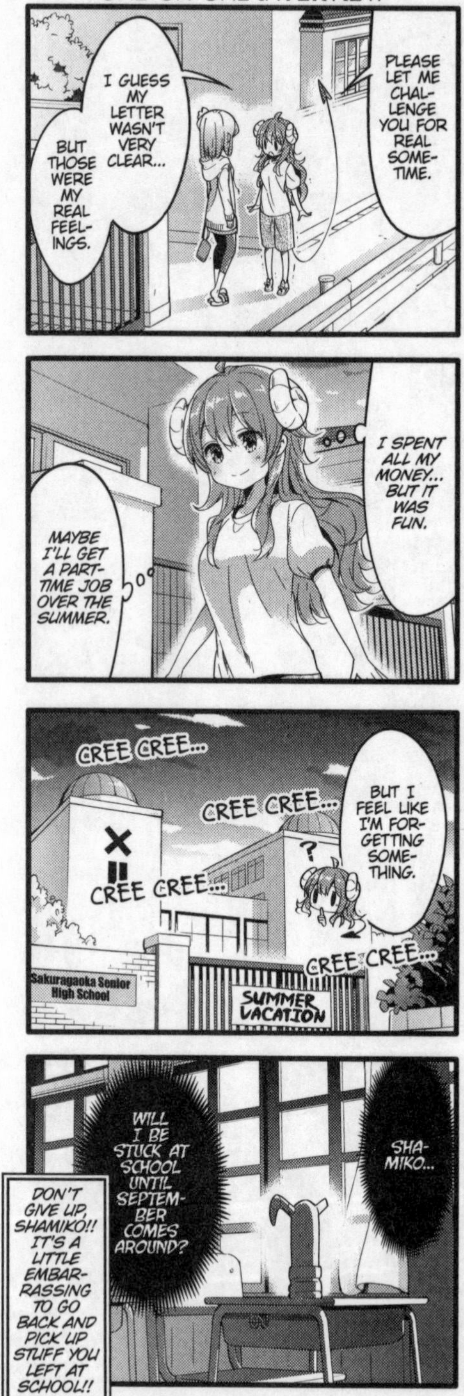
PLEASE LET ME CHALLENGE YOU FOR REAL SOMETIME.
I GUESS MY LETTER WASN'T VERY CLEAR...
BUT THOSE WERE MY REAL FEELINGS.
I SPENT ALL MY MONEY... BUT IT WAS FUN.
MAYBE I'LL GET A PART-TIME JOB OVER THE SUMMER.
BUT I FEEL LIKE I'M FORGETTING SOMETHING.
CREE CREE...
CREE CREE...
CREE CREE...
CREE CREE...
Sakuragaoka Senior High School
SUMMER VACATION
SHA-MIKO...
WILL I BE STUCK AT SCHOOL UNTIL SEPTEMBER COMES AROUND?
DON'T GIVE UP, SHAMIKO!! IT'S A LITTLE EMBARRASSING TO GO BACK AND PICK UP STUFF YOU LEFT AT SCHOOL!!

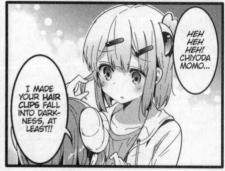

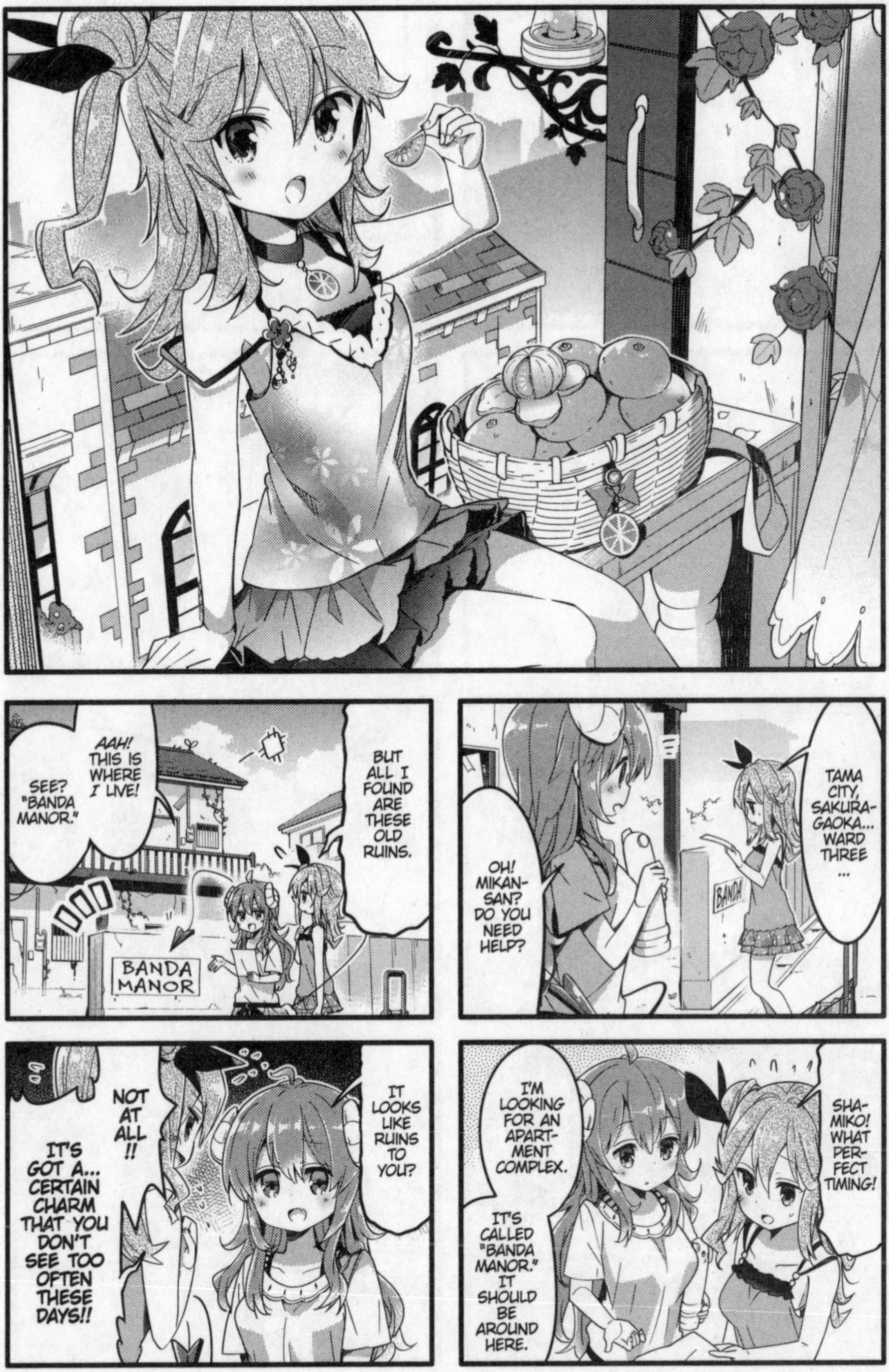
TAMA CITY, SAKURAGAOKA... WARD THREE ...
BANDA
OH! MIKAN-SAN? DO YOU NEED HELP?
BUT ALL I FOUND ARE THESE OLD RUINS.
AAH! THIS IS WHERE I LIVE!
SEE? "BANDA MANOR."
BANDA MANOR
SHAMIKO! WHAT PERFECT TIMING!
I'M LOOKING FOR AN APARTMENT COMPLEX.
IT'S CALLED "BANDA MANOR." IT SHOULD BE AROUND HERE.
IT LOOKS LIKE RUINS TO YOU?
NOT AT ALL!!
IT'S GOT A... CERTAIN CHARM THAT YOU DON'T SEE TOO OFTEN THESE DAYS!!

CHEAPER THAN THE AVERAGE DRINK

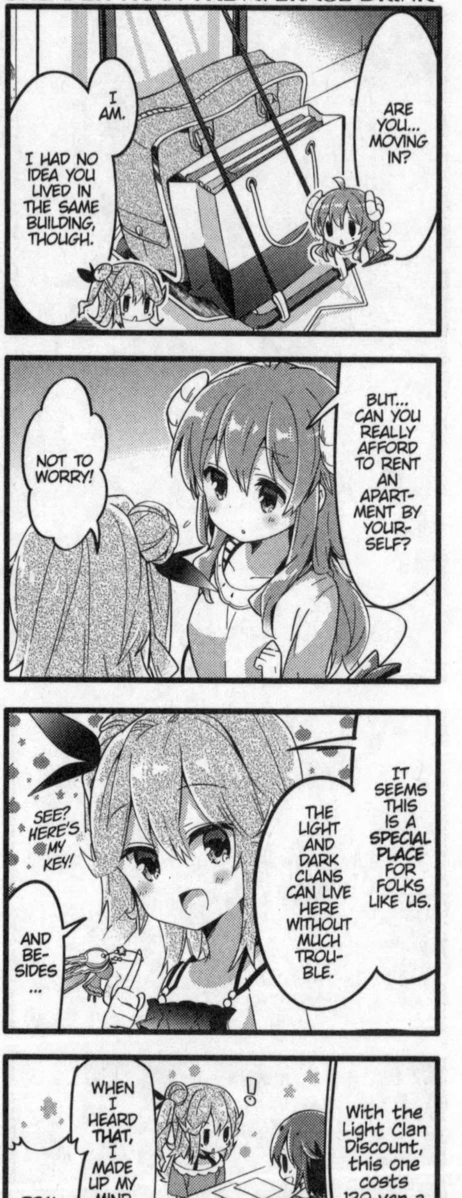
ARE YOU... MOVING IN?
I AM.
I HAD NO IDEA YOU LIVED IN THE SAME BUILDING, THOUGH.
BUT... CAN YOU REALLY AFFORD TO RENT AN APARTMENT BY YOURSELF?
NOT TO WORRY!
IT SEEMS THIS IS A SPECIAL PLACE FOR FOLKS LIKE US.
THE LIGHT AND DARK CLANS CAN LIVE HERE WITHOUT MUCH TROUBLE.
SEE? HERE'S MY KEY!
AND BESIDES...
With the Light Clan Discount, this one costs 120 yen a month.
!
WHEN I HEARD THAT, I MADE UP MY MIND ON THE SPOT!!
REALLY?! IT'S LIKE A STUDENT DISCOUNT!

DIFFERENT TASTES

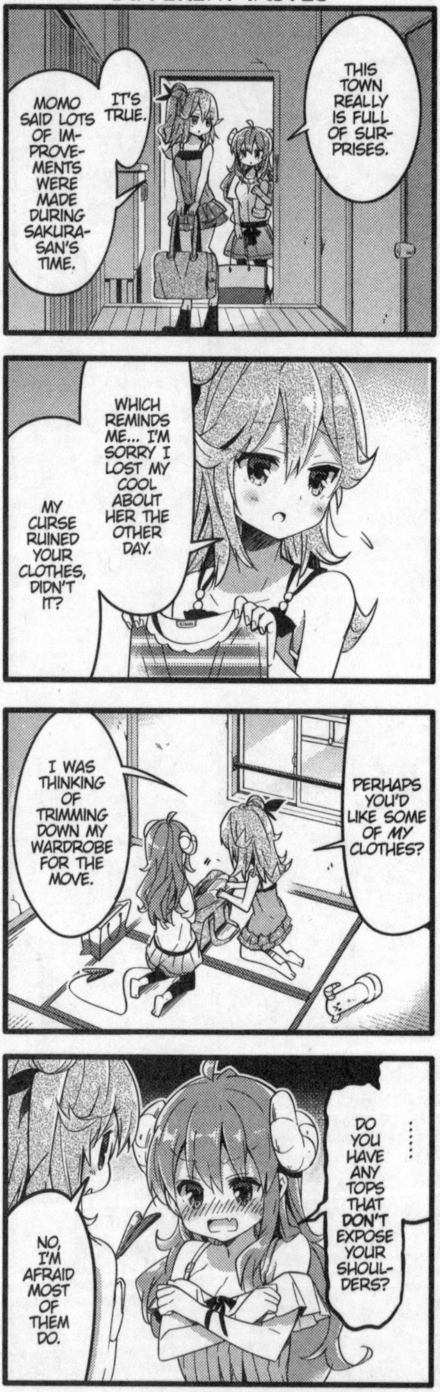
THIS TOWN REALLY IS FULL OF SURPRISES.
IT'S TRUE.
MOMO SAID LOTS OF IMPROVEMENTS WERE MADE DURING SAKURA-SAN'S TIME.
WHICH REMINDS ME... I'M SORRY I LOST MY COOL ABOUT HER THE OTHER DAY.
MY CURSE RUINED YOUR CLOTHES, DIDN'T IT?
PERHAPS YOU'D LIKE SOME OF MY CLOTHES?
I WAS THINKING OF TRIMMING DOWN MY WARDROBE FOR THE MOVE.
......
DO YOU HAVE ANY TOPS THAT DON'T EXPOSE YOUR SHOULDERS?
NO, I'M AFRAID MOST OF THEM DO.

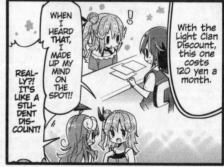

NIGHT OWL

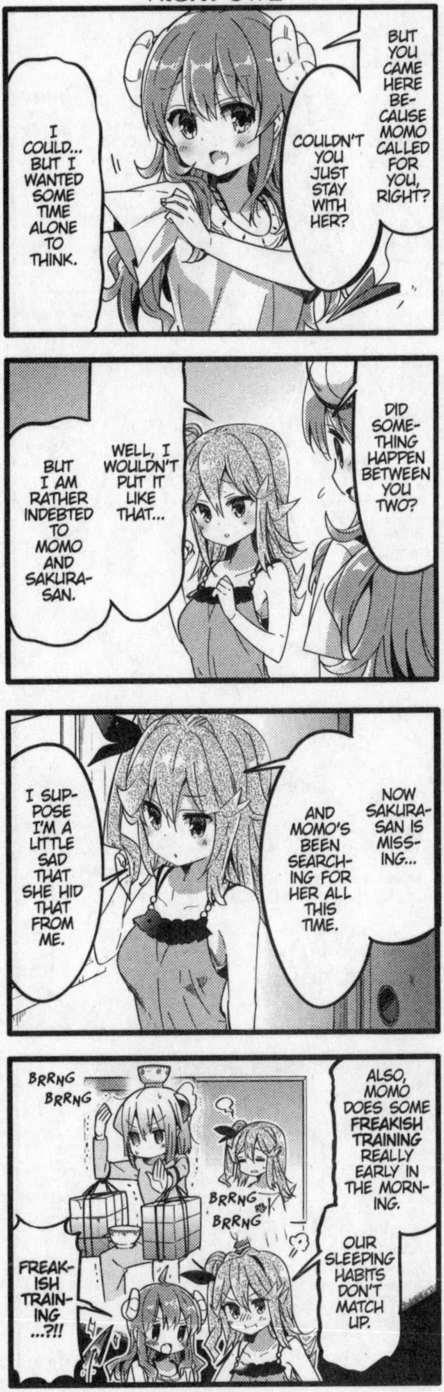

BUT YOU CAME HERE BECAUSE MOMO CALLED FOR YOU, RIGHT?
COULDN'T YOU JUST STAY WITH HER?
I COULD... BUT I WANTED SOME TIME ALONE TO THINK.
DID SOMETHING HAPPEN BETWEEN YOU TWO?
WELL, I WOULDN'T PUT IT LIKE THAT...
BUT I AM RATHER INDEBTED TO MOMO AND SAKURA-SAN.
NOW SAKURA-SAN IS MISSING...
AND MOMO'S BEEN SEARCHING FOR HER ALL THIS TIME.
I SUPPOSE I'M A LITTLE SAD THAT SHE HID THAT FROM ME.
ALSO, MOMO DOES SOME FREAKISH TRAINING REALLY EARLY IN THE MORNING.
BRRNG BRRNG
BRRNG BRRNG
OUR SLEEPING HABITS DON'T MATCH UP.
FREAKISH TRAINING...?!!

(SELF-PROCLAIMED) INNOCENT DEMON

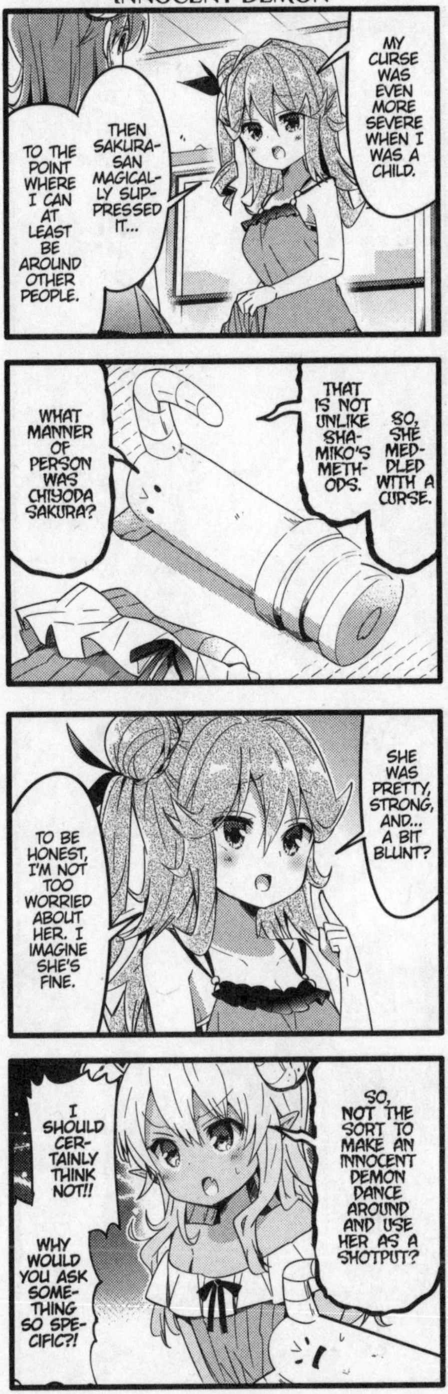

MY CURSE WAS EVEN MORE SEVERE WHEN I WAS A CHILD.
THEN SAKURA-SAN MAGICALLY SUPPRESSED IT...
TO THE POINT WHERE I CAN AT LEAST BE AROUND OTHER PEOPLE.
SO, SHE MEDDLED WITH A CURSE.
THAT IS NOT UNLIKE SHAMIKO'S METHODS.
WHAT MANNER OF PERSON WAS CHIYODA SAKURA?
SHE WAS PRETTY, STRONG, AND... A BIT BLUNT?
TO BE HONEST, I'M NOT TOO WORRIED ABOUT HER. I IMAGINE SHE'S FINE.
SO, NOT THE SORT TO MAKE AN INNOCENT DEMON DANCE AROUND AND USE HER AS A SHOTPUT?
I SHOULD CERTAINLY THINK NOT!!
WHY WOULD YOU ASK SOMETHING SO SPECIFIC?!

THE SECRET BEHIND THE BARGAIN

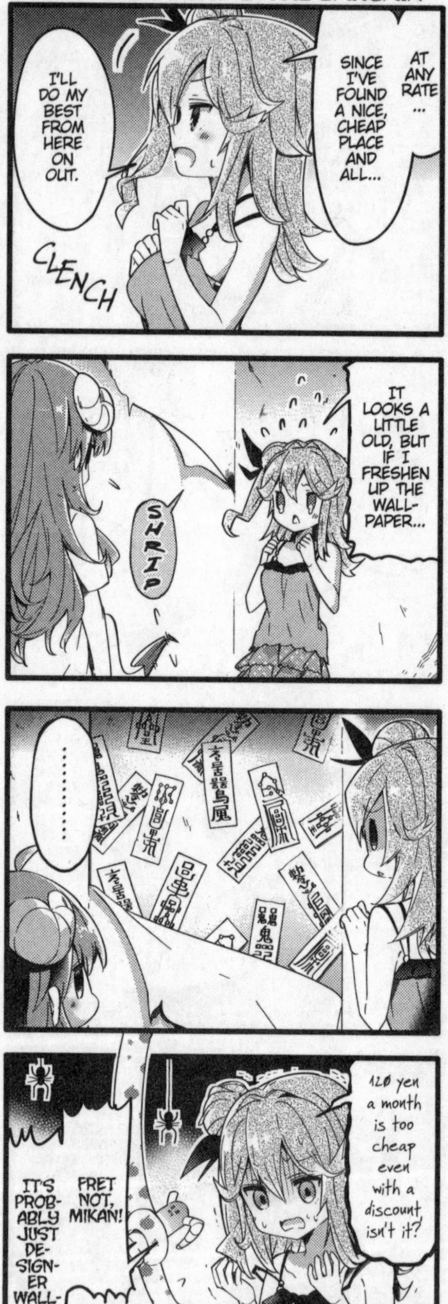
AT ANY RATE...
SINCE I'VE FOUND A NICE, CHEAP PLACE AND ALL...
I'LL DO MY BEST FROM HERE ON OUT.
CLENCH
IT LOOKS A LITTLE OLD, BUT IF I FRESHEN UP THE WALL-PAPER...
SHRIP
......
120 yen a month is too cheap even with a discount, isn't it?
FRET NOT, MIKAN!
IT'S PROBABLY JUST DE-SIGNER WALL-PAPER!
SHUDDER SHUDDER SHUDDER SHUDDER SHUDDER

COLD SHOULDER

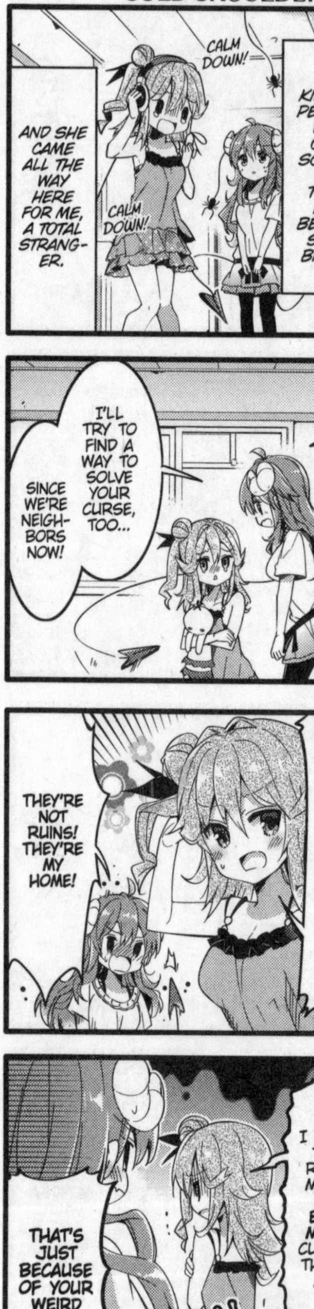
MIKAN-SAN MIGHT BE...
THE KIND OF PERSON WHO GETS SCARED BUT TRIES HER BEST TO SEEM BRAVE.
CALM DOWN!
AND SHE CAME ALL THE WAY HERE FOR ME, A TOTAL STRANGER.
CALM DOWN!
UM, MIKAN-SAN...
I'LL TRY TO FIND A WAY TO SOLVE YOUR CURSE, TOO...
SINCE WE'RE NEIGH-BORS NOW!
NEIGH-BORS, YOU SAY?!
I'M AL-READY PLAN-NING MY ESCAPE FROM THESE CRAZY RUINS!
THEY'RE NOT RUINS! THEY'RE MY HOME!
BUT MY SHOUL-DERS FEEL SUCH A CHILL...
I THINK THIS ROOM MIGHT BE EVEN MORE CURSED THAN I AM!
THAT'S JUST BECAUSE OF YOUR WEIRD TOP!
SHIVER...

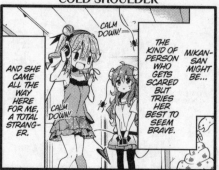

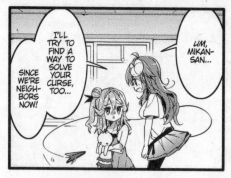

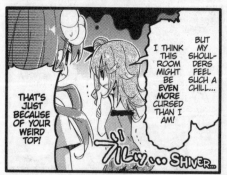

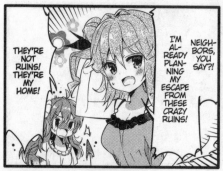

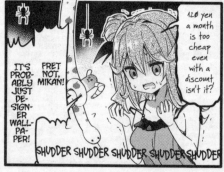

BECOME A DEMON WHO KEEPS THINGS IN ORDER

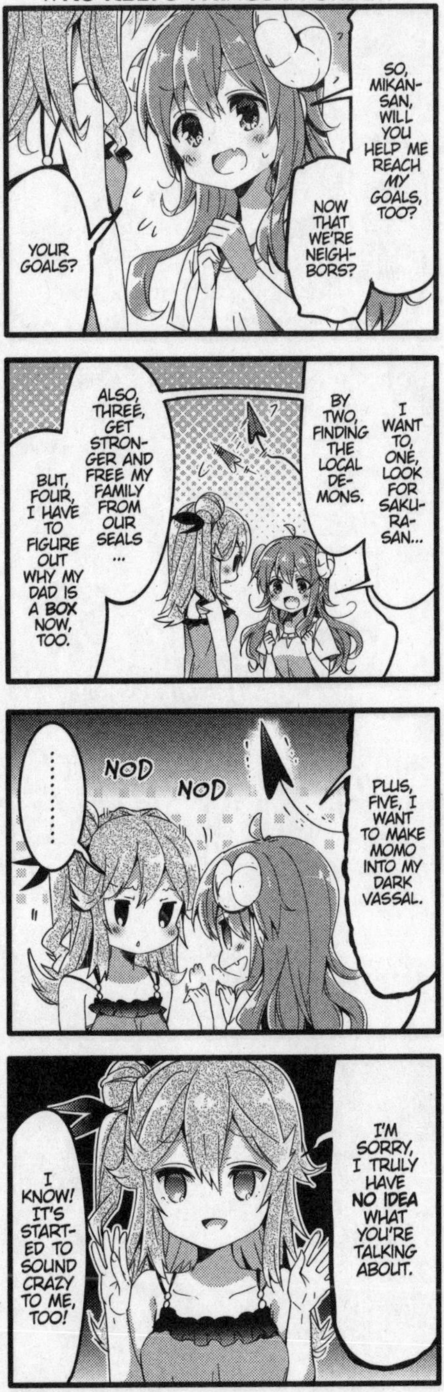
SO, MIKAN-SAN, WILL YOU HELP ME REACH MY GOALS, TOO?
NOW THAT WE'RE NEIGHBORS?
YOUR GOALS?
I WANT TO, ONE, LOOK FOR SAKURA-SAN...
BY TWO, FINDING THE LOCAL DEMONS.
ALSO, THREE, GET STRONGER AND FREE MY FAMILY FROM OUR SEALS ...
BUT, FOUR, I HAVE TO FIGURE OUT WHY MY DAD IS A BOX NOW, TOO.
PLUS, FIVE, I WANT TO MAKE MOMO INTO MY DARK VASSAL.
NOD
NOD
......
I'M SORRY, I TRULY HAVE NO IDEA WHAT YOU'RE TALKING ABOUT.
I KNOW! IT'S STARTED TO SOUND CRAZY TO ME, TOO!

DYSTOPIA IN ROOM 203

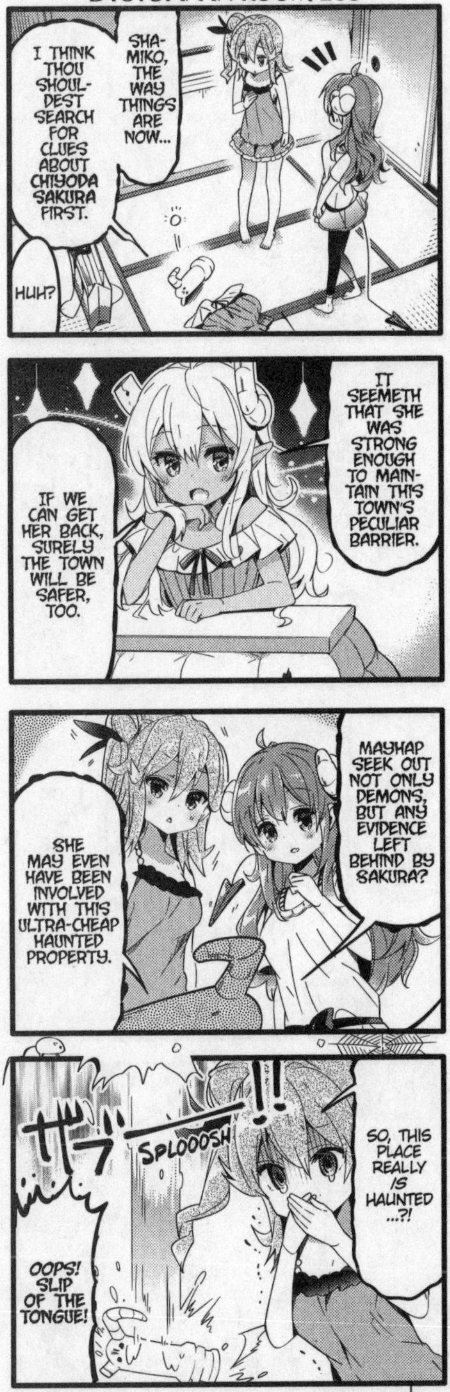
SHAMIKO, THE WAY THINGS ARE NOW...
I THINK THOU SHOULDEST SEARCH FOR CLUES ABOUT CHIYODA SAKURA FIRST.
HUH?
IT SEEMETH THAT SHE WAS STRONG ENOUGH TO MAINTAIN THIS TOWN'S PECULIAR BARRIER.
IF WE CAN GET HER BACK, SURELY THE TOWN WILL BE SAFER, TOO.
MAYHAP SEEK OUT NOT ONLY DEMONS, BUT ANY EVIDENCE LEFT BEHIND BY SAKURA?
SHE MAY EVEN HAVE BEEN INVOLVED WITH THIS ULTRA-CHEAP HAUNTED PROPERTY.
SO, THIS PLACE REALLY *IS* HAUNTED...?!
SPLOOOSH
OOPS! SLIP OF THE TONGUE!

ANCESTOR AIN'T GIVIN' UP

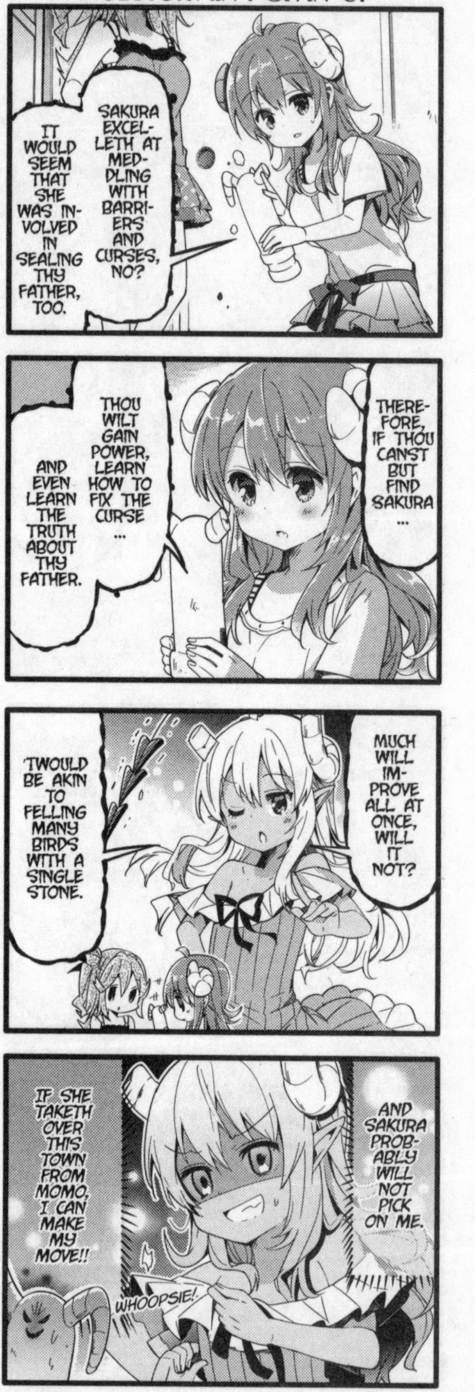
SAKURA EXCELLETH AT MEDDLING WITH BARRIERS AND CURSES, NO?
IT WOULD SEEM THAT SHE WAS INVOLVED IN SEALING THY FATHER, TOO.
THEREFORE, IF THOU CANST BUT FIND SAKURA ...
THOU WILT GAIN POWER, LEARN HOW TO FIX THE CURSE ...
AND EVEN LEARN THE TRUTH ABOUT THY FATHER.
MUCH WILL IMPROVE ALL AT ONCE, WILL IT NOT?
'TWOULD BE AKIN TO FELLING MANY BIRDS WITH A SINGLE STONE.
AND SAKURA PROBABLY WILL NOT PICK ON ME.
IF SHE TAKETH OVER THIS TOWN FROM MOMO, I CAN MAKE MY MOVE!!
WHOOPSIE!

THE ANCESTOR'S BIG MORALITY SCENE

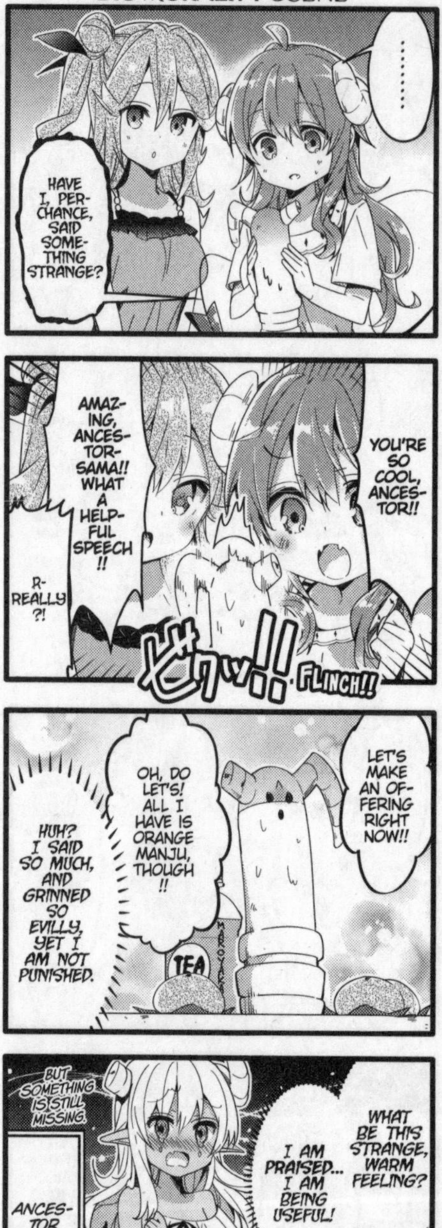
......
HAVE I, PERCHANCE, SAID SOMETHING STRANGE?
YOU'RE SO COOL, ANCESTOR!!
AMAZING, ANCESTOR-SAMA!! WHAT A HELPFUL SPEECH!!
R-REALLY?!
FLINCH!!
LET'S MAKE AN OFFERING RIGHT NOW!!
OH, DO LET'S! ALL I HAVE IS ORANGE MANJU, THOUGH!!
HUH? I SAID SO MUCH, AND GRINNED SO EVILLY, YET I AM NOT PUNISHED.
TEA
WHAT BE THIS STRANGE, WARM FEELING?
I AM PRAISED... I AM BEING USEFUL!
BUT SOMETHING IS STILL MISSING.
ANCESTOR HAS OPENED UP A NEW DOOR!!

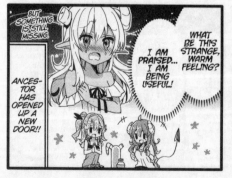

OMINOUS PINK AURA

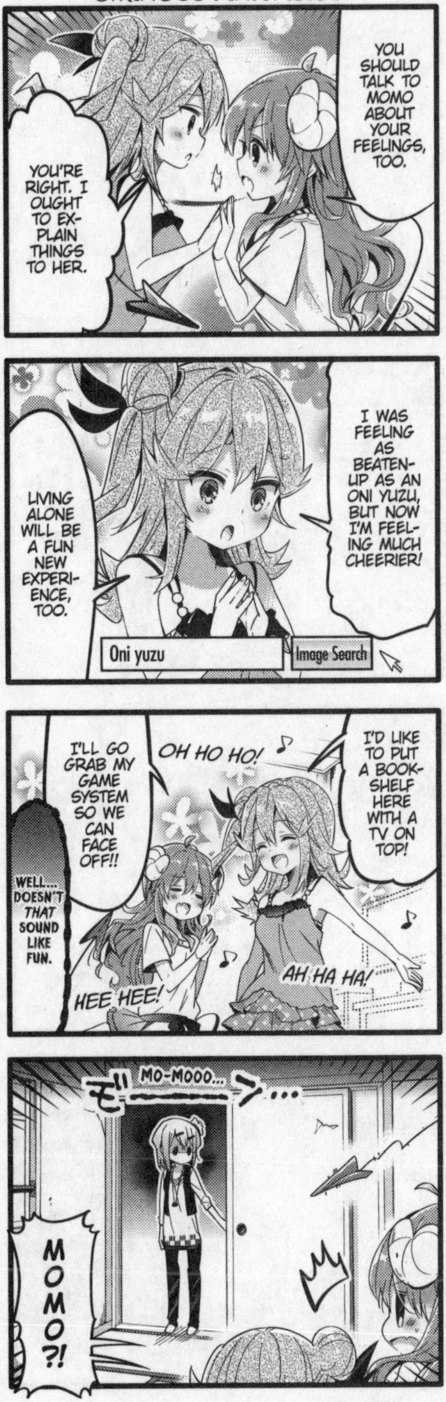
YOU SHOULD TALK TO MOMO ABOUT YOUR FEELINGS, TOO.
YOU'RE RIGHT. I OUGHT TO EXPLAIN THINGS TO HER.
I WAS FEELING AS BEATEN-UP AS AN ONI YUZU, BUT NOW I'M FEELING MUCH CHEERIER!
LIVING ALONE WILL BE A FUN NEW EXPERIENCE, TOO.
Oni yuzu
Image Search
I'D LIKE TO PUT A BOOKSHELF HERE WITH A TV ON TOP!
OH HO HO!
I'LL GO GRAB MY GAME SYSTEM SO WE CAN FACE OFF!!
WELL... DOESN'T THAT SOUND LIKE FUN.
AH HA HA!
HEE HEE!
MO-MOOO...
MOMO?!

A BOX WITH SHARP CORNERS

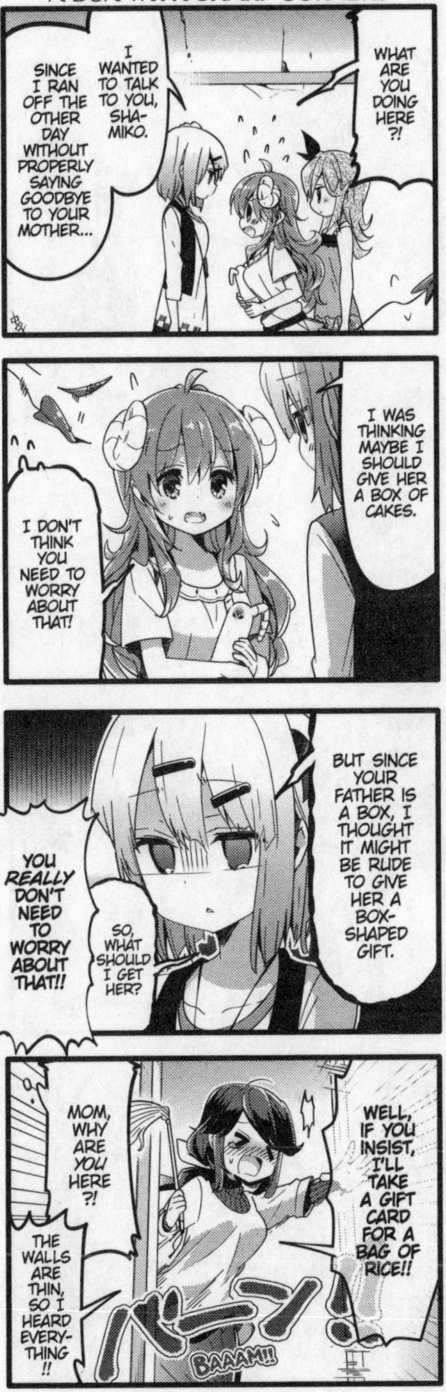
WHAT ARE YOU DOING HERE?!
I WANTED TO TALK TO YOU, SHAMIKO.
SINCE I RAN OFF THE OTHER DAY WITHOUT PROPERLY SAYING GOODBYE TO YOUR MOTHER...
I WAS THINKING MAYBE I SHOULD GIVE HER A BOX OF CAKES.
I DON'T THINK YOU NEED TO WORRY ABOUT THAT!
BUT SINCE YOUR FATHER IS A BOX, I THOUGHT IT MIGHT BE RUDE TO GIVE HER A BOX-SHAPED GIFT.
SO, WHAT SHOULD I GET HER?
YOU *REALLY* DON'T NEED TO WORRY ABOUT THAT!!
WELL, IF YOU INSIST, I'LL TAKE A GIFT CARD FOR A BAG OF RICE!!
MOM, WHY ARE *YOU* HERE?!
THE WALLS ARE THIN, SO I HEARD EVERYTHING!!
BAAAM!!

OUT OF THE FRYING PEACH

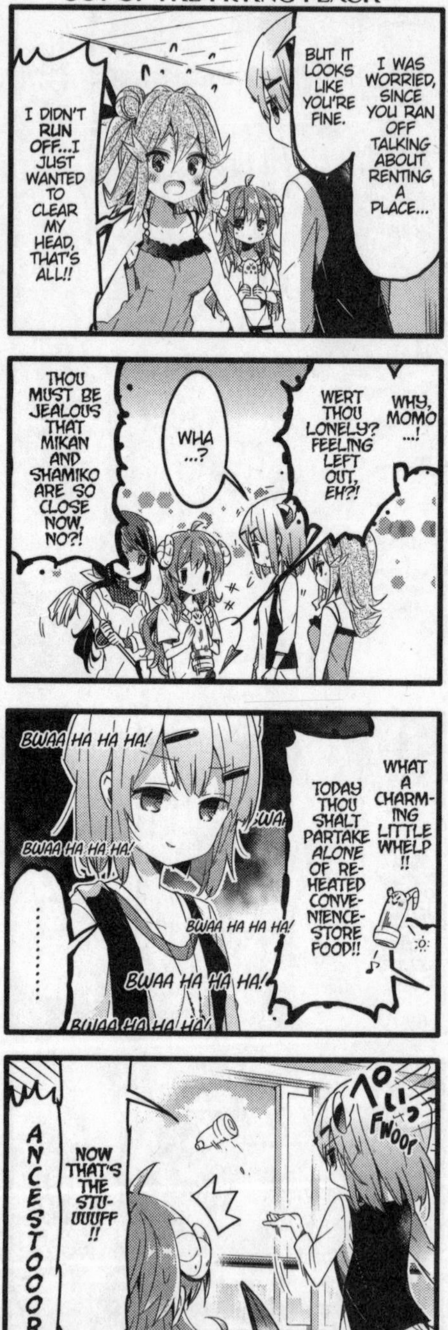
I WAS WORRIED, SINCE YOU RAN OFF TALKING ABOUT RENTING A PLACE...
BUT IT LOOKS LIKE YOU'RE FINE.
I DIDN'T RUN OFF...I JUST WANTED TO CLEAR MY HEAD, THAT'S ALL!!
WHY, MOMO...!
WERT THOU LONELY? FEELING LEFT OUT, EH?!
WHA...?
THOU MUST BE JEALOUS THAT MIKAN AND SHAMIKO ARE SO CLOSE NOW, NO?!
WHAT A CHARMING LITTLE WHELP!!
TODAY THOU SHALT PARTAKE ALONE OF RE-HEATED CONVENIENCE-STORE FOOD!!
BWAA HA HA HA!
BWAA HA HA HA!
BWAA HA HA HA!
BWAA HA HA HA!
BWAA HA HA HA!
....
FWOOP
NOW THAT'S THE STU-UUUFF!!
ANCESTOOOOR!!

MAGICAL GIRL OTHELLO

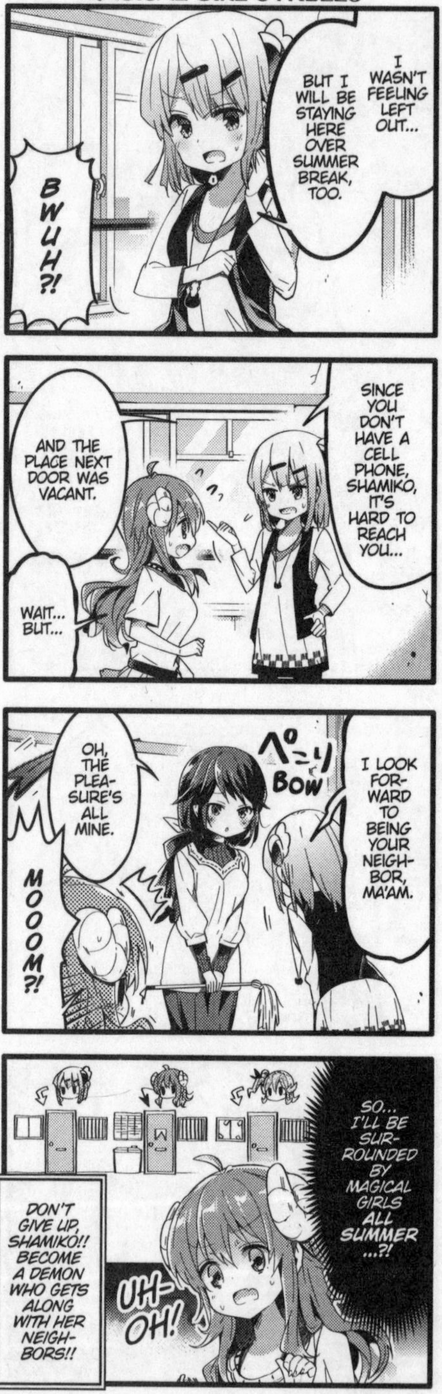
I WASN'T FEELING LEFT OUT...
BUT I WILL BE STAYING HERE OVER SUMMER BREAK, TOO.
BWUH?!
SINCE YOU DON'T HAVE A CELL PHONE, SHAMIKO, IT'S HARD TO REACH YOU...
AND THE PLACE NEXT DOOR WAS VACANT.
WAIT... BUT...
I LOOK FOR-WARD TO BEING YOUR NEIGHBOR, MA'AM.
ぺこり BOW
OH, THE PLEA-SURE'S ALL MINE.
MOOOOM?!
SO... I'LL BE SUR-ROUNDED BY MAGICAL GIRLS ALL SUMMER...?!
UH-OH!
DON'T GIVE UP, SHAMIKO!! BECOME A DEMON WHO GETS ALONG WITH HER NEIGH-BORS!!

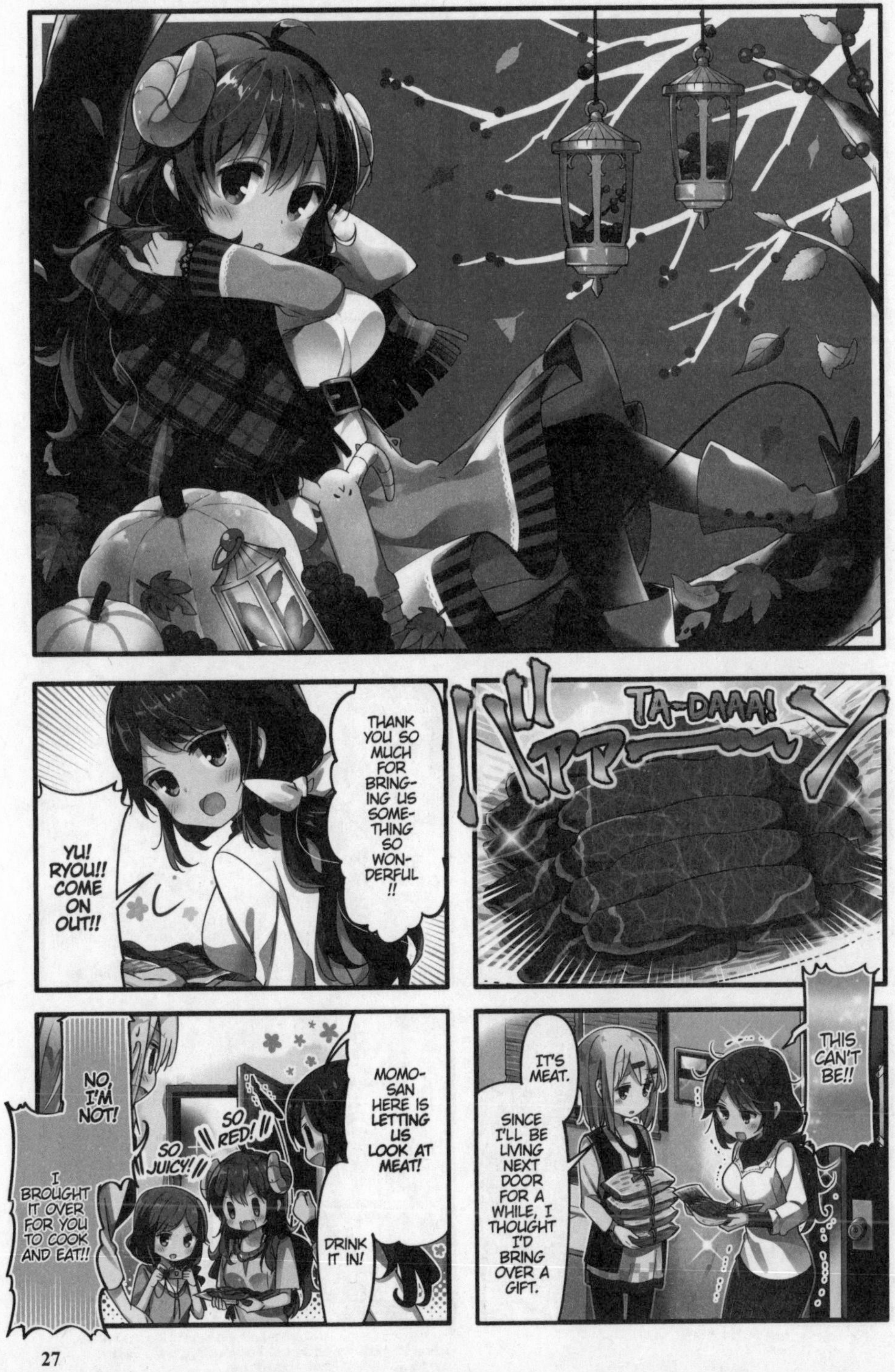
TA-DAAA!
IT'S MEAT.
SINCE I'LL BE LIVING NEXT DOOR FOR A WHILE, I THOUGHT I'D BRING OVER A GIFT.
THIS CAN'T BE!!
THANK YOU SO MUCH FOR BRINGING US SOMETHING SO WONDERFUL!!
YU! RYOU!! COME ON OUT!!
MOMO-SAN HERE IS LETTING US LOOK AT MEAT!
DRINK IT IN!
SO RED!
SO JUICY!
NO, I'M NOT!
I BROUGHT IT OVER FOR YOU TO COOK AND EAT!!

CONVENIENCE FACTOR

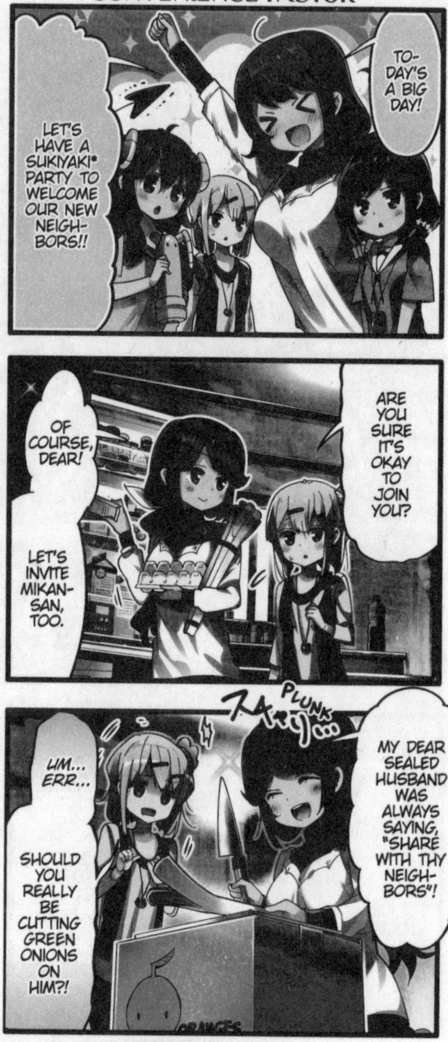
TO-DAY'S A BIG DAY!
LET'S HAVE A SUKIYAKI* PARTY TO WELCOME OUR NEW NEIGH-BORS!!
ARE YOU SURE IT'S OKAY TO JOIN YOU?
OF COURSE, DEAR!
LET'S INVITE MIKAN-SAN, TOO.
PLUNK
MY DEAR SEALED HUSBAND WAS ALWAYS SAYING, "SHARE WITH THY NEIGH-BORS"!
UM... ERR...
SHOULD YOU REALLY BE CUTTING GREEN ONIONS ON HIM?!
ORANGES
DON'T WORRY, DADBOX CAN ERASE ANY STAINS IN THREE MINUTES OR LESS.
HE'S VERY STURDY, TOO!
IT STILL FEELS WRONG!!
I'LL GO GET MY CUTTING BOARD!!

EGGSCELLENT ARRANGEMENTS

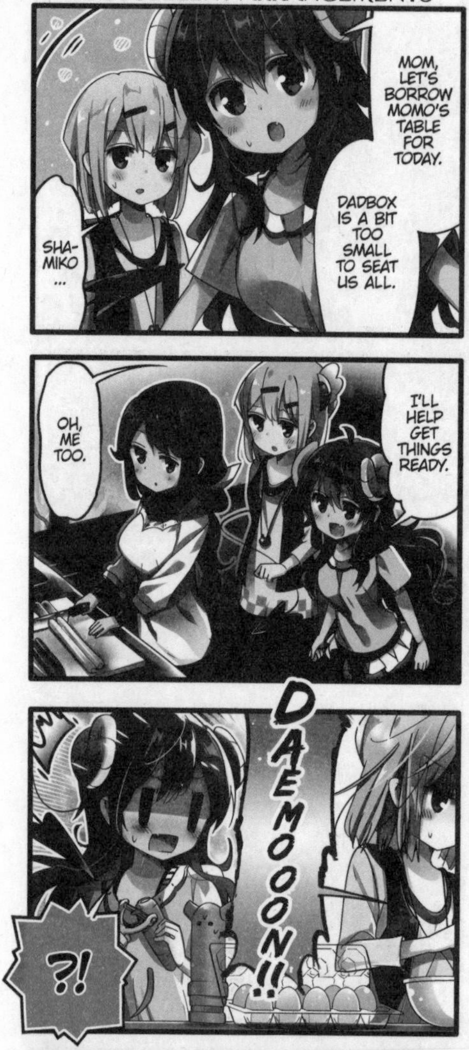
MOM, LET'S BORROW MOMO'S TABLE FOR TODAY.
DADBOX IS A BIT TOO SMALL TO SEAT US ALL.
SHA-MIKO...
I'LL HELP GET THINGS READY.
OH, ME TOO.
DAEMOOOON!!
?!
SHA-MIKO... I MESSED UP THE EGG.
HOW THE HECK DID *THAT* HAPPEN?!
ARE YOU FREAKED OUT *NOW*, MOMO?!

**Sukiyaki is thinly sliced meat and vegetables, cooked at the table with a soy-based sauce. The food is usually dipped in raw, beaten eggs after being cooked.*

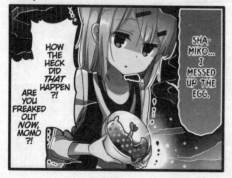

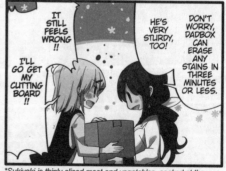

THE PINK MAGICAL GIRL FALLS CLOSER TO DARKNESS

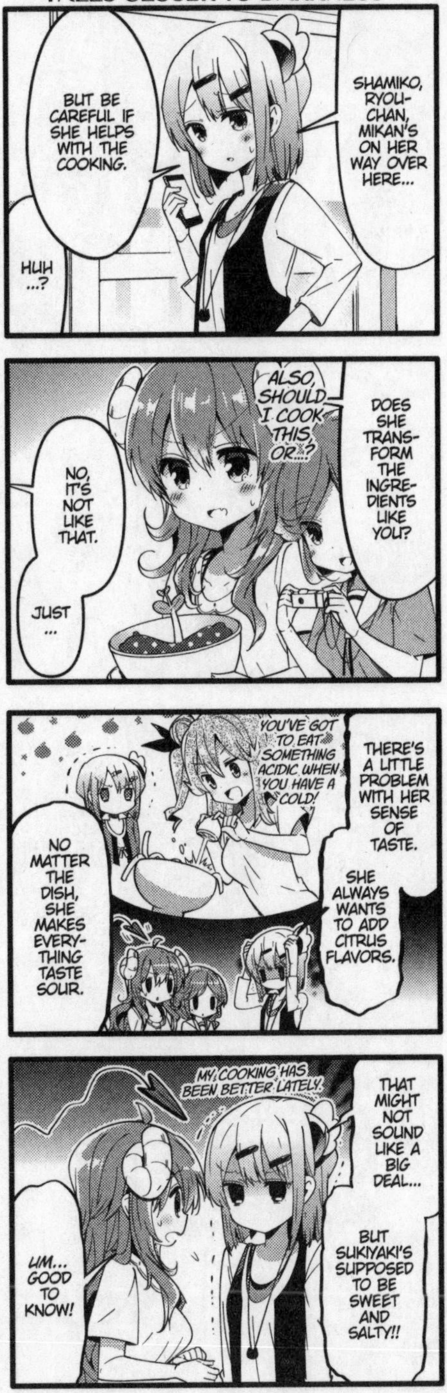
SHAMIKO, RYOU-CHAN, MIKAN'S ON HER WAY OVER HERE...
BUT BE CAREFUL IF SHE HELPS WITH THE COOKING.
HUH ...?
DOES SHE TRANSFORM THE INGREDIENTS LIKE YOU?
ALSO, SHOULD I COOK THIS, OR...?
NO, IT'S NOT LIKE THAT.
JUST ...
THERE'S A LITTLE PROBLEM WITH HER SENSE OF TASTE.
SHE ALWAYS WANTS TO ADD CITRUS FLAVORS.
YOU'VE GOT TO EAT SOMETHING ACIDIC WHEN YOU HAVE A COLD!
NO MATTER THE DISH, SHE MAKES EVERYTHING TASTE SOUR.
THAT MIGHT NOT SOUND LIKE A BIG DEAL...
BUT SUKIYAKI'S SUPPOSED TO BE SWEET AND SALTY!!
MY COOKING HAS BEEN BETTER LATELY.
UM... GOOD TO KNOW!

CITRUS TO SPARE

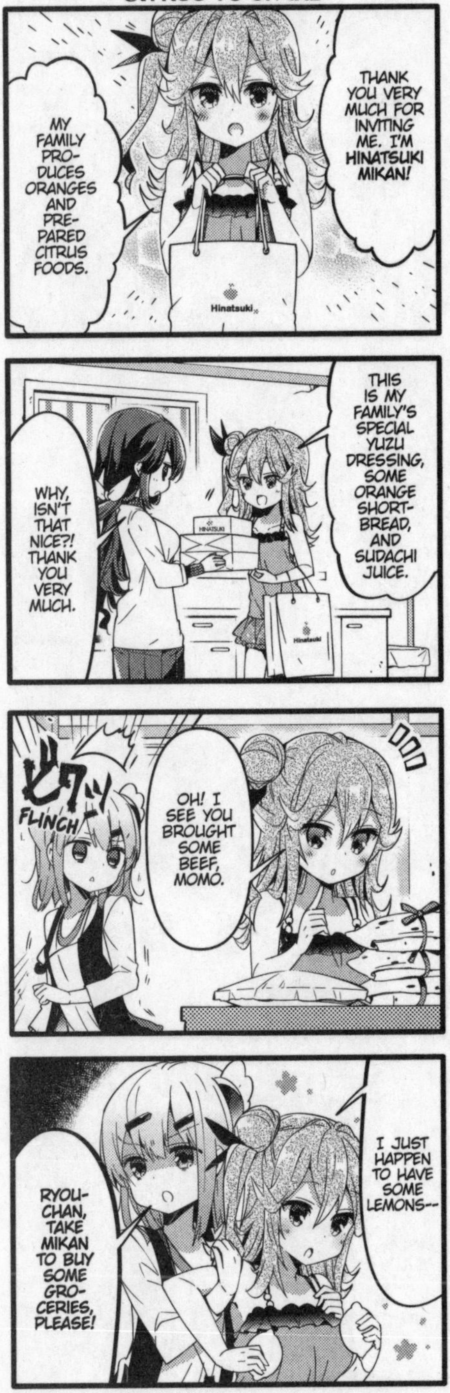
THANK YOU VERY MUCH FOR INVITING ME. I'M HINATSUKI MIKAN!
MY FAMILY PRODUCES ORANGES AND PREPARED CITRUS FOODS.
Hinatsuki
THIS IS MY FAMILY'S SPECIAL YUZU DRESSING, SOME ORANGE SHORTBREAD, AND SUDACHI JUICE.
WHY, ISN'T THAT NICE?! THANK YOU VERY MUCH.
OH! I SEE YOU BROUGHT SOME BEEF, MOMO.
FLINCH
I JUST HAPPEN TO HAVE SOME LEMONS--
RYOU-CHAN, TAKE MIKAN TO BUY SOME GROCERIES, PLEASE!

NOT A "YELLOW RIBBON" SITUATION

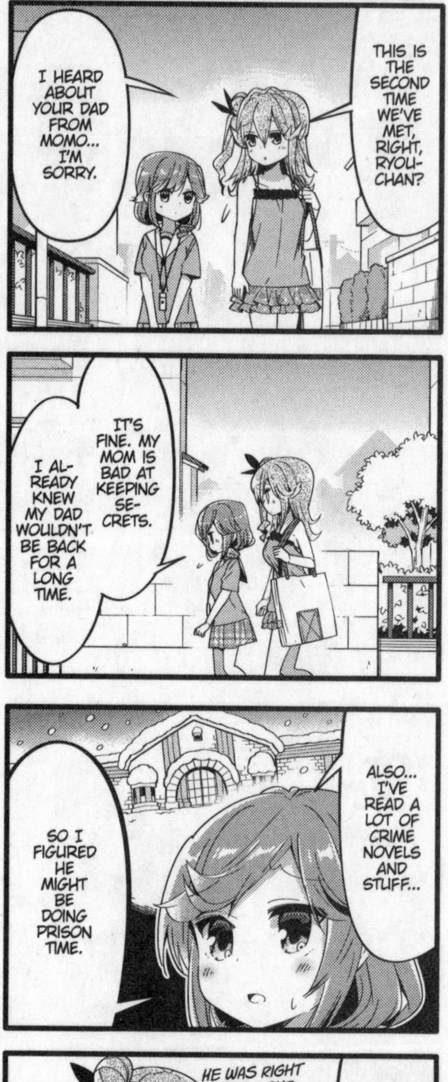
THIS IS THE SECOND TIME WE'VE MET, RIGHT, RYOU-CHAN?
I HEARD ABOUT YOUR DAD FROM MOMO... I'M SORRY.
IT'S FINE. MY MOM IS BAD AT KEEPING SECRETS.
I ALREADY KNEW MY DAD WOULDN'T BE BACK FOR A LONG TIME.
ALSO... I'VE READ A LOT OF CRIME NOVELS AND STUFF...
SO I FIGURED HE MIGHT BE DOING PRISON TIME.
HE WAS RIGHT UNDER OUR NOSES.
I'M JUST RELIEVED THAT HE'S CLOSER TO US THAN I REALIZED.
WOW, YOU'VE GOT SOME GRIT!!

NUMBER-ONE CITRUS FAN

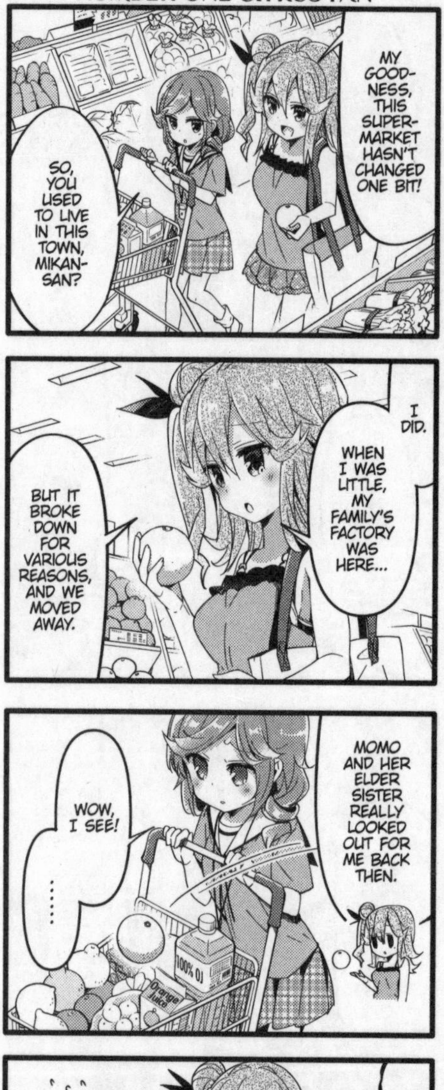
MY GOODNESS, THIS SUPERMARKET HASN'T CHANGED ONE BIT!
SO, YOU USED TO LIVE IN THIS TOWN, MIKAN-SAN?
I DID.
WHEN I WAS LITTLE, MY FAMILY'S FACTORY WAS HERE...
BUT IT BROKE DOWN FOR VARIOUS REASONS, AND WE MOVED AWAY.
MOMO AND HER ELDER SISTER REALLY LOOKED OUT FOR ME BACK THEN.
WOW, I SEE!
......
100% OJ
Orange Juice
UM, MIKAN-SAN... WE SHOULD BUY MORE THAN JUST CITRUS STUFF.
I'M SO SORRY... FORCE OF HABIT!!

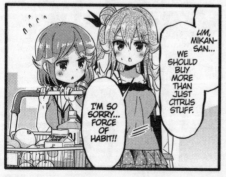

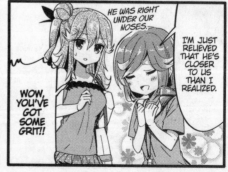

THE ENDS JUSTIFY THE MAGICAL MEANS

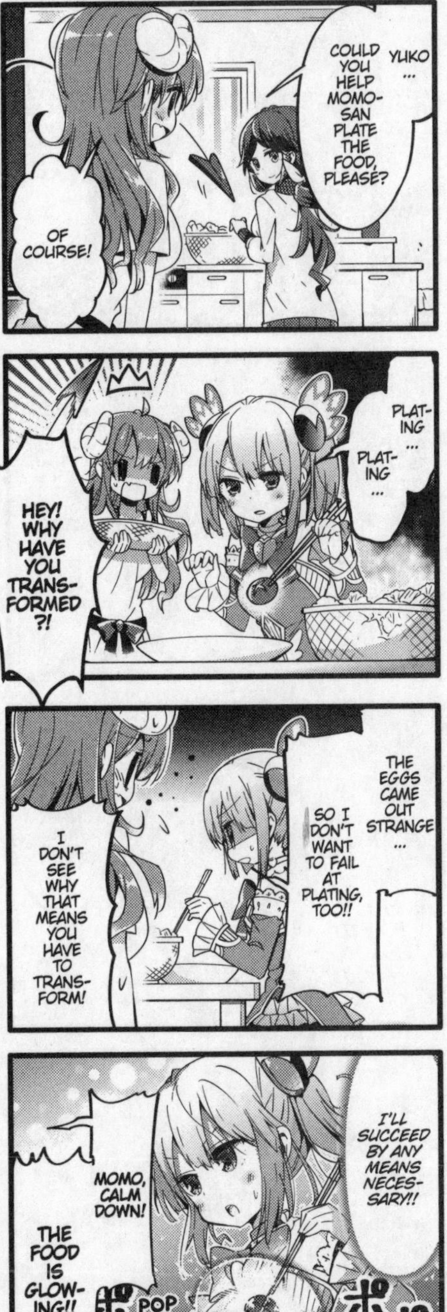
YUKO...
COULD YOU HELP MOMO-SAN PLATE THE FOOD, PLEASE?
OF COURSE!
PLATING... PLATING...
HEY! WHY HAVE YOU TRANSFORMED?!
THE EGGS CAME OUT STRANGE...
SO I DON'T WANT TO FAIL AT PLATING, TOO!!
I DON'T SEE WHY THAT MEANS YOU HAVE TO TRANSFORM!
I'LL SUCCEED BY ANY MEANS NECESSARY!!
MOMO, CALM DOWN!
THE FOOD IS GLOWING!!
ポ POP ポ POP ポ POP ポ POP

BECOME A DEMON WHO INSPIRES CONFIDENCE

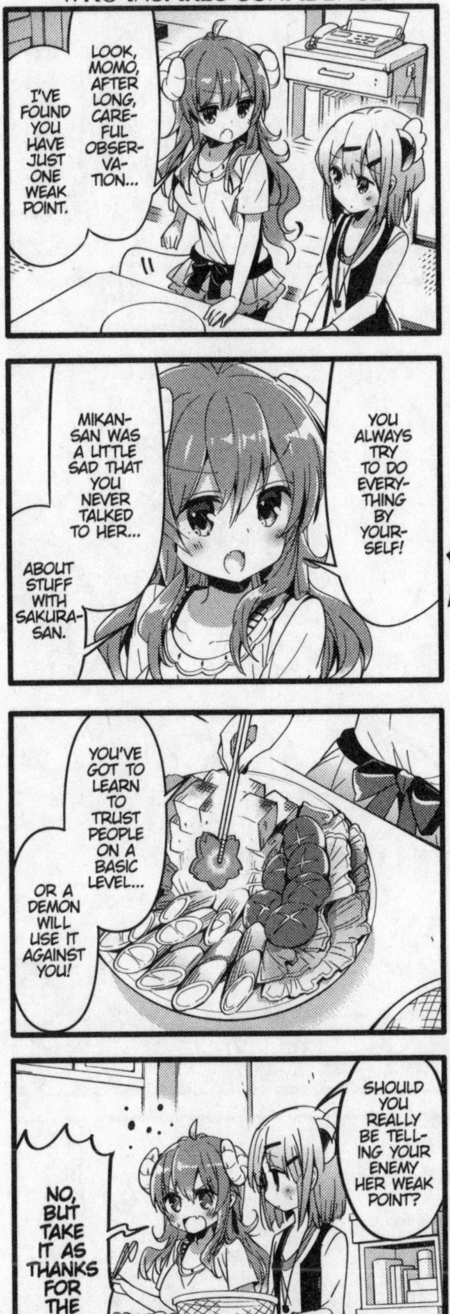
LOOK, MOMO, AFTER LONG, CAREFUL OBSERVATION...
I'VE FOUND YOU HAVE JUST ONE WEAK POINT.
YOU ALWAYS TRY TO DO EVERYTHING BY YOURSELF!
MIKAN-SAN WAS A LITTLE SAD THAT YOU NEVER TALKED TO HER...
ABOUT STUFF WITH SAKURA-SAN.
YOU'VE GOT TO LEARN TO TRUST PEOPLE ON A BASIC LEVEL...
OR A DEMON WILL USE IT AGAINST YOU!
SHOULD YOU REALLY BE TELLING YOUR ENEMY HER WEAK POINT?
NO, BUT TAKE IT AS THANKS FOR THE MEAT!!

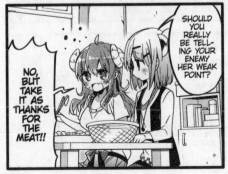

OUT-OF-THIS-WORLD FLAVOR

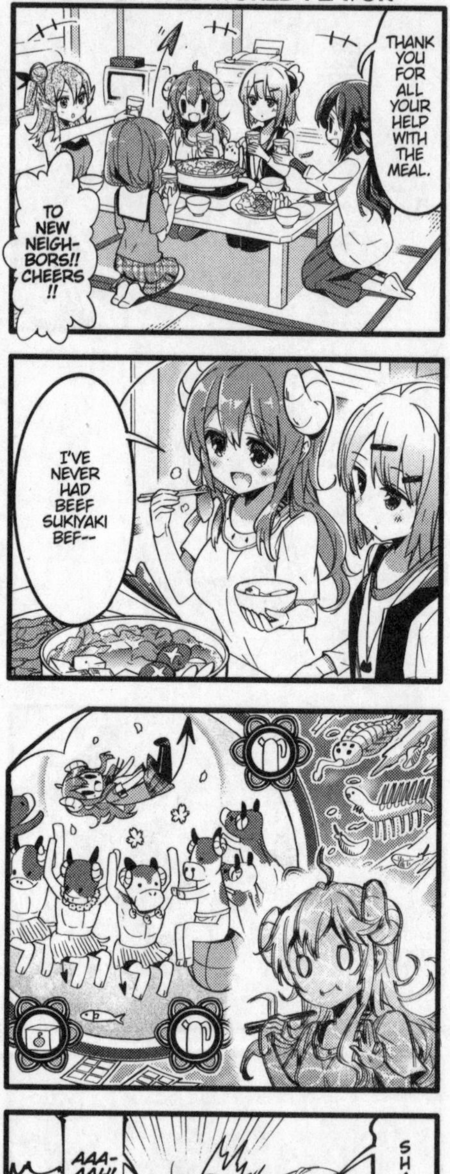
THANK YOU FOR ALL YOUR HELP WITH THE MEAL.
TO NEW NEIGHBORS!! CHEERS!!
I'VE NEVER HAD BEEF SUKIYAKI BEF--
SHAMIKO?!!
AAAAAH!
SORRY, IT WAS MORE YUMMY THAN I COULD PROCESS!

COMPULSORY OBSERVATION

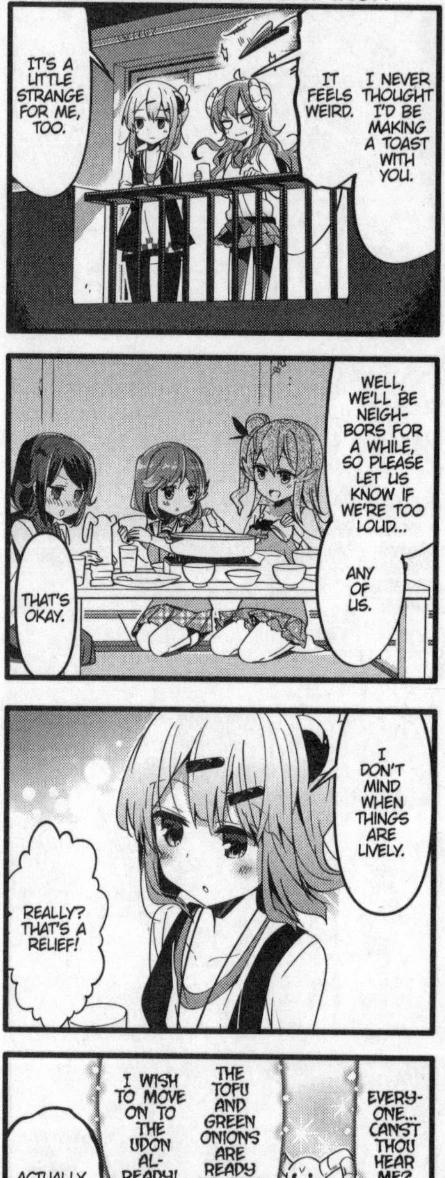
I NEVER THOUGHT I'D BE MAKING A TOAST WITH YOU.
IT FEELS WEIRD.
IT'S A LITTLE STRANGE FOR ME, TOO.
WELL, WE'LL BE NEIGHBORS FOR A WHILE, SO PLEASE LET US KNOW IF WE'RE TOO LOUD...
ANY OF US.
THAT'S OKAY.
I DON'T MIND WHEN THINGS ARE LIVELY.
REALLY? THAT'S A RELIEF!
EVERYONE... CANST THOU HEAR ME?
THE TOFU AND GREEN ONIONS ARE READY TO EAT! FINISH THEM!
I WISH TO MOVE ON TO THE UDON ALREADY!
ACTUALLY, HEARING THINGS DIRECTLY IN MY BRAIN IS PRETTY ANNOYING, THOUGH.

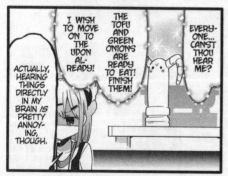

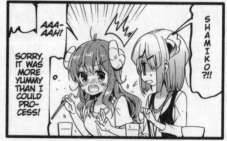

CRIME OF CONSCIENCE

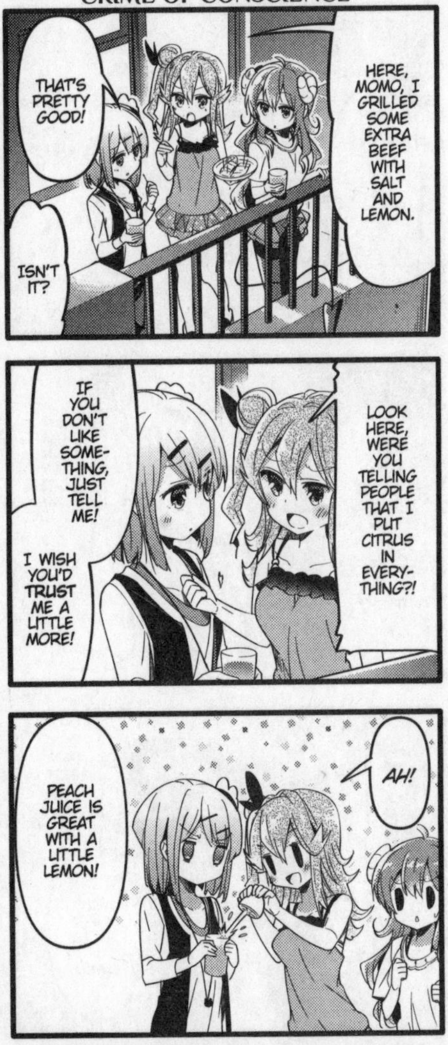
HERE, MOMO, I GRILLED SOME EXTRA BEEF WITH SALT AND LEMON.
THAT'S PRETTY GOOD!
ISN'T IT?
LOOK HERE, WERE YOU TELLING PEOPLE THAT I PUT CITRUS IN EVERYTHING?!
IF YOU DON'T LIKE SOMETHING, JUST TELL ME!
I WISH YOU'D TRUST ME A LITTLE MORE!
AH!
PEACH JUICE IS GREAT WITH A LITTLE LEMON!
HEY, WHAT'S WITH THE FACE?
IF I'M SURE IT'LL TURN OUT GOOD, I'M GOING TO TRY IT!

SHOCHU* ON THE ROCKS IS TOO STRONG FOR HER

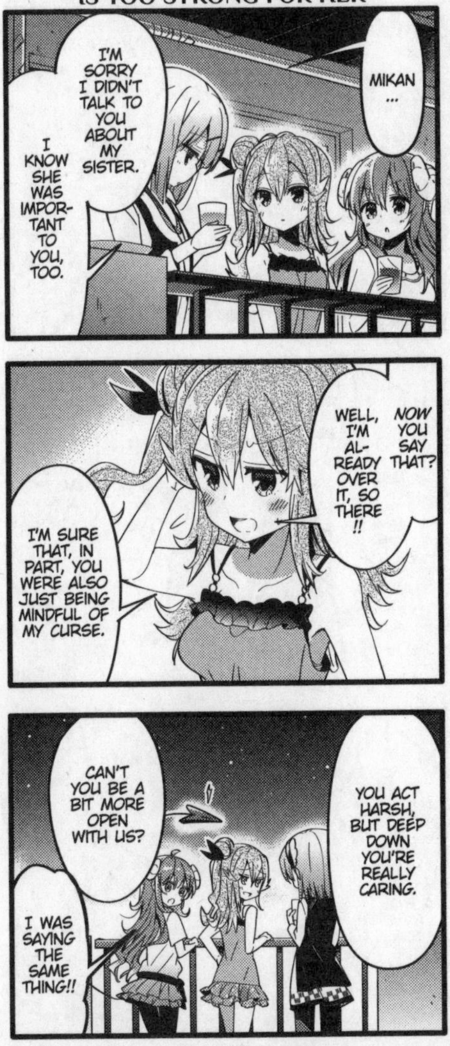
MIKAN ...
I'M SORRY I DIDN'T TALK TO YOU ABOUT MY SISTER.
I KNOW SHE WAS IMPORTANT TO YOU, TOO.
NOW YOU SAY THAT?
WELL, I'M ALREADY OVER IT, SO THERE!!
I'M SURE THAT, IN PART, YOU WERE ALSO JUST BEING MINDFUL OF MY CURSE.
YOU ACT HARSH, BUT DEEP DOWN YOU'RE REALLY CARING.
CAN'T YOU BE A BIT MORE OPEN WITH US?
I WAS SAYING THE SAME THING!!
SEIKO... THESE YOUNG FOLK ARE UNBEARABLY AWKWARD.
I'M STILL QUITE YOUNG COMPARED TO YOU, ANCESTOR-SAMA.
FACE THE TRUTH, SEIKO.

**Shochu is a distilled alcoholic drink typically made from rice, barley, sweet potato, buckwheat, or brown sugar. It is weaker than whiskey or vodka, but stronger than sake or wine.*

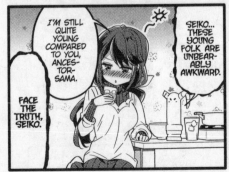

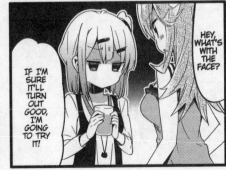

MASS-PRODUCED DADS

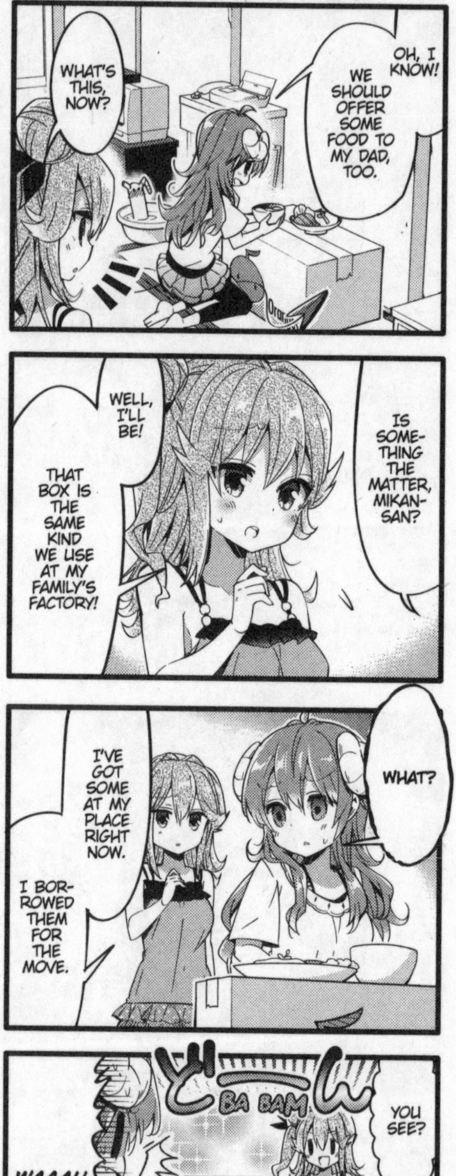
OH, I KNOW! WE SHOULD OFFER SOME FOOD TO MY DAD, TOO.
WHAT'S THIS, NOW?
IS SOMETHING THE MATTER, MIKAN-SAN?
WELL, I'LL BE!
THAT BOX IS THE SAME KIND WE USE AT MY FAMILY'S FACTORY!
WHAT?
I'VE GOT SOME AT MY PLACE RIGHT NOW.
I BORROWED THEM FOR THE MOVE.
どーん
BA BAM
YOU SEE?
WAAAH, SO MANY DADS!!

MIGHTY CARDBOARD PAPA RANGERS

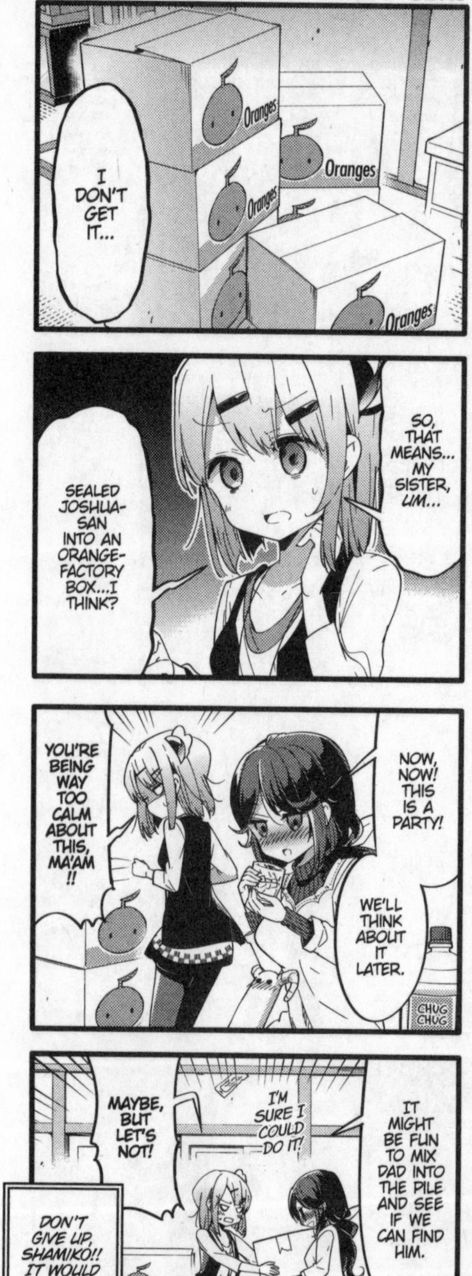
I DON'T GET IT...
SO, THAT MEANS... MY SISTER, UM...
SEALED JOSHUA-SAN INTO AN ORANGE-FACTORY BOX...I THINK?
NOW, NOW! THIS IS A PARTY!
WE'LL THINK ABOUT IT LATER.
YOU'RE BEING WAY TOO CALM ABOUT THIS, MA'AM!!
CHUG CHUG
IT MIGHT BE FUN TO MIX DAD INTO THE PILE AND SEE IF WE CAN FIND HIM.
I'M SURE I COULD DO IT!
MAYBE, BUT LET'S NOT!
DON'T GIVE UP, SHAMIKO!! IT WOULD BE A BIT HURTFUL IF YOU LOST AT THAT GAME!!

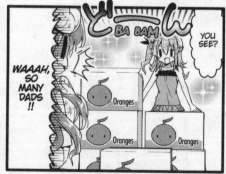

SECONDS!! DEMON GIRL NEXT DOOR

(CHAPTER 27)

~ DEMON VS. DIFFICULT KANJI ~

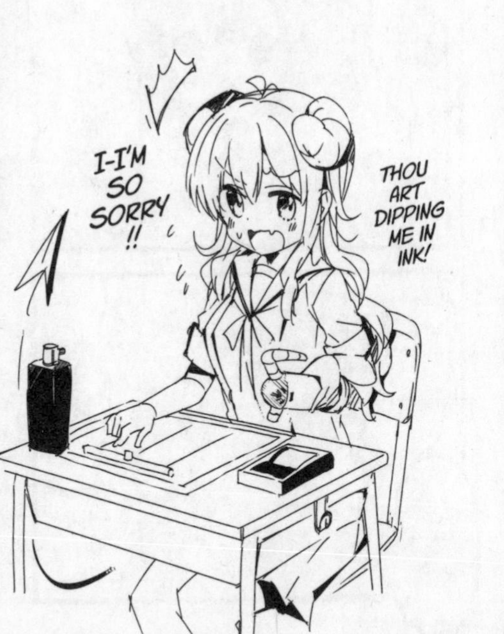
THOU ART DIPPING ME IN INK!
I-I'M SO SORRY!!

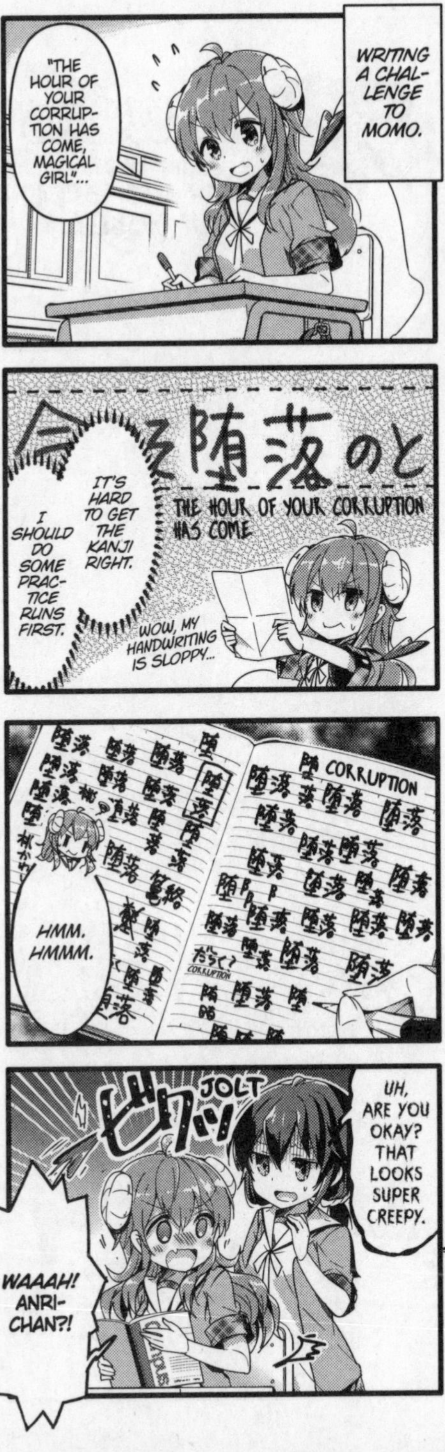
WRITING A CHALLENGE TO MOMO.
"THE HOUR OF YOUR CORRUPTION HAS COME, MAGICAL GIRL"...
THE HOUR OF YOUR CORRUPTION HAS COME
IT'S HARD TO GET THE KANJI RIGHT.
I SHOULD DO SOME PRACTICE RUNS FIRST.
WOW, MY HANDWRITING IS SLOPPY...
CORRUPTION
HMM. HMMM.
UH, ARE YOU OKAY? THAT LOOKS SUPER CREEPY.
JOLT
WAAAH! ANRI-CHAN?!

SECONDS!! DEMON GIRL NEXT DOOR

(CHAPTER 29)

~ "29" CAN ALSO BE READ AS "NIKU" (MEAT)! ~

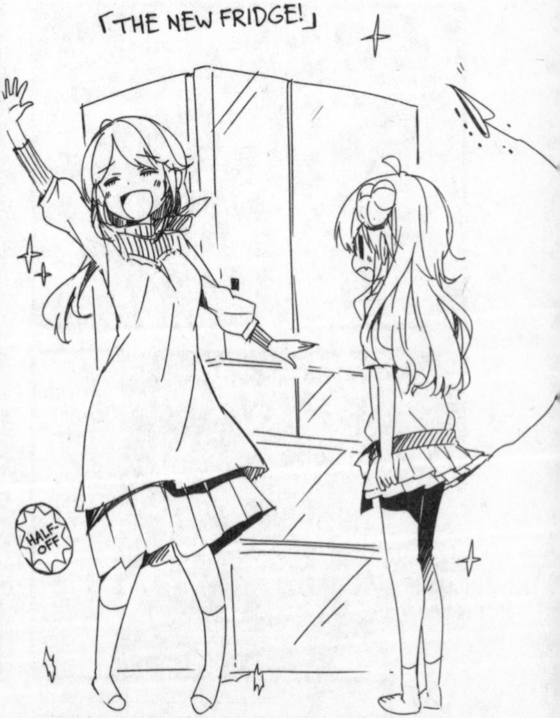
「THE NEW FRIDGE!」
HALF-OFF

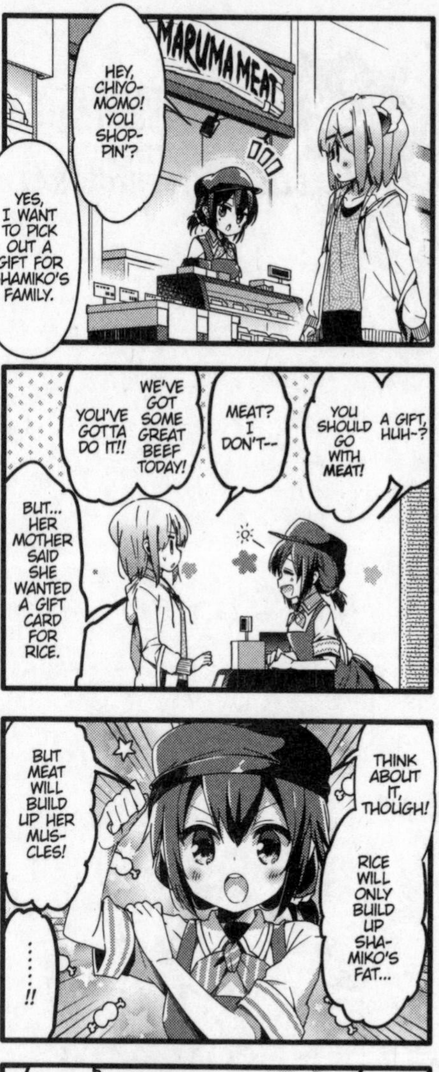
MARUMA MEAT
HEY, CHIYOMOMO! YOU SHOPPIN'?
YES, I WANT TO PICK OUT A GIFT FOR SHAMIKO'S FAMILY.
A GIFT, HUH~?
YOU SHOULD GO WITH MEAT!
MEAT? I DON'T--
WE'VE GOT SOME GREAT BEEF TODAY!
YOU'VE GOTTA DO IT!!
BUT... HER MOTHER SAID SHE WANTED A GIFT CARD FOR RICE.
THINK ABOUT IT, THOUGH!
RICE WILL ONLY BUILD UP SHAMIKO'S FAT...
BUT MEAT WILL BUILD UP HER MUSCLES!
......!!
YOU'VE SOLD ME ON THE MEAT.
GOOD CALL!! WANT ME TO PUT IT IN A GIFT BOX?
N-NO... NO BOXES, PLEASE.

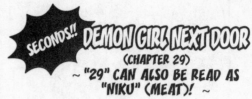

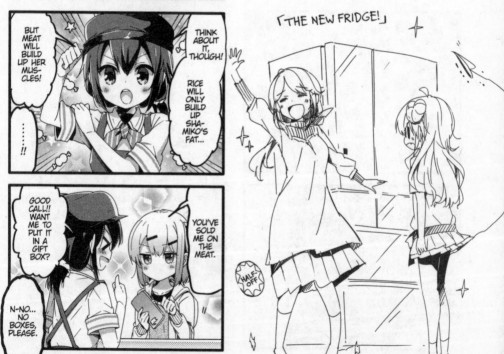

The Demon Girl Next Door

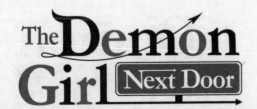

The Demon Girl Next Door

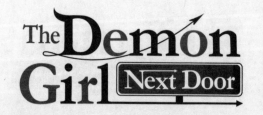

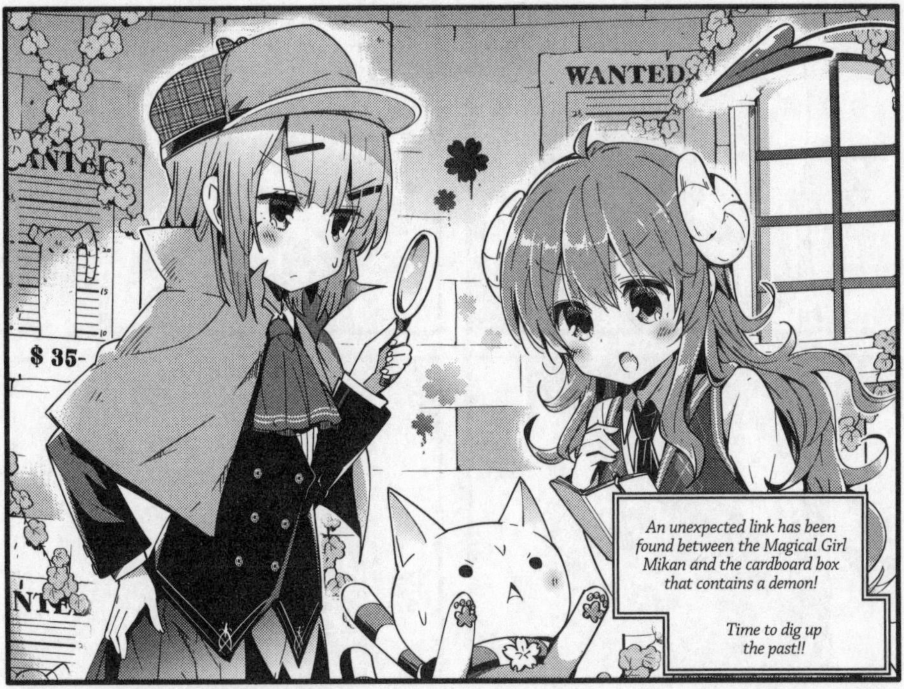
WANTED
$ 35-
An unexpected link has been found between the Magical Girl Mikan and the cardboard box that contains a demon!
Time to dig up the past!!

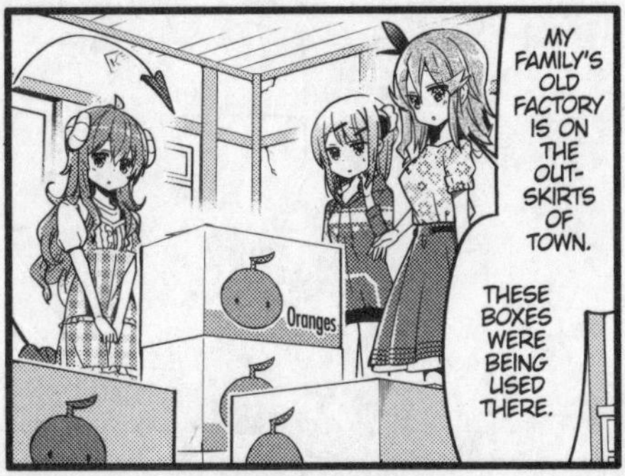
MY FAMILY'S OLD FACTORY IS ON THE OUT-SKIRTS OF TOWN.
THESE BOXES WERE BEING USED THERE.
Oranges

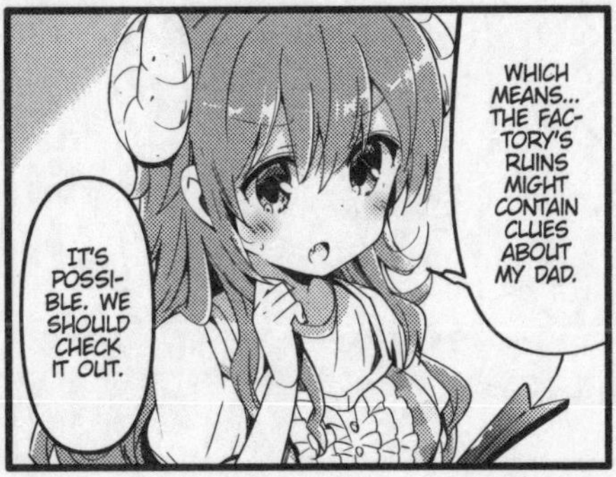
WHICH MEANS... THE FAC-TORY'S RUINS MIGHT CONTAIN CLUES ABOUT MY DAD.
IT'S POSSI-BLE. WE SHOULD CHECK IT OUT.

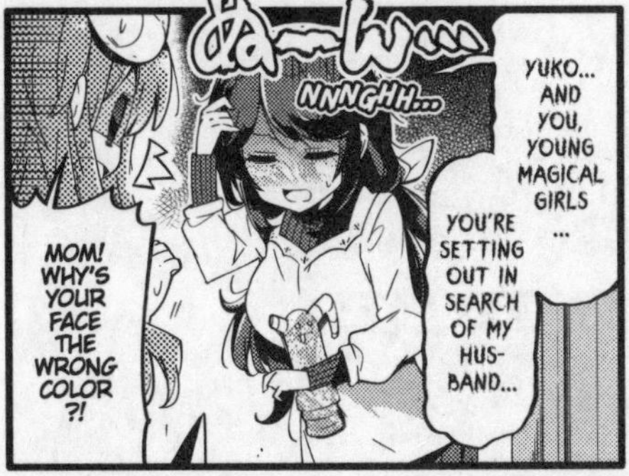
ぬ〜ん…
NNNGHH...
YUKO... AND YOU, YOUNG MAGICAL GIRLS ...
YOU'RE SETTING OUT IN SEARCH OF MY HUS-BAND...
MOM! WHY'S YOUR FACE THE WRONG COLOR ?!

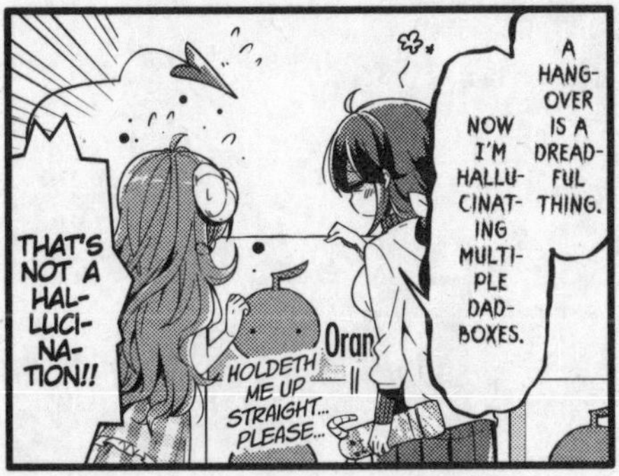
A HANG-OVER IS A DREAD-FUL THING.
NOW I'M HALLU-CINAT-ING MULTI-PLE DAD-BOXES.
THAT'S NOT A HAL-LUCI-NA-TION!!
Oran
HOLDETH ME UP STRAIGHT... PLEASE...

OPENING UP OLD WOUNDS

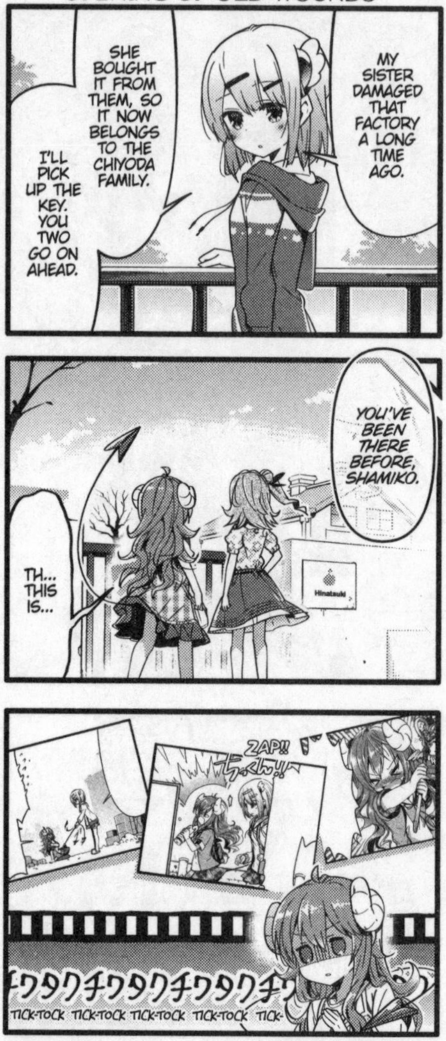
MY SISTER DAMAGED THAT FACTORY A LONG TIME AGO.
SHE BOUGHT IT FROM THEM, SO IT NOW BELONGS TO THE CHIYODA FAMILY.
I'LL PICK UP THE KEY. YOU TWO GO ON AHEAD.
YOU'VE BEEN THERE BEFORE, SHAMIKO.
Hinatsuki
TH... THIS IS...
ZAP!!
TICK-TOCK TICK-TOCK TICK-TOCK TICK-TOCK TICK-
THIS IS THE DEMON TRAUMA FACTORY!!
TROPHE!
ASS
CAT
BRR
EXCUSE ME?! IT WAS NO SUCH THING!!
THIS FACTORY PRODUCED WONDERFUL SNACKS, I'LL HAVE YOU KNOW!!

SHAMIKO'S INTEREST: PIQUED

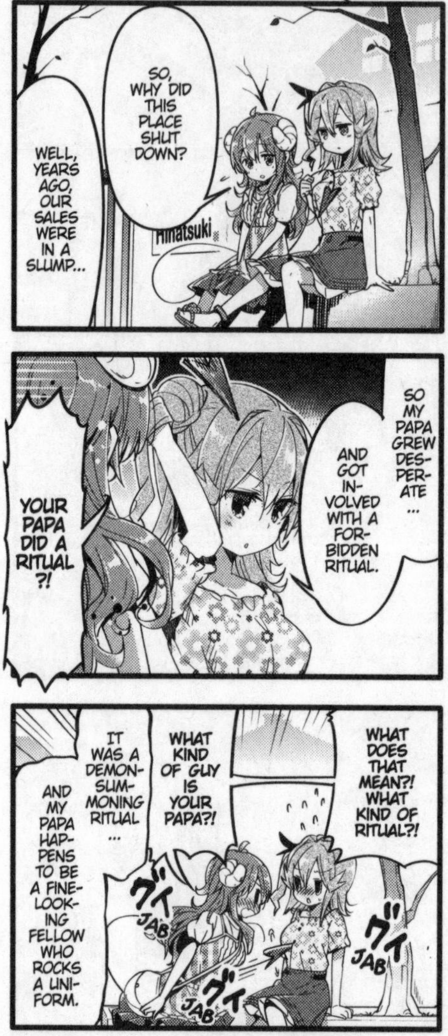
SO, WHY DID THIS PLACE SHUT DOWN?
WELL, YEARS AGO, OUR SALES WERE IN A SLUMP...
Hinatsuki
SO MY PAPA GREW DESPERATE...
AND GOT INVOLVED WITH A FORBIDDEN RITUAL.
YOUR PAPA DID A RITUAL?!
WHAT DOES THAT MEAN?! WHAT KIND OF RITUAL?!
WHAT KIND OF GUY IS YOUR PAPA?!
IT WAS A DEMON-SUMMONING RITUAL...
AND MY PAPA HAPPENS TO BE A FINE-LOOKING FELLOW WHO ROCKS A UNIFORM.
JAB
JAB
JAB
TELL ME MORE!
WHY ARE YOU SO EXCITED?!
I'M SORRY! YOU JUST SAID A LOT OF COOL-SOUNDING WORDS!!

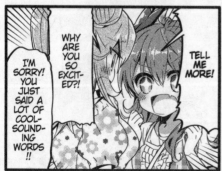

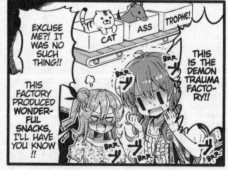

NEW DESTRUCTIVE TECHNIQUES

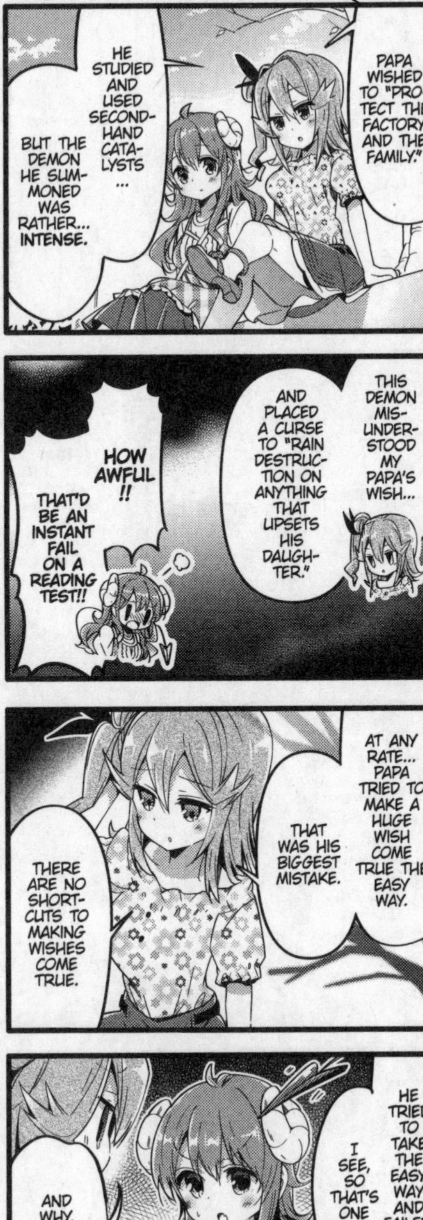
PAPA WISHED TO "PROTECT THE FACTORY AND THE FAMILY."
HE STUDIED AND USED SECOND-HAND CATALYSTS...
BUT THE DEMON HE SUMMONED WAS RATHER... INTENSE.
THIS DEMON MISUNDERSTOOD MY PAPA'S WISH...
AND PLACED A CURSE TO "RAIN DESTRUCTION ON ANYTHING THAT UPSETS HIS DAUGHTER."
HOW AWFUL!!
THAT'D BE AN INSTANT FAIL ON A READING TEST!!
AT ANY RATE... PAPA TRIED TO MAKE A HUGE WISH COME TRUE THE EASY WAY.
THAT WAS HIS BIGGEST MISTAKE.
THERE ARE NO SHORTCUTS TO MAKING WISHES COME TRUE.
HE TRIED TO TAKE THE EASY WAY AND FAILED.
I SEE, SO THAT'S ONE WAY...
AND WHY, MAY I ASK, ARE YOU TAKING NOTES?!

WHEN THE CAT'S AWAY...

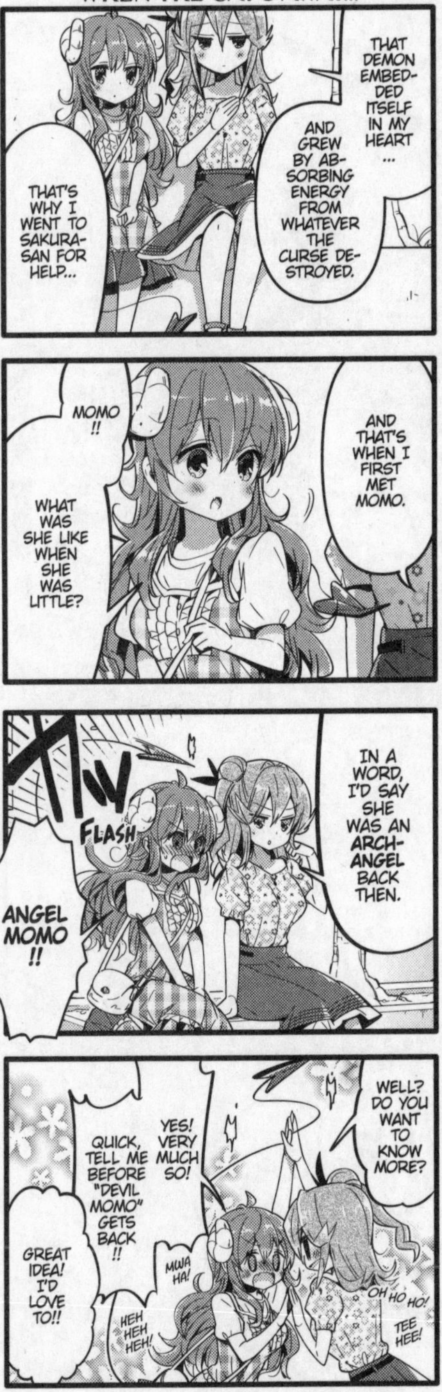
THAT DEMON EMBEDDED ITSELF IN MY HEART...
AND GREW BY ABSORBING ENERGY FROM WHATEVER THE CURSE DESTROYED.
THAT'S WHY I WENT TO SAKURA-SAN FOR HELP...
AND THAT'S WHEN I FIRST MET MOMO.
MOMO!!
WHAT WAS SHE LIKE WHEN SHE WAS LITTLE?
IN A WORD, I'D SAY SHE WAS AN ARCHANGEL BACK THEN.
FLASH
ANGEL MOMO!!
WELL? DO YOU WANT TO KNOW MORE?
YES! VERY MUCH SO!
QUICK, TELL ME BEFORE "DEVIL MOMO" GETS BACK!!
OH HO HO!
TEE HEE!
MWA HA!
HEH HEH HEH!
GREAT IDEA! I'D LOVE TO!!

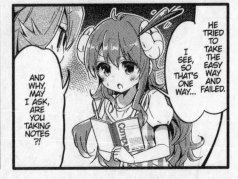

MIKAN'S SPECIAL SECRET, REVEALED!! ①

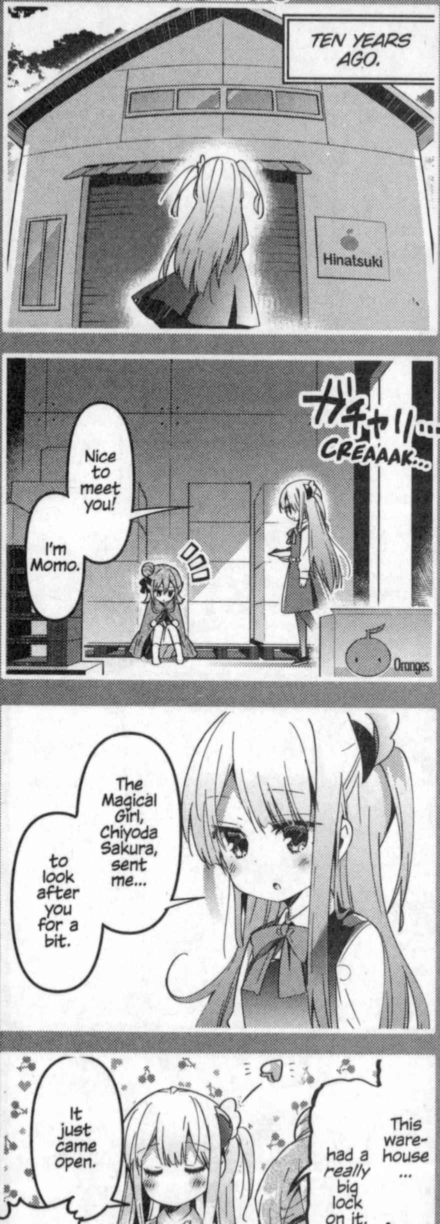
TEN YEARS AGO.
Hinatsuki
ガチャリ… CREAAAK...
Nice to meet you!
I'm Momo.
Oranges
The Magical Girl, Chiyoda Sakura, sent me...
to look after you for a bit.
This warehouse...
had a really big lock on it.
It just came open.
You broke it!!

MIKAN'S SPECIAL SECRET, REVEALED!! ②

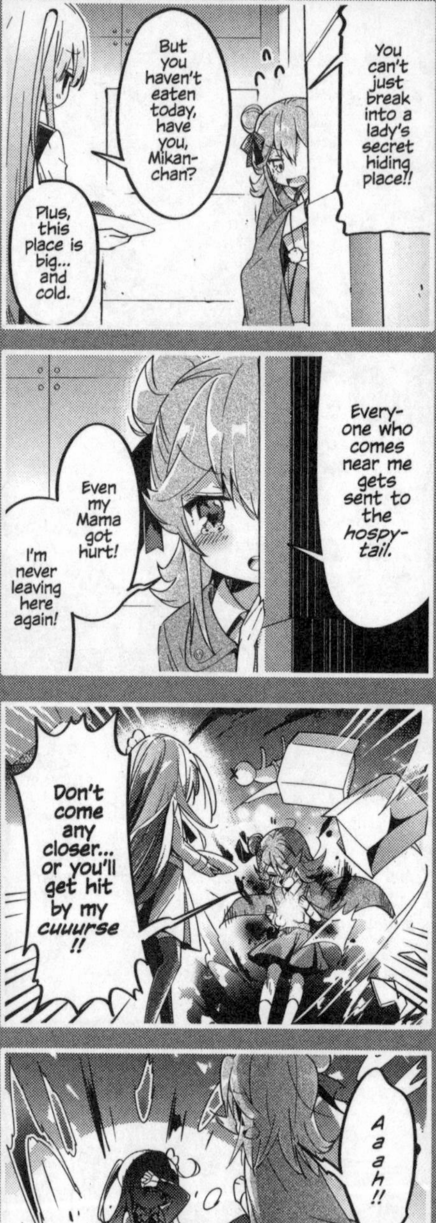
You can't just break into a lady's secret hiding place!!
But you haven't eaten today, have you, Mikan-chan?
Plus, this place is big... and cold.
Everyone who comes near me gets sent to the *hospytail*.
Even my Mama got hurt!
I'm never leaving here again!
Don't come any closer... or you'll get hit by my *cuuurse* !!
Aaaah!!
DWM DWM DWM DWM DWM

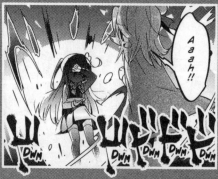

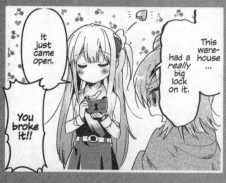

PINK POWER RICE BALLS

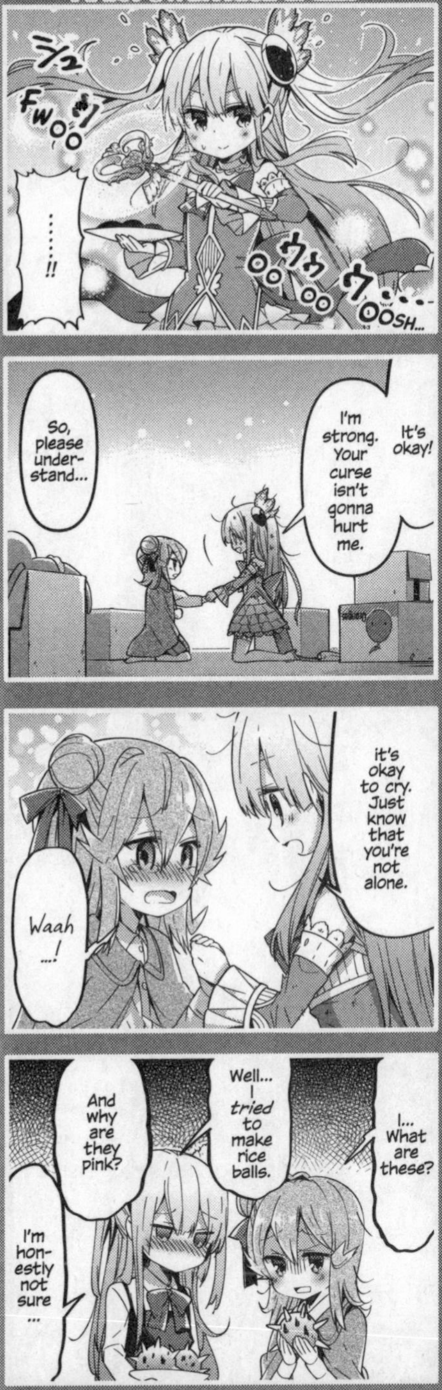
FWOO
......!!
OOOOOOO
OOSH...
It's okay!
I'm strong. Your curse isn't gonna hurt me.
So, please understand...
it's okay to cry. Just know that you're not alone.
Waah...!
I... What are these?
Well... I *tried* to make rice balls.
And why are they pink?
I'm honestly not sure...

MOMO'S ANGEL EPISODES, NOT REVEALED!!

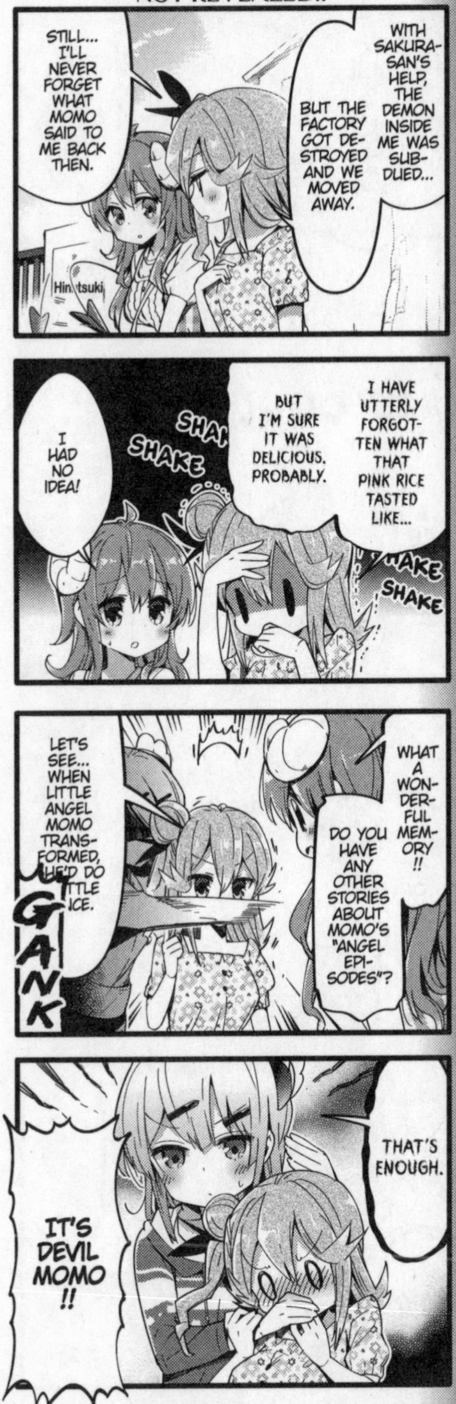
WITH SAKURA-SAN'S HELP, THE DEMON INSIDE ME WAS SUBDUED...
BUT THE FACTORY GOT DESTROYED AND WE MOVED AWAY.
STILL... I'LL NEVER FORGET WHAT MOMO SAID TO ME BACK THEN.
I HAVE UTTERLY FORGOTTEN WHAT THAT PINK RICE TASTED LIKE...
BUT I'M SURE IT WAS DELICIOUS. PROBABLY.
SHAKE
SHAKE
SHAKE
I HAD NO IDEA!
WHAT A WONDERFUL MEMORY!!
DO YOU HAVE ANY OTHER STORIES ABOUT MOMO'S "ANGEL EPISODES"?
LET'S SEE... WHEN LITTLE ANGEL MOMO TRANSFORMED,
GANK
THAT'S ENOUGH.
IT'S DEVIL MOMO!!

MEMORIES DESTROYED

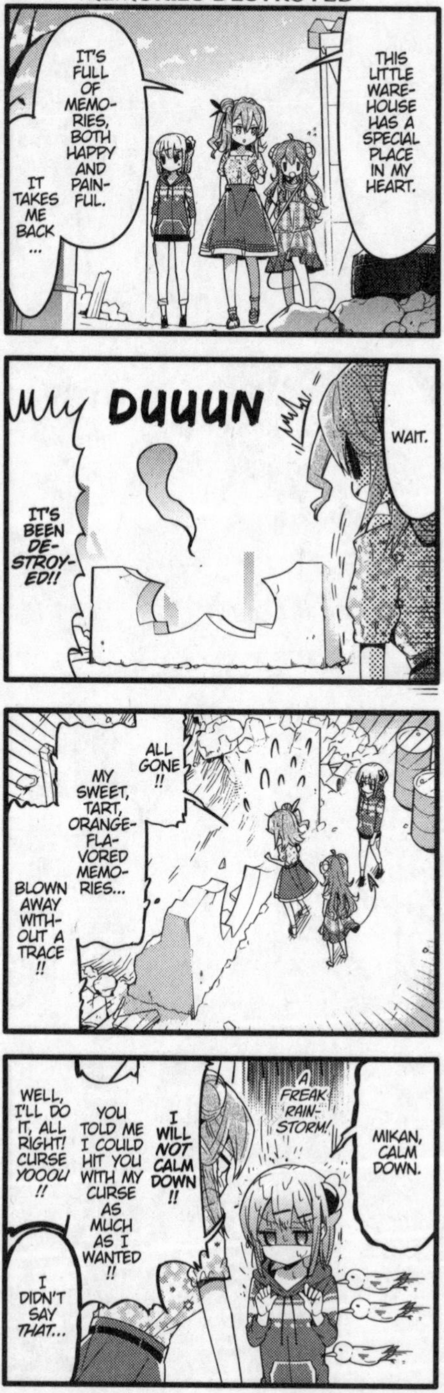
THIS LITTLE WAREHOUSE HAS A SPECIAL PLACE IN MY HEART.
IT'S FULL OF MEMORIES, BOTH HAPPY AND PAINFUL.
IT TAKES ME BACK...
WAIT.
DUUUN
IT'S BEEN DESTROYED!!
ALL GONE!!
MY SWEET, TART, ORANGE-FLAVORED MEMORIES...
BLOWN AWAY WITHOUT A TRACE!!
MIKAN, CALM DOWN.
A FREAK RAINSTORM!
I WILL NOT CALM DOWN!!
YOU TOLD ME I COULD HIT YOU WITH MY CURSE AS MUCH AS I WANTED!!
WELL, I'LL DO IT, ALL RIGHT! CURSE YOOOU!!
I DIDN'T SAY THAT...

THE POWER OF PINK RICE BALLS

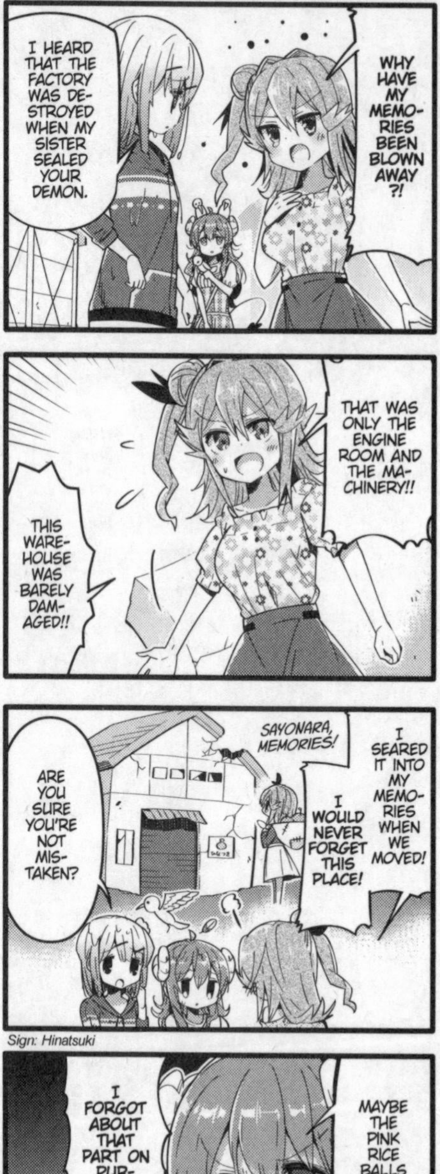
WHY HAVE MY MEMORIES BEEN BLOWN AWAY?!
I HEARD THAT THE FACTORY WAS DESTROYED WHEN MY SISTER SEALED YOUR DEMON.
THAT WAS ONLY THE ENGINE ROOM AND THE MACHINERY!!
THIS WAREHOUSE WAS BARELY DAMAGED!!
I SEARED IT INTO MY MEMORIES WHEN WE MOVED!
SAYONARA, MEMORIES!
I WOULD NEVER FORGET THIS PLACE!
ARE YOU SURE YOU'RE NOT MISTAKEN?
MAYBE THE PINK RICE BALLS ERASED YOUR MEMORIES!
I FORGOT ABOUT THAT PART ON PURPOSE!
COULD YOU TWO STOP TALKING ABOUT MY COOKING?

Sign: Hinatsuki

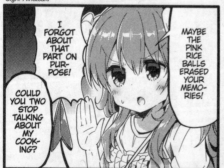

INFORMATION LEAK

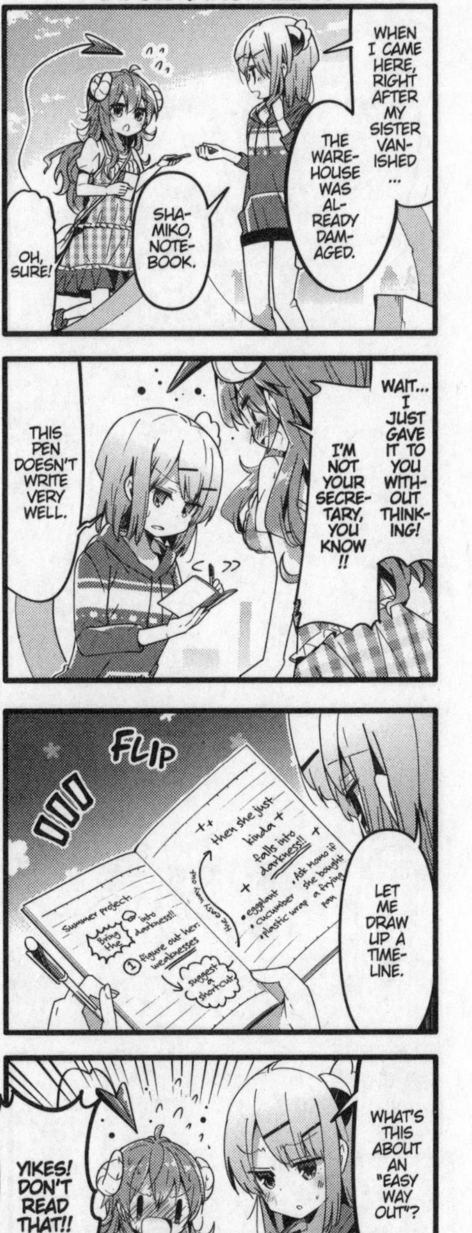
WHEN I CAME HERE, RIGHT AFTER MY SISTER VANISHED...
THE WAREHOUSE WAS ALREADY DAMAGED.
SHAMIKO, NOTEBOOK.
OH, SURE!
WAIT... I JUST GAVE IT TO YOU WITHOUT THINKING!
I'M NOT YOUR SECRETARY, YOU KNOW!!
THIS PEN DOESN'T WRITE VERY WELL.
LET ME DRAW UP A TIMELINE.
FLIP
then she just kinda falls into darkness!!
eggplant
cucumber
plastic wrap
Summer project:
Bring the into darkness!!
① Figure out her weaknesses
suggest a shortcut
WHAT'S THIS ABOUT AN "EASY WAY OUT"?
YIKES! DON'T READ THAT!! DON'T TURN THE PAAAGE!!!

PINK MENTAL OLYMPICS

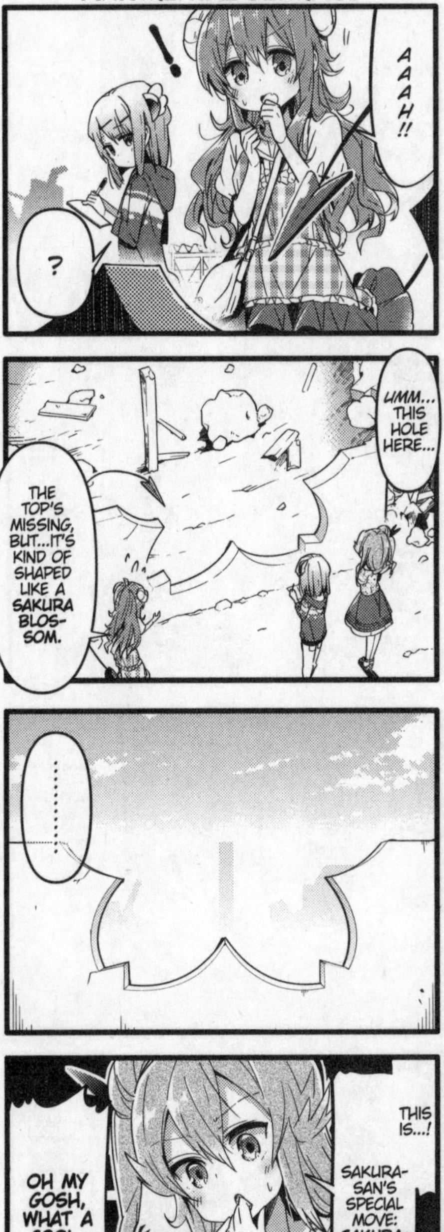
AAAAH!!
!
?
UMM... THIS HOLE HERE...
THE TOP'S MISSING, BUT...IT'S KIND OF SHAPED LIKE A SAKURA BLOSSOM.
......
THIS IS...!
SAKURA-SAN'S SPECIAL MOVE: SAKURAMENT CANNON!!
OH MY GOSH, WHAT A COOL-SOUNDING PHRASE!!

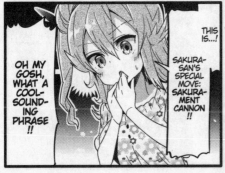

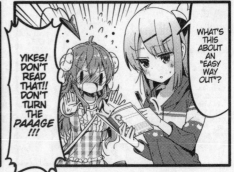

PINK COMMENTARY SEAL

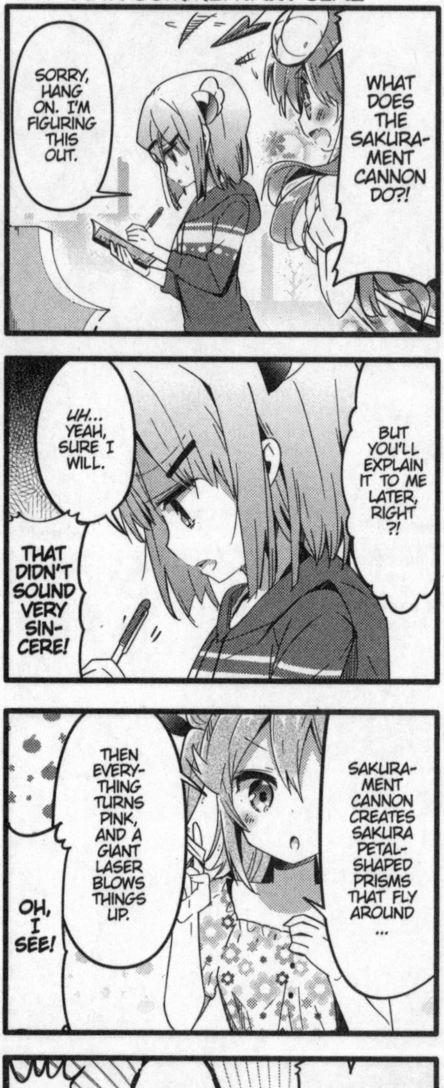
WHAT DOES THE SAKURAMENT CANNON DO?!
SORRY, HANG ON. I'M FIGURING THIS OUT.
BUT YOU'LL EXPLAIN IT TO ME LATER, RIGHT?!
UH... YEAH, SURE I WILL.
THAT DIDN'T SOUND VERY SINCERE!
SAKURAMENT CANNON CREATES SAKURA PETAL-SHAPED PRISMS THAT FLY AROUND...
THEN EVERYTHING TURNS PINK, AND A GIANT LASER BLOWS THINGS UP.
OH, I SEE!
BY THE WAY, FRESH PEACH HEART SHOWER IS--
MMPH!
YOU GUYS ARE WAY TOO CHATTY.
MIKAN-SAAAN!!

BECOME AN ADAPTABLE DEMON

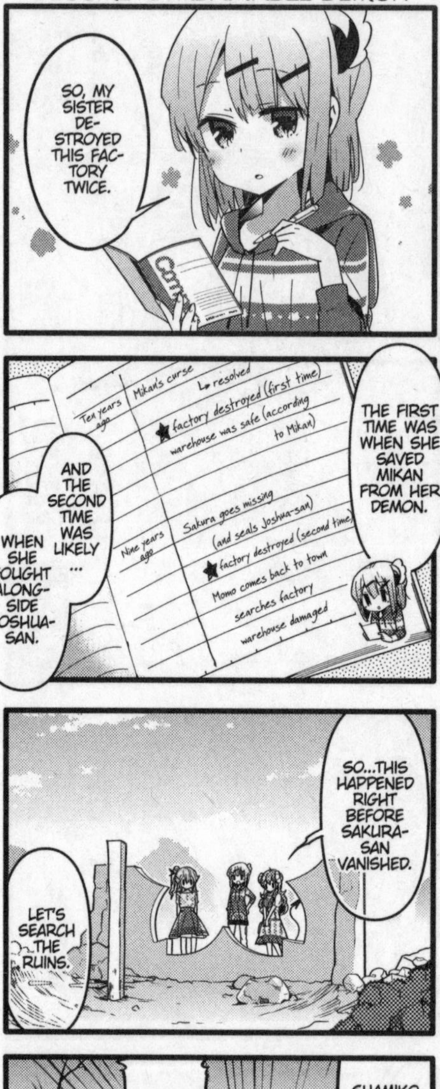
SO, MY SISTER DESTROYED THIS FACTORY TWICE.
THE FIRST TIME WAS WHEN SHE SAVED MIKAN FROM HER DEMON.
Ten years ago
Mikan's curse
↳ resolved
factory destroyed (first time)
warehouse was safe (according to Mikan)
Nine years ago
Sakura goes missing
(and seals Joshua-san)
factory destroyed (second time)
Momo comes back to town
searches factory
warehouse damaged
AND THE SECOND TIME WAS LIKELY...
WHEN SHE FOUGHT ALONGSIDE JOSHUA-SAN.
SO...THIS HAPPENED RIGHT BEFORE SAKURA-SAN VANISHED.
LET'S SEARCH THE RUINS.
SHAMIKO, DO YOU HAVE A SHOVEL AND STUFF?
OF COURSE I DON'T, DARN IT!!
THAT'S HEAVY!!
DON'T GIVE UP, SHAMIKO!! BECOME A DEMON WHO'S READY FOR ALL KINDS OF SITUATIONS!!

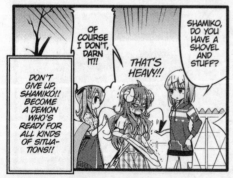

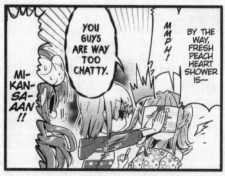

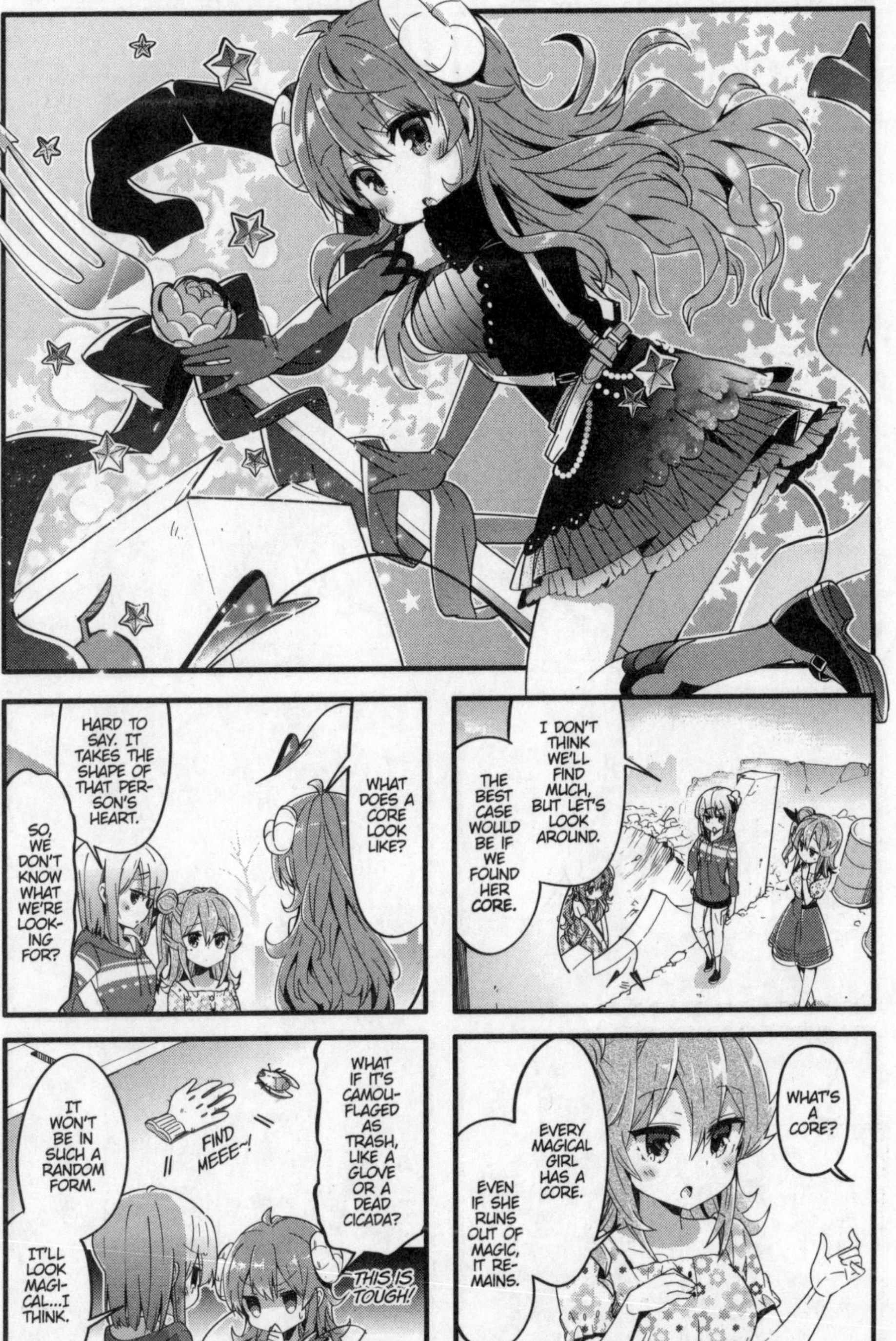

I DON'T THINK WE'LL FIND MUCH, BUT LET'S LOOK AROUND.
THE BEST CASE WOULD BE IF WE FOUND HER CORE.
WHAT DOES A CORE LOOK LIKE?
HARD TO SAY. IT TAKES THE SHAPE OF THAT PERSON'S HEART.
SO, WE DON'T KNOW WHAT WE'RE LOOKING FOR?
WHAT'S A CORE?
EVERY MAGICAL GIRL HAS A CORE.
EVEN IF SHE RUNS OUT OF MAGIC, IT REMAINS.
WHAT IF IT'S CAMOUFLAGED AS TRASH, LIKE A GLOVE OR A DEAD CICADA?
FIND MEEE~!
IT WON'T BE IN SUCH A RANDOM FORM.
THIS IS TOUGH!
IT'LL LOOK MAGICAL...I THINK.

ALL ABOUT THE MUSCLES

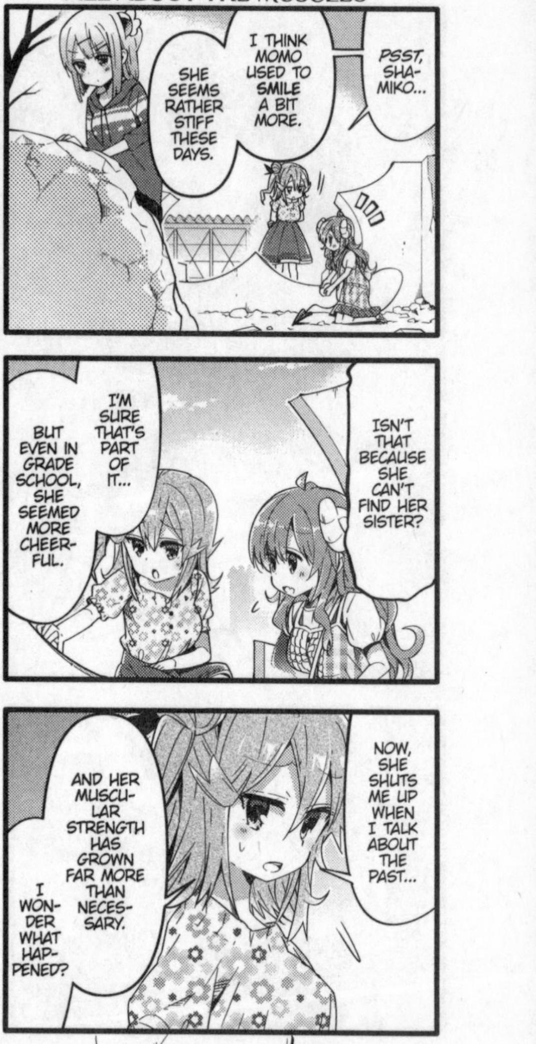
PSST, SHAMIKO...
I THINK MOMO USED TO SMILE A BIT MORE.
SHE SEEMS RATHER STIFF THESE DAYS.
ISN'T THAT BECAUSE SHE CAN'T FIND HER SISTER?
I'M SURE THAT'S PART OF IT...
BUT EVEN IN GRADE SCHOOL, SHE SEEMED MORE CHEERFUL.
NOW, SHE SHUTS ME UP WHEN I TALK ABOUT THE PAST...
AND HER MUSCULAR STRENGTH HAS GROWN FAR MORE THAN NECESSARY.
I WONDER WHAT HAPPENED?
SHE TOLD ME HER MUSCLES WERE ENHANCED BY MAGIC.
DID SHE JUST DIG UP THAT ROCK?
NO, THAT'S A BIT MUCH, EVEN FOR A MAGICAL GIRL.

RECEIVING A DEMON SIGNAL

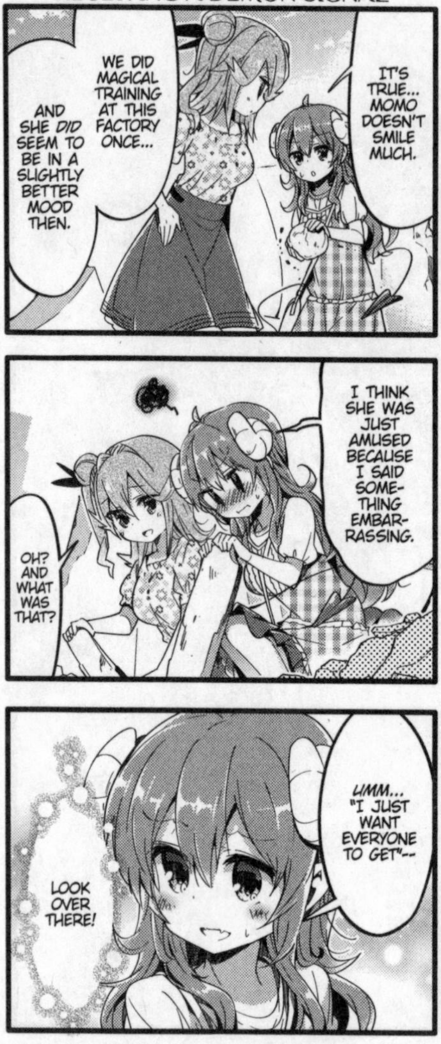
IT'S TRUE... MOMO DOESN'T SMILE MUCH.
WE DID MAGICAL TRAINING AT THIS FACTORY ONCE...
AND SHE *DID* SEEM TO BE IN A SLIGHTLY BETTER MOOD THEN.
I THINK SHE WAS JUST AMUSED BECAUSE I SAID SOMETHING EMBARRASSING.
OH? AND WHAT WAS THAT?
UMM... "I JUST WANT EVERYONE TO GET"--
LOOK OVER THERE!
DID YOU JUST SAY SOMETHING, MIKAN-SAN?
EH ?!
NO, NOT A THING.

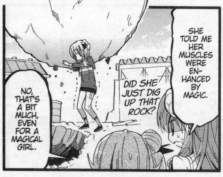

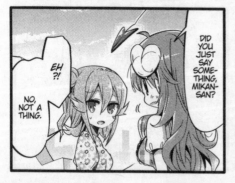

DEMON DISCOVERY

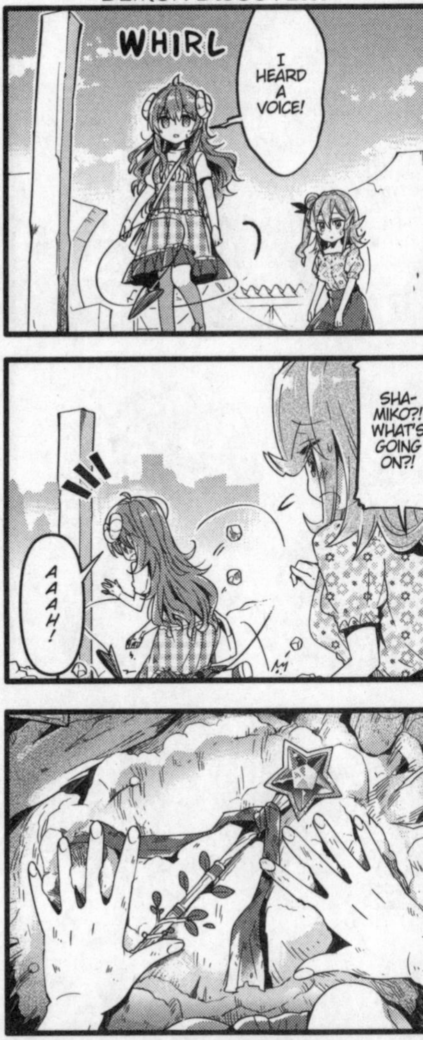
WHIRL
I HEARD A VOICE!
SHA-MIKO?! WHAT'S GOING ON?!
AAAH!
I'VE...
I'VE FOUND SOMETHING BIG!!
NEW WEAPON ACQUIRED!!

THE DEMON MAKES THINGS AWKWARD

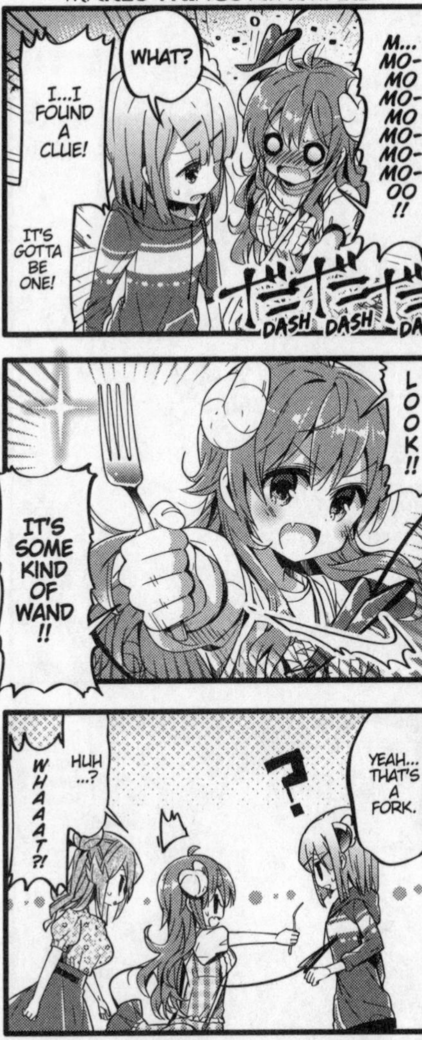
M... MOMOMOMO-MOMOMOMO-MOMOMOO!!
WHAT?
I...I FOUND A CLUE!
IT'S GOTTA BE ONE!
DASH DASH DASH
LOOK!!
IT'S SOME KIND OF WAND!!
YEAH... THAT'S A FORK.
HUH...?
WHAAAAT?!
NO!!
UHH... IT WAS A WAND JUST A MINUTE AGO! HUH?!
SHAMIKO, ARE YOU HUNGRY?
DON'T LOOK AT ME LIKE THAT!!

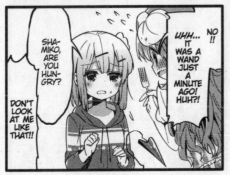

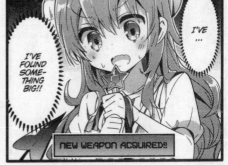

LIKE THEY'RE LOOKING AT A SICK PERSON

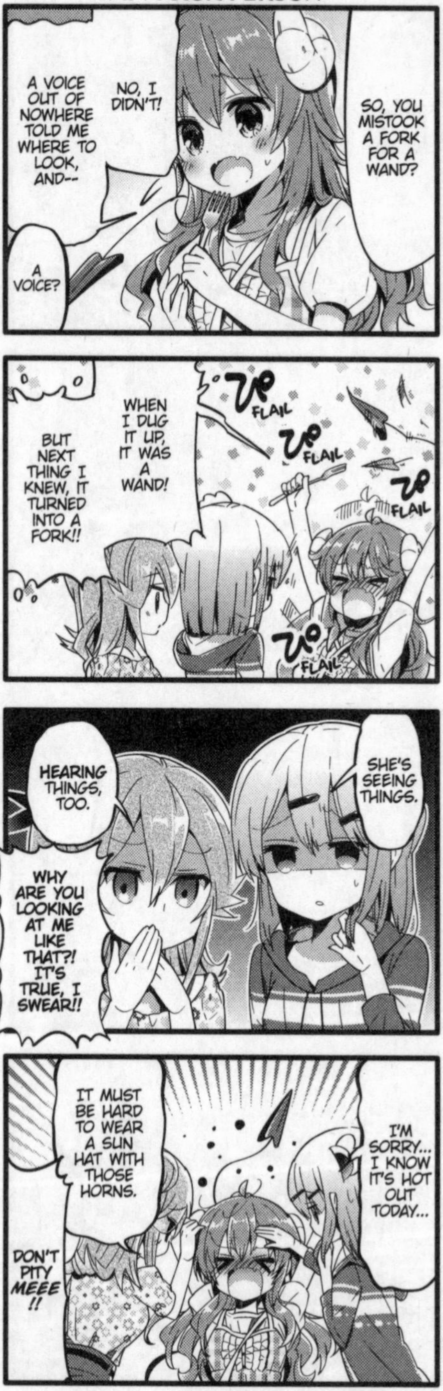
SO, YOU MISTOOK A FORK FOR A WAND?
NO, I DIDN'T!
A VOICE OUT OF NOWHERE TOLD ME WHERE TO LOOK, AND--
A VOICE?
FLAIL
FLAIL
WHEN I DUG IT UP, IT WAS A WAND!
FLAIL
BUT NEXT THING I KNEW, IT TURNED INTO A FORK!!
FLAIL
SHE'S SEEING THINGS.
HEARING THINGS, TOO.
WHY ARE YOU LOOKING AT ME LIKE THAT?! IT'S TRUE, I SWEAR!!
I'M SORRY... I KNOW IT'S HOT OUT TODAY...
IT MUST BE HARD TO WEAR A SUN HAT WITH THOSE HORNS.
DON'T PITY *MEEE*!!

A YOSHIDA FAMILY TREASURE

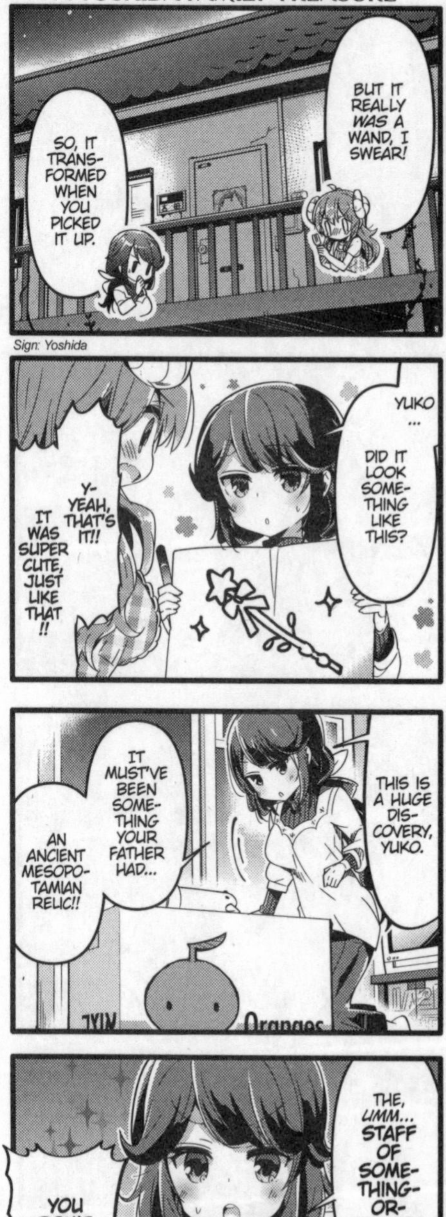
BUT IT REALLY *WAS* A WAND, I SWEAR!
SO, IT TRANSFORMED WHEN YOU PICKED IT UP.
YUKO... DID IT LOOK SOMETHING LIKE THIS?
Y-YEAH, THAT'S IT!!
IT WAS SUPER CUTE, JUST LIKE THAT!!
THIS IS A HUGE DISCOVERY, YUKO.
IT MUST'VE BEEN SOMETHING YOUR FATHER HAD...
AN ANCIENT MESOPOTAMIAN RELIC!!
THE, *UMM*... STAFF OF SOMETHING-OR-OTHER!
YOU DON'T REMEMBER WHAT IT'S CALLED?!

Sign: Yoshida

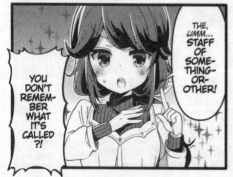

A CHEAP SHOCHU HANGOVER IS HELL

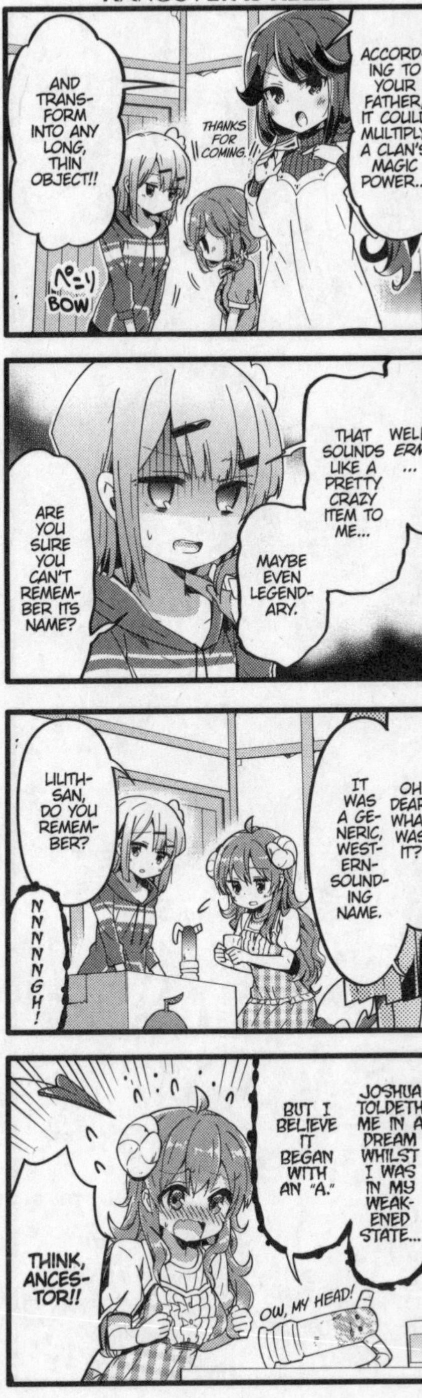
ACCORDING TO YOUR FATHER, IT COULD MULTIPLY A CLAN'S MAGIC POWER...
AND TRANSFORM INTO ANY LONG, THIN OBJECT!!
THANKS FOR COMING.
ぺこり
BOW
WELL, *ERM* ...
THAT SOUNDS LIKE A PRETTY CRAZY ITEM TO ME...
MAYBE EVEN LEGENDARY.
ARE YOU SURE YOU CAN'T REMEMBER ITS NAME?
OH DEAR, WHAT WAS IT?
IT WAS A GENERIC, WESTERN-SOUNDING NAME.
LILITH-SAN, DO YOU REMEMBER?
NNNNNNGH!
JOSHUA TOLDETH ME IN A DREAM WHILST I WAS IN MY WEAKENED STATE...
BUT I BELIEVE IT BEGAN WITH AN "A."
OW, MY HEAD!
THINK, ANCESTOR!!

THE ANCESTOR SQUEEZES OUT A SPEECH

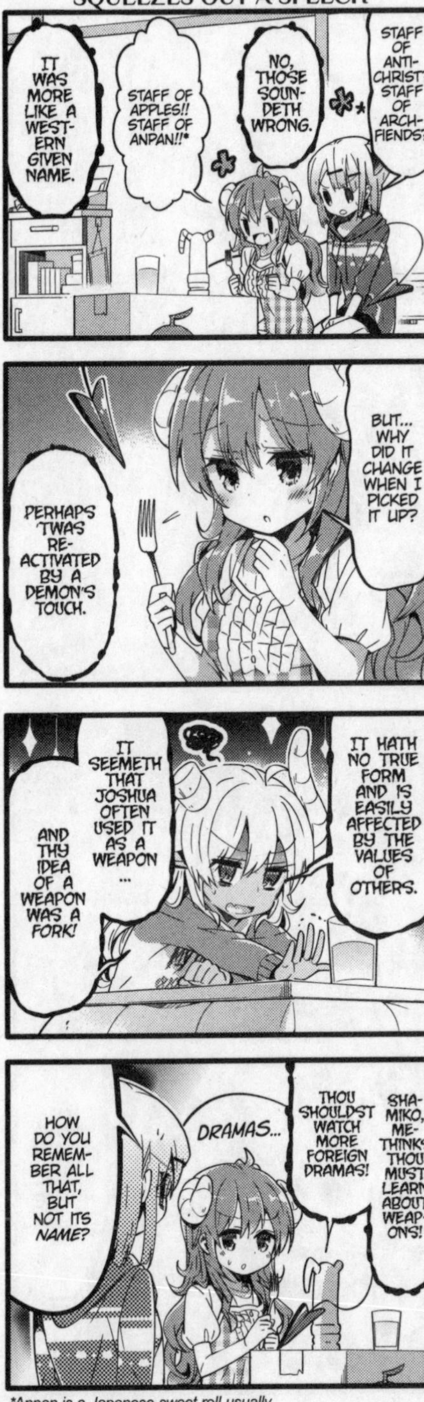
STAFF OF ANTI-CHRIST? STAFF OF ARCH-FIENDS?
NO, THOSE SOUNDETH WRONG.
STAFF OF APPLES!! STAFF OF ANPAN!!*
IT WAS MORE LIKE A WESTERN GIVEN NAME.
BUT... WHY DID IT CHANGE WHEN I PICKED IT UP?
PERHAPS TWAS REACTIVATED BY A DEMON'S TOUCH.
IT HATH NO TRUE FORM AND IS EASILY AFFECTED BY THE VALUES OF OTHERS.
IT SEEMETH THAT JOSHUA OFTEN USED IT AS A WEAPON ...
AND THY IDEA OF A WEAPON WAS A FORK!
SHAMIKO, METHINKS THOU MUST LEARN ABOUT WEAPONS!
THOU SHOULDST WATCH MORE FOREIGN DRAMAS!
DRAMAS...
HOW DO YOU REMEMBER ALL THAT, BUT NOT ITS *NAME*?

**Anpan is a Japanese sweet roll usually filled with red bean paste.*

PRECIOUS FAMILY HEIRLOOM (WHATEVER IT'S CALLED)

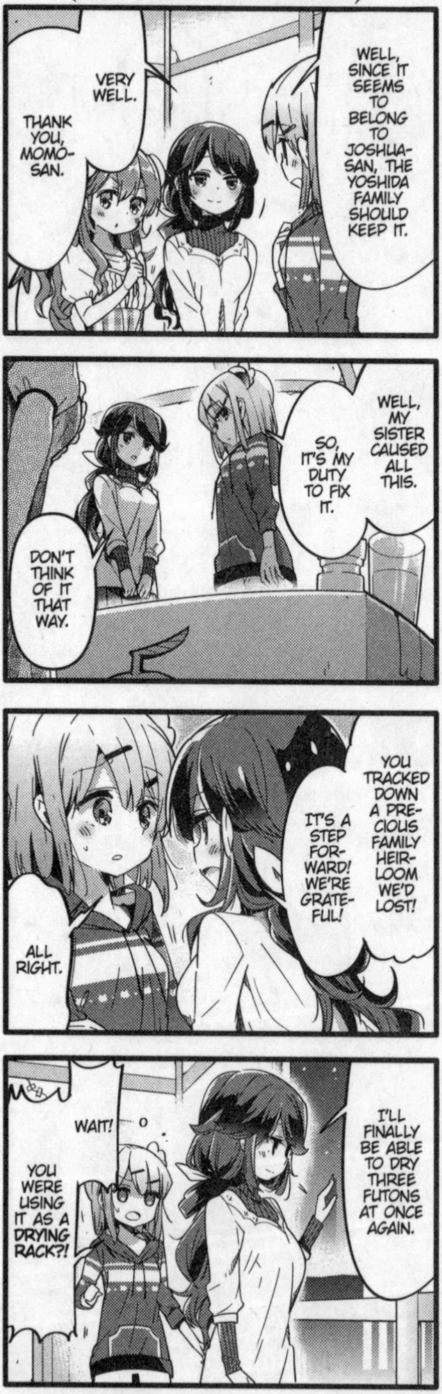
WELL, SINCE IT SEEMS TO BELONG TO JOSHUA-SAN, THE YOSHIDA FAMILY SHOULD KEEP IT.
VERY WELL.
THANK YOU, MOMO-SAN.
WELL, MY SISTER CAUSED ALL THIS.
SO, IT'S MY DUTY TO FIX IT.
DON'T THINK OF IT THAT WAY.
YOU TRACKED DOWN A PRECIOUS FAMILY HEIRLOOM WE'D LOST!
IT'S A STEP FORWARD! WE'RE GRATEFUL!
ALL RIGHT.
I'LL FINALLY BE ABLE TO DRY THREE FUTONS AT ONCE AGAIN.
WAIT!
YOU WERE USING IT AS A DRYING RACK?!

DEMONS GET WORKED UP ABOUT WEIRD THINGS

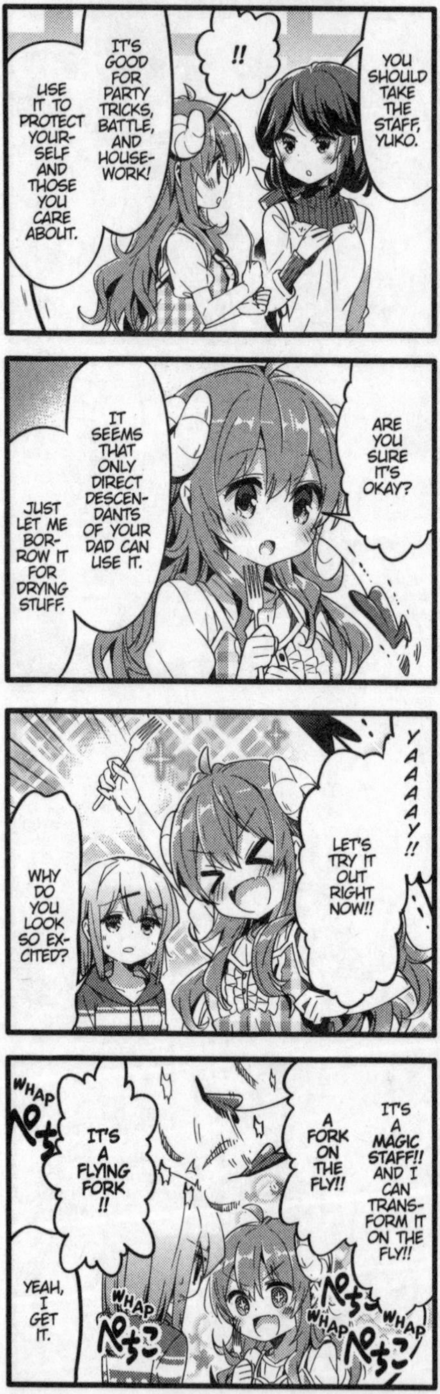
YOU SHOULD TAKE THE STAFF, YUKO.
!!
IT'S GOOD FOR PARTY TRICKS, BATTLE, AND HOUSEWORK!
USE IT TO PROTECT YOURSELF AND THOSE YOU CARE ABOUT.
ARE YOU SURE IT'S OKAY?
IT SEEMS THAT ONLY DIRECT DESCENDANTS OF YOUR DAD CAN USE IT.
JUST LET ME BORROW IT FOR DRYING STUFF.
YAAAAAY!!
LET'S TRY IT OUT RIGHT NOW!!
WHY DO YOU LOOK SO EXCITED?
IT'S A MAGIC STAFF!! AND I CAN TRANSFORM IT ON THE FLY!!
A FORK ON THE FLY!!
IT'S A FLYING FORK!!
WHAP
YEAH, I GET IT.
WHAP
WHAP
WHAP
WHAP

A SIMPLE REALIZATION

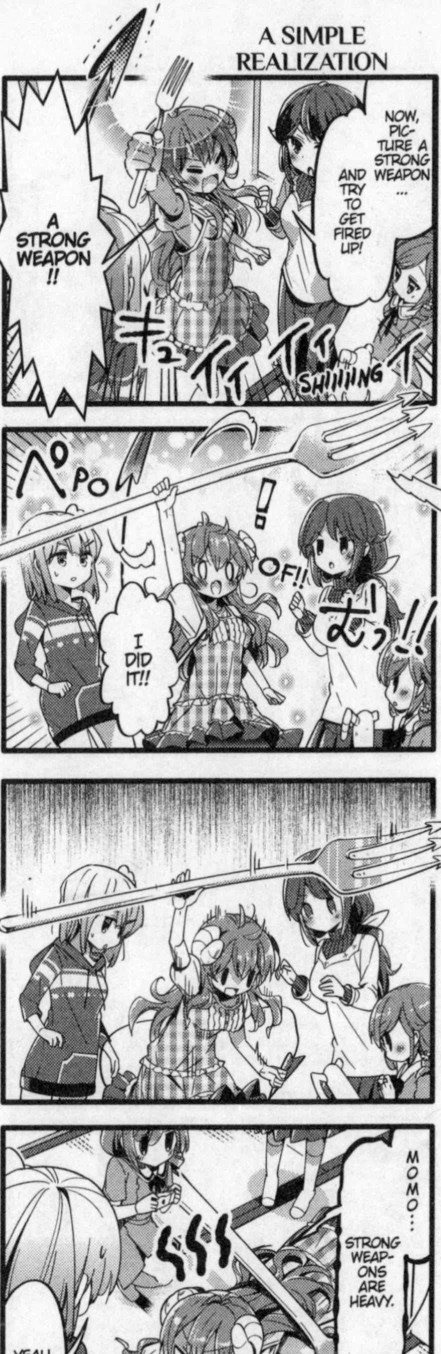
NOW, PICTURE A STRONG WEAPON ...
AND TRY TO GET FIRED UP!
A STRONG WEAPON !!
SHIIIIING
PO
!
OF!!
I DID IT!!
MOMO...
STRONG WEAPONS ARE HEAVY.
YEAH, I KNOW.

HOMEMAKER DEMON

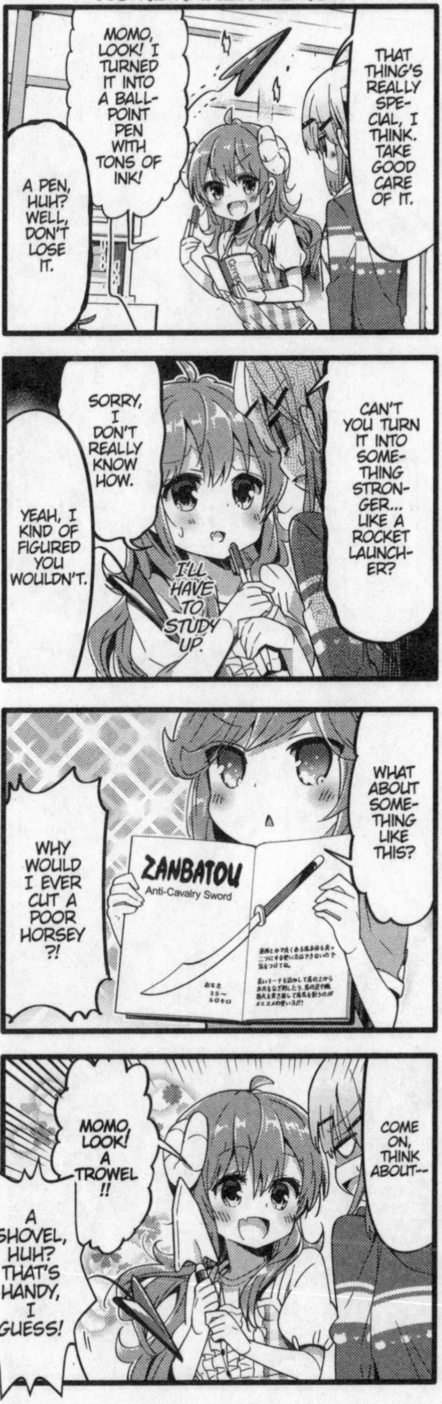
THAT THING'S REALLY SPECIAL, I THINK. TAKE GOOD CARE OF IT.
MOMO, LOOK! I TURNED IT INTO A BALLPOINT PEN WITH TONS OF INK!
A PEN, HUH? WELL, DON'T LOSE IT.
CAN'T YOU TURN IT INTO SOMETHING STRONGER... LIKE A ROCKET LAUNCHER?
SORRY, I DON'T REALLY KNOW HOW.
YEAH, I KIND OF FIGURED YOU WOULDN'T.
I'LL HAVE TO STUDY UP.
WHAT ABOUT SOMETHING LIKE THIS?
ZANBATOU
Anti-Cavalry Sword
WHY WOULD I EVER CUT A POOR HORSEY ?!
COME ON, THINK ABOUT--
MOMO, LOOK! A TROWEL !!
A SHOVEL, HUH? THAT'S HANDY, I GUESS!

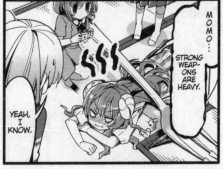

BECOME A DEMON WITH TALENT

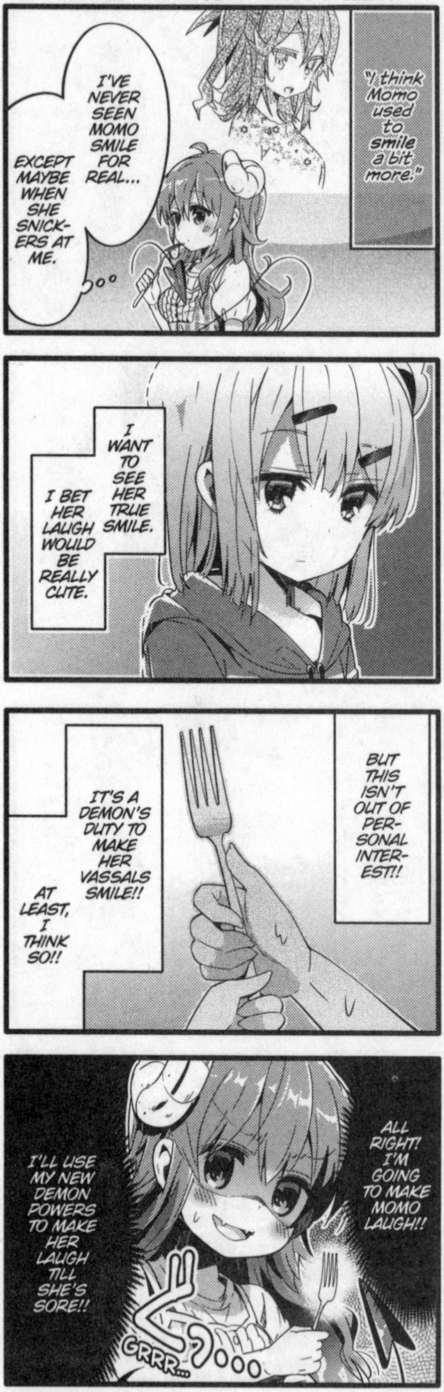
"I think Momo used to smile a bit more."
I'VE NEVER SEEN MOMO SMILE FOR REAL...
EXCEPT MAYBE WHEN SHE SNICKERS AT ME.
I WANT TO SEE HER TRUE SMILE.
I BET HER LAUGH WOULD BE REALLY CUTE.
BUT THIS ISN'T OUT OF PERSONAL INTEREST!!
IT'S A DEMON'S DUTY TO MAKE HER VASSALS SMILE!!
AT LEAST, I THINK SO!!
ALL RIGHT! I'M GOING TO MAKE MOMO LAUGH!!
I'LL USE MY NEW DEMON POWERS TO MAKE HER LAUGH TILL SHE'S SORE!!
GRRR...

DEMONIC DELIVERY

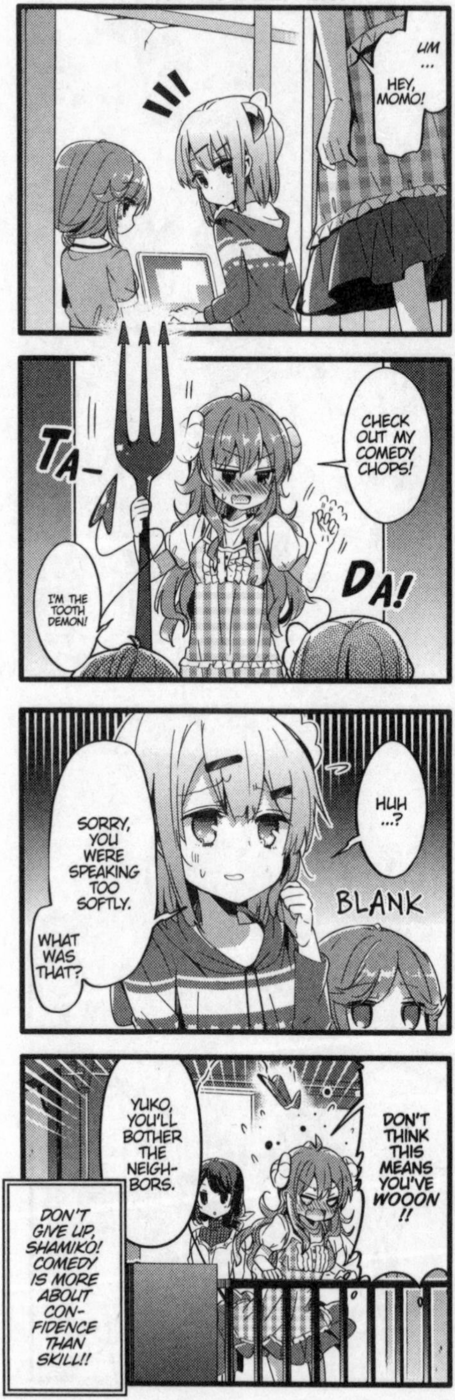
UM ...
HEY, MOMO!
CHECK OUT MY COMEDY CHOPS!
TA-
DA!
I'M THE TOOTH DEMON!
HUH ...?
BLANK
SORRY, YOU WERE SPEAKING TOO SOFTLY.
WHAT WAS THAT?
DON'T THINK THIS MEANS YOU'VE WOOON !!
YUKO, YOU'LL BOTHER THE NEIGHBORS.
DON'T GIVE UP, SHAMIKO! COMEDY IS MORE ABOUT CONFIDENCE THAN SKILL!!

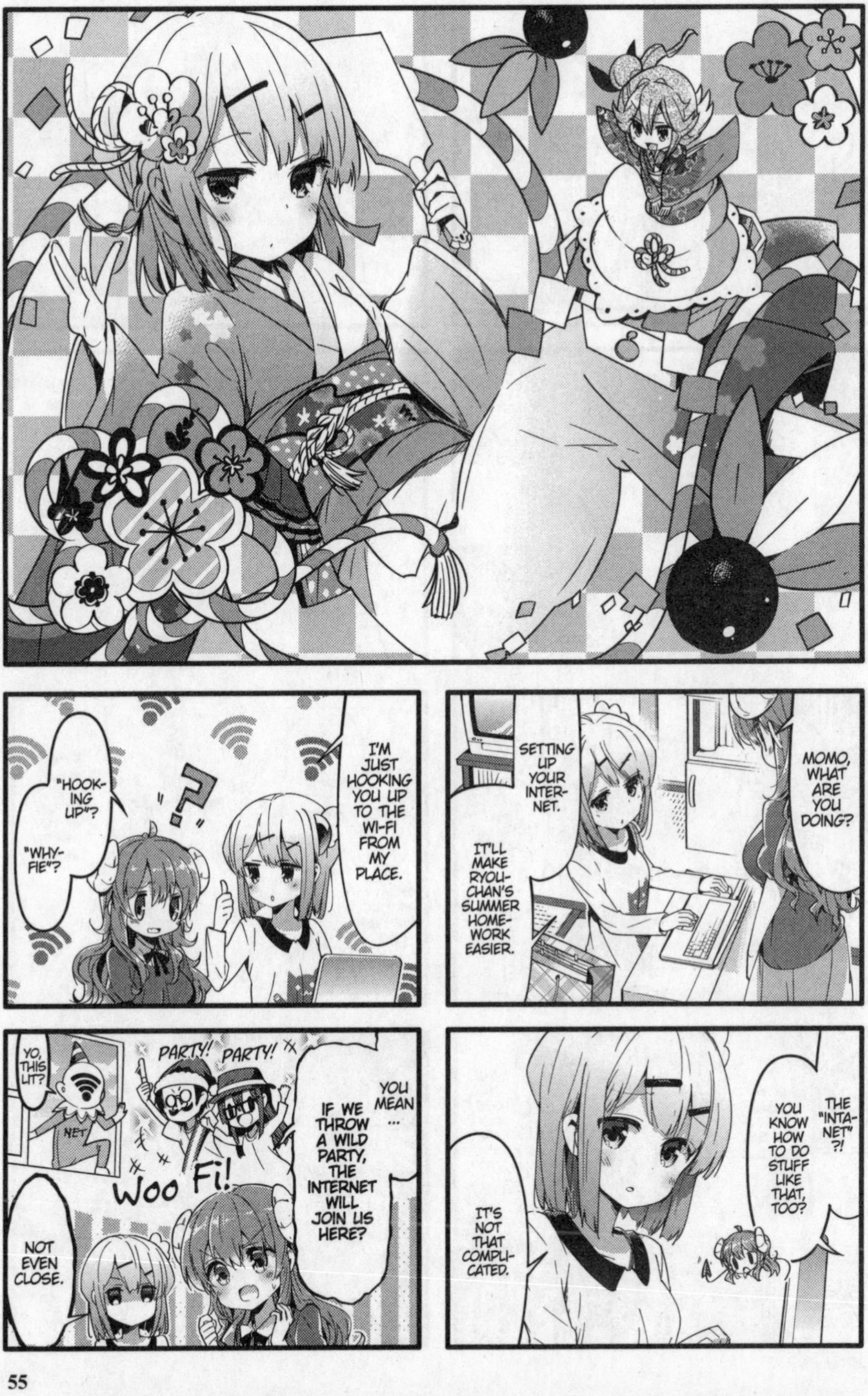
MOMO, WHAT ARE YOU DOING?
SETTING UP YOUR INTERNET.
IT'LL MAKE RYOU-CHAN'S SUMMER HOMEWORK EASIER.
I'M JUST HOOKING YOU UP TO THE WI-FI FROM MY PLACE.
"?!"
"HOOKING UP"?
"WHYFIE"?
THE "INTANET"?!
YOU KNOW HOW TO DO STUFF LIKE THAT, TOO?
IT'S NOT THAT COMPLICATED.
YOU MEAN ...
IF WE THROW A WILD PARTY, THE INTERNET WILL JOIN US HERE?
PARTY!
PARTY!
YO, THIS LIT?
NET
Woo Fi!
NOT EVEN CLOSE.

INFORMATION-AGE DEMON

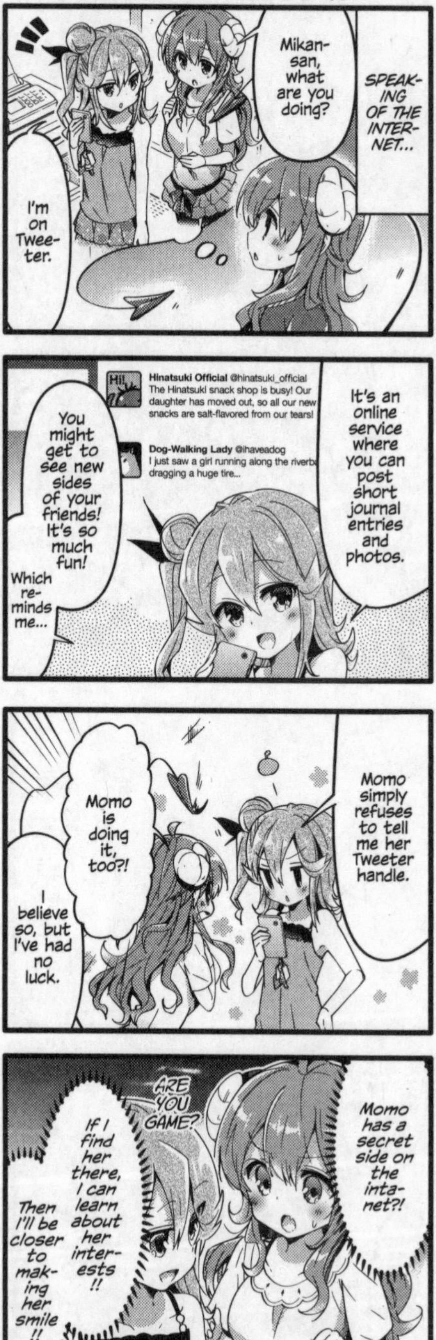
SPEAKING OF THE INTERNET...
Mikan-san, what are you doing?
I'm on Tweeter.
It's an online service where you can post short journal entries and photos.
Hinatsuki Official @hinatsuki_official
The Hinatsuki snack shop is busy! Our daughter has moved out, so all our new snacks are salt-flavored from our tears!
Dog-Walking Lady @ihaveadog
I just saw a girl running along the riverb
dragging a huge tire...
You might get to see new sides of your friends! It's so much fun!
Which reminds me...
Momo simply refuses to tell me her Tweeter handle.
Momo is doing it, too?!
I believe so, but I've had no luck.
Momo has a secret side on the intanet?!
ARE YOU GAME?
If I find her there, I can learn about her interests!!
Then I'll be closer to making her smile!!

PEOPLE CALL THAT "CYBERSTALKING"

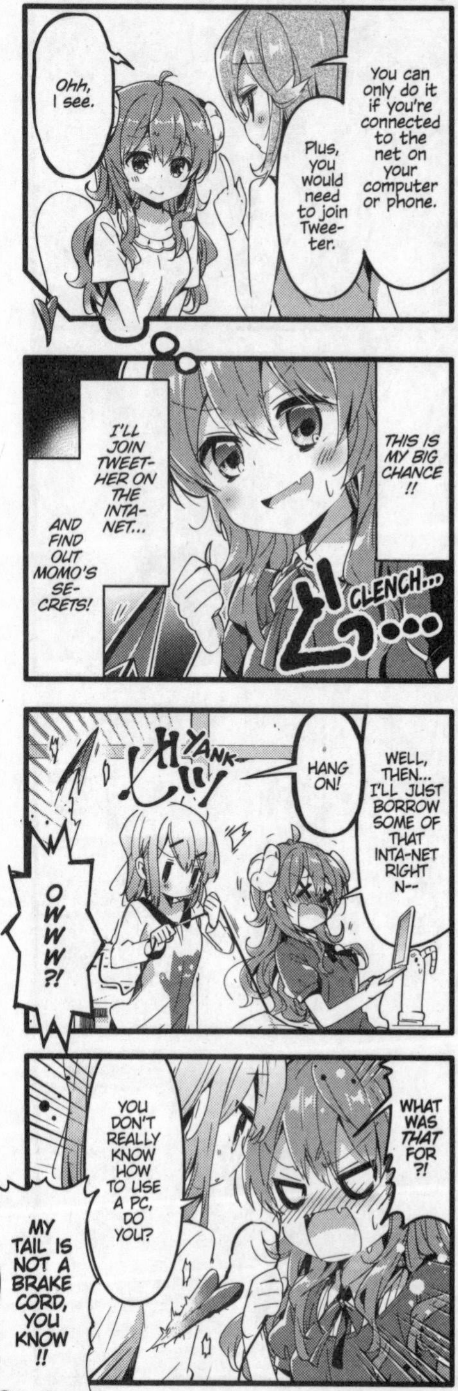
You can only do it if you're connected to the net on your computer or phone.
Plus, you would need to join Tweeter.
Ohh, I see.
THIS IS MY BIG CHANCE!!
I'LL JOIN TWEETER ON THE INTA-NET...
AND FIND OUT MOMO'S SECRETS!
CLENCH...
WELL, THEN... I'LL JUST BORROW SOME OF THAT INTA-NET RIGHT N--
HANG ON!
YANK
OWWW?!
WHAT WAS THAT FOR?!
YOU DON'T REALLY KNOW HOW TO USE A PC, DO YOU?
MY TAIL IS NOT A BRAKE CORD, YOU KNOW!!

MOM SENSES A MEETING

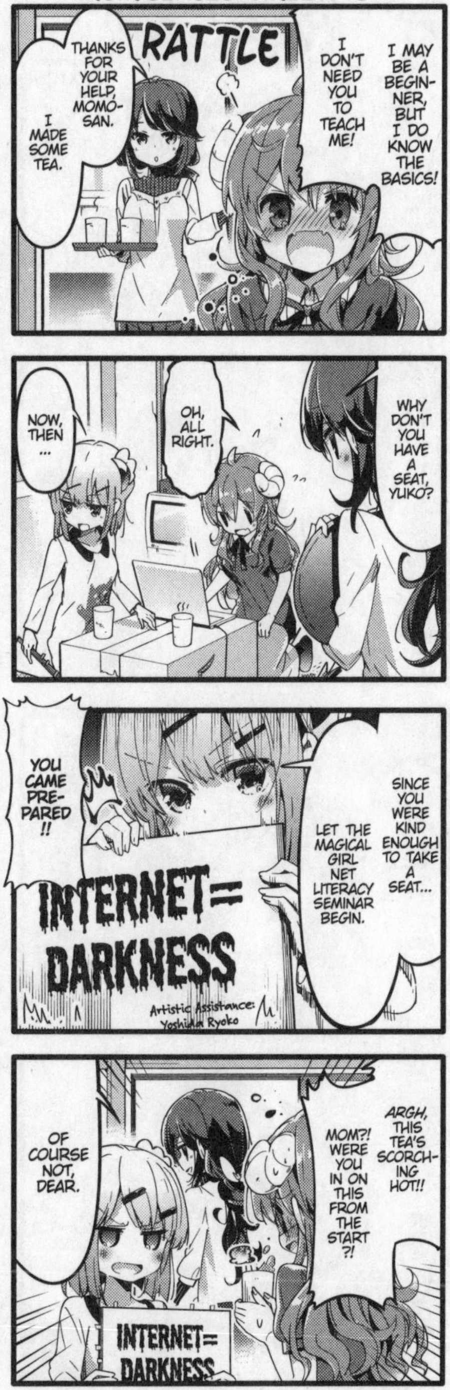
I MAY BE A BEGINNER, BUT I DO KNOW THE BASICS!
I DON'T NEED YOU TO TEACH ME!
RATTLE
THANKS FOR YOUR HELP, MOMO-SAN.
I MADE SOME TEA.
WHY DON'T YOU HAVE A SEAT, YUKO?
OH, ALL RIGHT.
NOW, THEN...
SINCE YOU WERE KIND ENOUGH TO TAKE A SEAT...
LET THE MAGICAL GIRL NET LITERACY SEMINAR BEGIN.
YOU CAME PREPARED!!
INTERNET= DARKNESS
Artistic Assistance: Yoshida Ryoko
ARGH, THIS TEA'S SCORCHING HOT!!
MOM?! WERE YOU IN ON THIS FROM THE START?!
OF COURSE NOT, DEAR.
INTERNET= DARKNESS

THE DARKNESS OF THE INTERNET IS DEEP

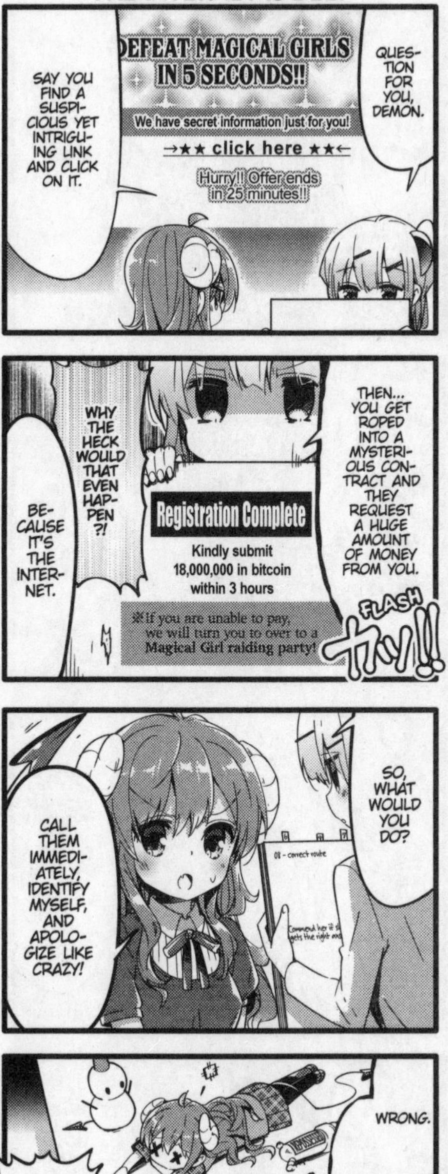
QUESTION FOR YOU, DEMON.
DEFEAT MAGICAL GIRLS IN 5 SECONDS!!
We have secret information just for you!
→★★ click here ★★←
Hurry!! Offer ends in 25 minutes!!
SAY YOU FIND A SUSPICIOUS YET INTRIGUING LINK AND CLICK ON IT.
THEN... YOU GET ROPED INTO A MYSTERIOUS CONTRACT AND THEY REQUEST A HUGE AMOUNT OF MONEY FROM YOU.
FLASH カッ!!
Registration Complete
Kindly submit 18,000,000 in bitcoin within 3 hours
※If you are unable to pay, we will turn you to over to a Magical Girl raiding party!
WHY THE HECK WOULD THAT EVEN HAPPEN?!
BECAUSE IT'S THE INTERNET.
SO, WHAT WOULD YOU DO?
08 - correct route
CALL THEM IMMEDIATELY, IDENTIFY MYSELF, AND APOLOGIZE LIKE CRAZY!
WRONG.
THE DEMON HAS DIED.
You are Dead
WAIT, I COULD DIE?!

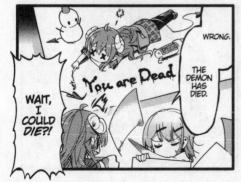

SUSPICIOUS ACT

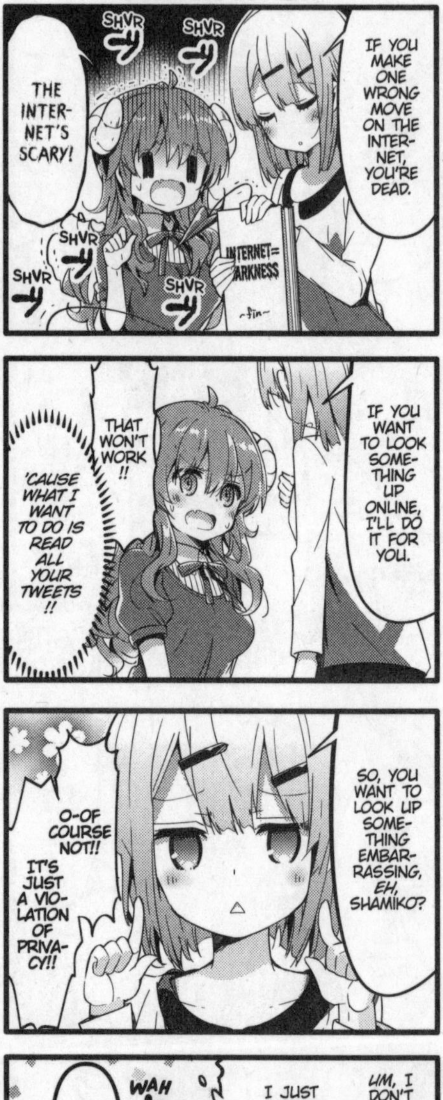
IF YOU MAKE ONE WRONG MOVE ON THE INTERNET, YOU'RE DEAD.
SHVR
SHVR
THE INTERNET'S SCARY!
INTERNET= ARKNESS
SHVR
SHVR
SHVR
~fin~
IF YOU WANT TO LOOK SOMETHING UP ONLINE, I'LL DO IT FOR YOU.
THAT WON'T WORK!!
'CAUSE WHAT I WANT TO DO IS READ ALL YOUR TWEETS!!
SO, YOU WANT TO LOOK UP SOMETHING EMBARRASSING, EH, SHAMIKO?
O-OF COURSE NOT!!
IT'S JUST A VIOLATION OF PRIVACY!!
UM, I DON'T MEAN I WANT TO VIOLATE YOUR PRIVACY, SPECIFICALLY...
I JUST DON'T WANT YOU TO INVADE MINE! DON'T GET THE WRONG IDEA!
WAH わ
WAH わ
UM, I GOT THAT.
WHY ARE YOU BABBLING SO MUCH?
わ WAH
わ WAH

CLAIRVOYANT PEACH

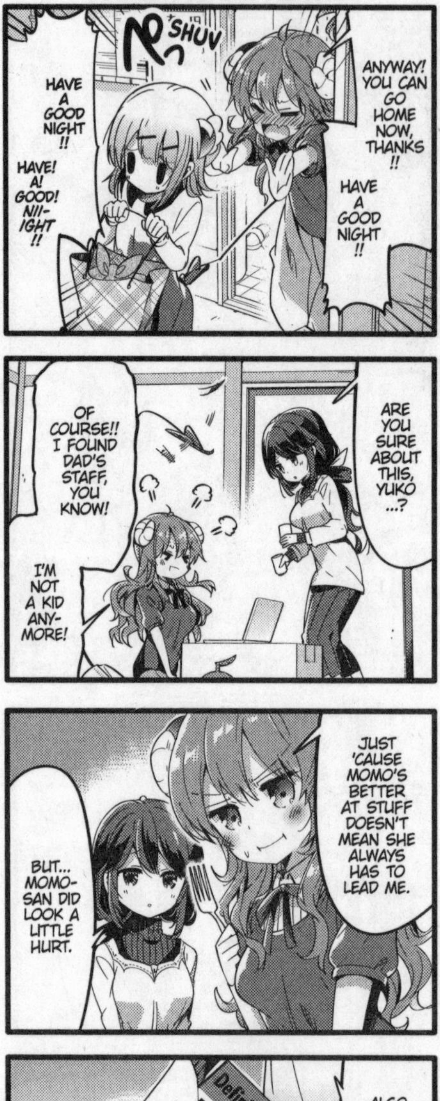
ANYWAY! YOU CAN GO HOME NOW, THANKS!!
HAVE A GOOD NIGHT!!
SHUV
HAVE A GOOD NIGHT!!
HAVE! A! GOOD! NI!-IGHT!!
ARE YOU SURE ABOUT THIS, YUKO...?
OF COURSE!! I FOUND DAD'S STAFF, YOU KNOW!
I'M NOT A KID ANYMORE!
JUST 'CAUSE MOMO'S BETTER AT STUFF DOESN'T MEAN SHE ALWAYS HAS TO LEAD ME.
BUT... MOMO-SAN DID LOOK A LITTLE HURT.
ALSO, SHE SAID, "I THOUGHT THIS MIGHT HAPPEN," AND LEFT THIS FOR YOU.
BE SURE TO RETURN IT LATER.
Definitive Edition
Even Toucan Do It:
Computers & Internet
DARN HER!! BUT I GUESS I'LL READ IT!!

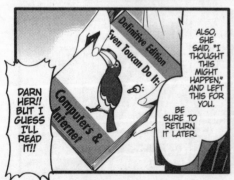

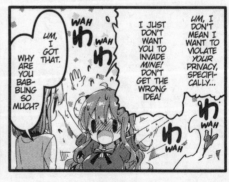

IT WORKED ON OLD TVS

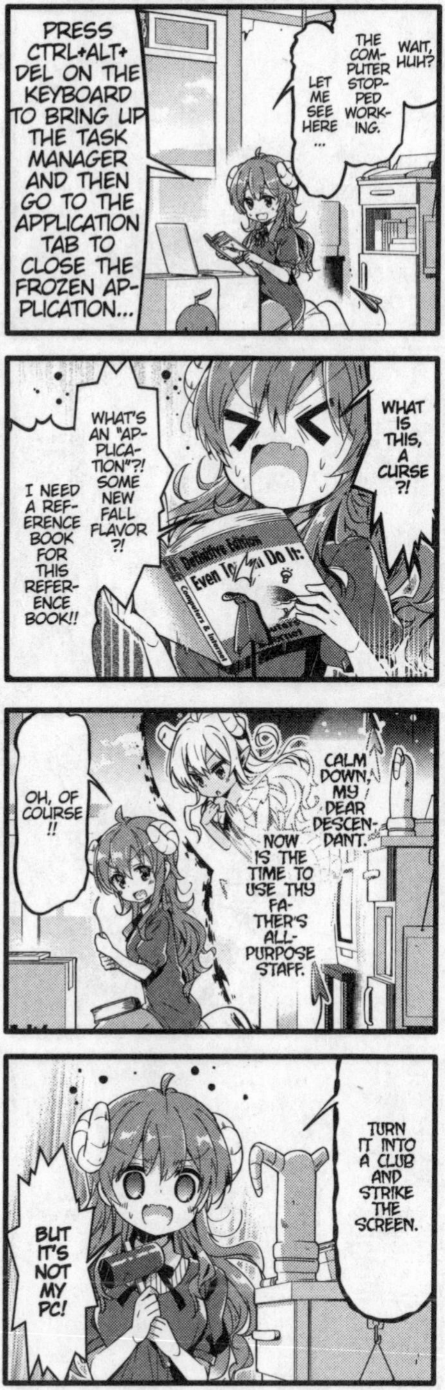
WAIT, HUH?
THE COMPUTER STOPPED WORKING.
LET ME SEE HERE...
PRESS CTRL+ALT+DEL ON THE KEYBOARD TO BRING UP THE TASK MANAGER AND THEN GO TO THE APPLICATION TAB TO CLOSE THE FROZEN APPLICATION...
WHAT IS THIS, A CURSE?!
WHAT'S AN "APPLICATION"?! SOME NEW FALL FLAVOR?!
I NEED A REFERENCE BOOK FOR THIS REFERENCE BOOK!!
Definitive Edition
Computers & Internet
CALM DOWN, MY DEAR DESCENDANT.
NOW IS THE TIME TO USE THY FATHER'S ALL-PURPOSE STAFF.
OH, OF COURSE!!
TURN IT INTO A CLUB AND STRIKE THE SCREEN.
BUT IT'S NOT MY PC!

YOUR (USER)NAME

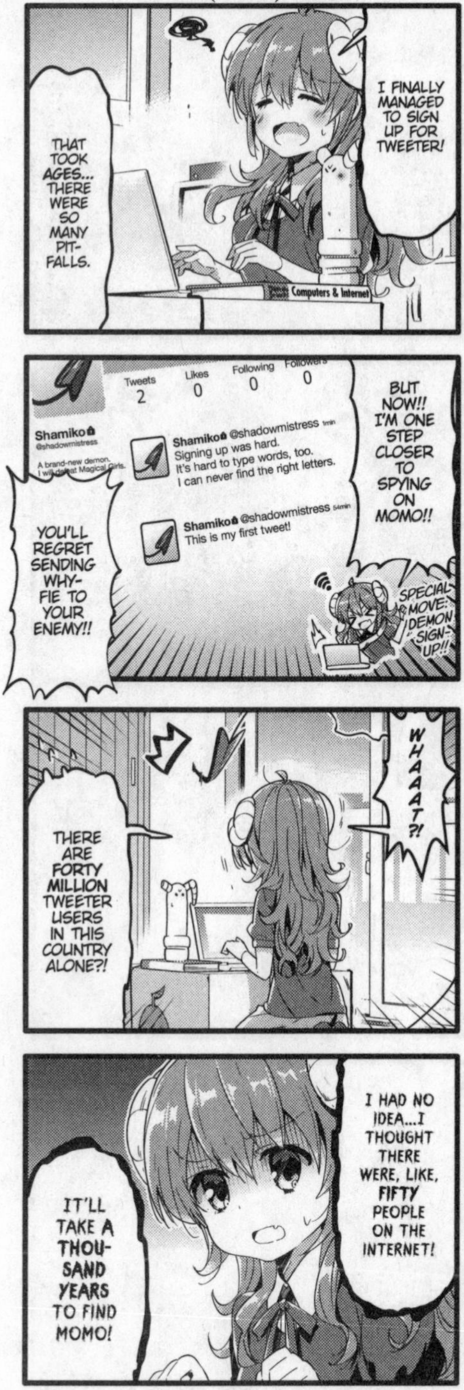
I FINALLY MANAGED TO SIGN UP FOR TWEETER!
THAT TOOK AGES... THERE WERE SO MANY PITFALLS.
Computers & Internet
BUT NOW!! I'M ONE STEP CLOSER TO SPYING ON MOMO!!
Tweets 2 Likes 0 Following 0 Followers 0
Shamiko @shadowmistress
Shamiko @shadowmistress 1min
Signing up was hard.
It's hard to type words, too.
I can never find the right letters.
Shamiko @shadowmistress 54min
This is my first tweet!
SPECIAL MOVE: DEMON SIGN-UP!!
YOU'LL REGRET SENDING WHYFIE TO YOUR ENEMY!!
WHAAAAT?!
THERE ARE FORTY MILLION TWEETER USERS IN THIS COUNTRY ALONE?!
I HAD NO IDEA...I THOUGHT THERE WERE, LIKE, FIFTY PEOPLE ON THE INTERNET!
IT'LL TAKE A THOUSAND YEARS TO FIND MOMO!

A DEMON WHO CAN USE HER WEAPONS

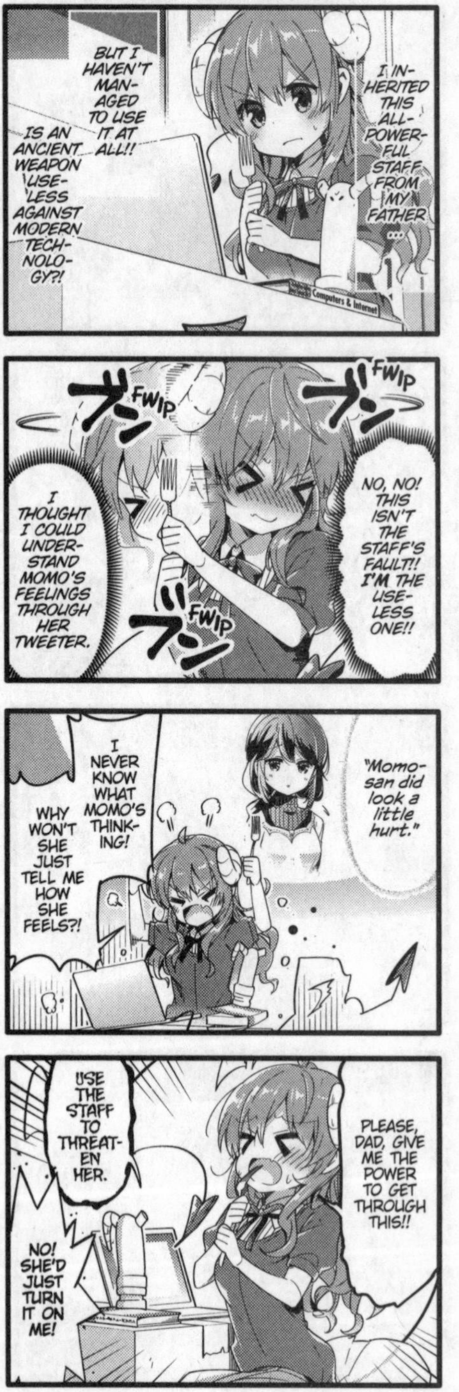
I INHERITED THIS ALL-POWERFUL STAFF FROM MY FATHER...
BUT I HAVEN'T MANAGED TO USE IT AT ALL!!
IS AN ANCIENT WEAPON USELESS AGAINST MODERN TECHNOLOGY?!
Computers & Internet
FWIP
FWIP
NO, NO! THIS ISN'T THE STAFF'S FAULT!! I'M THE USELESS ONE!!
I THOUGHT I COULD UNDERSTAND MOMO'S FEELINGS THROUGH HER TWEETER.
FWIP
"Momo-san did look a little hurt."
I NEVER KNOW WHAT MOMO'S THINKING!
WHY WON'T SHE JUST TELL ME HOW SHE FEELS?!
PLEASE, DAD, GIVE ME THE POWER TO GET THROUGH THIS!!
USE THE STAFF TO THREATEN HER.
NO! SHE'D JUST TURN IT ON ME!

THE STAFF FANS THE FLAMES

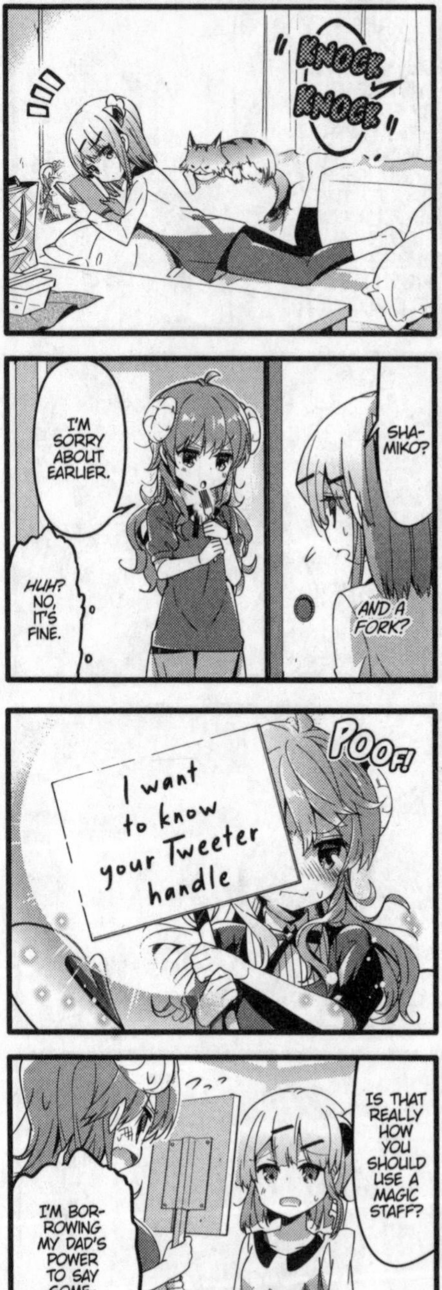
KNOCK KNOCK
SHAMIKO?
I'M SORRY ABOUT EARLIER.
AND A FORK?
HUH? NO, IT'S FINE.
POOF!
I want to know your Tweeter handle
IS THAT REALLY HOW YOU SHOULD USE A MAGIC STAFF?
I'M BORROWING MY DAD'S POWER TO SAY SOMETHING THAT'S HARD!!

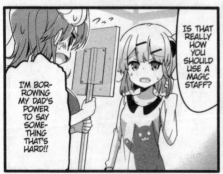

MYSTERY CREATURE

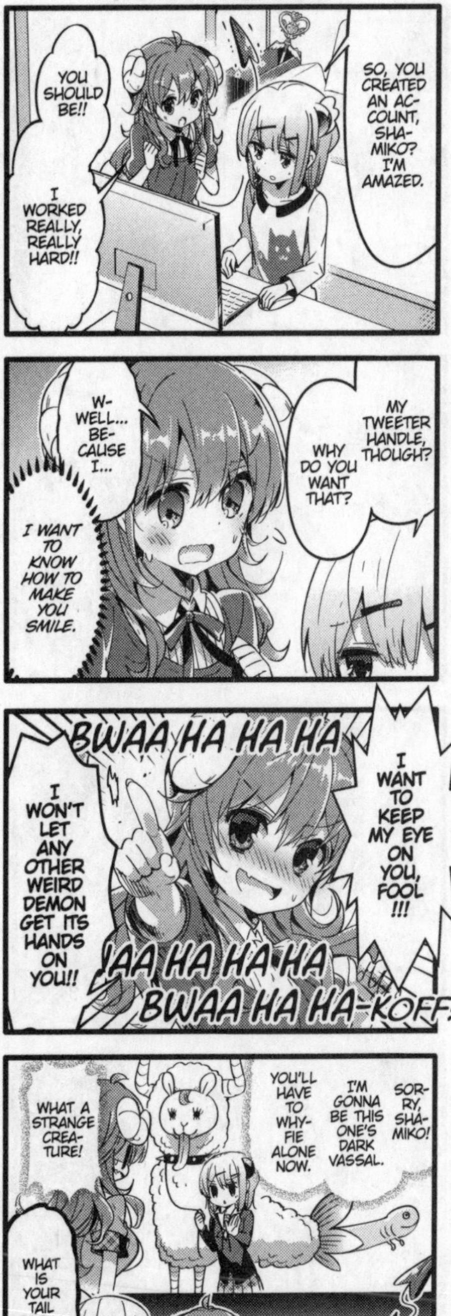
SO, YOU CREATED AN AC-COUNT, SHA-MIKO? I'M AMAZED.
YOU SHOULD BE!!
I WORKED REALLY, REALLY HARD!!
MY TWEETER HANDLE, THOUGH? WHY DO YOU WANT THAT?
W-WELL... BE-CAUSE I...
I WANT TO KNOW HOW TO MAKE YOU SMILE.
I WANT TO KEEP MY EYE ON YOU, FOOL!!!
BWAA HA HA HA
I WON'T LET ANY OTHER WEIRD DEMON GET ITS HANDS ON YOU!!
AA HA HA HA HA BWAA HA HA-KOFF!
SOR-RY, SHA-MIKO!
I'M GONNA BE THIS ONE'S DARK VASSAL.
YOU'LL HAVE TO WHY-FIE ALONE NOW.
WHAT A STRANGE CREA-TURE!
WHAT IS YOUR TAIL SAYING NOW?

PEACH STRAIGHT FLUSH

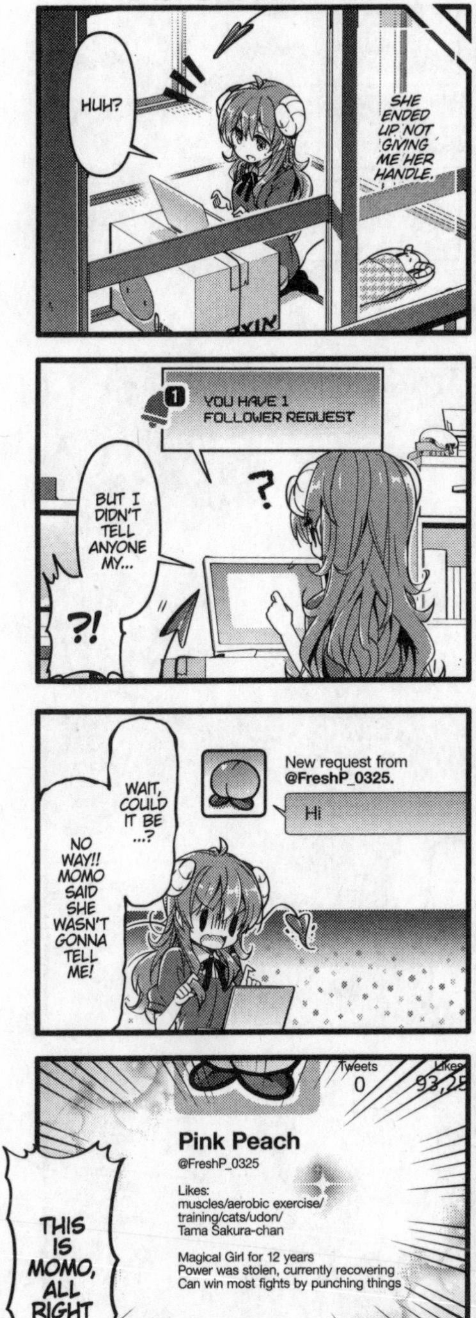
SHE ENDED UP NOT GIVING ME HER HANDLE.
HUH?
1
YOU HAVE 1 FOLLOWER REQUEST
?
BUT I DIDN'T TELL ANYONE MY...
?!
New request from @FreshP_0325.
Hi
WAIT, COULD IT BE ...?
NO WAY!! MOMO SAID SHE WASN'T GONNA TELL ME!
Tweets
0
Likes
Pink Peach
@FreshP_0325
Likes:
muscles/aerobic exercise/
training/cats/udon/
Tama Sakura-chan
Magical Girl for 12 years
Power was stolen, currently recovering
Can win most fights by punching things
THIS IS MOMO, ALL RIGHT!!

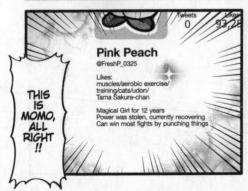

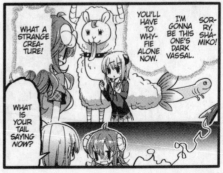

NEW SOURCE OF PEACH INFORMATION

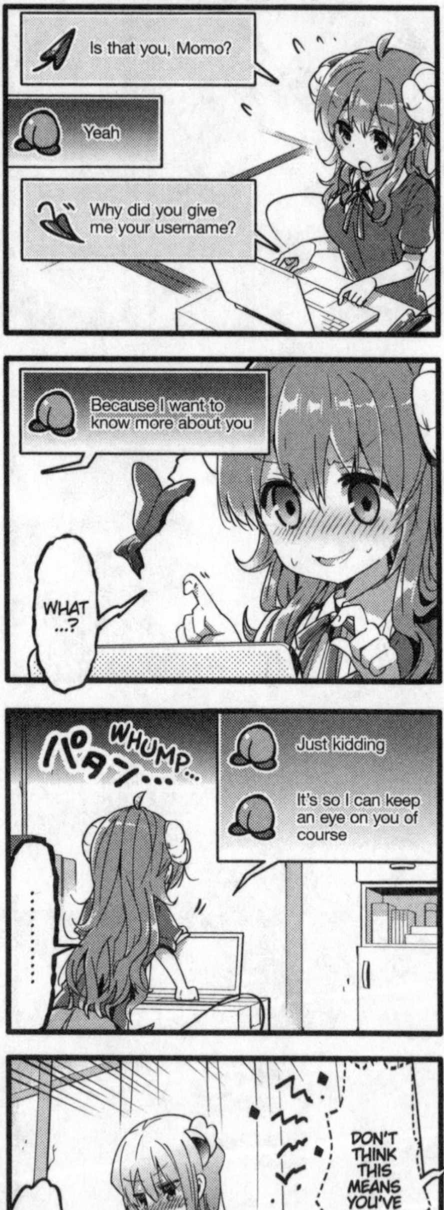

Is that you, Momo?
Yeah
Why did you give me your username?
Because I want to know more about you
WHAT ...?
WHUMP...
パタン...
Just kidding
It's so I can keep an eye on you of course
DON'T THINK THIS MEANS YOU'VE WOOON !!
THESE WALLS ARE SO THIN.

HAVING A WHY-FIE PARTY

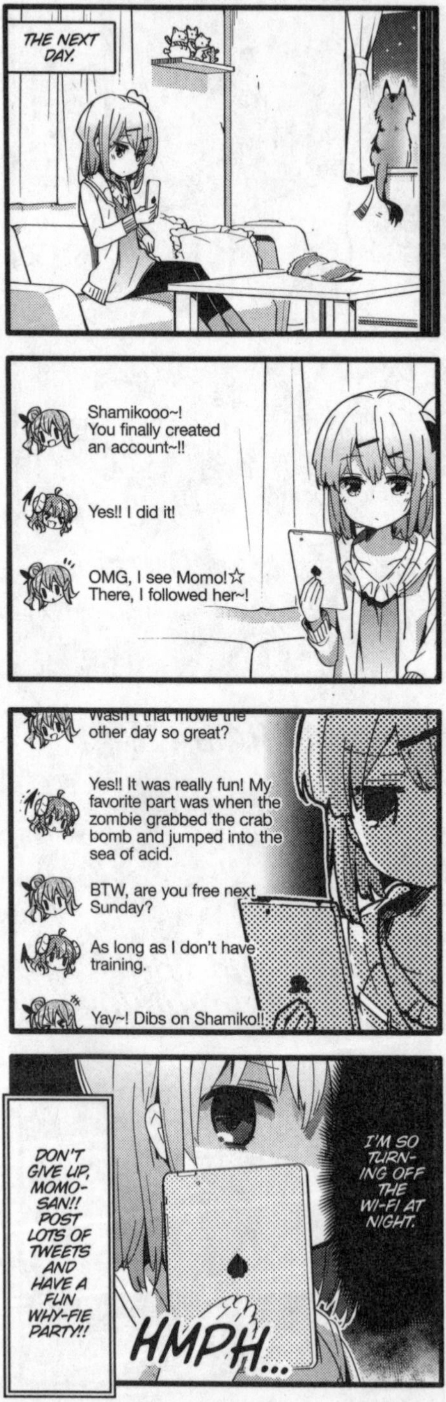

THE NEXT DAY.
Shamikooo~! You finally created an account~!!
Yes!! I did it!
OMG, I see Momo!☆ There, I followed her~!
other day so great?
Yes!! It was really fun! My favorite part was when the zombie grabbed the crab bomb and jumped into the sea of acid.
BTW, are you free next Sunday?
As long as I don't have training.
Yay~! Dibs on Shamiko!!
I'M SO TURNING OFF THE WI-FI AT NIGHT.
HMPH...
DON'T GIVE UP, MOMO-SAN!! POST LOTS OF TWEETS AND HAVE A FUN WHY-FIE PARTY!!

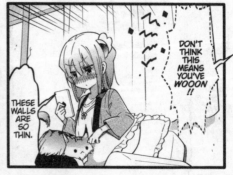

The Demon Girl Next Door

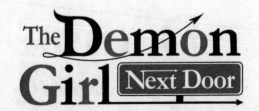

The Demon Girl Next Door

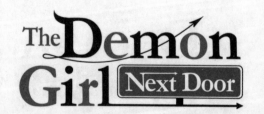

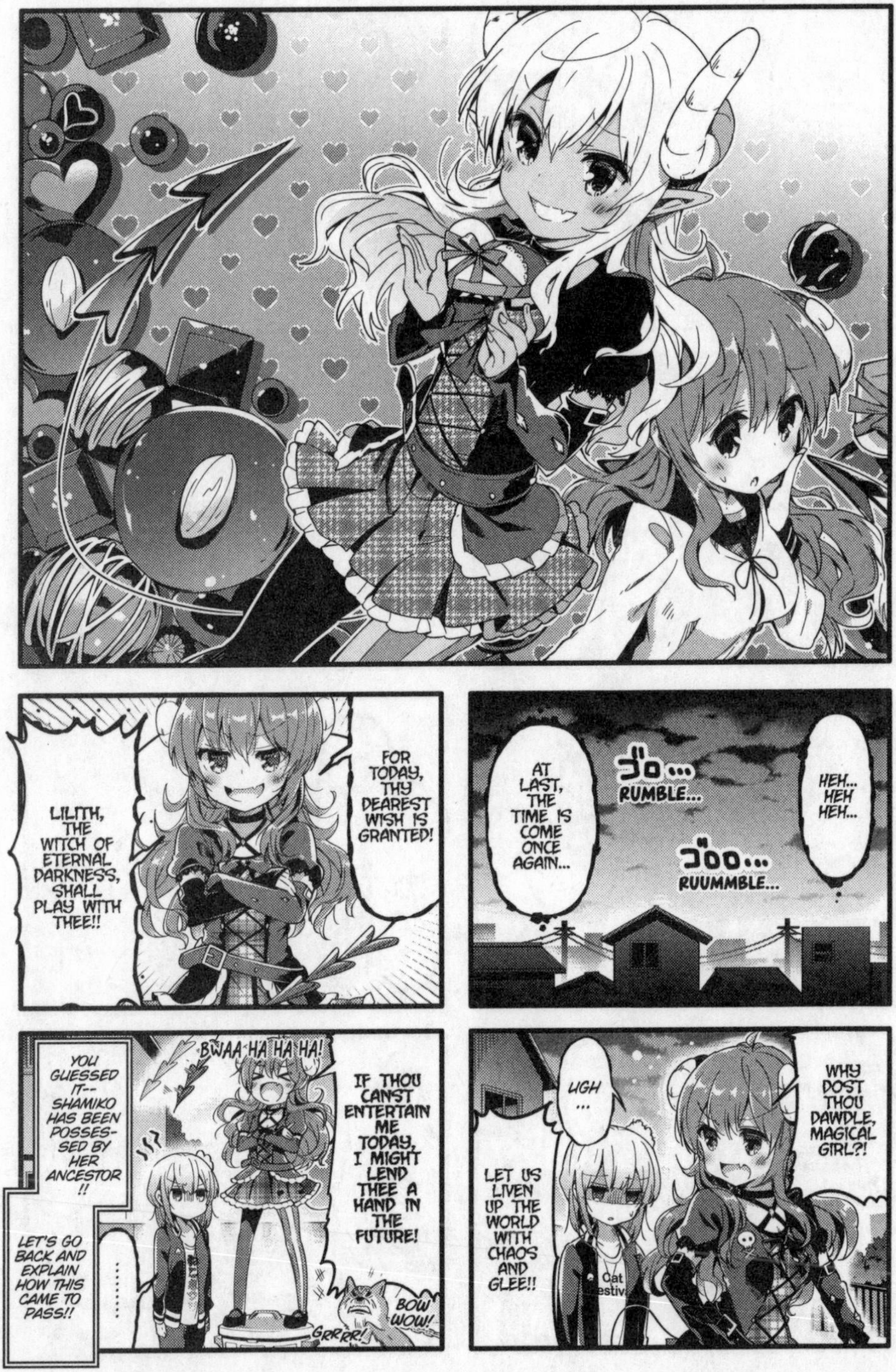
HEH... HEH HEH...
ゴロ... RUMBLE...
AT LAST, THE TIME IS COME ONCE AGAIN...
ゴロロ... RUUMMBLE...
FOR TODAY, THY DEAREST WISH IS GRANTED!
LILITH, THE WITCH OF ETERNAL DARKNESS, SHALL PLAY WITH THEE!!
WHY DOST THOU DAWDLE, MAGICAL GIRL?!
UGH ...
LET US LIVEN UP THE WORLD WITH CHAOS AND GLEE!!
BWAA HA HA HA!
IF THOU CANST ENTERTAIN ME TODAY, I MIGHT LEND THEE A HAND IN THE FUTURE!
YOU GUESSED IT-- SHAMIKO HAS BEEN POSSES-SED BY HER ANCESTOR!!
......
BOW WOW!
GRRRR!
LET'S GO BACK AND EXPLAIN HOW THIS CAME TO PASS!!

VARIETY BRIBE SET

ONE DAY AGO.
What manner of trickery is this?
It's a bribe--I mean, offering.
I have something to ask you today, Lilith-san.
WHUMP
どさっ
Based on what Shamiko's mother has said...
I assume that Joshua-san once carried you around.
Do you recall seeing Chiyoda Sakura at that time?
Heh heh... prepare to be amazed.
I have no idea.
All right, we're done for the day.
Aaah! Come back! I was still eating thoooose!
SHF SHF SHF SHF SHF
スススススス

THE ANCESTOR'S SECRET, REVEALED!!

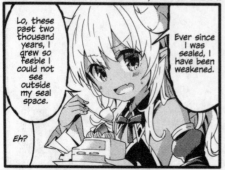

Ever since I was sealed, I have been weakened.
Lo, these past two thousand years, I grew so feeble I could not see outside my seal space.
Eh?
Ten years ago, my mind cleared, and I could see the outside world again...
but I scarcely remember my weakened years.
You mean you were totally sealed up for two thousand years?
Well, yes, more or less.
I could meddle with the dreams of my brethren from time to time...
but until Shamiko could hear my voice, I was most frightfully bored.
Wipe that look off thy face! I do not need thy pity!!
No!! Give me not offerings in terrifying silence!!
And Shamiko, stop crying!!

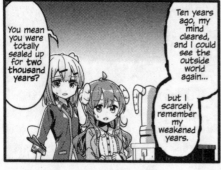

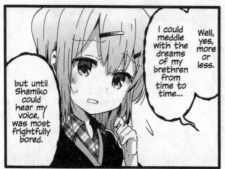

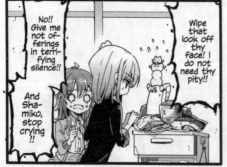

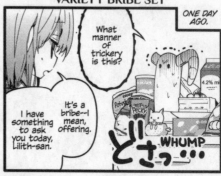

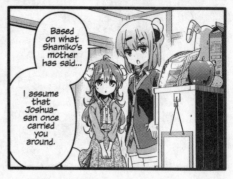

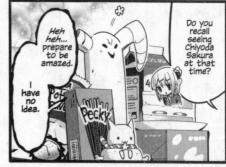

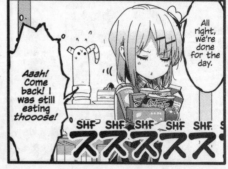

FUN ANCESTOR MEMORIES

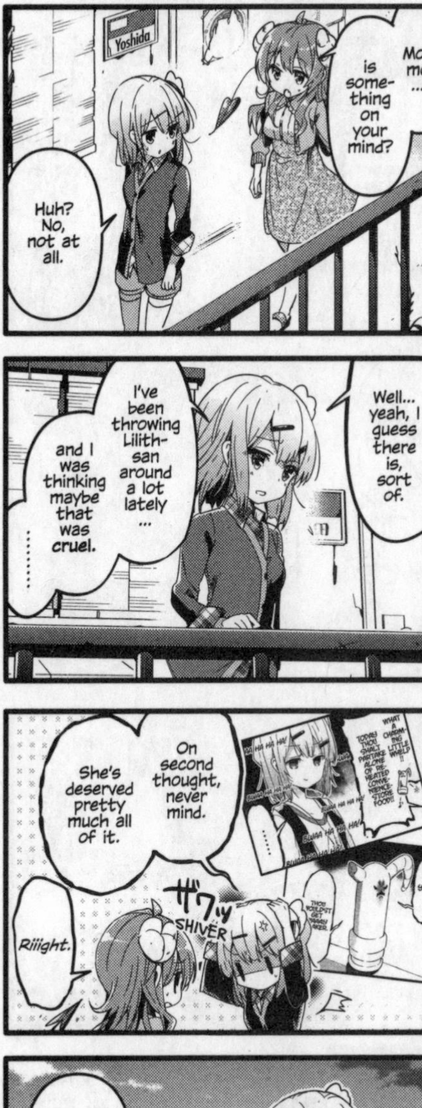
Yoshida
Momo... is something on your mind?
Huh? No, not at all.
Well... yeah, I guess there is, sort of.
I've been throwing Lilith-san around a lot lately...
and I was thinking maybe that was cruel.
......
On second thought, never mind.
She's deserved pretty much all of it.
......
ザワッ SHIVER
Riiight.
Um, so, I have an idea.

THE STAFF BECOMES A TORTURE DEVICE

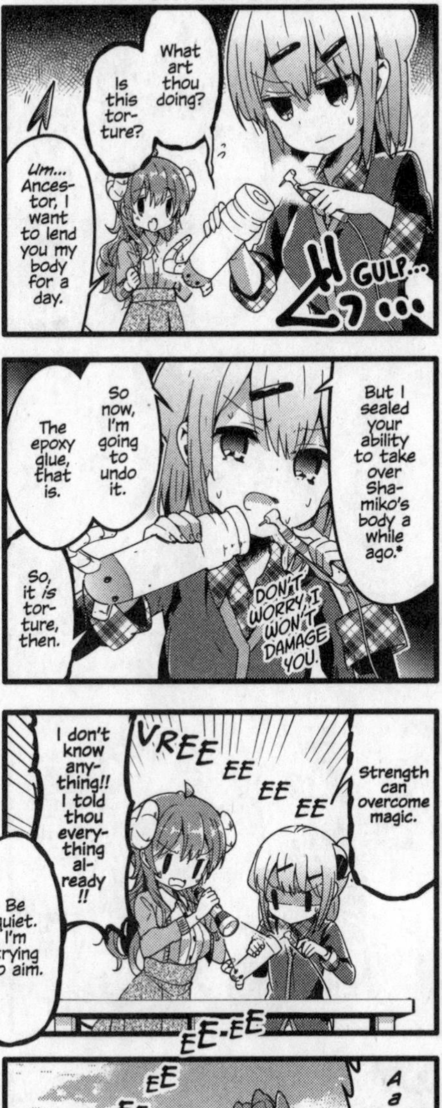
What art thou doing?
Is this torture?
Um... Ancestor, I want to lend you my body for a day.
GULP...
But I sealed your ability to take over Shamiko's body a while ago.*
So now, I'm going to undo it.
The epoxy glue, that is.
So, it is torture, then.
DON'T WORRY, I WON'T DAMAGE YOU.
Strength can overcome magic.
VREEEEEEEEE
I don't know anything!! I told thou everything already!!
Be quiet. I'm trying to aim.
EE-EE EE EEEEE!
Aaaaaaaaaaaaaaaaa!
※Please enjoy these pretty Dutch flowers while the Ancestatue is getting drilled.

*See Volume 1.

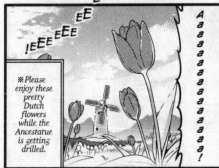

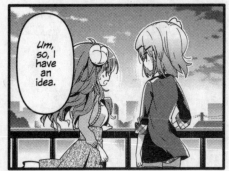

THE MEDIATOR EXITS

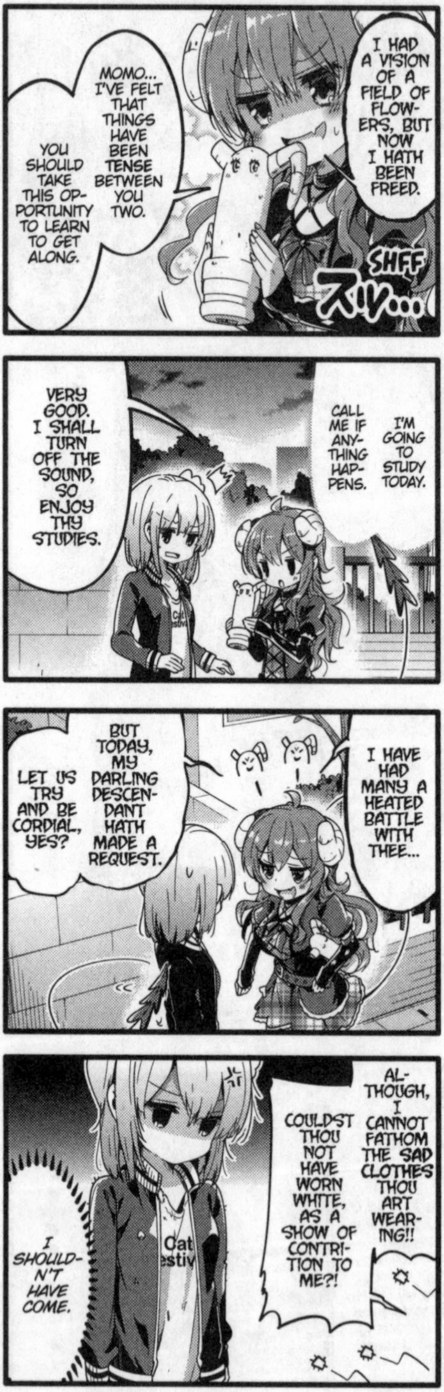
I HAD A VISION OF A FIELD OF FLOWERS, BUT NOW I HATH BEEN FREED.
MOMO... I'VE FELT THAT THINGS HAVE BEEN TENSE BETWEEN YOU TWO.
YOU SHOULD TAKE THIS OPPORTUNITY TO LEARN TO GET ALONG.
SHFF
スッ...
I'M GOING TO STUDY TODAY.
CALL ME IF ANYTHING HAPPENS.
VERY GOOD. I SHALL TURN OFF THE SOUND, SO ENJOY THY STUDIES.
I HAVE HAD MANY A HEATED BATTLE WITH THEE...
BUT TODAY, MY DARLING DESCENDANT HATH MADE A REQUEST.
LET US TRY AND BE CORDIAL, YES?
ALTHOUGH, I CANNOT FATHOM THE SAD CLOTHES THOU ART WEARING!!
COULDST THOU NOT HAVE WORN WHITE, AS A SHOW OF CONTRITION TO ME?!
I SHOULDN'T HAVE COME.

MOMO GAINS A DARKNESS POINT

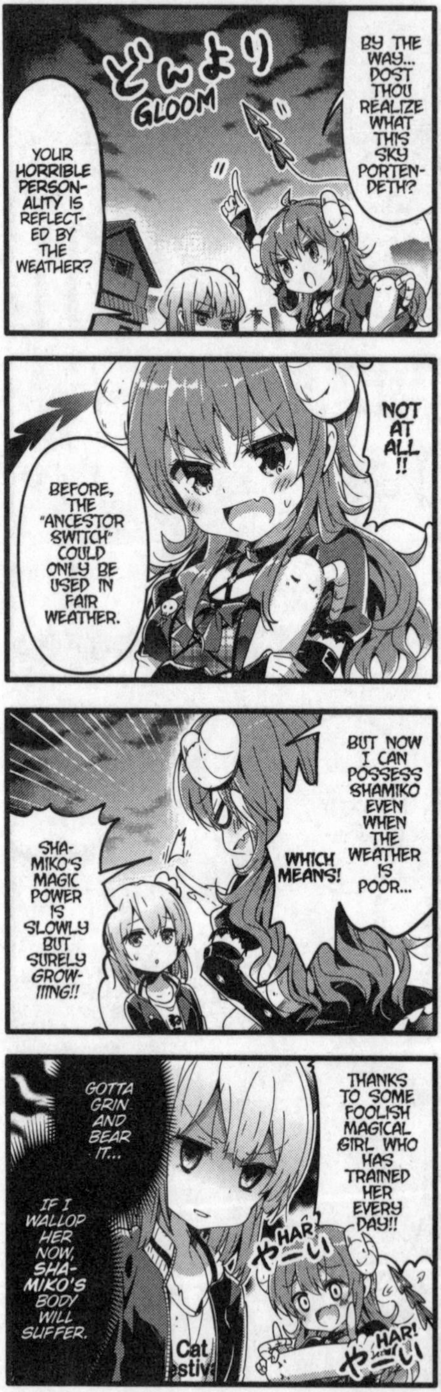
BY THE WAY... DOST THOU REALIZE WHAT THIS SKY PORTENDETH?
どんより
GLOOM
YOUR HORRIBLE PERSONALITY IS REFLECTED BY THE WEATHER?
NOT AT ALL!!
BEFORE, THE "ANCESTOR SWITCH" COULD ONLY BE USED IN FAIR WEATHER.
BUT NOW I CAN POSSESS SHAMIKO EVEN WHEN THE WEATHER IS POOR...
WHICH MEANS!
SHAMIKO'S MAGIC POWER IS SLOWLY BUT SURELY GROWIIIING!!
THANKS TO SOME FOOLISH MAGICAL GIRL WHO HAS TRAINED HER EVERY DAY!!
HAR!
やーい
HAR!
やーい
GOTTA GRIN AND BEAR IT...
IF I WALLOP HER NOW, SHAMIKO'S BODY WILL SUFFER.

ANTSY ANCESTOR THROWS A TANTRUM

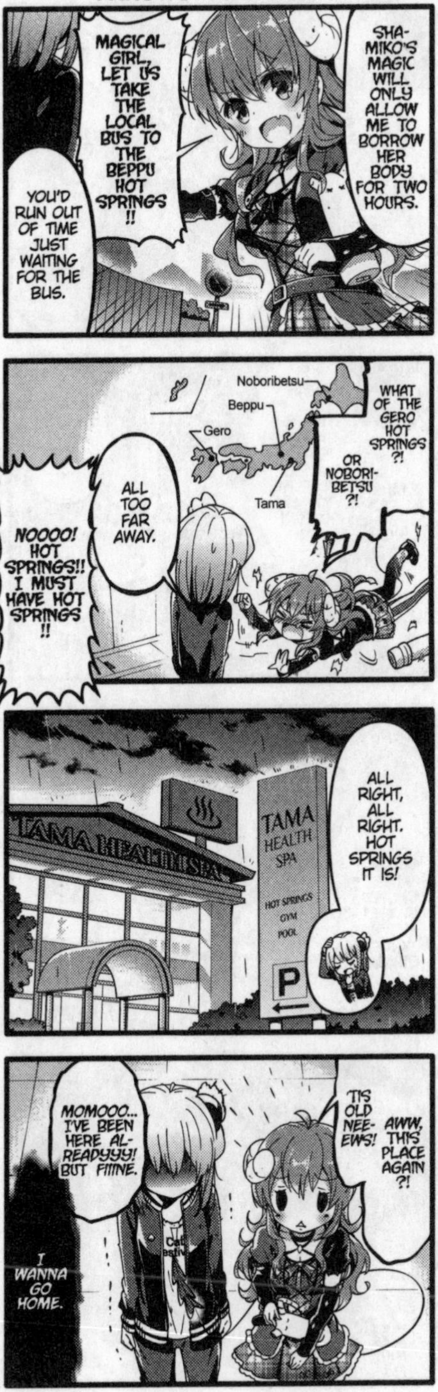
SHA-MIKO'S MAGIC WILL ONLY ALLOW ME TO BORROW HER BODY FOR TWO HOURS.
MAGICAL GIRL, LET US TAKE THE LOCAL BUS TO THE BEPPU HOT SPRINGS!!
YOU'D RUN OUT OF TIME JUST WAITING FOR THE BUS.
WHAT OF THE GERO HOT SPRINGS?!
OR NOBORI-BETSU?!
Noboribetsu
Beppu
Gero
Tama
ALL TOO FAR AWAY.
NOOOO! HOT SPRINGS!! I MUST HAVE HOT SPRINGS!!
ALL RIGHT, ALL RIGHT. HOT SPRINGS IT IS!
TAMA HEALTH SPA
HOT SPRINGS
GYM
POOL
P
TAMA HEALTH SPA
'TIS OLD NEE-EWS!
AWW, THIS PLACE AGAIN?!
MOMOOO... I'VE BEEN HERE AL-READYYY! BUT FIIINE.
I WANNA GO HOME.

SHE'S BEEN SLACKING OFF LATELY

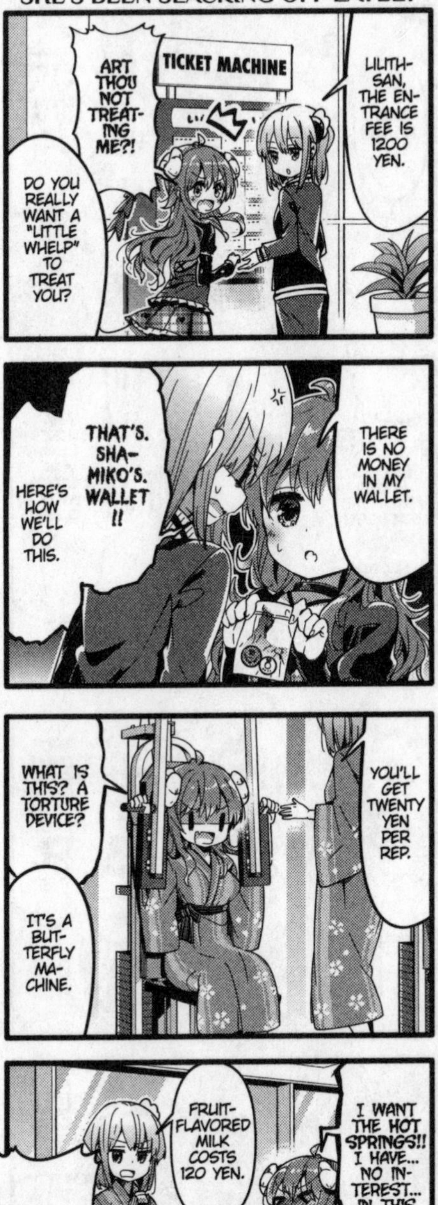
LILITH-SAN, THE EN-TRANCE FEE IS 1200 YEN.
TICKET MACHINE
ART THOU NOT TREAT-ING ME?!
DO YOU REALLY WANT A "LITTLE WHELP" TO TREAT YOU?
THERE IS NO MONEY IN MY WALLET.
THAT'S. SHA-MIKO'S. WALLET!!
HERE'S HOW WE'LL DO THIS.
YOU'LL GET TWENTY YEN PER REP.
WHAT IS THIS? A TORTURE DEVICE?
IT'S A BUT-TERFLY MA-CHINE.
I WANT THE HOT SPRINGS!! I HAVE... NO IN-TEREST... IN THIS FOOLISH DEVICE...
FRUIT-FLAVORED MILK COSTS 120 YEN.
VERY WELL! SIX MORE REPS!!

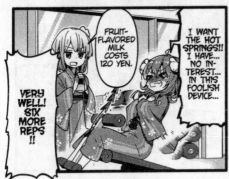

ANTSY ANCESTOR'S BRILLIANT DEDUCTION

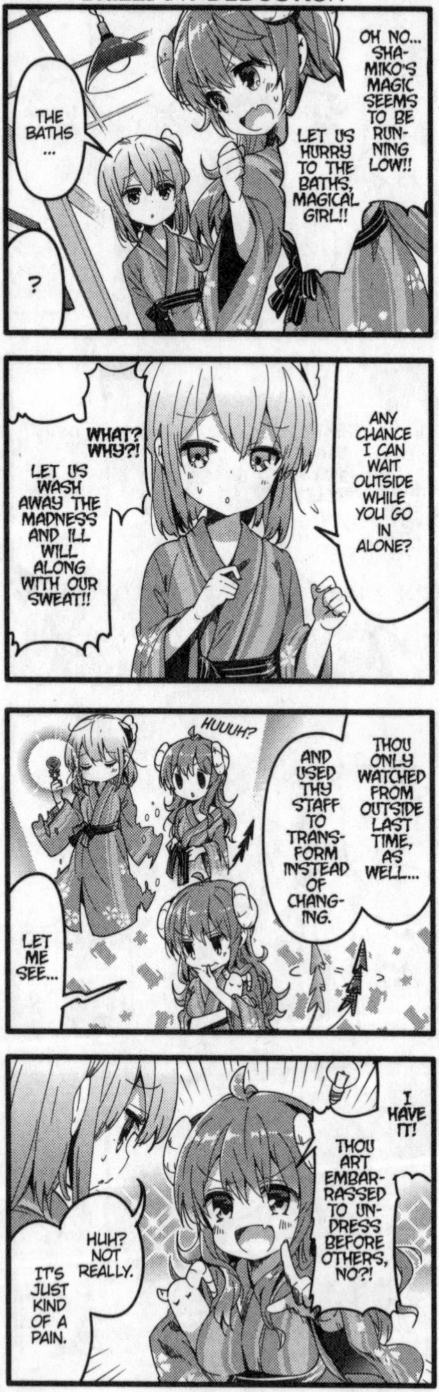
OH NO... SHAMIKO'S MAGIC SEEMS TO BE RUNNING LOW!!
LET US HURRY TO THE BATHS, MAGICAL GIRL!!
THE BATHS...
?
ANY CHANCE I CAN WAIT OUTSIDE WHILE YOU GO IN ALONE?
WHAT? WHY?!
LET US WASH AWAY THE MADNESS AND ILL WILL ALONG WITH OUR SWEAT!!
HUUUH?
THOU ONLY WATCHED FROM OUTSIDE LAST TIME, AS WELL...
AND USED THY STAFF TO TRANSFORM INSTEAD OF CHANGING.
LET ME SEE...
I HAVE IT!
THOU ART EMBARRASSED TO UNDRESS BEFORE OTHERS, NO?!
HUH? NOT REALLY.
IT'S JUST KIND OF A PAIN.

ANTSY ANCESTOR'S BRILLIANT BARGAINING

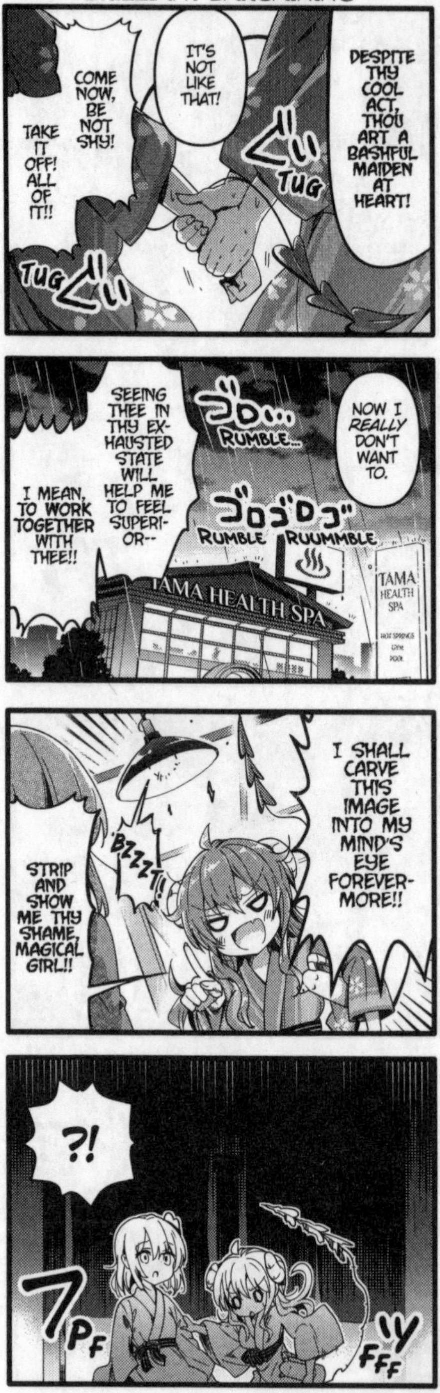
DESPITE THY COOL ACT, THOU ART A BASHFUL MAIDEN AT HEART!
IT'S NOT LIKE THAT!
ぐい TUG
COME NOW, BE NOT SHY!
TAKE IT OFF! ALL OF IT!!
TUG ぐい
NOW I REALLY DON'T WANT TO.
ゴロ… RUMBLE...
SEEING THEE IN THY EXHAUSTED STATE WILL HELP ME TO FEEL SUPERIOR--
I MEAN, TO WORK TOGETHER WITH THEE!!
RUMBLE RUUMMBLE
TAMA HEALTH SPA
TAMA HEALTH SPA
I SHALL CARVE THIS IMAGE INTO MY MIND'S EYE FOREVERMORE!!
BZZZT!
STRIP AND SHOW ME THY SHAME, MAGICAL GIRL!!
?!
PF
FFF

THE WEAKNESS OF THE WITCH OF DARKNESS, REVEALED!

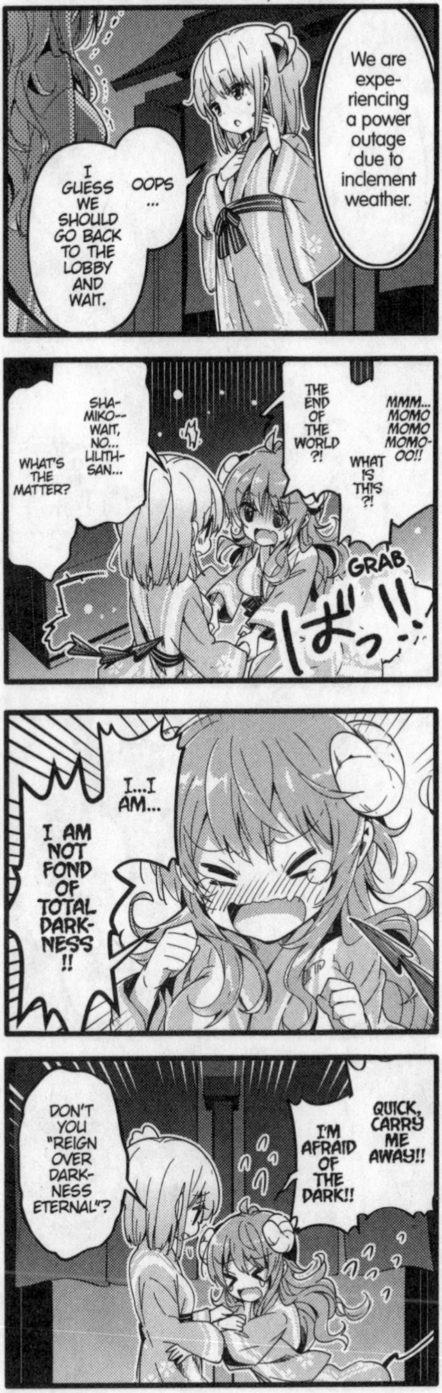

We are experiencing a power outage due to inclement weather.
OOPS...
I GUESS WE SHOULD GO BACK TO THE LOBBY AND WAIT.
MMM... MOMO MOMO MOMO-OO!!
WHAT IS THIS?!
THE END OF THE WORLD?!
SHAMIKO-- WAIT, NO... LILITH-SAN...
WHAT'S THE MATTER?
GRAB
ばっ!!
I...I AM...
I AM NOT FOND OF TOTAL DARKNESS!!
QUICK, CARRY ME AWAY!!
I'M AFRAID OF THE DARK!!
DON'T YOU "REIGN OVER DARKNESS ETERNAL"?

PEACH PLAYLIST: VIDEO SITE EDITION

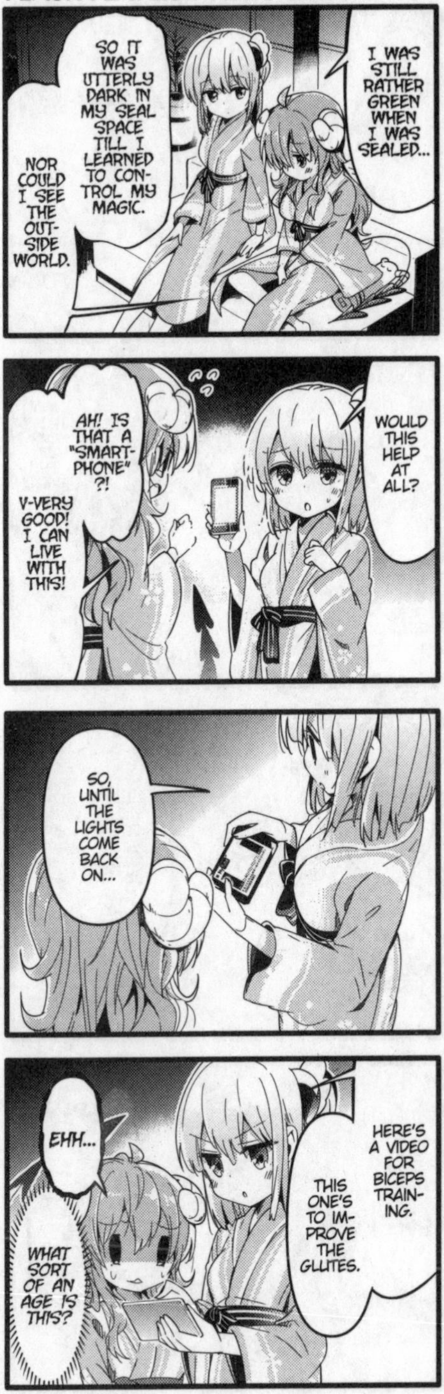

I WAS STILL RATHER GREEN WHEN I WAS SEALED...
SO IT WAS UTTERLY DARK IN MY SEAL SPACE TILL I LEARNED TO CONTROL MY MAGIC.
NOR COULD I SEE THE OUTSIDE WORLD.
WOULD THIS HELP AT ALL?
AH! IS THAT A "SMARTPHONE"?!
V-VERY GOOD! I CAN LIVE WITH THIS!
SO, UNTIL THE LIGHTS COME BACK ON...
HERE'S A VIDEO FOR BICEPS TRAINING.
THIS ONE'S TO IMPROVE THE GLUTES.
EHH...
WHAT SORT OF AN AGE IS THIS?

BATH, TAKE TWO

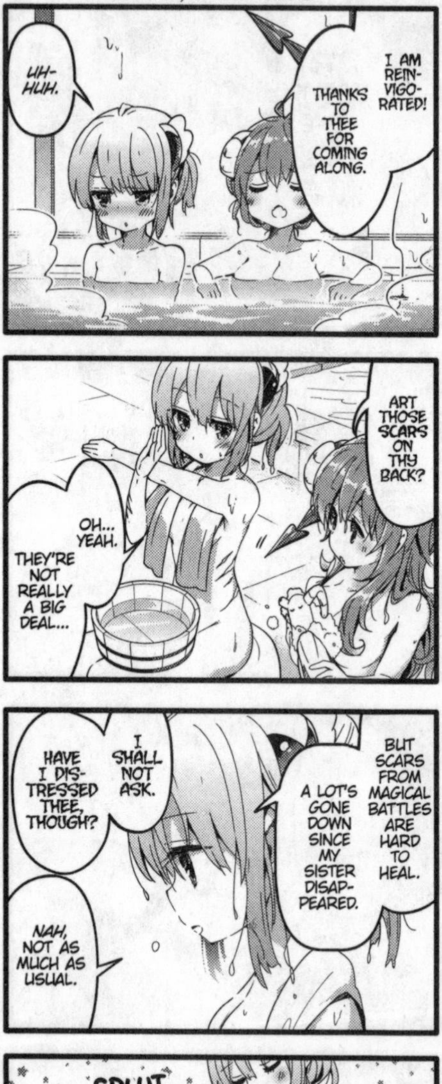
I AM REINVIGORATED!
THANKS TO THEE FOR COMING ALONG.
UH-HUH.
ART THOSE SCARS ON THY BACK?
OH... YEAH.
THEY'RE NOT REALLY A BIG DEAL...
BUT SCARS FROM MAGICAL BATTLES ARE HARD TO HEAL.
A LOT'S GONE DOWN SINCE MY SISTER DISAPPEARED.
I SHALL NOT ASK.
HAVE I DISTRESSED THEE, THOUGH?
NAH, NOT AS MUCH AS USUAL.
SPLUT
SPLUT
WHAT'S THIS?! THE BUBBLES WILL NOT CEASE!!
DOTH EXPENSIVE SHAMPOO PRODUCE THIS MUCH FOAM?!
SPLUT

SHAMIKO RETURNS

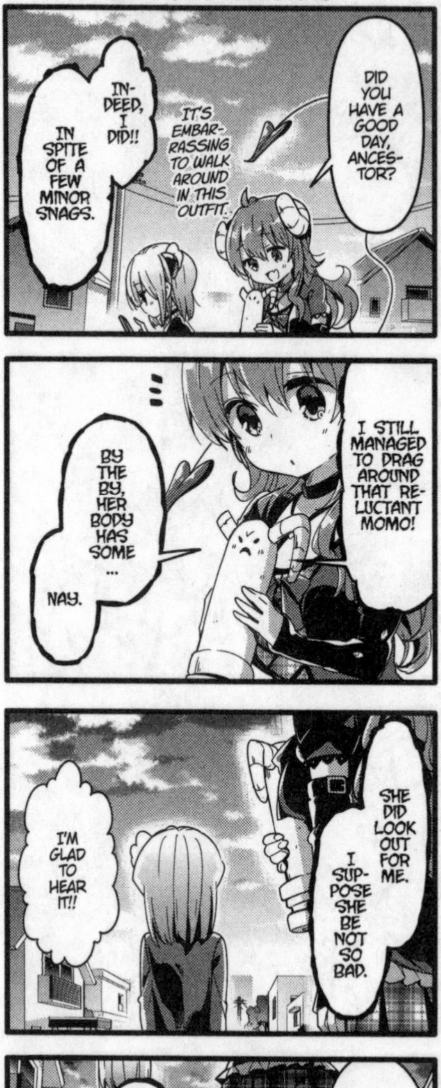
DID YOU HAVE A GOOD DAY, ANCESTOR?
IT'S EMBARRASSING TO WALK AROUND IN THIS OUTFIT.
INDEED, I DID!!
IN SPITE OF A FEW MINOR SNAGS.
I STILL MANAGED TO DRAG AROUND THAT RELUCTANT MOMO!
BY THE BY, HER BODY HAS SOME ...
NAY.
SHE DID LOOK OUT FOR ME.
I SUPPOSE SHE BE NOT SO BAD.
I'M GLAD TO HEAR IT!!
WE CAN DO THIS AGAIN SOMETIME.
I DON'T MIND BEING CARRIED AROUND BY THEE EITHER, SHAMIKO.
REALLY? YOU DON'T?

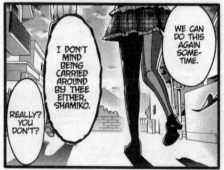

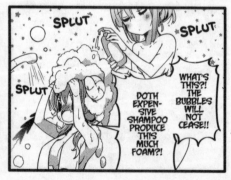

~~BLACKMAIL~~ PINKMAIL

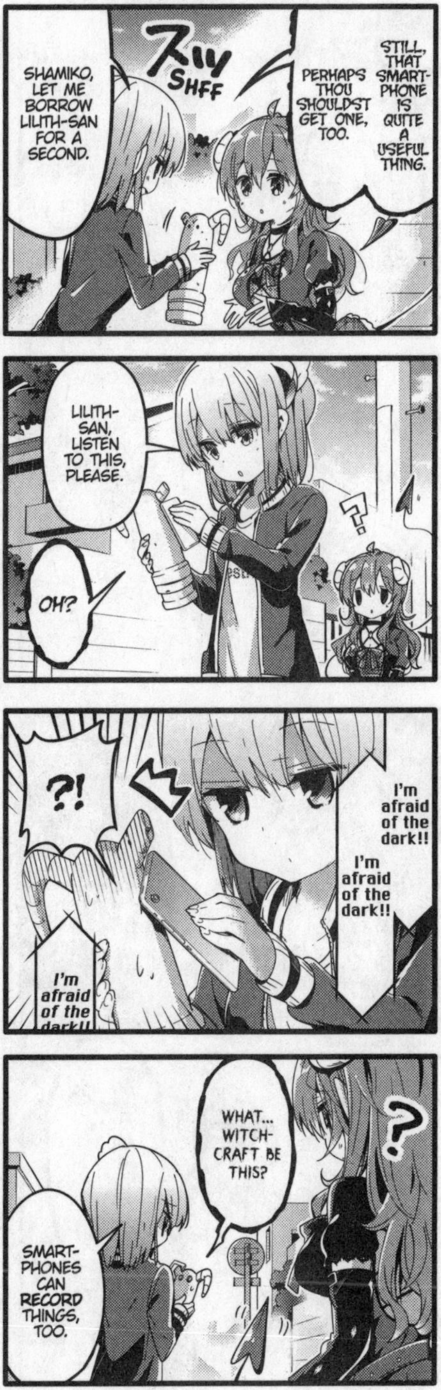
STILL, THAT SMARTPHONE IS QUITE A USEFUL THING.
PERHAPS THOU SHOULDST GET ONE, TOO.
スッ SHFF
SHAMIKO, LET ME BORROW LILITH-SAN FOR A SECOND.
LILITH-SAN, LISTEN TO THIS, PLEASE.
?
OH?
I'm afraid of the dark!!
I'm afraid of the dark!!
?!
I'm afraid of the dark!!
?
WHAT... WITCHCRAFT BE THIS?
SMARTPHONES CAN RECORD THINGS, TOO.

ANCESTOR, CAUGHT BY THE TAIL

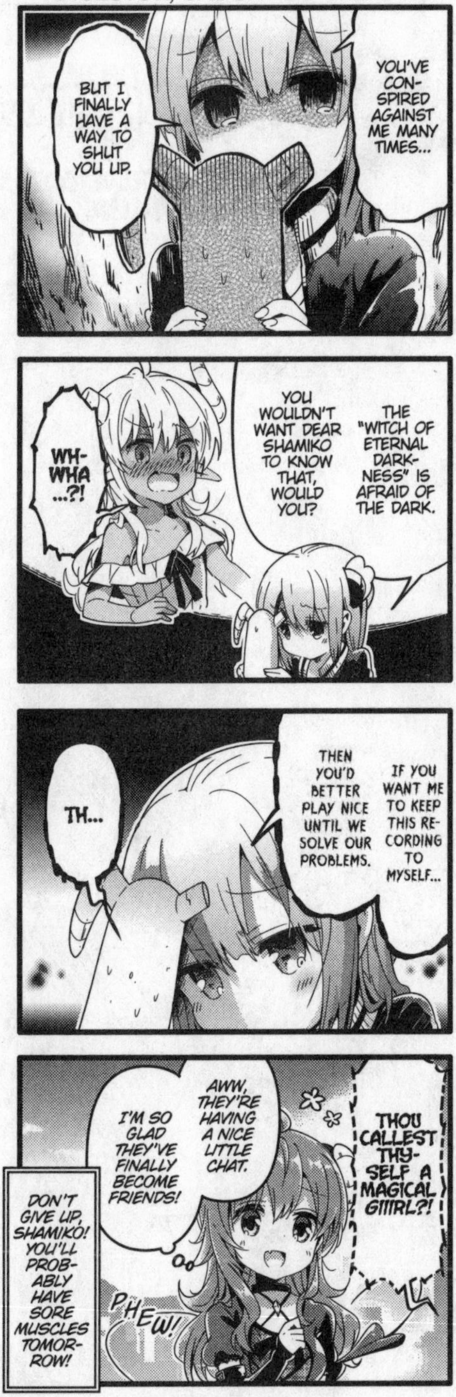
YOU'VE CONSPIRED AGAINST ME MANY TIMES...
BUT I FINALLY HAVE A WAY TO SHUT YOU UP.
THE "WITCH OF ETERNAL DARKNESS" IS AFRAID OF THE DARK.
YOU WOULDN'T WANT DEAR SHAMIKO TO KNOW THAT, WOULD YOU?
WH-WHA...?!
IF YOU WANT ME TO KEEP THIS RECORDING TO MYSELF...
THEN YOU'D BETTER PLAY NICE UNTIL WE SOLVE OUR PROBLEMS.
TH...
THOU CALLEST THYSELF A MAGICAL GIIIRL?!
AWW, THEY'RE HAVING A NICE LITTLE CHAT.
I'M SO GLAD THEY'VE FINALLY BECOME FRIENDS!
PHEW!
DON'T GIVE UP, SHAMIKO! YOU'LL PROBABLY HAVE SORE MUSCLES TOMORROW!

SECONDS!!

DEMON GIRL NEXT DOOR

(CHAPTER 33)

~ THE SECRET OF THE ANCESTOR'S OUTFIT, REVEALED! ~

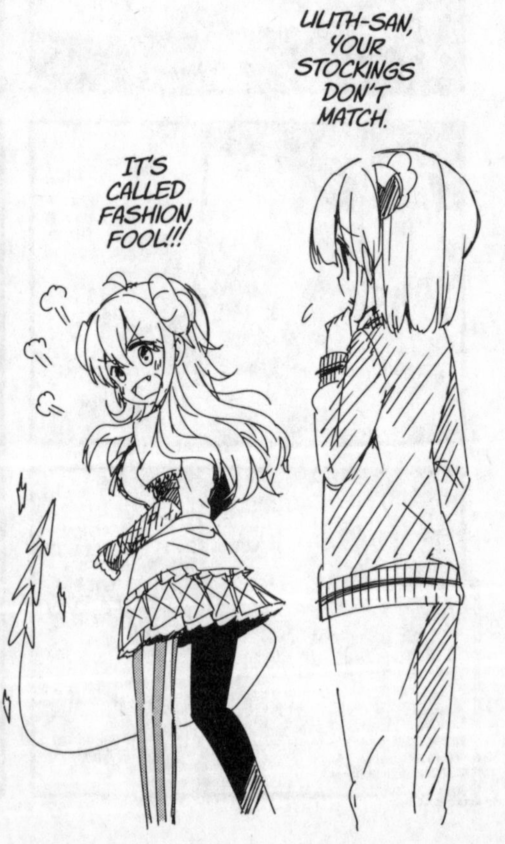
ULITH-SAN, YOUR STOCKINGS DON'T MATCH.
IT'S CALLED FASHION, FOOL!!!

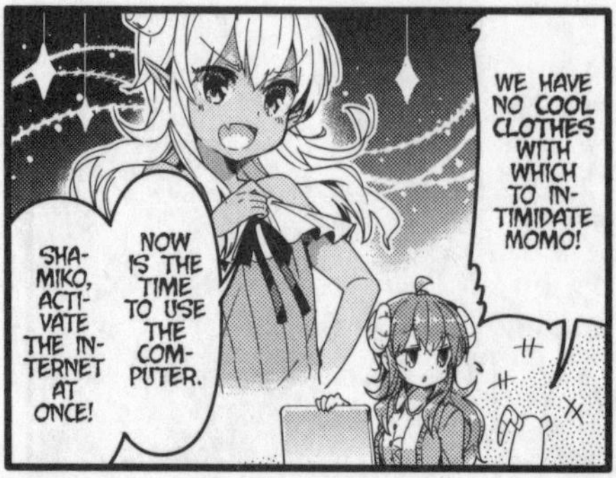
WE HAVE NO COOL CLOTHES WITH WHICH TO INTIMIDATE MOMO!
NOW IS THE TIME TO USE THE COMPUTER.
SHAMIKO, ACTIVATE THE INTERNET AT ONCE!

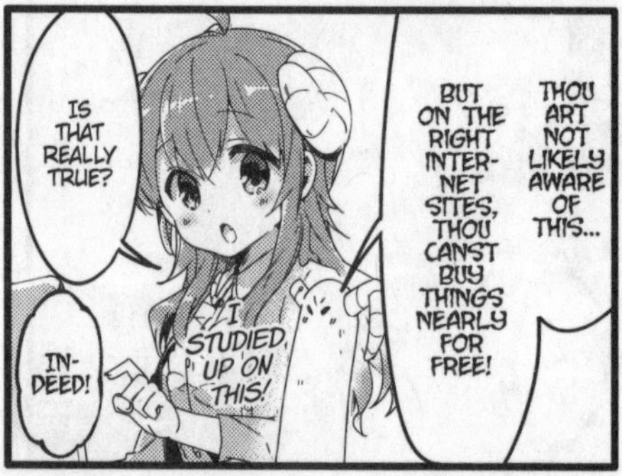
THOU ART NOT LIKELY AWARE OF THIS...
BUT ON THE RIGHT INTERNET SITES, THOU CANST BUY THINGS NEARLY FOR FREE!
IS THAT REALLY TRUE?
I STUDIED UP ON THIS!
INDEED!

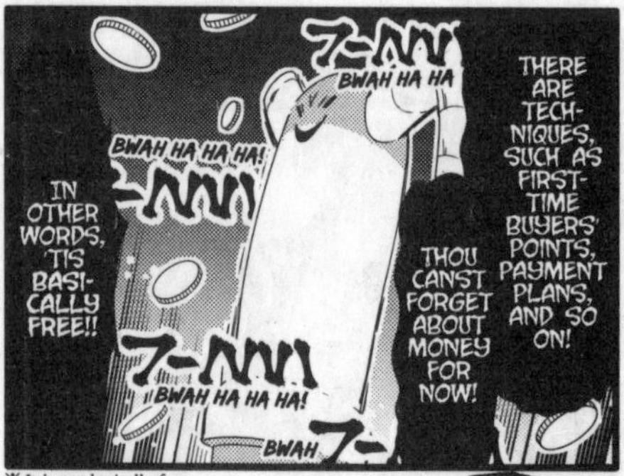
BWAH HA HA
THERE ARE TECHNIQUES, SUCH AS FIRST-TIME BUYERS' POINTS, PAYMENT PLANS, AND SO ON!
BWAH HA HA HA!
THOU CANST FORGET ABOUT MONEY FOR NOW!
IN OTHER WORDS, 'TIS BASICALLY FREE!!
BWAH HA HA HA!
BWAH

※ It is not basically free.

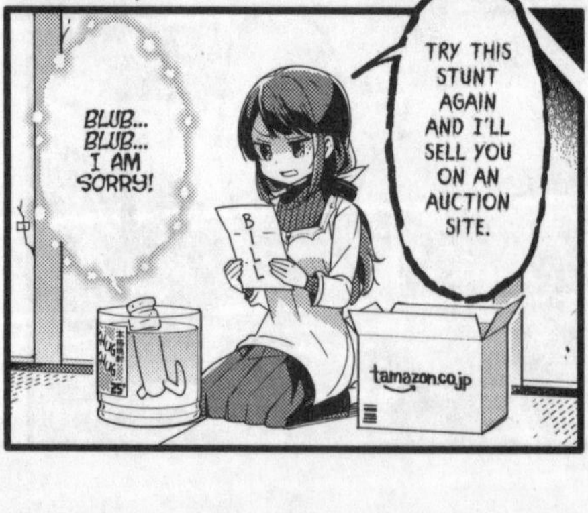
TRY THIS STUNT AGAIN AND I'LL SELL YOU ON AN AUCTION SITE.
BLUB... BLUB... I AM SORRY!
BILL
tamazon.co.jp

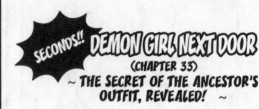

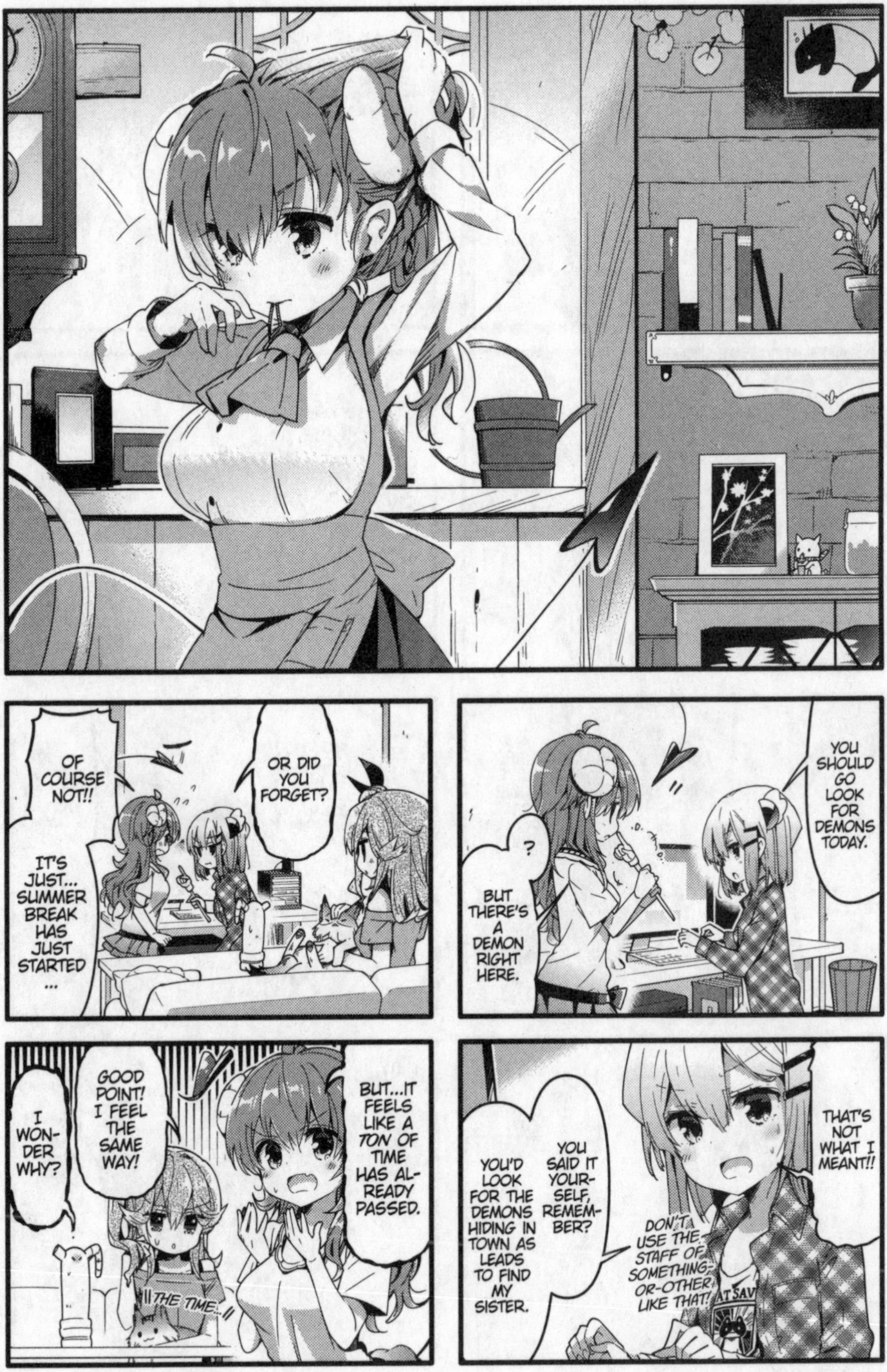
YOU SHOULD GO LOOK FOR DEMONS TODAY.
?
BUT THERE'S A DEMON RIGHT HERE.
THAT'S NOT WHAT I MEANT!!
DON'T USE THE STAFF OF SOMETHING-OR-OTHER LIKE THAT!
YOU SAID IT YOURSELF, REMEMBER?
YOU'D LOOK FOR THE DEMONS HIDING IN TOWN AS LEADS TO FIND MY SISTER.
OR DID YOU FORGET?
OF COURSE NOT!!
IT'S JUST... SUMMER BREAK HAS JUST STARTED...
BUT...IT FEELS LIKE A *TON* OF TIME HAS ALREADY PASSED.
GOOD POINT! I FEEL THE SAME WAY!
I WONDER WHY?
THE TIME...

A DEMON WHO LOVES ERRANDS

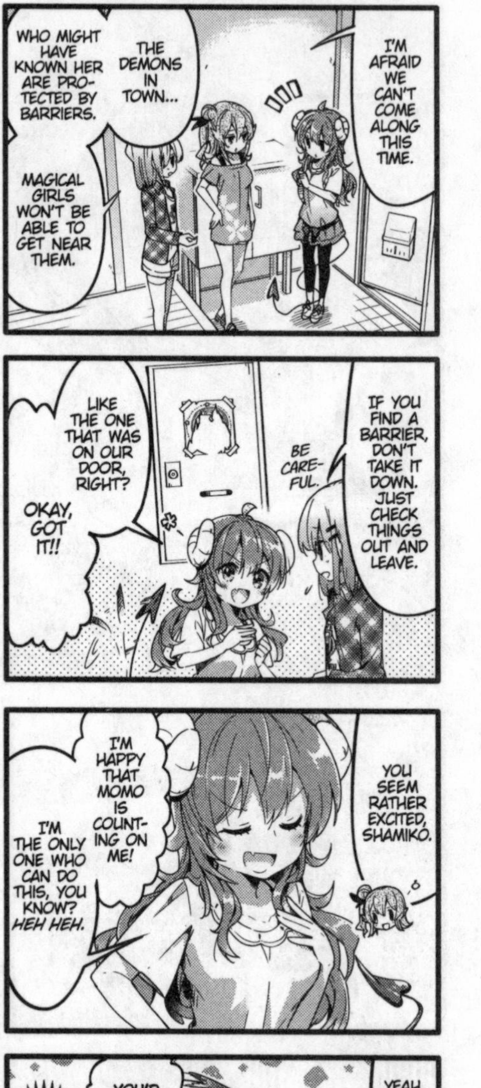
I'M AFRAID WE CAN'T COME ALONG THIS TIME.
THE DEMONS IN TOWN...
WHO MIGHT HAVE KNOWN HER ARE PROTECTED BY BARRIERS.
MAGICAL GIRLS WON'T BE ABLE TO GET NEAR THEM.
IF YOU FIND A BARRIER, DON'T TAKE IT DOWN. JUST CHECK THINGS OUT AND LEAVE.
BE CAREFUL.
LIKE THE ONE THAT WAS ON OUR DOOR, RIGHT?
OKAY, GOT IT!!
YOU SEEM RATHER EXCITED, SHAMIKO.
I'M HAPPY THAT MOMO IS COUNTING ON ME!
I'M THE ONLY ONE WHO CAN DO THIS, YOU KNOW? HEH HEH.
YEAH. THANKS A BUNCH.
ALSO, GRAB SOME GROCERIES FOR DINNER ON YOUR WAY BACK.
YOU'D BETTER WAIT ON THE EDGE OF YOUR SEATS!!
SHAMIKO... CLEARLY, THOU ART BEING USED.

LOTS OF WEIRDOS IN THIS TOWN

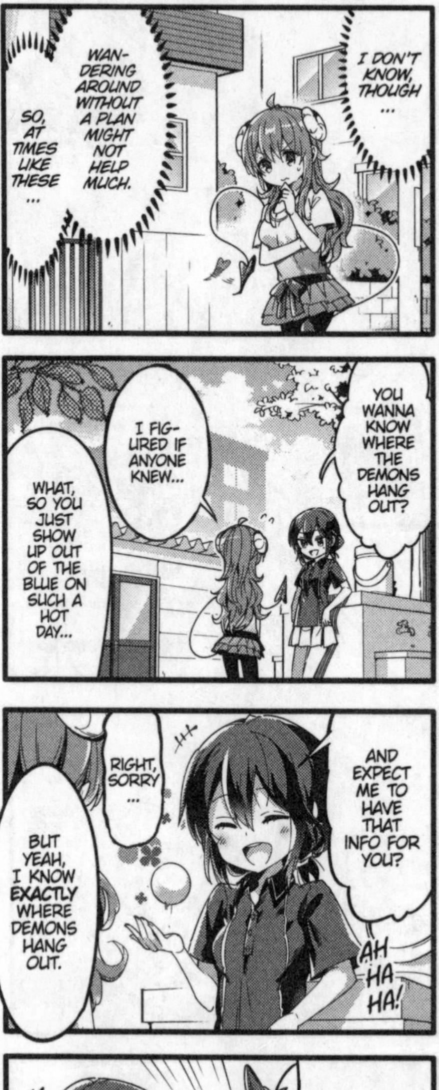
I DON'T KNOW, THOUGH ...
WANDERING AROUND WITHOUT A PLAN MIGHT NOT HELP MUCH.
SO, AT TIMES LIKE THESE ...
YOU WANNA KNOW WHERE THE DEMONS HANG OUT?
I FIGURED IF ANYONE KNEW...
WHAT, SO YOU JUST SHOW UP OUT OF THE BLUE ON SUCH A HOT DAY...
AND EXPECT ME TO HAVE THAT INFO FOR YOU?
RIGHT, SORRY ...
BUT YEAH, I KNOW EXACTLY WHERE DEMONS HANG OUT.
AH HA HA!
OF COURSE... EVEN YOU WOULDN'T JUST--
WAIT, WHAT?!
I KNOW A PLACE WHERE YOU CAN ALWAYS SEE A DEMON.

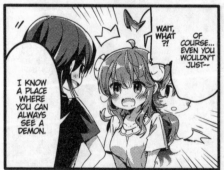

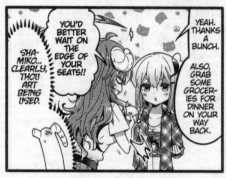

FIRST DEMON, SPOTTED

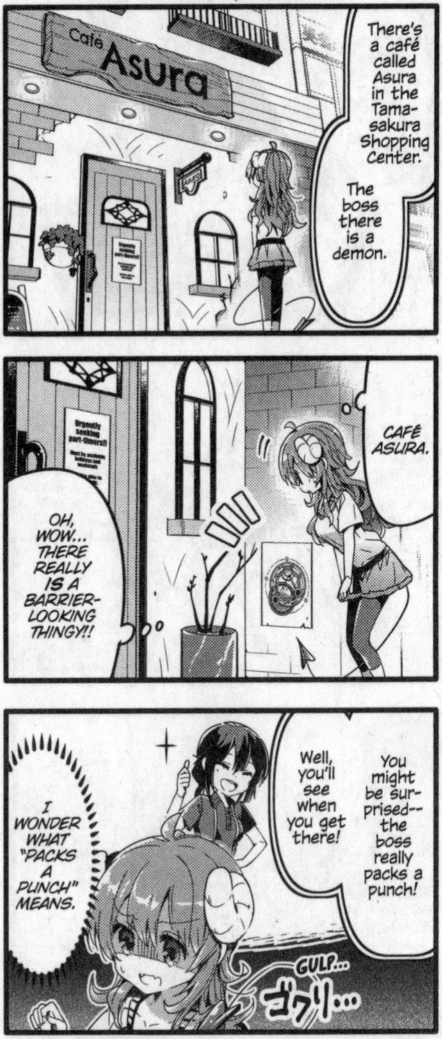
Café
Asura
There's a café called Asura in the Tamasakura Shopping Center.
The boss there is a demon.
CAFÉ ASURA.
OH, WOW... THERE REALLY IS A BARRIER-LOOKING THINGY!!
You might be surprised--the boss really packs a punch!
Well, you'll see when you get there!
I WONDER WHAT "PACKS A PUNCH" MEANS.
GULP...
ゴクリ…
WELL... YOU CAN'T CATCH A DEMON WITHOUT ENTERING THEIR LAIR!!
BAM!!
'SCUSE MEEE!!

ARE YOU THE BOSS?

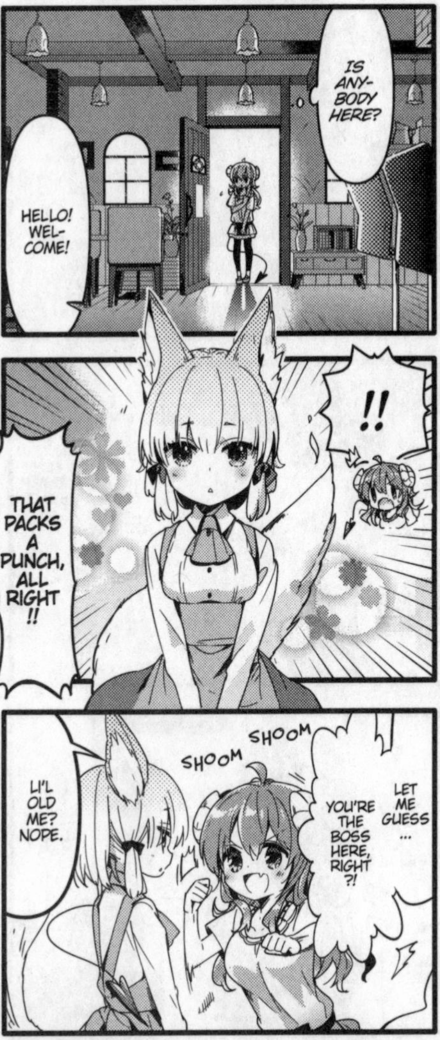
IS ANYBODY HERE?
HELLO! WELCOME!
!!
THAT PACKS A PUNCH, ALL RIGHT!!
LET ME GUESS...
YOU'RE THE BOSS HERE, RIGHT?!
SHOOM SHOOM
LI'L OLD ME? NOPE.
I PACKED A PUNCH, HUH?
ERM... I'M REALLY, REALLY SORRY...

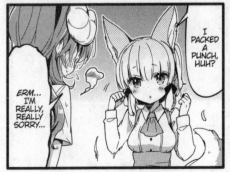

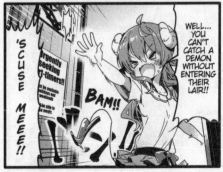

NOW *THAT'S* A PUNCH

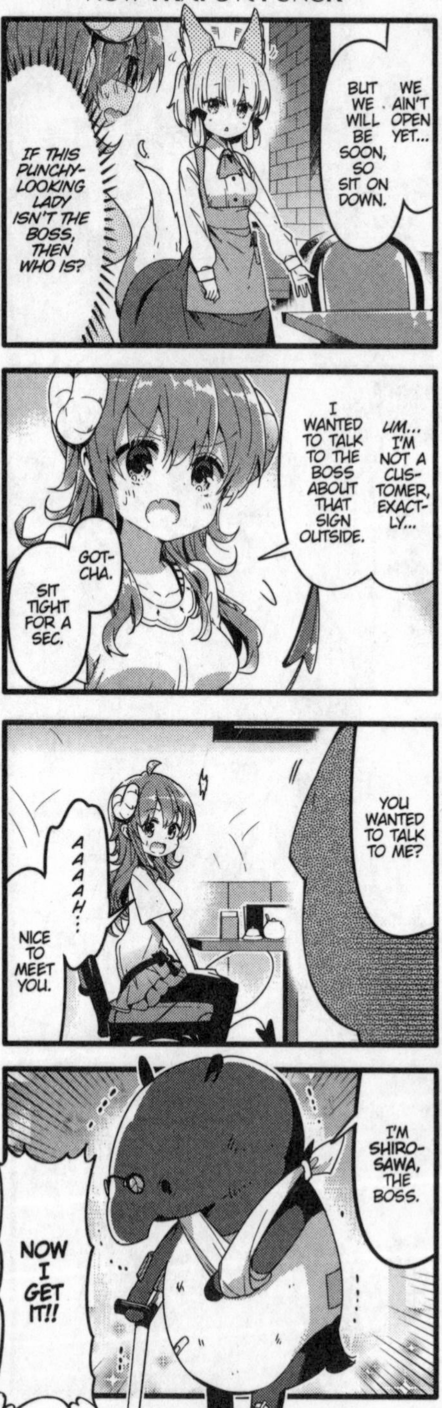
WE AIN'T OPEN YET...
BUT WE WILL BE SOON, SO SIT ON DOWN.
IF THIS PUNCHY-LOOKING LADY ISN'T THE BOSS, THEN WHO IS?
UM... I'M NOT A CUSTOMER, EXACTLY...
I WANTED TO TALK TO THE BOSS ABOUT THAT SIGN OUTSIDE.
GOTCHA.
SIT TIGHT FOR A SEC.
YOU WANTED TO TALK TO ME?
AAAAAH...
NICE TO MEET YOU.
I'M SHIROSAWA, THE BOSS.
NOW I GET IT!!

DOUBLE DITZ SYSTEM

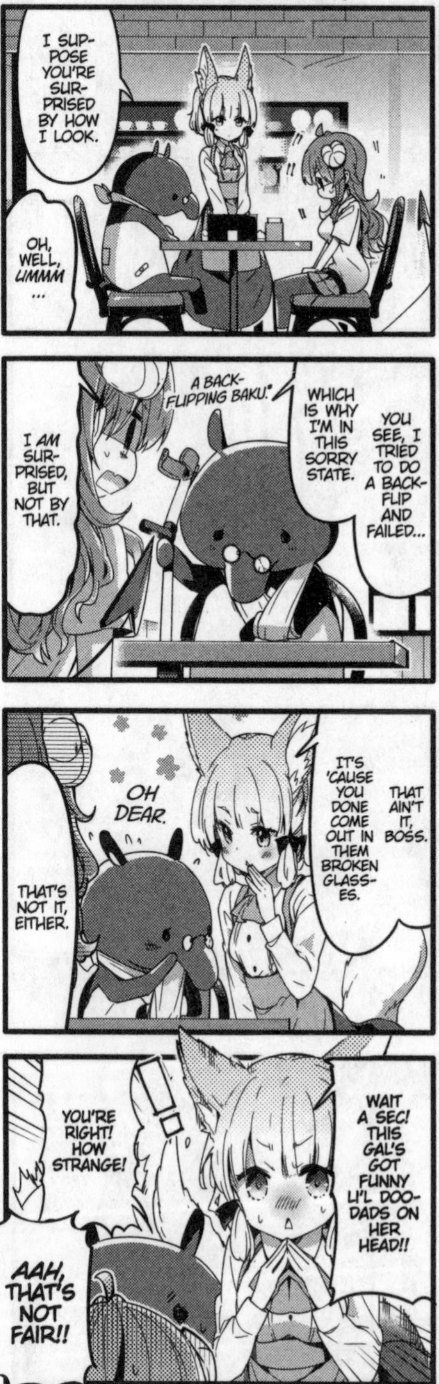
I SUPPOSE YOU'RE SURPRISED BY HOW I LOOK.
OH, WELL, UMMM...
YOU SEE, I TRIED TO DO A BACKFLIP AND FAILED...
WHICH IS WHY I'M IN THIS SORRY STATE.
A BACK-FLIPPING BAKU.*
I AM SURPRISED, BUT NOT BY THAT.
THAT AIN'T IT, BOSS.
IT'S 'CAUSE YOU DONE COME OUT IN THEM BROKEN GLASSES.
OH DEAR.
THAT'S NOT IT, EITHER.
WAIT A SEC! THIS GAL'S GOT FUNNY LI'L DOODADS ON HER HEAD!!
YOU'RE RIGHT! HOW STRANGE!
AAH, THAT'S NOT FAIR!!

** Shirosawa is a baku, which in Japanese means both a mythical nightmare-eating creature and the real-world tapir.*

HARD LINES ARE HARD

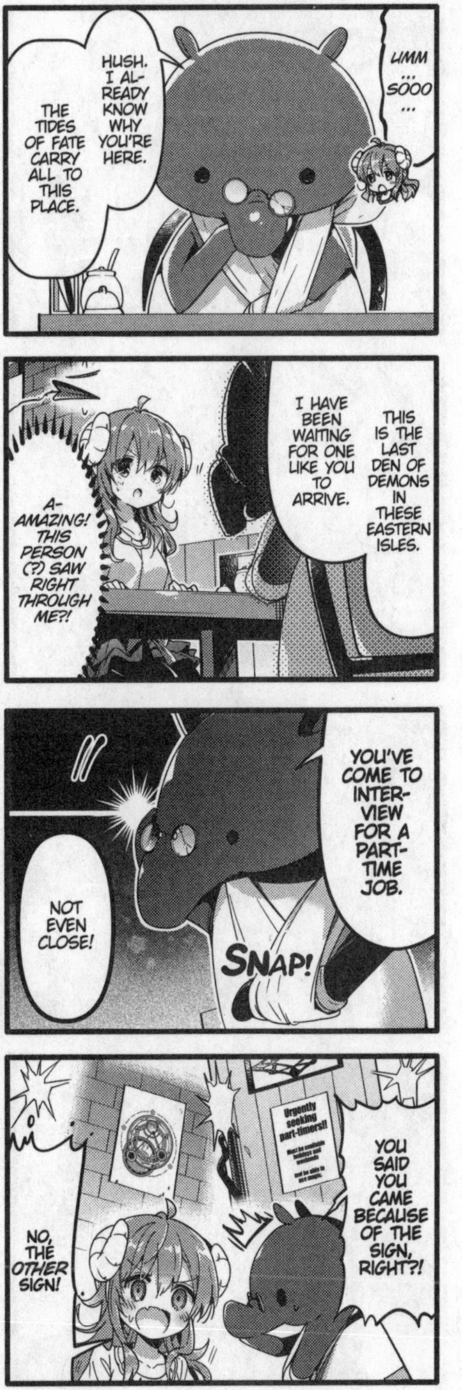
UMM ... SOOO ...
HUSH. I ALREADY KNOW WHY YOU'RE HERE.
THE TIDES OF FATE CARRY ALL TO THIS PLACE.
THIS IS THE LAST DEN OF DEMONS IN THESE EASTERN ISLES.
I HAVE BEEN WAITING FOR ONE LIKE YOU TO ARRIVE.
A-AMAZING! THIS PERSON (?) SAW RIGHT THROUGH ME?!
YOU'VE COME TO INTERVIEW FOR A PART-TIME JOB.
SNAP!
NOT EVEN CLOSE!
Urgently seeking part-timers!!
YOU SAID YOU CAME BECAUSE OF THE SIGN, RIGHT?!
NO, THE OTHER SIGN!

BAKU CAN BE SCARY

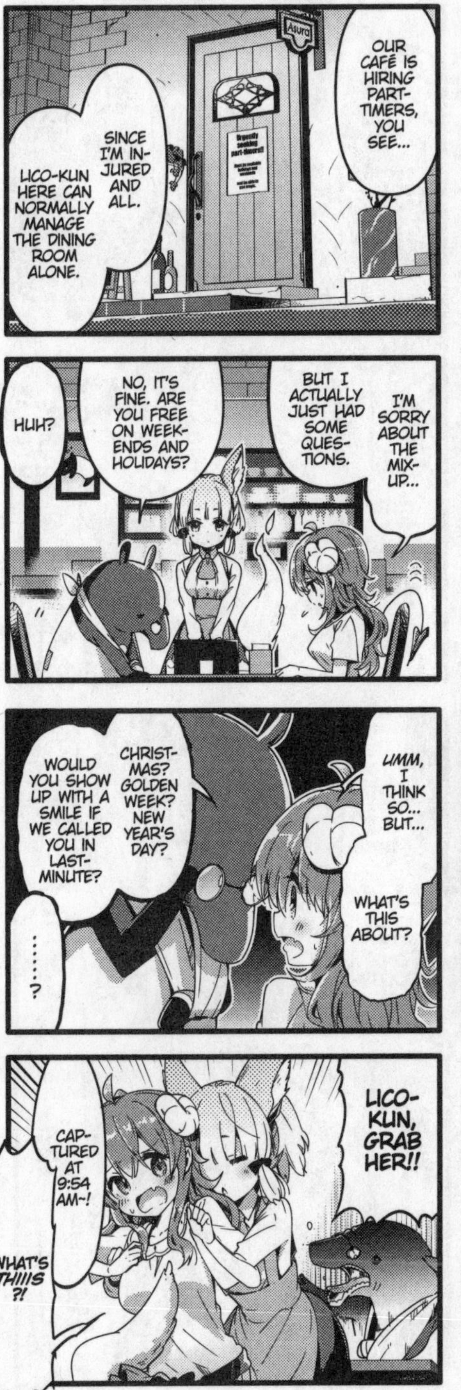
Asura
Urgently seeking part-timers!!
OUR CAFÉ IS HIRING PART-TIMERS, YOU SEE...
SINCE I'M INJURED AND ALL.
LICO-KUN HERE CAN NORMALLY MANAGE THE DINING ROOM ALONE.
I'M SORRY ABOUT THE MIX-UP...
BUT I ACTUALLY JUST HAD SOME QUESTIONS.
NO, IT'S FINE. ARE YOU FREE ON WEEKENDS AND HOLIDAYS?
HUH?
UMM, I THINK SO... BUT...
WHAT'S THIS ABOUT?
CHRISTMAS? GOLDEN WEEK? NEW YEAR'S DAY?
WOULD YOU SHOW UP WITH A SMILE IF WE CALLED YOU IN LAST-MINUTE?
......?
LICO-KUN, GRAB HER!!
CAPTURED AT 9:54 AM~!
WHAT'S THIIIS?!

A DEMON'S FIRST PLEA

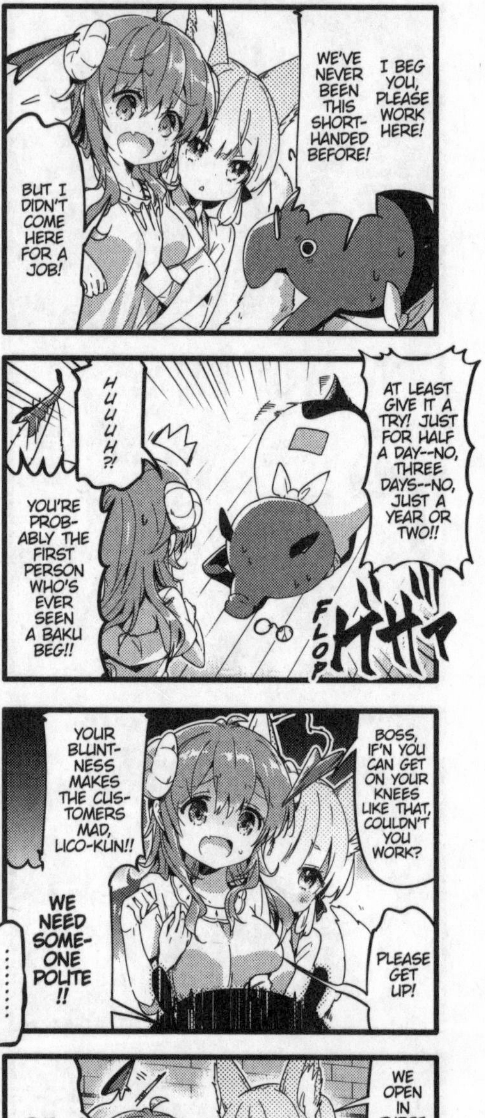
I BEG YOU, PLEASE WORK HERE!
WE'VE NEVER BEEN THIS SHORT-HANDED BEFORE!
BUT I DIDN'T COME HERE FOR A JOB!
AT LEAST GIVE IT A TRY! JUST FOR HALF A DAY--NO, THREE DAYS--NO, JUST A YEAR OR TWO!!
HUUUH?!
YOU'RE PROBABLY THE FIRST PERSON WHO'S EVER SEEN A BAKU BEG!!
FLOP
BOSS, IF'N YOU CAN GET ON YOUR KNEES LIKE THAT, COULDN'T YOU WORK?
YOUR BLUNTNESS MAKES THE CUSTOMERS MAD, LICO-KUN!!
PLEASE GET UP!
WE NEED SOMEONE POLITE!!
......
WE OPEN IN THREE MINUTES, 'KAAAY~?
FINE, JUST FOR TODAY.
SO, THIS HERE IS THE TABLE NUMBER CHART, 'KAAAY~?

A CAFÉ THAT CAN FORM A LINE

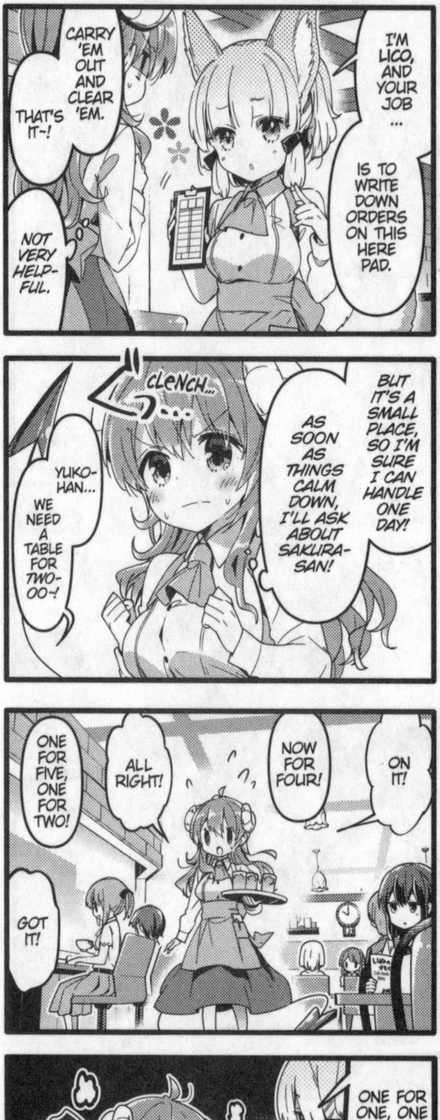
I'M LICO, AND YOUR JOB ... IS TO WRITE DOWN ORDERS ON THIS HERE PAD.
CARRY 'EM OUT AND CLEAR 'EM. THAT'S IT~!
NOT VERY HELPFUL.
BUT IT'S A SMALL PLACE, SO I'M SURE I CAN HANDLE ONE DAY!
AS SOON AS THINGS CALM DOWN, I'LL ASK ABOUT SAKURA-SAN!
CLENCH...
YUKO-HAN... WE NEED A TABLE FOR TWO-OO~!
ON IT!
NOW FOR FOUR!
ALL RIGHT!
ONE FOR FIVE, ONE FOR TWO!
GOT IT!
ONE FOR ONE, ONE FOR ONE, ONE FOR FOUR, ONE FOR FIVE, ONE FOR TWELVE PLUS A CHILD, ONE FOR FOUR...
WHY ARE THERE SO MANY CUSTOMERS?

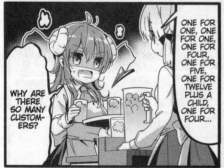

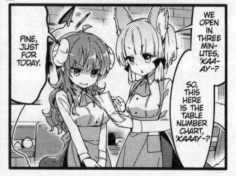

SHADOW MISTRESS YUKO

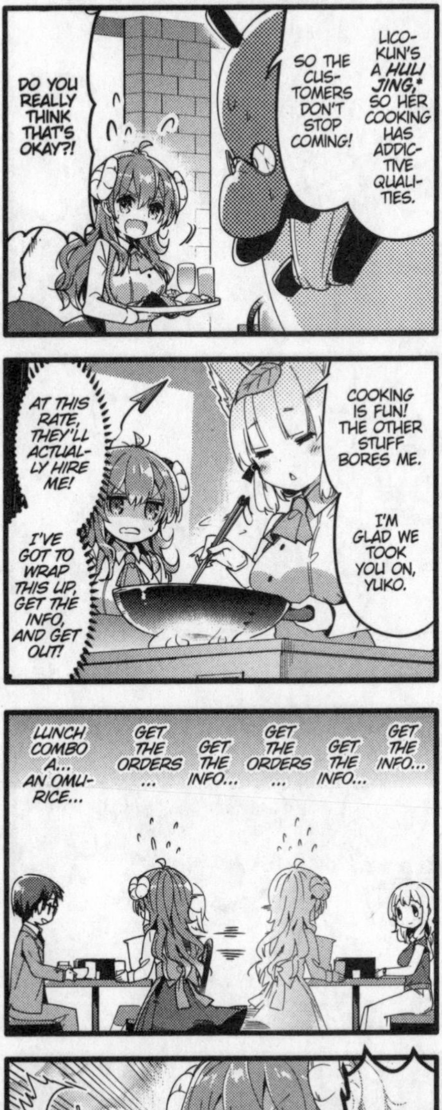
LICO-KUN'S A *HULI JING,** SO HER COOKING HAS ADDICTIVE QUALITIES.
SO THE CUSTOMERS DON'T STOP COMING!
DO YOU REALLY THINK THAT'S OKAY?!
COOKING IS FUN! THE OTHER STUFF BORES ME.
I'M GLAD WE TOOK YOU ON, YUKO.
AT THIS RATE, THEY'LL ACTUALLY HIRE ME!
I'VE GOT TO WRAP THIS UP, GET THE INFO, AND GET OUT!
GET THE INFO...
GET THE INFO...
GET THE ORDERS...
GET THE INFO...
GET THE ORDERS...
LUNCH COMBO A... AN OMURICE...
CURRY AND LUNCH COMBO B FOR TABLE FIVE!!
THE DEMON HAS EVOLVED INTO A WAITRESS!

A huli jing is a shapeshifting fox spirit from Chinese mythology, not unlike the Japanese kitsune.

A LUNCH FROM WHICH THERE IS NO ESCAPE

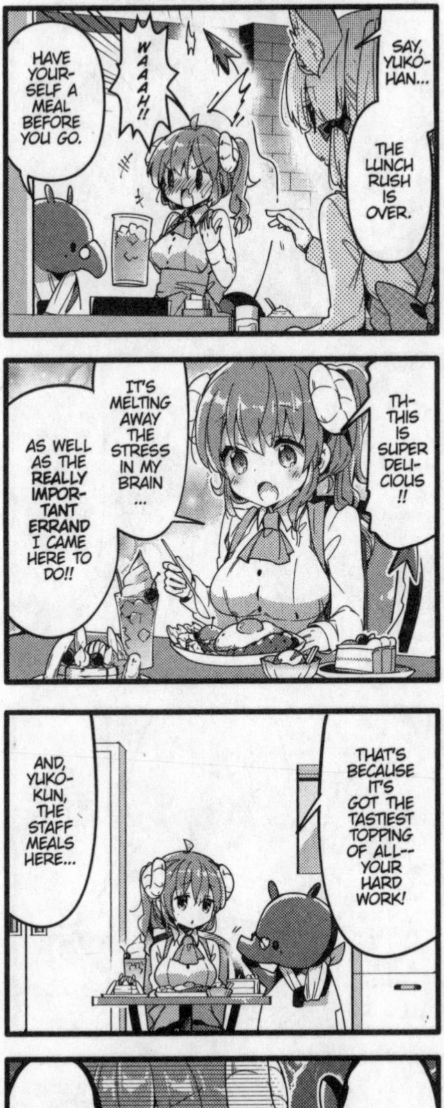
SAY, YUKO-HAN...
THE LUNCH RUSH IS OVER.
WAAAAH!!
HAVE YOURSELF A MEAL BEFORE YOU GO.
TH-THIS IS SUPER DELICIOUS!!
IT'S MELTING AWAY THE STRESS IN MY BRAIN...
AS WELL AS THE REALLY IMPORTANT ERRAND I CAME HERE TO DO!!
THAT'S BECAUSE IT'S GOT THE TASTIEST TOPPING OF ALL-- YOUR HARD WORK!
AND, YUKO-KUN, THE STAFF MEALS HERE...
ARE ALWAYS FREE...
AND ALL-YOU-CAN-EAT!
??!!

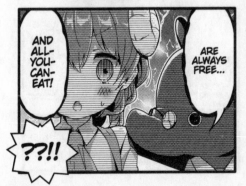

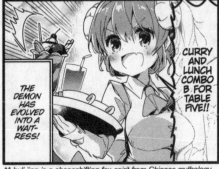

LIKE DINNER?

WELCOME BACK.

HOW DID IT GO?

HEEEY, I'M HOO-OME!!

MOMO, I...

AND I LEARNED SOMETHING REALLY IMPORTANT!

HM?

I GOT A PART-TIME JOB!

IT'S THE TASTIEST TOPPING OF ALL!!

HARD WORK!

LEARN THE VALUE OF HARD WORK AND EAT EVEN TASTIER FOOD!!

DON'T GIVE UP, SHA-MIKO!!

DID YOU FORGET THE ENTIRE POINT OF YOUR TRIP?

A BALANCED DIET

SHA-MIKO'S AW-FULLY LATE...

AND I'M QUITE HUN-GRY.

NO, NOT YET. LET'S TRUST IN SHA-MIKO.

OUR STRATEGY MEETING IS OVER, SO SHALL WE POP OUT TO THE CON-VENIENCE STORE?

I'M SURE SHE'LL COME BACK WITH USEFUL INFORMA-TION AND INGREDI-ENTS FOR A TASTY MEAL.

SHE DOES GET RESULTS, EVEN IF IT TAKES A WHILE.

ARE THEY STARTING TO CON-SIDER SHAMIKO THEIR LIFELINE?

UH-HUH.

|| GURGLE ||

|| GURGLE ||

YOU'RE RIGHT... PLUS WE HAD CON-VENIENCE STORE FOOD FOR LUNCH ALREADY!!

"THE TIME HATH

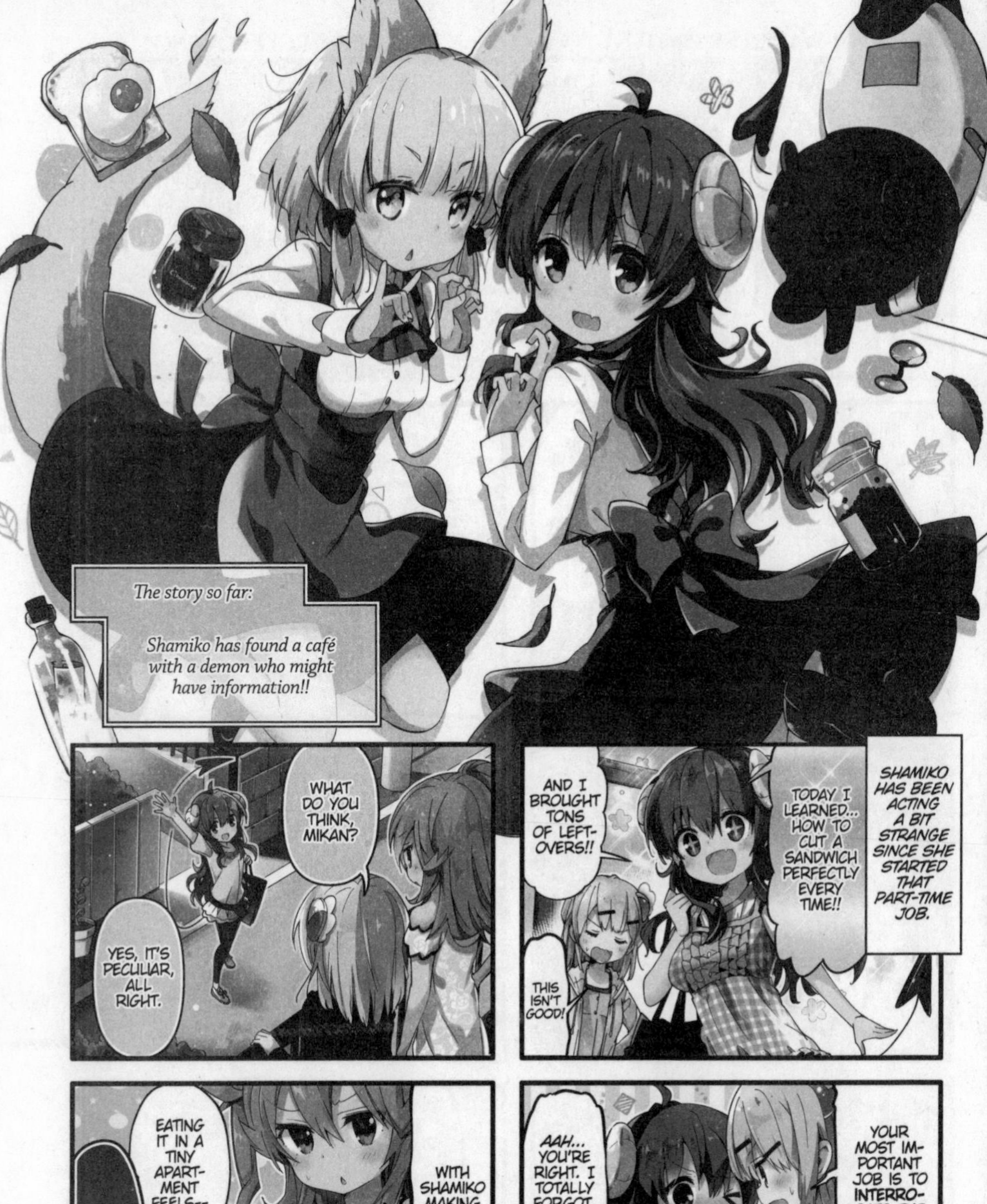
The story so far:
Shamiko has found a café with a demon who might have information!!
SHAMIKO HAS BEEN ACTING A BIT STRANGE SINCE SHE STARTED THAT PART-TIME JOB.
TODAY I LEARNED... HOW TO CUT A SANDWICH PERFECTLY EVERY TIME!!
AND I BROUGHT TONS OF LEFTOVERS!!
THIS ISN'T GOOD!
WHAT DO YOU THINK, MIKAN?
YES, IT'S PECULIAR, ALL RIGHT.
YOUR MOST IMPORTANT JOB IS TO INTERROGATE THE DEMON!!
AAH... YOU'RE RIGHT. I TOTALLY FORGOT.
I'LL ASK TOMORROW, FOR SURE.
WITH SHAMIKO MAKING SUCH HIP CAFÉ FOOD NOW...
EATING IT IN A TINY APARTMENT FEELS--
THAT'S WEIRD TOO, BUT NOT WHAT I MEANT.

TWO GIRLS ROLEPLAYING

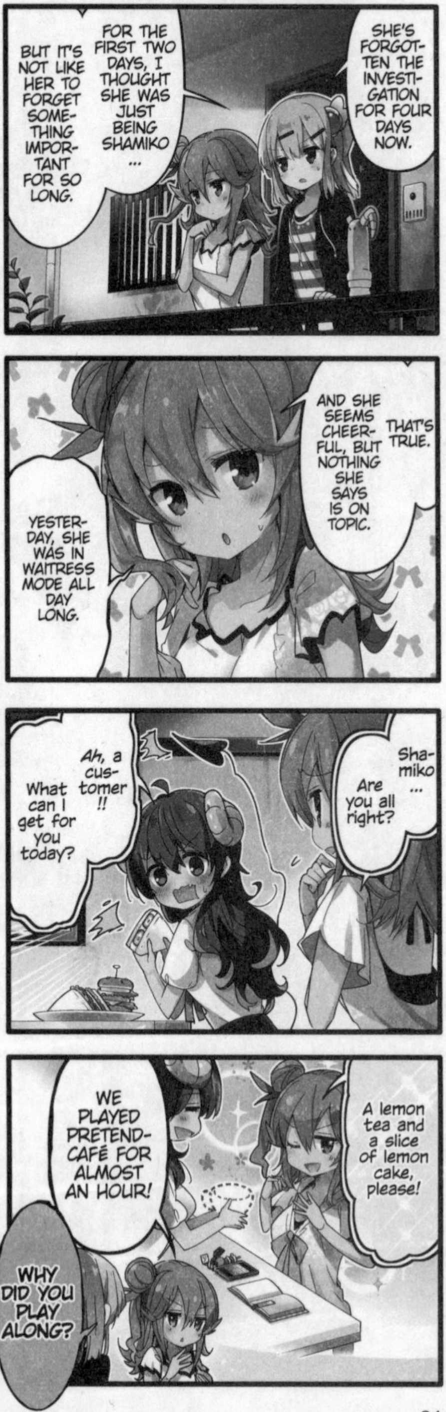
SHE'S FORGOTTEN THE INVESTIGATION FOR FOUR DAYS NOW.
FOR THE FIRST TWO DAYS, I THOUGHT SHE WAS JUST BEING SHAMIKO ...
BUT IT'S NOT LIKE HER TO FORGET SOMETHING IMPORTANT FOR SO LONG.
THAT'S TRUE.
AND SHE SEEMS CHEERFUL, BUT NOTHING SHE SAYS IS ON TOPIC.
YESTERDAY, SHE WAS IN WAITRESS MODE ALL DAY LONG.
Shamiko ... Are you all right?
Ah, a customer!!
What can I get for you today?
A lemon tea and a slice of lemon cake, please!
WE PLAYED PRETEND-CAFÉ FOR ALMOST AN HOUR!
WHY DID YOU PLAY ALONG?

ANTI-WAITRESS PROTEST

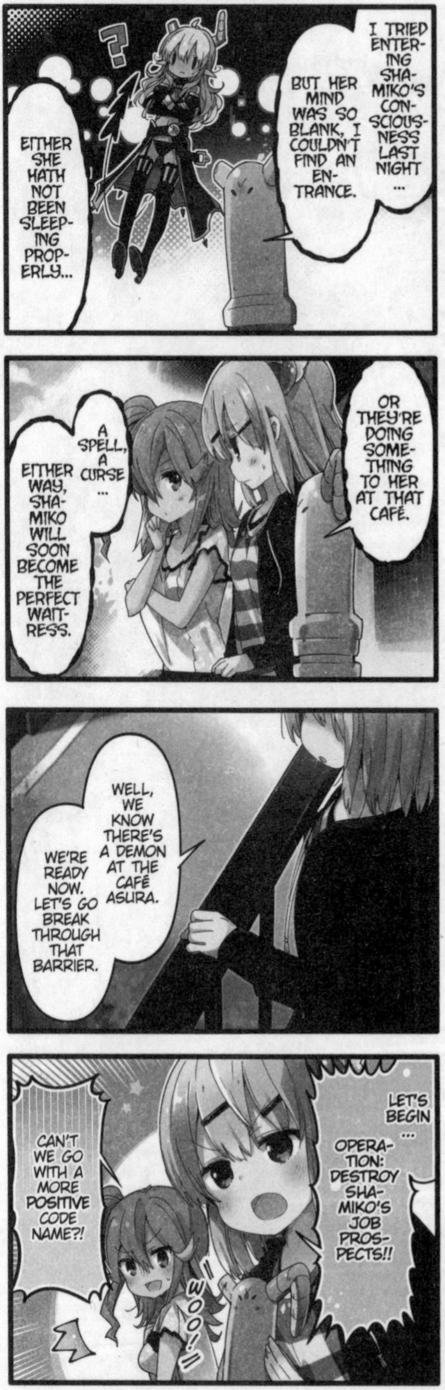
I TRIED ENTERING SHAMIKO'S CONSCIOUSNESS LAST NIGHT ...
BUT HER MIND WAS SO BLANK, I COULDN'T FIND AN ENTRANCE.
?
EITHER SHE HATH NOT BEEN SLEEPING PROPERLY...
OR THEY'RE DOING SOMETHING TO HER AT THAT CAFÉ.
A SPELL, A CURSE ...
EITHER WAY, SHAMIKO WILL SOON BECOME THE PERFECT WAITRESS.
WELL, WE KNOW THERE'S A DEMON AT THE CAFÉ ASURA.
WE'RE READY NOW. LET'S GO BREAK THROUGH THAT BARRIER.
LET'S BEGIN ...
OPERATION: DESTROY SHAMIKO'S JOB PROSPECTS!!
WOO!!
CAN'T WE GO WITH A MORE POSITIVE CODE NAME?!

STAGE FRIGHT

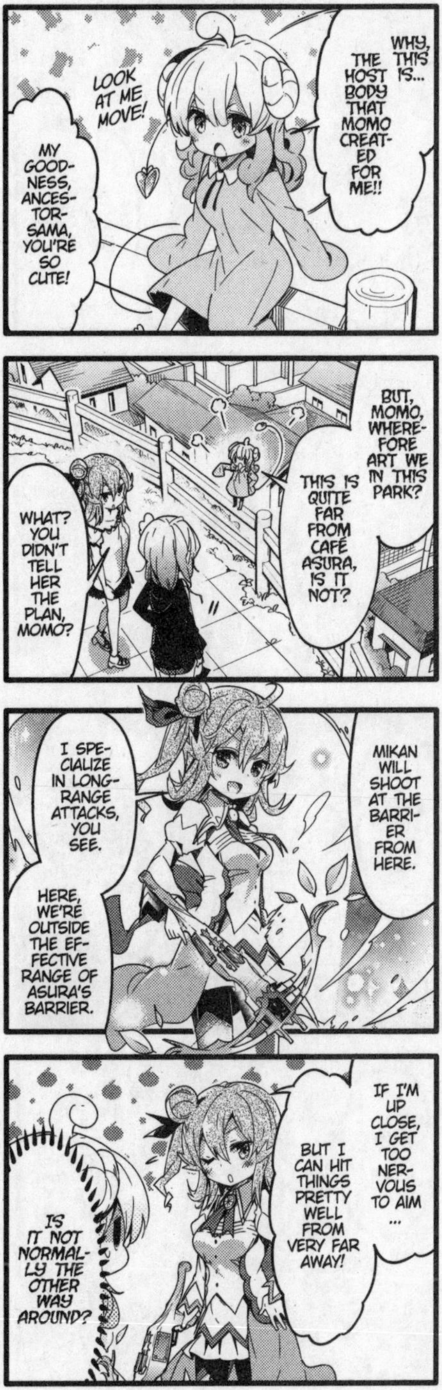
WHY, THIS IS... THE HOST BODY THAT MOMO CREATED FOR ME!!
LOOK AT ME MOVE!
MY GOODNESS, ANCESTOR-SAMA, YOU'RE SO CUTE!
BUT, MOMO, WHEREFORE ART WE IN THIS PARK?
THIS IS QUITE FAR FROM CAFÉ ASURA, IS IT NOT?
WHAT? YOU DIDN'T TELL HER THE PLAN, MOMO?
MIKAN WILL SHOOT AT THE BARRIER FROM HERE.
I SPECIALIZE IN LONG-RANGE ATTACKS, YOU SEE.
HERE, WE'RE OUTSIDE THE EFFECTIVE RANGE OF ASURA'S BARRIER.
IF I'M UP CLOSE, I GET TOO NERVOUS TO AIM...
BUT I CAN HIT THINGS PRETTY WELL FROM VERY FAR AWAY!
IS IT NOT NORMALLY THE OTHER WAY AROUND?

LILITH SKYWALKER

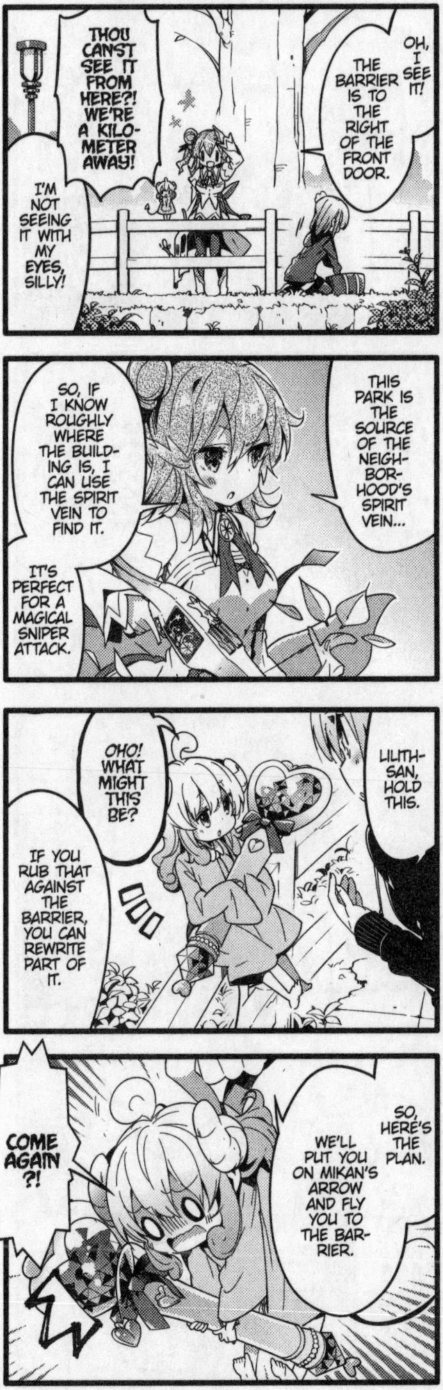
OH, I SEE IT!
THE BARRIER IS TO THE RIGHT OF THE FRONT DOOR.
THOU CANST SEE IT FROM HERE?! WE'RE A KILOMETER AWAY!
I'M NOT SEEING IT WITH MY EYES, SILLY!
THIS PARK IS THE SOURCE OF THE NEIGHBORHOOD'S SPIRIT VEIN...
SO, IF I KNOW ROUGHLY WHERE THE BUILDING IS, I CAN USE THE SPIRIT VEIN TO FIND IT.
IT'S PERFECT FOR A MAGICAL SNIPER ATTACK.
LILITH-SAN, HOLD THIS.
OHO! WHAT MIGHT THIS BE?
IF YOU RUB THAT AGAINST THE BARRIER, YOU CAN REWRITE PART OF IT.
SO, HERE'S THE PLAN.
WE'LL PUT YOU ON MIKAN'S ARROW AND FLY YOU TO THE BARRIER.
COME AGAIN?!

A HUNDRED THOUSAND CENTIMETERS PER SECOND

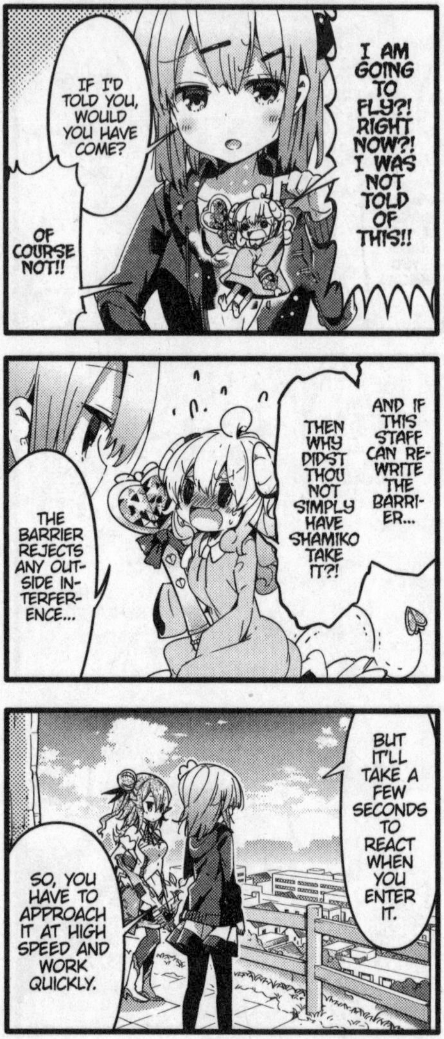
I AM GOING TO FLY?! RIGHT NOW?! I WAS NOT TOLD OF THIS!!
IF I'D TOLD YOU, WOULD YOU HAVE COME?
OF COURSE NOT!!
AND IF THIS STAFF CAN RE-WRITE THE BARRI-ER...
THEN WHY DIDST THOU NOT SIMPLY HAVE SHAMIKO TAKE IT?!
THE BARRIER REJECTS ANY OUT-SIDE IN-TERFER-ENCE...
BUT IT'LL TAKE A FEW SECONDS TO REACT WHEN YOU ENTER IT.
SO, YOU HAVE TO APPROACH IT AT HIGH SPEED AND WORK QUICKLY.
ASURA'S BARRIER IS ABOUT A KILO-METER FROM HERE...
I CAN GET YOU THERE IN ONE SECOND.
SO, I AM ABOUT TO BE FIRED AT A THOU-SAND METERS PER SECOND?

ANCESTRAL SELF-AWARENESS

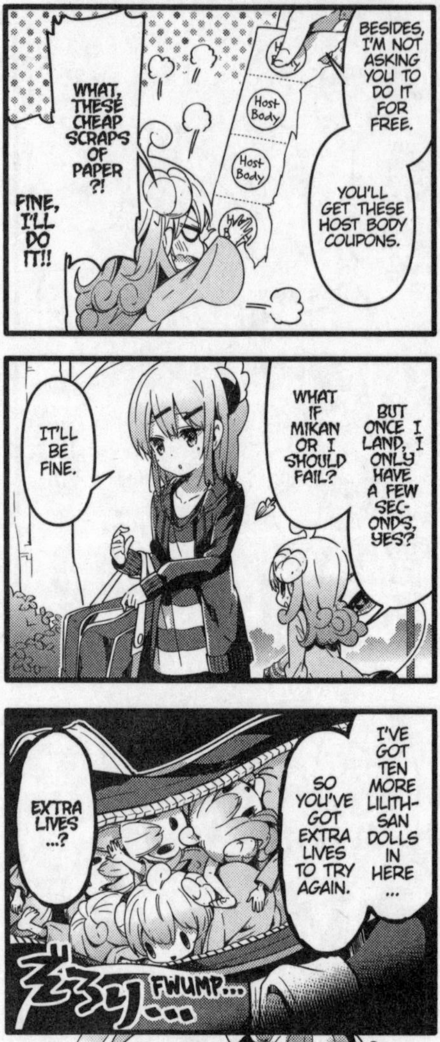
BESIDES, I'M NOT ASKING YOU TO DO IT FOR FREE.
YOU'LL GET THESE HOST BODY COUPONS.
Host Body
Host Body
WHAT, THESE CHEAP SCRAPS OF PAPER ?!
FINE, I'LL DO IT!!
BUT ONCE I LAND, I ONLY HAVE A FEW SEC-ONDS, YES?
WHAT IF MIKAN OR I SHOULD FAIL?
IT'LL BE FINE.
I'VE GOT TEN MORE LILITH-SAN DOLLS IN HERE...
SO YOU'VE GOT EXTRA LIVES TO TRY AGAIN.
EXTRA LIVES ...?
ぞろり...
FWUMP...
OKAY... LET THE BATTLE TO STEAL SHAMIKO BACK BEGIIIN!
I HAVE EXTRA LIVES?

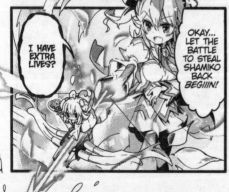

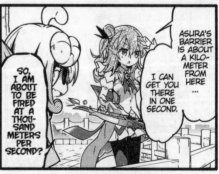

A LETTER ON AN ARROW

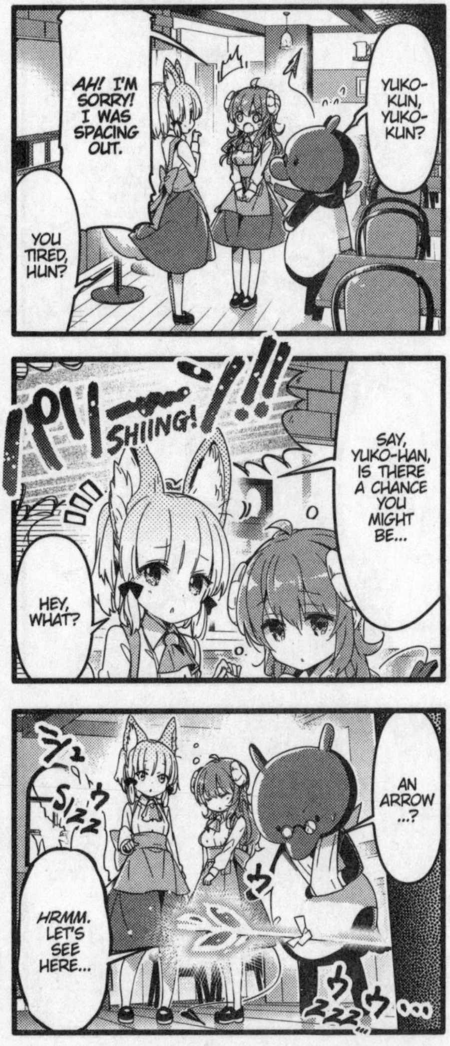
YUKO-KUN, YUKO-KUN?
AH! I'M SORRY! I WAS SPACING OUT.
YOU TIRED, HUN?
SHIING!
SAY, YUKO-HAN, IS THERE A CHANCE YOU MIGHT BE...
HEY, WHAT?
AN ARROW ...?
SIZZZ
HRMM. LET'S SEE HERE...
A LETTER ON AN ARROW?!
AWW, HOW NICE! JUST LIKE OLD TIMES. I'VE ALWAYS WANTED ONE.
If you try to run, I'll shoot. Please just wait quietly. I'm sorry about this.
Hinatsuki
IT'S NOT NICE AT ALL!! THIS MESSAGE SOUNDS VERY THREAT-ENING!!

LICO-KUN ADDS FUEL TO THE FIRE

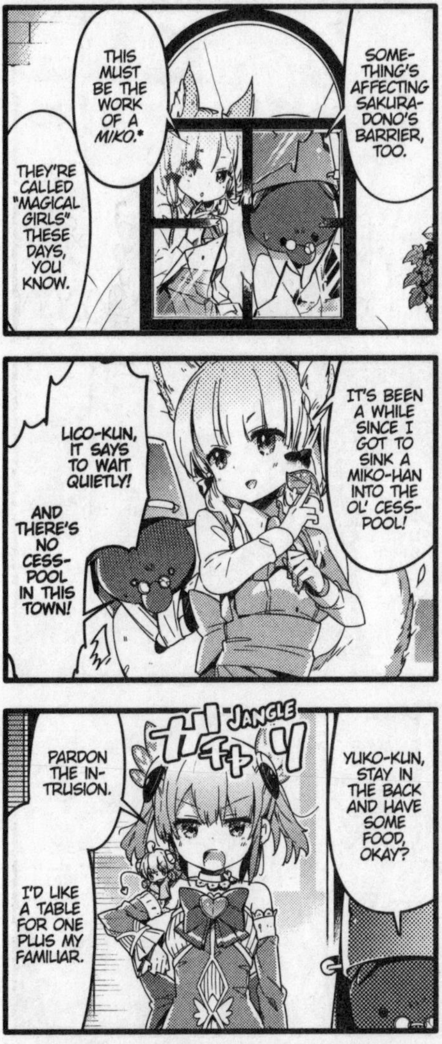
SOME-THING'S AFFECTING SAKURA-DONO'S BARRIER, TOO.
THIS MUST BE THE WORK OF A MIKO.*
THEY'RE CALLED "MAGICAL GIRLS" THESE DAYS, YOU KNOW.
IT'S BEEN A WHILE SINCE I GOT TO SINK A MIKO-HAN INTO THE OL' CESS-POOL!
LICO-KUN, IT SAYS TO WAIT QUIETLY!
AND THERE'S NO CESS-POOL IN THIS TOWN!
YUKO-KUN, STAY IN THE BACK AND HAVE SOME FOOD, OKAY?
JANGLE
PARDON THE IN-TRUSION.
I'D LIKE A TABLE FOR ONE PLUS MY FAMILIAR.
MY, THAT'S SOME OUTFIT YOU'VE GOT ON THERE, MISS~!
ALL WE'VE GOT TODAY IS BUBUZUKE.** THAT ALL RIGHT?
LICO-KUN ?!

** A miko is a Shinto priestess, usually a young woman, who performs dances and ceremonies at shrines. In pre-modern times they were seen as having mystical powers.*

***Bubuzuke is a Kyoto term for ochazuke, which is rice with green tea poured over it.*

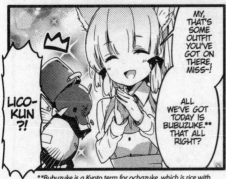

A YUKO-SAN FAN

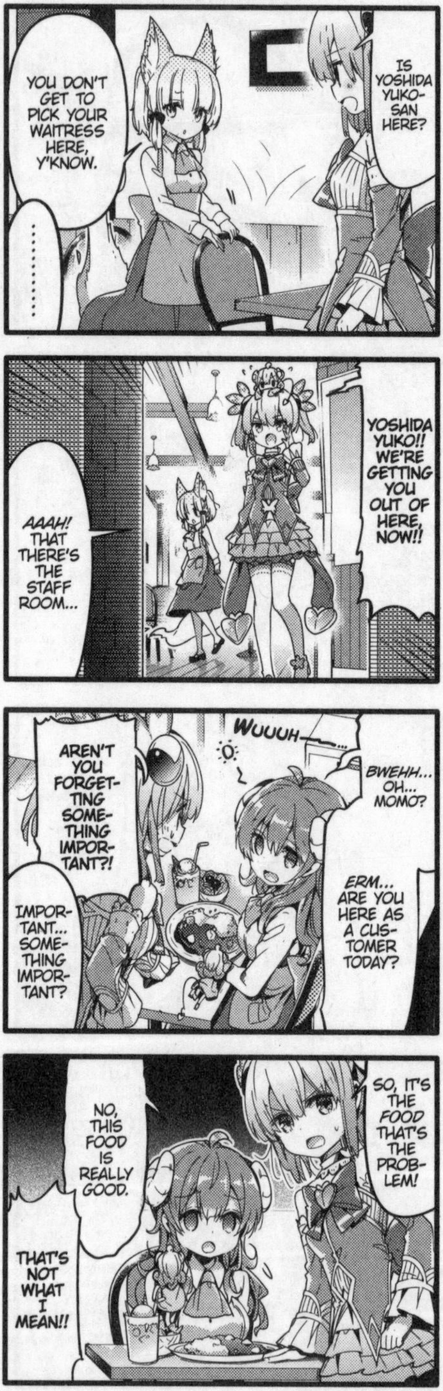
IS YOSHIDA YUKO-SAN HERE?
YOU DON'T GET TO PICK YOUR WAITRESS HERE, Y'KNOW.
......
YOSHIDA YUKO!! WE'RE GETTING YOU OUT OF HERE, NOW!!
AAAH! THAT THERE'S THE STAFF ROOM...
WUUUH—...
BWEHH... OH... MOMO?
ERM... ARE YOU HERE AS A CUSTOMER TODAY?
AREN'T YOU FORGETTING SOMETHING IMPORTANT?!
IMPORTANT... SOMETHING IMPORTANT?
SO, IT'S THE FOOD THAT'S THE PROBLEM!
NO, THIS FOOD IS REALLY GOOD.
THAT'S NOT WHAT I MEAN!!

LICO-KUN'S FRIENDLY FIRE

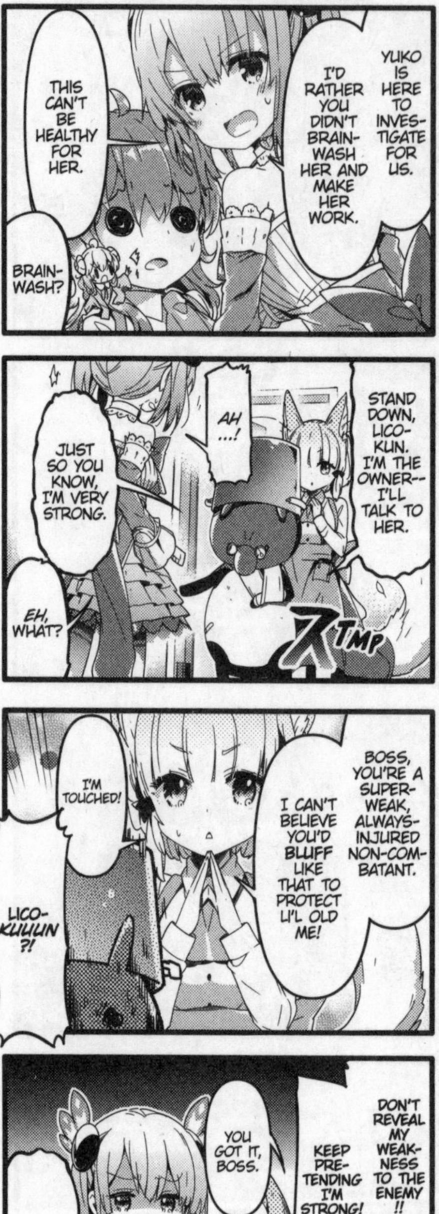
YUKO IS HERE TO INVESTIGATE FOR US.
I'D RATHER YOU DIDN'T BRAINWASH HER AND MAKE HER WORK.
THIS CAN'T BE HEALTHY FOR HER.
BRAINWASH?
STAND DOWN, LICO-KUN. I'M THE OWNER-- I'LL TALK TO HER.
AH ...!
JUST SO YOU KNOW, I'M VERY STRONG.
EH, WHAT?
TMP
BOSS, YOU'RE A SUPER-WEAK, ALWAYS-INJURED NON-COMBATANT.
I CAN'T BELIEVE YOU'D BLUFF LIKE THAT TO PROTECT LI'L OLD ME!
I'M TOUCHED!
LICO-KUUUN?!
DON'T REVEAL MY WEAKNESS TO THE ENEMY!!
KEEP PRETENDING I'M STRONG!
YOU GOT IT, BOSS.
UH... I CAN HEAR YOU, YOU KNOW.

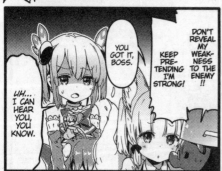

GARLIC-LIKE EFFECT?

x 1

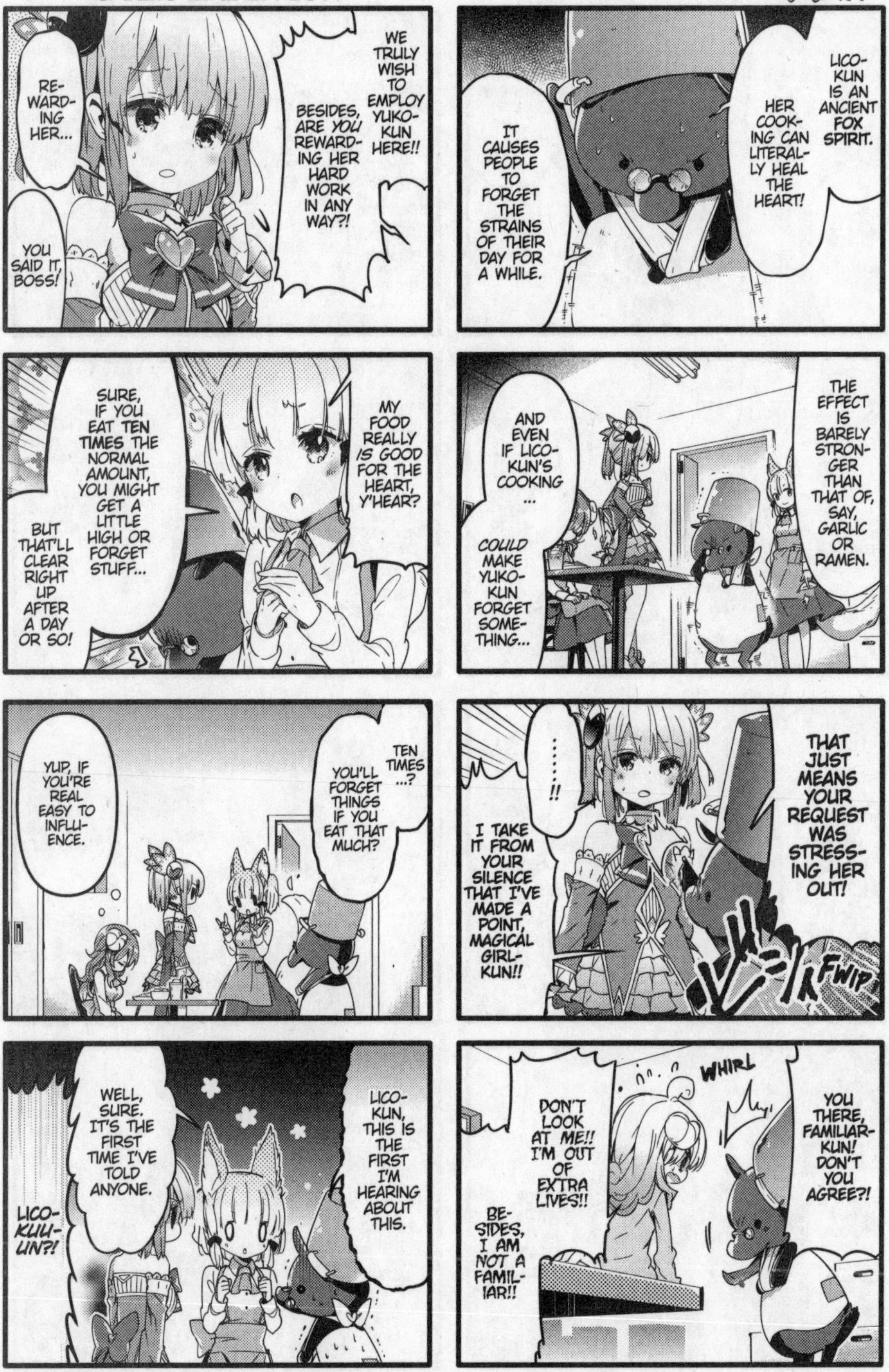

LICO-KUN IS AN ANCIENT FOX SPIRIT.
HER COOKING CAN LITERALLY HEAL THE HEART!
IT CAUSES PEOPLE TO FORGET THE STRAINS OF THEIR DAY FOR A WHILE.
WE TRULY WISH TO EMPLOY YUKO-KUN HERE!!
BESIDES, ARE *YOU* REWARDING HER HARD WORK IN ANY WAY?!
RE-WARDING HER...
YOU SAID IT, BOSS!
THE EFFECT IS BARELY STRONGER THAN THAT OF, SAY, GARLIC OR RAMEN.
AND EVEN IF LICO-KUN'S COOKING...
COULD MAKE YUKO-KUN FORGET SOMETHING...
MY FOOD REALLY *IS* GOOD FOR THE HEART, Y'HEAR?
SURE, IF YOU EAT TEN TIMES THE NORMAL AMOUNT, YOU MIGHT GET A LITTLE HIGH OR FORGET STUFF...
BUT THAT'LL CLEAR RIGHT UP AFTER A DAY OR SO!
THAT JUST MEANS YOUR REQUEST WAS STRESSING HER OUT!
......!!
I TAKE IT FROM YOUR SILENCE THAT I'VE MADE A POINT, MAGICAL GIRL-KUN!!
FWIP
TEN TIMES ...?
YOU'LL FORGET THINGS IF YOU EAT THAT MUCH?
YUP, IF YOU'RE REAL EASY TO INFLUENCE.
YOU THERE, FAMILIAR-KUN! DON'T YOU AGREE?!
WHIRL
DON'T LOOK AT ME!! I'M OUT OF EXTRA LIVES!!
BESIDES, I AM NOT A FAMILIAR!!
LICO-KUN, THIS IS THE FIRST I'M HEARING ABOUT THIS.
WELL, SURE. IT'S THE FIRST TIME I'VE TOLD ANYONE.
LICO-KUUUN?!

A DEMON'S BIG SLIDING APOLOGY SCENE

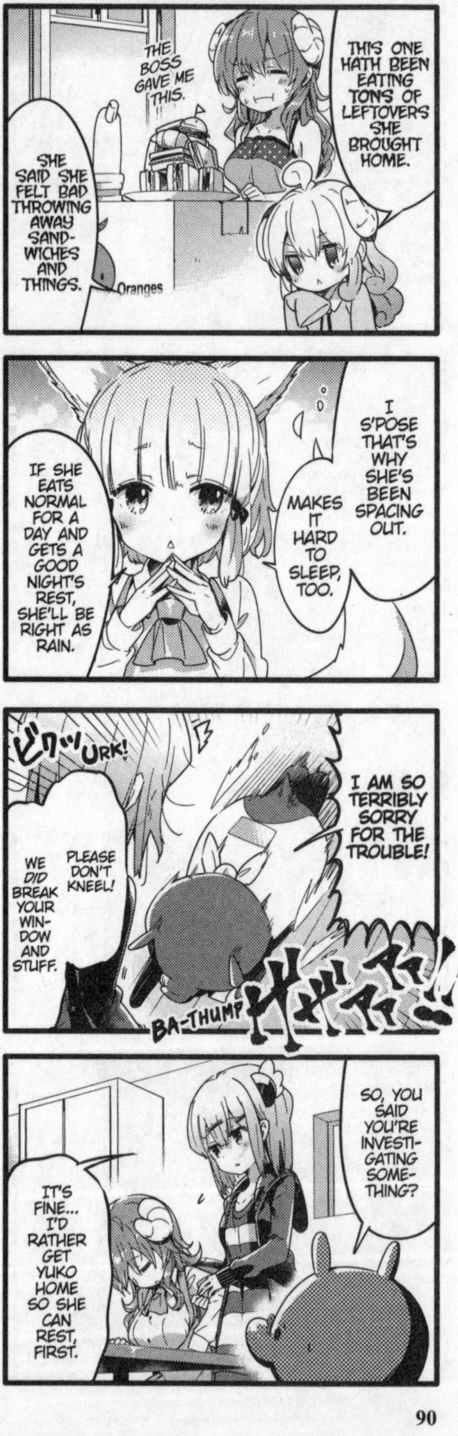
THIS ONE HATH BEEN EATING TONS OF LEFTOVERS SHE BROUGHT HOME.
THE BOSS GAVE ME THIS.
SHE SAID SHE FELT BAD THROWING AWAY SANDWICHES AND THINGS.
Oranges
I S'POSE THAT'S WHY SHE'S BEEN SPACING OUT.
MAKES IT HARD TO SLEEP, TOO.
IF SHE EATS NORMAL FOR A DAY AND GETS A GOOD NIGHT'S REST, SHE'LL BE RIGHT AS RAIN.
ビクッ URK!
I AM SO TERRIBLY SORRY FOR THE TROUBLE!
PLEASE DON'T KNEEL!
WE *DID* BREAK YOUR WINDOW AND STUFF.
BA-THUMP
SO, YOU SAID YOU'RE INVESTIGATING SOMETHING?
IT'S FINE... I'D RATHER GET YUKO HOME SO SHE CAN REST, FIRST.

BECOME A LESS AWKWARD MAGICAL GIRL

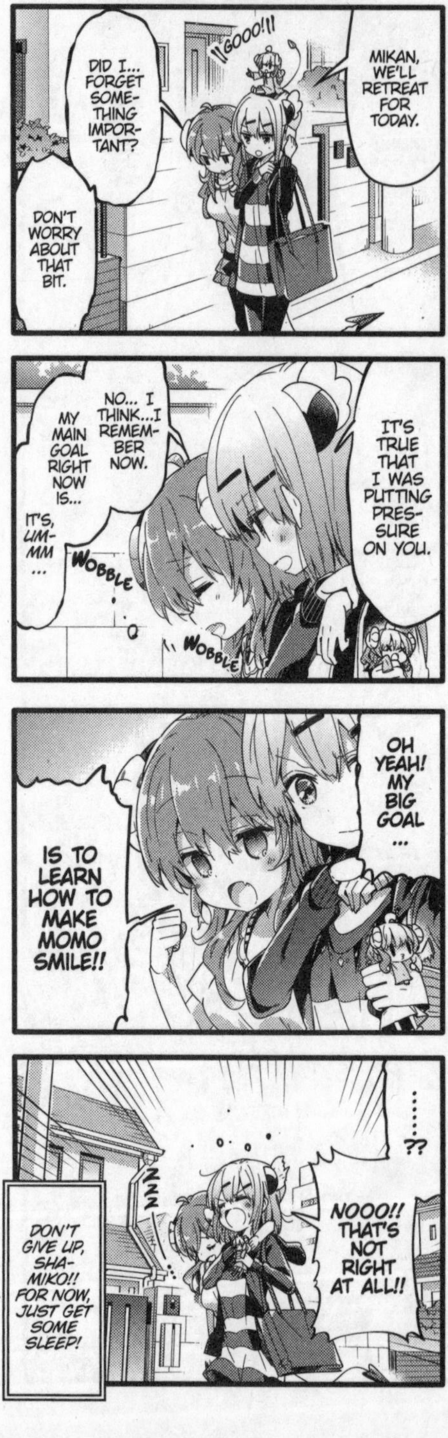
MIKAN, WE'LL RETREAT FOR TODAY.
GOOO!!
DID I... FORGET SOMETHING IMPORTANT?
DON'T WORRY ABOUT THAT BIT.
IT'S TRUE THAT I WAS PUTTING PRESSURE ON YOU.
NO... I THINK...I REMEMBER NOW.
MY MAIN GOAL RIGHT NOW IS...
IT'S, UMMM ...
WOBBLE
WOBBLE
OH YEAH! MY BIG GOAL ...
IS TO LEARN HOW TO MAKE MOMO SMILE!!
......??
NOOO!! THAT'S NOT RIGHT AT ALL!!
ZZZ
DON'T GIVE UP, SHAMIKO!! FOR NOW, JUST GET SOME SLEEP!

The Demon Girl Next Door

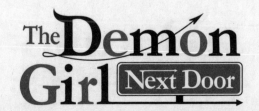

The Demon Girl Next Door

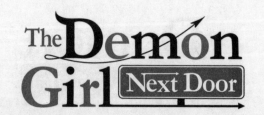

SHAMIKO IS EX-HAUSTED AFTER THE EVENTS AT THE CAFÉ.

YOU DON'T HAVE TO DO THIS. I'M NOT SICK.

YEAH, BUT...

JUST TELL ME! ANYTHING AT ALL!

OKAY, THEN...

AN ICE CREAM MONAKA?*

I WANT HOST BODY COUPONS!

"ARE YOU REWARD-ING HER FOR HER HARD WORK IN ANY WAY?!"

SHAMIKO, IS THERE ANYTHING YOU WANT?

HUH? WHAT'S THIS ALL ABOUT?

NO, THAT'LL BE GONE ONCE YOU EAT IT.

BUT YOU SAID, "ANY-THING AT ALL"!!

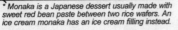

* Monaka is a Japanese dessert usually made with sweet red bean paste between two rice wafers. An ice cream monaka has an ice cream filling instead.

A DEMON'S BIG FLYING SCENE

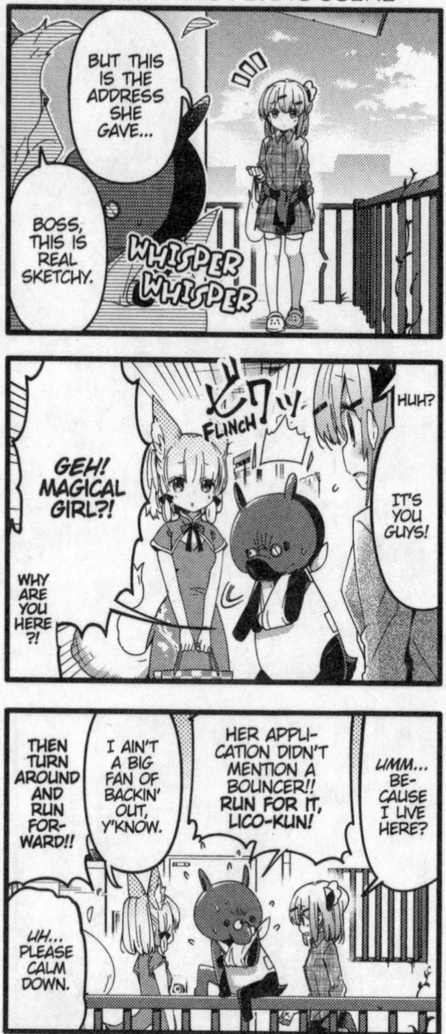
BUT THIS IS THE ADDRESS SHE GAVE...
BOSS, THIS IS REAL SKETCHY.
WHISPER WHISPER
HUH?
IT'S YOU GUYS!
FLINCH
GEH! MAGICAL GIRL?!
WHY ARE YOU HERE?!
UMM... BE-CAUSE I LIVE HERE?
HER APPLI-CATION DIDN'T MENTION A BOUNCER!! RUN FOR IT, LICO-KUN!
I AIN'T A BIG FAN OF BACKIN' OUT, Y'KNOW.
THEN TURN AROUND AND RUN FOR-WARD!!
UH... PLEASE CALM DOWN.
I'M OUTTA HEEE-ERE!!
OH DEAR...
HEEEY?!

SHE LIKES EATING OTHER PEOPLE'S FOOD, TOO

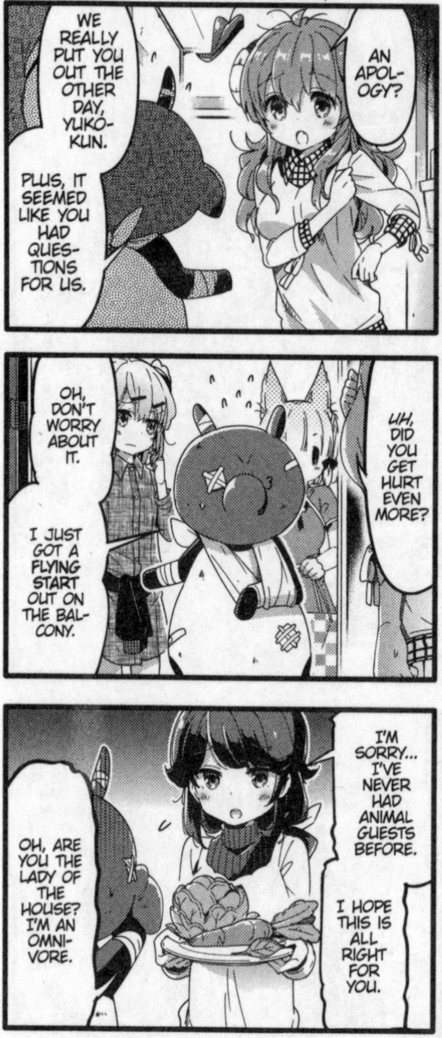
AN APOL-OGY?
WE REALLY PUT YOU OUT THE OTHER DAY, YUKO-KUN.
PLUS, IT SEEMED LIKE YOU HAD QUES-TIONS FOR US.
UH, DID YOU GET HURT EVEN MORE?
OH, DON'T WORRY ABOUT IT.
I JUST GOT A FLYING START OUT ON THE BAL-CONY.
I'M SORRY... I'VE NEVER HAD ANIMAL GUESTS BEFORE.
I HOPE THIS IS ALL RIGHT FOR YOU.
OH, ARE YOU THE LADY OF THE HOUSE? I'M AN OMNI-VORE.
I'VE GOT A HAN-KERIN' FOR INARI SUSHI.*
WITH NO VINEGAR, IF YOU PLEASE.
LICO-KUN, STOP THAT AT ONCE!

Inari sushi is rice wrapped in deep-fried tofu. It's named after Inari, a Shinto goddess (often represented as a fox) who has a fondness for tofu.

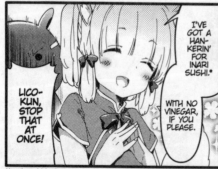

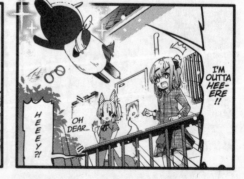

RYO-DONO'S IMPRESSIVE TECH SKILLS

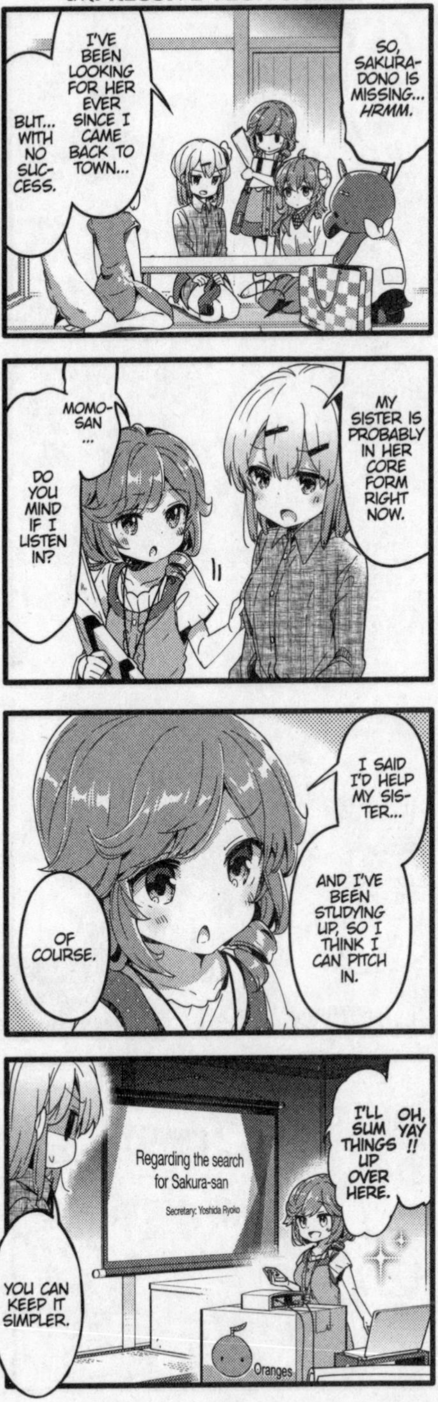
SO, SAKURA-DONO IS MISSING... *HRMM.*
I'VE BEEN LOOKING FOR HER EVER SINCE I CAME BACK TO TOWN...
BUT... WITH NO SUCCESS.
MY SISTER IS PROBABLY IN HER CORE FORM RIGHT NOW.
MOMO-SAN ...
DO YOU MIND IF I LISTEN IN?
I SAID I'D HELP MY SISTER...
AND I'VE BEEN STUDYING UP, SO I THINK I CAN PITCH IN.
OF COURSE.
OH, YAY!!
I'LL SUM THINGS UP OVER HERE.
Regarding the search for Sakura-san
Secretary: Yoshida Ryoko
Oranges
YOU CAN KEEP IT SIMPLER.

THE BOSS'S INFORMATION, REVEALED!

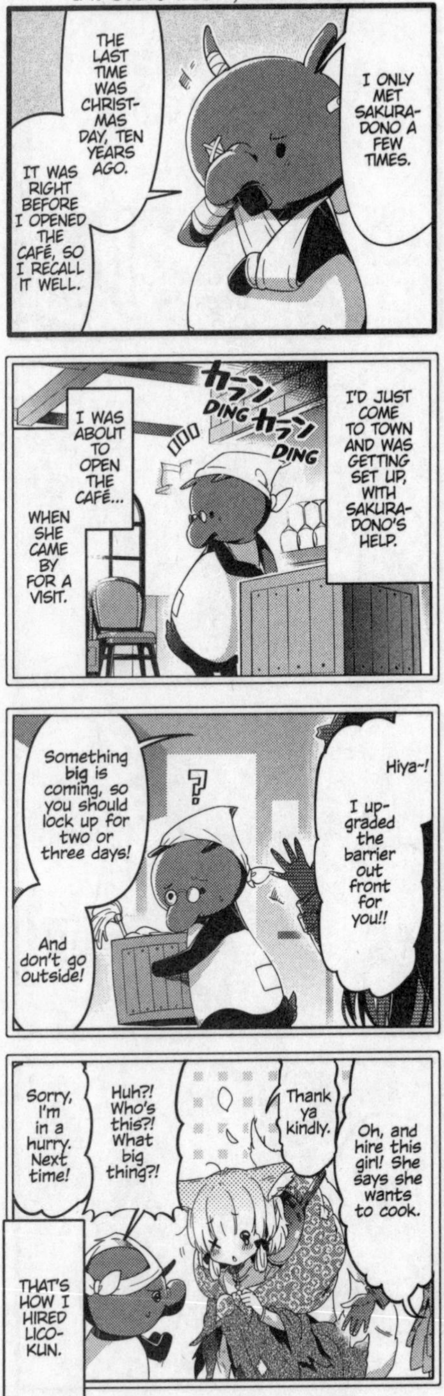
I ONLY MET SAKURA-DONO A FEW TIMES.
THE LAST TIME WAS CHRISTMAS DAY, TEN YEARS AGO.
IT WAS RIGHT BEFORE I OPENED THE CAFÉ, SO I RECALL IT WELL.
I'D JUST COME TO TOWN AND WAS GETTING SET UP, WITH SAKURA-DONO'S HELP.
カラン DING
カラン DING
I WAS ABOUT TO OPEN THE CAFÉ...
WHEN SHE CAME BY FOR A VISIT.
Hiya~!
I upgraded the barrier out front for you!!
Something big is coming, so you should lock up for two or three days!
And don't go outside!
Oh, and hire this girl! She says she wants to cook.
Thank ya kindly.
Huh?! Who's this?! What big thing?!
Sorry, I'm in a hurry. Next time!
THAT'S HOW I HIRED LICO-KUN.

THE SECRET OF THE CORE, REVEALED!

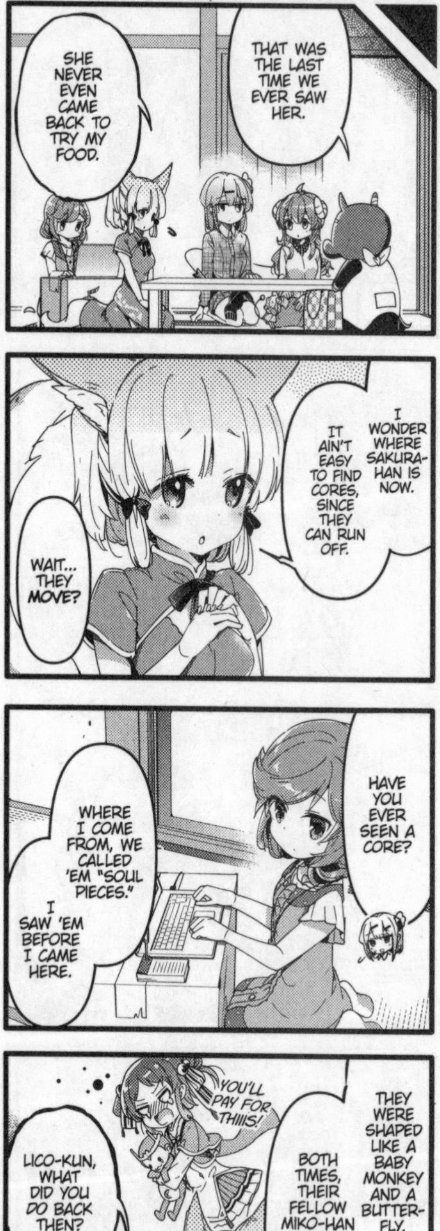
THAT WAS THE LAST TIME WE EVER SAW HER.
SHE NEVER EVEN CAME BACK TO TRY MY FOOD.
I WONDER WHERE SAKURA-HAN IS NOW.
IT AIN'T EASY TO FIND CORES, SINCE THEY CAN RUN OFF.
WAIT... THEY MOVE?
HAVE YOU EVER SEEN A CORE?
WHERE I COME FROM, WE CALLED 'EM "SOUL PIECES."
I SAW 'EM BEFORE I CAME HERE.
THEY WERE SHAPED LIKE A BABY MONKEY AND A BUTTERFLY.
BOTH TIMES, THEIR FELLOW MIKO-HAN WERE RUNNING AWAY WITH THEM.
YOU'LL PAY FOR THIIIS!
LICO-KUN, WHAT DID YOU DO BACK THEN?

DON'T PLAY RPGS IN OTHER PEOPLE'S HOMES

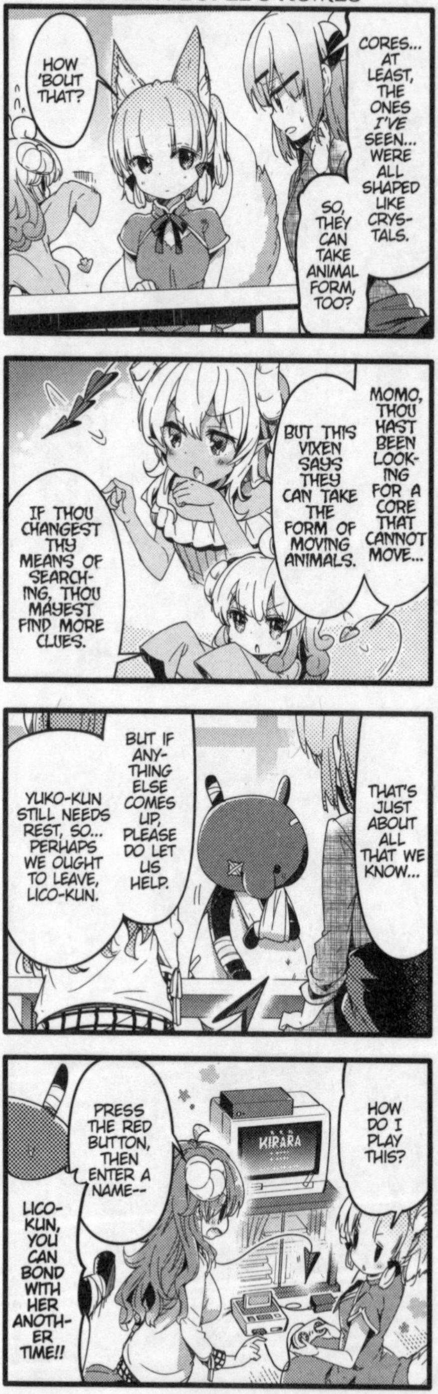
CORES... AT LEAST, THE ONES I'VE SEEN... WERE ALL SHAPED LIKE CRYSTALS.
SO, THEY CAN TAKE ANIMAL FORM, TOO?
HOW 'BOUT THAT?
MOMO, THOU HAST BEEN LOOKING FOR A CORE THAT CANNOT MOVE...
BUT THIS VIXEN SAYS THEY CAN TAKE THE FORM OF MOVING ANIMALS.
IF THOU CHANGEST THY MEANS OF SEARCHING, THOU MAYEST FIND MORE CLUES.
THAT'S JUST ABOUT ALL THAT WE KNOW...
BUT IF ANYTHING ELSE COMES UP, PLEASE DO LET US HELP.
YUKO-KUN STILL NEEDS REST, SO... PERHAPS WE OUGHT TO LEAVE, LICO-KUN.
HOW DO I PLAY THIS?
KIRARA
PRESS THE RED BUTTON, THEN ENTER A NAME--
LICO-KUN, YOU CAN BOND WITH HER ANOTHER TIME!!

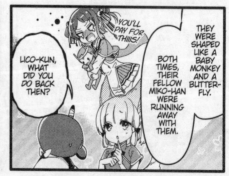

MESSED-UP RELATIONSHIP

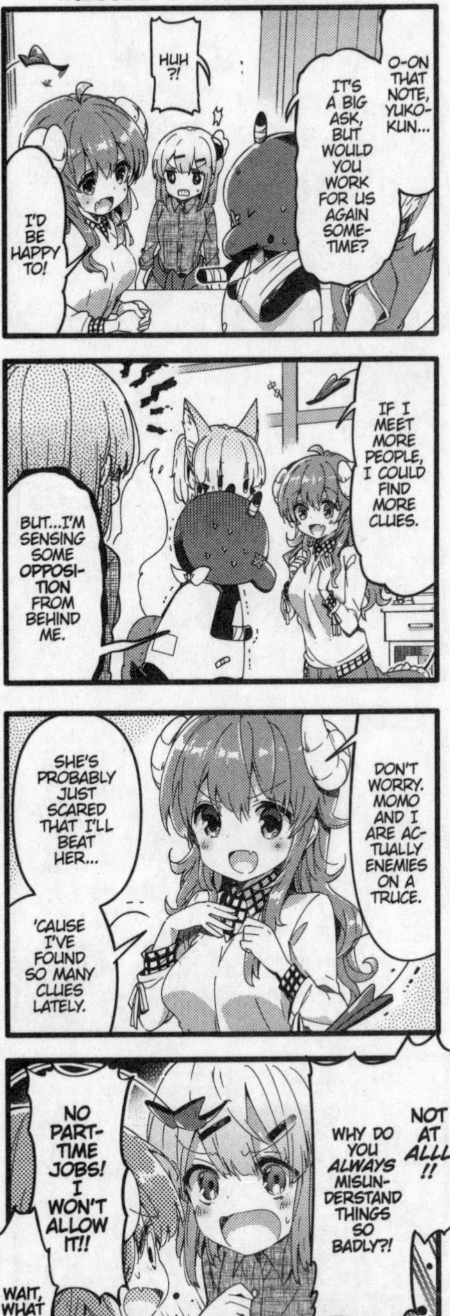
O-ON THAT NOTE, YUKO-KUN...
IT'S A BIG ASK, BUT WOULD YOU WORK FOR US AGAIN SOMETIME?
HUH?!
I'D BE HAPPY TO!
IF I MEET MORE PEOPLE, I COULD FIND MORE CLUES.
BUT...I'M SENSING SOME OPPOSITION FROM BEHIND ME.
DON'T WORRY. MOMO AND I ARE ACTUALLY ENEMIES ON A TRUCE.
SHE'S PROBABLY JUST SCARED THAT I'LL BEAT HER...
'CAUSE I'VE FOUND SO MANY CLUES LATELY.
NOT AT ALLL!!
WHY DO YOU ALWAYS MISUNDERSTAND THINGS SO BADLY?!
NO PART-TIME JOBS! I WON'T ALLOW IT!!
WAIT, WHAT?!

SUPPORT THE LOCAL MASCOT

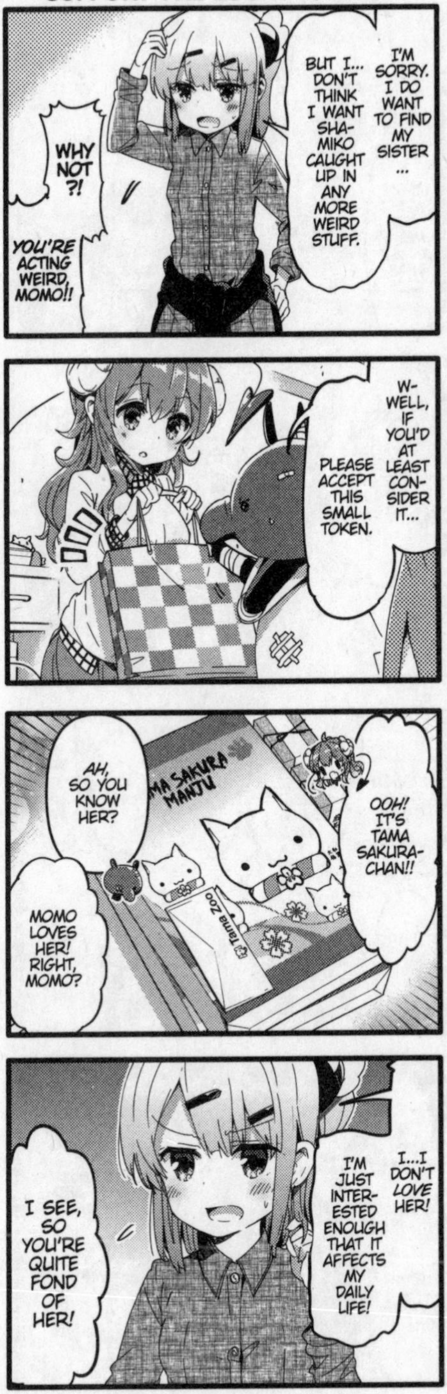
I'M SORRY. I DO WANT TO FIND MY SISTER...
BUT I... DON'T THINK I WANT SHAMIKO CAUGHT UP IN ANY MORE WEIRD STUFF.
WHY NOT?!
YOU'RE ACTING WEIRD, MOMO!!
W-WELL, IF YOU'D AT LEAST CONSIDER IT...
PLEASE ACCEPT THIS SMALL TOKEN.
OOH! IT'S TAMA SAKURA-CHAN!!
MA SAKURA MANJU
Tama Zoo
AH, SO YOU KNOW HER?
MOMO LOVES HER! RIGHT, MOMO?
I...I DON'T LOVE HER!
I'M JUST INTERESTED ENOUGH THAT IT AFFECTS MY DAILY LIFE!
I SEE, SO YOU'RE QUITE FOND OF HER!

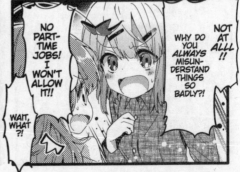

EVERYONE HAS THEIR PRICE

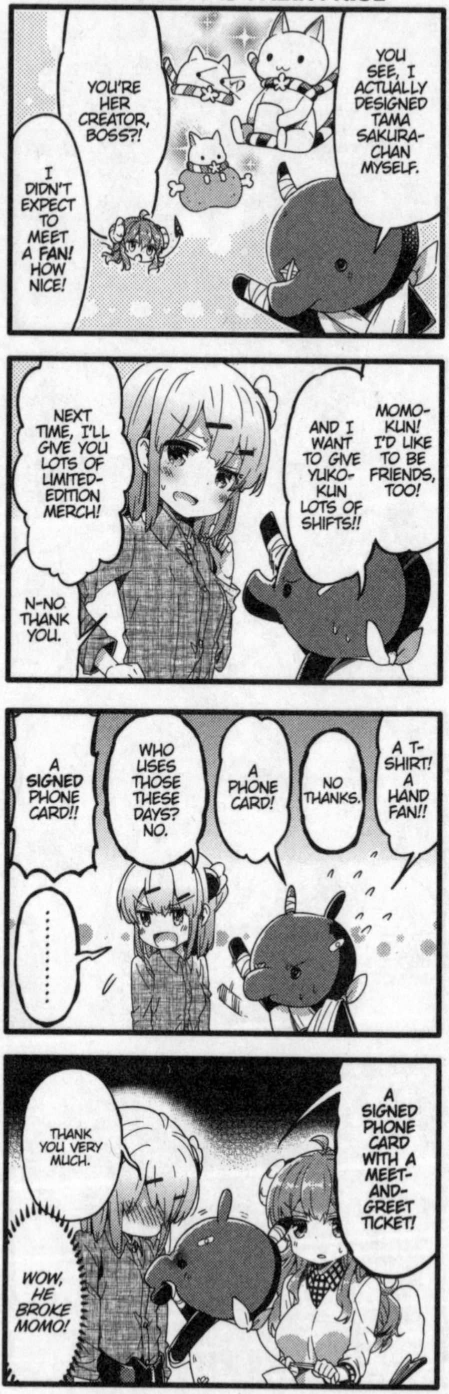
YOU SEE, I ACTUALLY DESIGNED TAMA SAKURA-CHAN MYSELF.
YOU'RE HER CREATOR, BOSS?!
I DIDN'T EXPECT TO MEET A FAN! HOW NICE!
MOMO-KUN! I'D LIKE TO BE FRIENDS, TOO!
AND I WANT TO GIVE YUKO-KUN LOTS OF SHIFTS!!
NEXT TIME, I'LL GIVE YOU LOTS OF LIMITED-EDITION MERCH!
N-NO THANK YOU.
A T-SHIRT! A HAND FAN!!
NO THANKS.
A PHONE CARD!
WHO USES THOSE THESE DAYS? NO.
A SIGNED PHONE CARD!!
......
A SIGNED PHONE CARD WITH A MEET-AND-GREET TICKET!
THANK YOU VERY MUCH.
WOW, HE BROKE MOMO!

THE DEPTH OF SAKURA'S MYSTERIES, REVEALED!

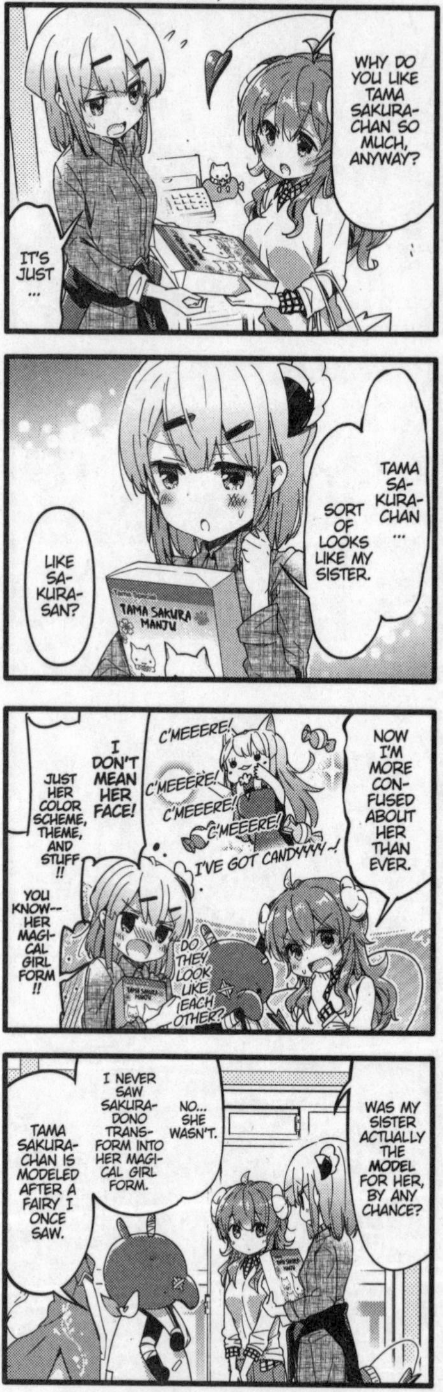
WHY DO YOU LIKE TAMA SAKURA-CHAN SO MUCH, ANYWAY?
IT'S JUST ...
TAMA SAKURA-CHAN ...
SORT OF LOOKS LIKE MY SISTER.
LIKE SAKURA-SAN?
TAMA SAKURA MANJU
NOW I'M MORE CONFUSED ABOUT HER THAN EVER.
C'MEEERE!
C'MEEERE!
C'MEEERE!
C'MEEERE!
I'VE GOT CANDYYYY~!
I DON'T MEAN HER FACE!
JUST HER COLOR SCHEME, THEME, AND STUFF!!
YOU KNOW--HER MAGICAL GIRL FORM!!
DO THEY LOOK LIKE EACH OTHER?
WAS MY SISTER ACTUALLY THE MODEL FOR HER, BY ANY CHANCE?
NO... SHE WASN'T.
I NEVER SAW SAKURA-DONO TRANSFORM INTO HER MAGICAL GIRL FORM.
TAMA SAKURA-CHAN IS MODELED AFTER A FAIRY I ONCE SAW.

A BAKU'S SCREAM IS HIGHER THAN YOU'D THINK

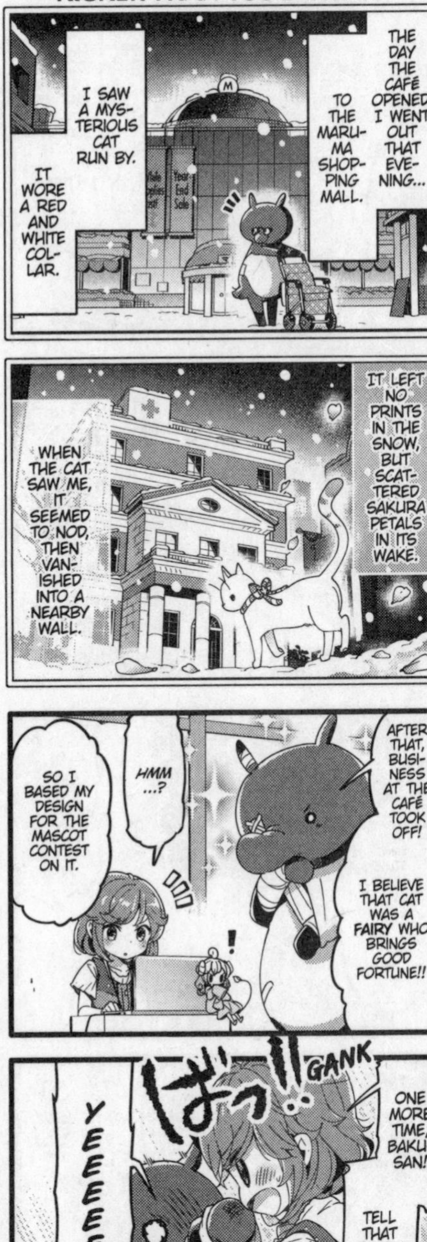
THE DAY THE CAFÉ OPENED, I WENT OUT THAT EVENING...
TO THE MARUMA SHOPPING MALL.
I SAW A MYSTERIOUS CAT RUN BY.
IT WORE A RED AND WHITE COLLAR.
IT LEFT NO PRINTS IN THE SNOW, BUT SCATTERED SAKURA PETALS IN ITS WAKE.
WHEN THE CAT SAW ME, IT SEEMED TO NOD, THEN VANISHED INTO A NEARBY WALL.
AFTER THAT, BUSINESS AT THE CAFÉ TOOK OFF!
I BELIEVE THAT CAT WAS A FAIRY WHO BRINGS GOOD FORTUNE!!
HMM ...?
SO I BASED MY DESIGN FOR THE MASCOT CONTEST ON IT.
ONE MORE TIME, BAKU-SAN!
TELL THAT STORY AGAIN !!
ばっ!! GANK
YEEEEEEK!!
RYOU ?!

THAT DOESN'T MEAN TO SQUEEZE HIS NOSE

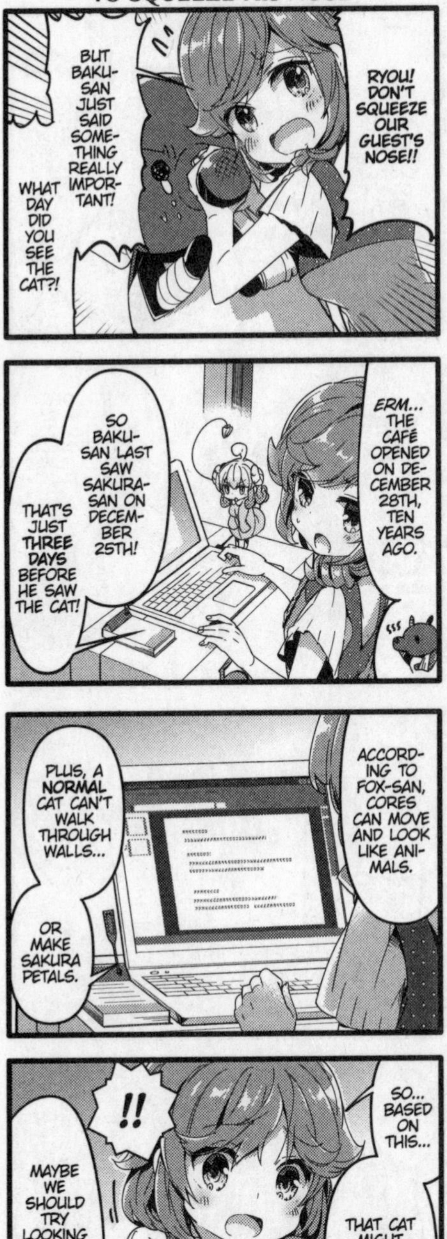
RYOU! DON'T SQUEEZE OUR GUEST'S NOSE!!
BUT BAKU-SAN JUST SAID SOMETHING REALLY IMPORTANT!
WHAT DAY DID YOU SEE THE CAT?!
ERM... THE CAFÉ OPENED ON DECEMBER 28TH, TEN YEARS AGO.
SO BAKU-SAN LAST SAW SAKURA-SAN ON DECEMBER 25TH!
THAT'S JUST THREE DAYS BEFORE HE SAW THE CAT!
ACCORDING TO FOX-SAN, CORES CAN MOVE AND LOOK LIKE ANIMALS.
PLUS, A NORMAL CAT CAN'T WALK THROUGH WALLS...
OR MAKE SAKURA PETALS.
SO... BASED ON THIS...
!!
THAT CAT MIGHT HAVE BEEN SAKURA-SAN'S CORE!
MAYBE WE SHOULD TRY LOOKING FOR A CAT WITH A RED AND WHITE COLLAR?

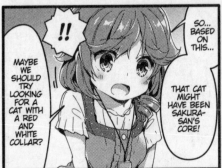

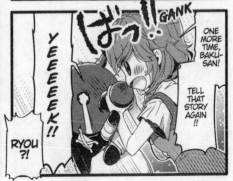

RYOU WANTS TO BE A STRATEGIST LIKE HER SISTER

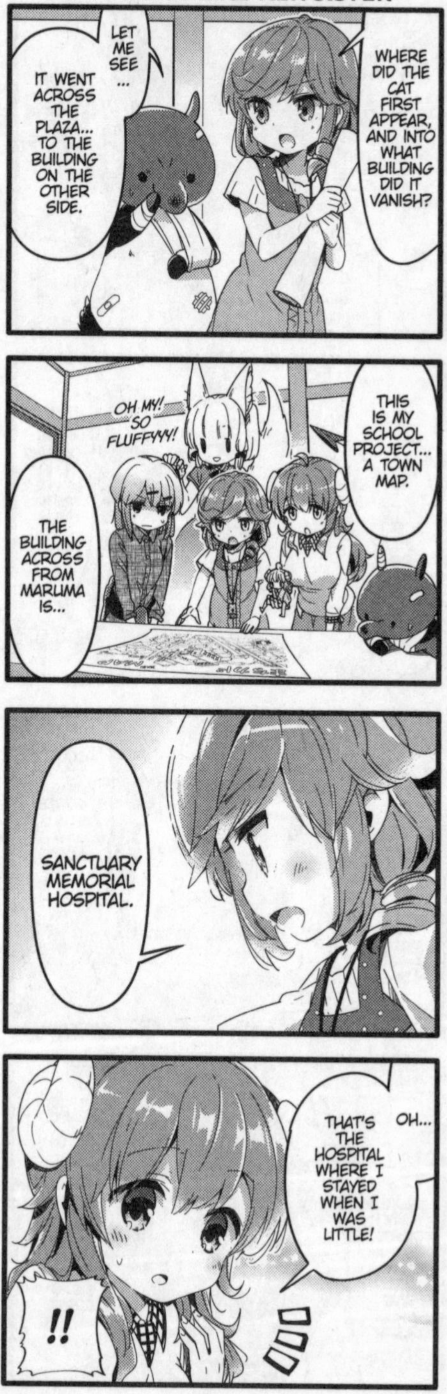
WHERE DID THE CAT FIRST APPEAR, AND INTO WHAT BUILDING DID IT VANISH?
LET ME SEE ...
IT WENT ACROSS THE PLAZA... TO THE BUILDING ON THE OTHER SIDE.
THIS IS MY SCHOOL PROJECT... A TOWN MAP.
OH MY! SO FLUFFYYY!
THE BUILDING ACROSS FROM MARUMA IS...
SANCTUARY MEMORIAL HOSPITAL.
OH...
THAT'S THE HOSPITAL WHERE I STAYED WHEN I WAS LITTLE!
!!

FOXES APPEAR WHEN YOU LEAST EXPECT THEM

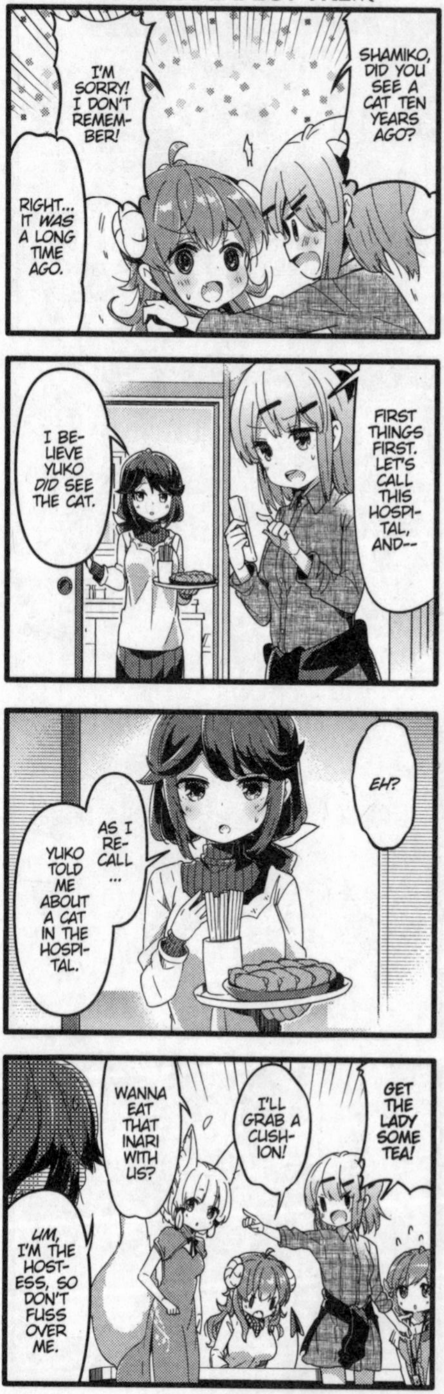
SHAMIKO, DID YOU SEE A CAT TEN YEARS AGO?
I'M SORRY! I DON'T REMEMBER!
RIGHT... IT *WAS* A LONG TIME AGO.
FIRST THINGS FIRST. LET'S CALL THIS HOSPITAL, AND--
I BELIEVE YUKO *DID* SEE THE CAT.
EH?
AS I RECALL...
YUKO TOLD ME ABOUT A CAT IN THE HOSPITAL.
GET THE LADY SOME TEA!
I'LL GRAB A CUSHION!
WANNA EAT THAT INARI WITH US?
UM, I'M THE HOSTESS, SO DON'T FUSS OVER ME.

THE CAT'S SECRET, REVEALED!

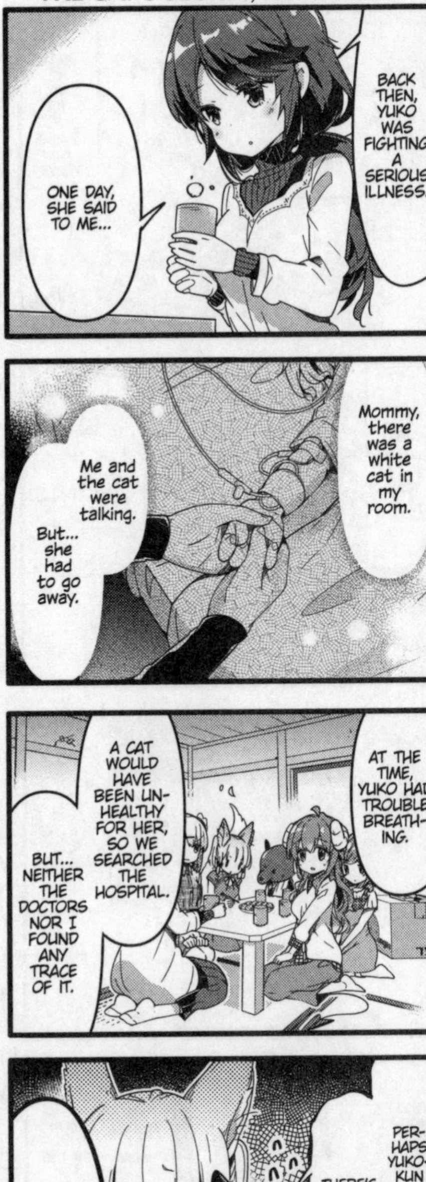
BACK THEN, YUKO WAS FIGHTING A SERIOUS ILLNESS.
ONE DAY, SHE SAID TO ME...
Mommy, there was a white cat in my room.
Me and the cat were talking.
But... she had to go away.
AT THE TIME, YUKO HAD TROUBLE BREATHING.
A CAT WOULD HAVE BEEN UNHEALTHY FOR HER, SO WE SEARCHED THE HOSPITAL.
BUT... NEITHER THE DOCTORS NOR I FOUND ANY TRACE OF IT.
PERHAPS YUKO-KUN WAS JUST DREAMING?
THERE'S NO SUCH THING AS A TALKING ANIMAL!
C'MON, BOSS... LOOK IN A MIRROR.

LICO-KUN CLEANED THE PLATE

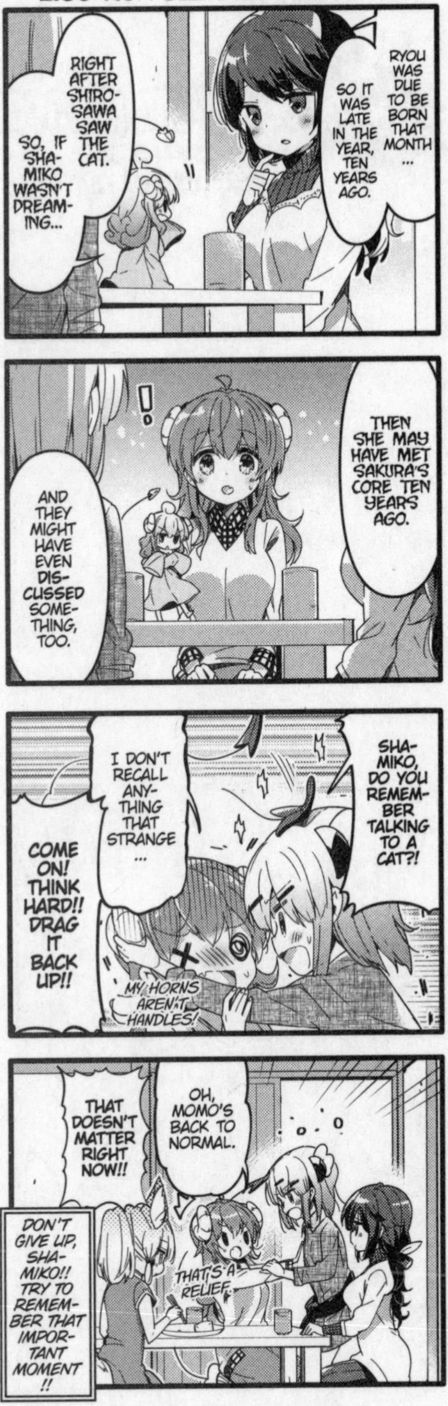
RYOU WAS DUE TO BE BORN THAT MONTH ...
SO IT WAS LATE IN THE YEAR, TEN YEARS AGO.
RIGHT AFTER SHIROSAWA SAW THE CAT.
SO, IF SHAMIKO WASN'T DREAMING...
THEN SHE MAY HAVE MET SAKURA'S CORE TEN YEARS AGO.
AND THEY MIGHT HAVE EVEN DISCUSSED SOMETHING, TOO.
SHAMIKO, DO YOU REMEMBER TALKING TO A CAT?!
I DON'T RECALL ANYTHING THAT STRANGE ...
COME ON! THINK HARD!! DRAG IT BACK UP!!
MY HORNS AREN'T HANDLES!
OH, MOMO'S BACK TO NORMAL.
THAT DOESN'T MATTER RIGHT NOW!!
THAT'S A RELIEF.
DON'T GIVE UP, SHAMIKO!! TRY TO REMEMBER THAT IMPORTANT MOMENT!!

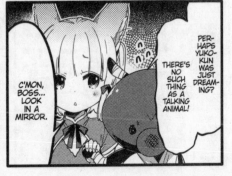

SECONDS!! DEMON GIRL NEXT DOOR

(CHAPTER 35)

~ A VERY USEFUL FEATURE ~

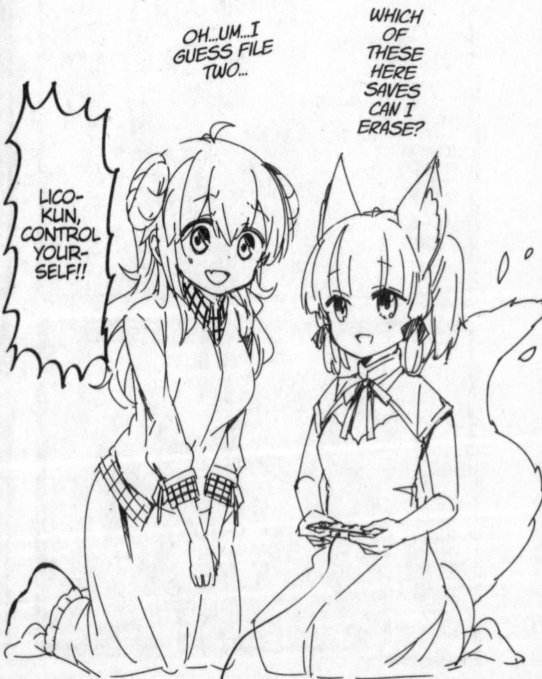
WHICH OF THESE HERE SAVES CAN I ERASE?
OH...UM...I GUESS FILE TWO...
LICO-KUN, CONTROL YOURSELF!!

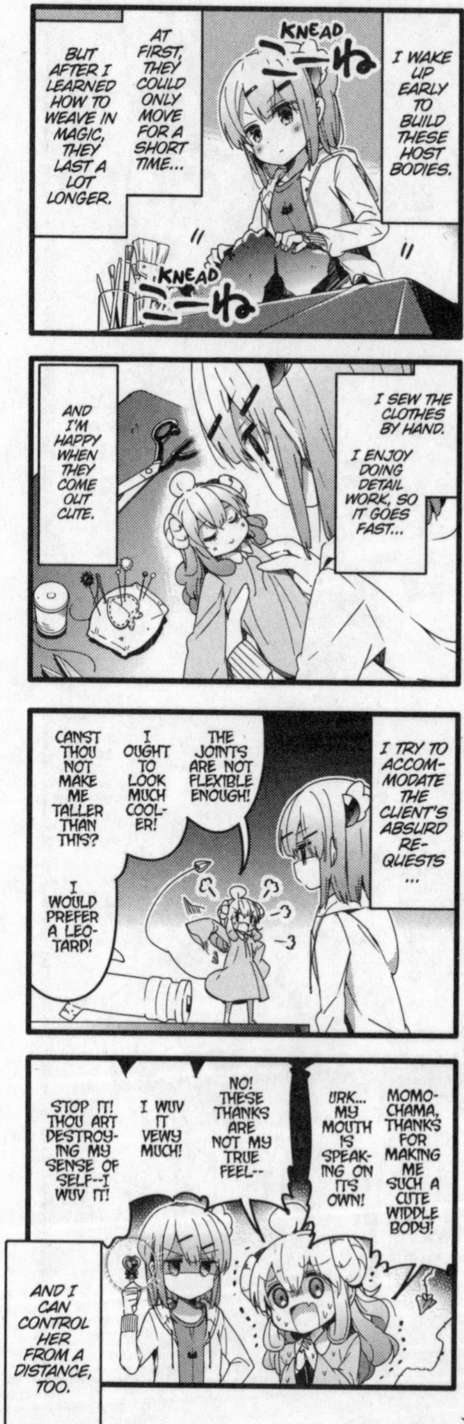
I WAKE UP EARLY TO BUILD THESE HOST BODIES.
KNEAD
AT FIRST, THEY COULD ONLY MOVE FOR A SHORT TIME...
BUT AFTER I LEARNED HOW TO WEAVE IN MAGIC, THEY LAST A LOT LONGER.
KNEAD
I SEW THE CLOTHES BY HAND.
I ENJOY DOING DETAIL WORK, SO IT GOES FAST...
AND I'M HAPPY WHEN THEY COME OUT CUTE.
I TRY TO ACCOMMODATE THE CLIENT'S ABSURD REQUESTS...
THE JOINTS ARE NOT FLEXIBLE ENOUGH!
I OUGHT TO LOOK MUCH COOLER!
CANST THOU NOT MAKE ME TALLER THAN THIS?
I WOULD PREFER A LEOTARD!
MOMOCHAMA, THANKS FOR MAKING ME SUCH A CUTE WIDDLE BODY!
URK... MY MOUTH IS SPEAKING ON ITS OWN!
NO! THESE THANKS ARE NOT MY TRUE FEEL--
I WUV IT VEWY MUCH!
STOP IT! THOU ART DESTROYING MY SENSE OF SELF--I WUV IT!
AND I CAN CONTROL HER FROM A DISTANCE, TOO.

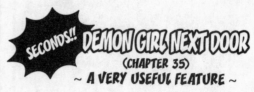

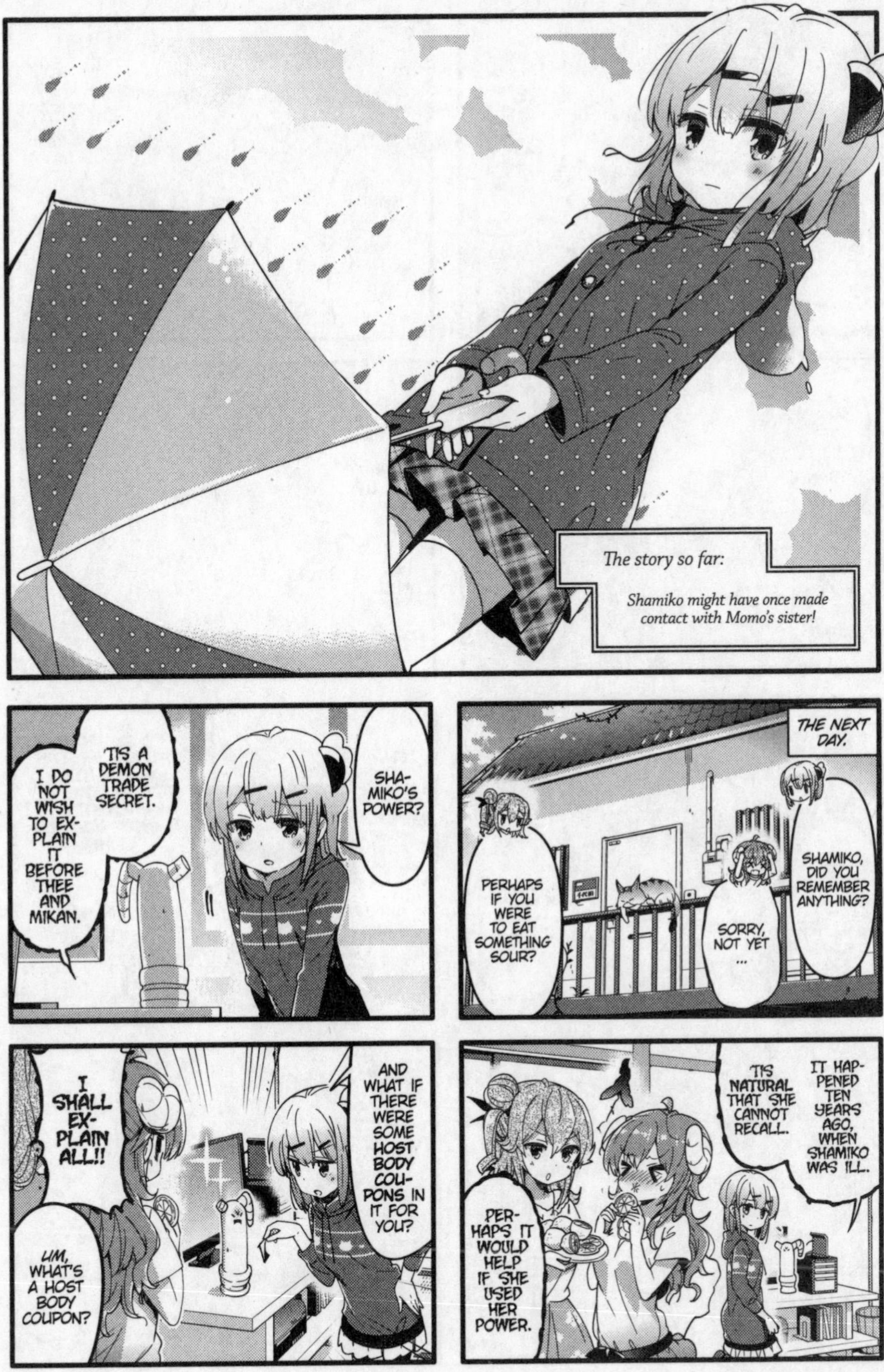
The story so far:
Shamiko might have once made contact with Momo's sister!
THE NEXT DAY.
SHAMIKO, DID YOU REMEMBER ANYTHING?
SORRY, NOT YET ...
PERHAPS IF YOU WERE TO EAT SOMETHING SOUR?
SHAMIKO'S POWER?
'TIS A DEMON TRADE SECRET.
I DO NOT WISH TO EXPLAIN IT BEFORE THEE AND MIKAN.
IT HAPPENED TEN YEARS AGO, WHEN SHAMIKO WAS ILL.
'TIS NATURAL THAT SHE CANNOT RECALL.
PERHAPS IT WOULD HELP IF SHE USED HER POWER.
AND WHAT IF THERE WERE SOME HOST BODY COUPONS IN IT FOR YOU?
I SHALL EXPLAIN ALL!!
UM, WHAT'S A HOST BODY COUPON?

SHAMIKO, SHAKEN OFF

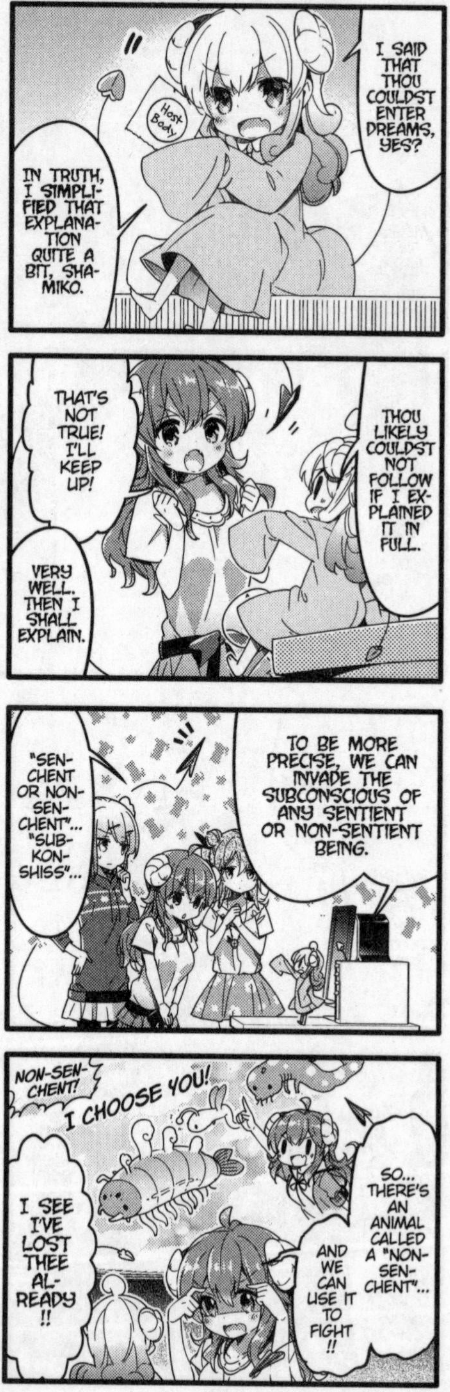
I SAID THAT THOU COULDST ENTER DREAMS, YES?
Host Body
IN TRUTH, I SIMPLIFIED THAT EXPLANATION QUITE A BIT, SHAMIKO.
THOU LIKELY COULDST NOT FOLLOW IF I EXPLAINED IT IN FULL.
THAT'S NOT TRUE! I'LL KEEP UP!
VERY WELL. THEN I SHALL EXPLAIN.
TO BE MORE PRECISE, WE CAN INVADE THE SUBCONSCIOUS OF ANY SENTIENT OR NON-SENTIENT BEING.
"SENCHENT OR NON-SENCHENT"... "SUBKONSHISS"...
SO... THERE'S AN ANIMAL CALLED A "NON-SENCHENT"...
AND WE CAN USE IT TO FIGHT!!
NON-SENCHENT!
I CHOOSE YOU!
I SEE I'VE LOST THEE ALREADY!!

A GIRL WHO CAN ASK QUESTIONS

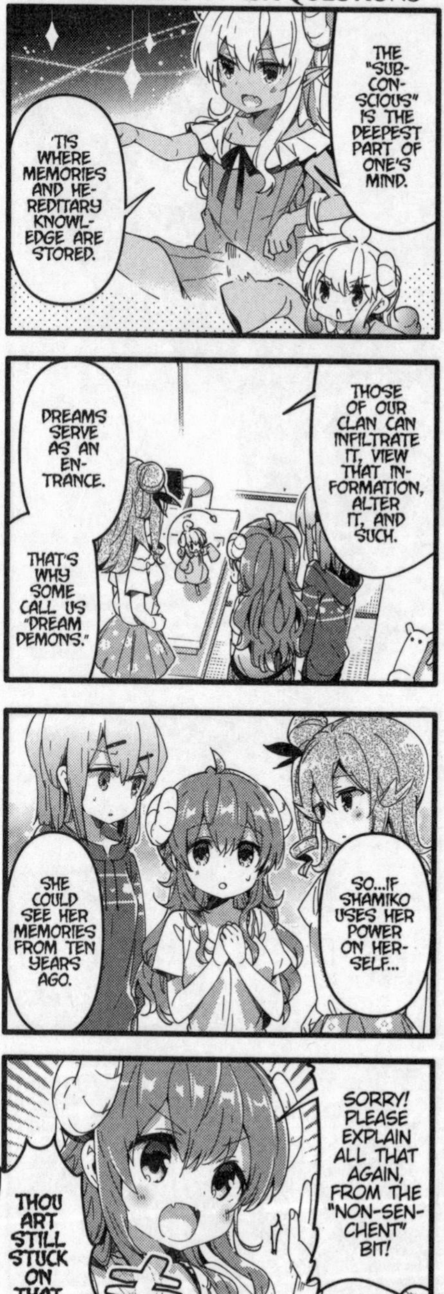
THE "SUBCONSCIOUS" IS THE DEEPEST PART OF ONE'S MIND.
'TIS WHERE MEMORIES AND HEREDITARY KNOWLEDGE ARE STORED.
THOSE OF OUR CLAN CAN INFILTRATE IT, VIEW THAT INFORMATION, ALTER IT, AND SUCH.
DREAMS SERVE AS AN ENTRANCE.
THAT'S WHY SOME CALL US "DREAM DEMONS."
SO...IF SHAMIKO USES HER POWER ON HERSELF...
SHE COULD SEE HER MEMORIES FROM TEN YEARS AGO.
SORRY! PLEASE EXPLAIN ALL THAT AGAIN, FROM THE "NON-SENCHENT" BIT!
THOU ART STILL STUCK ON THAT POINT?!
FROWN

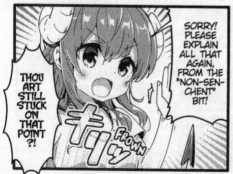

A DEMON WITH MANY SLEEP SCENES FOR A REASON

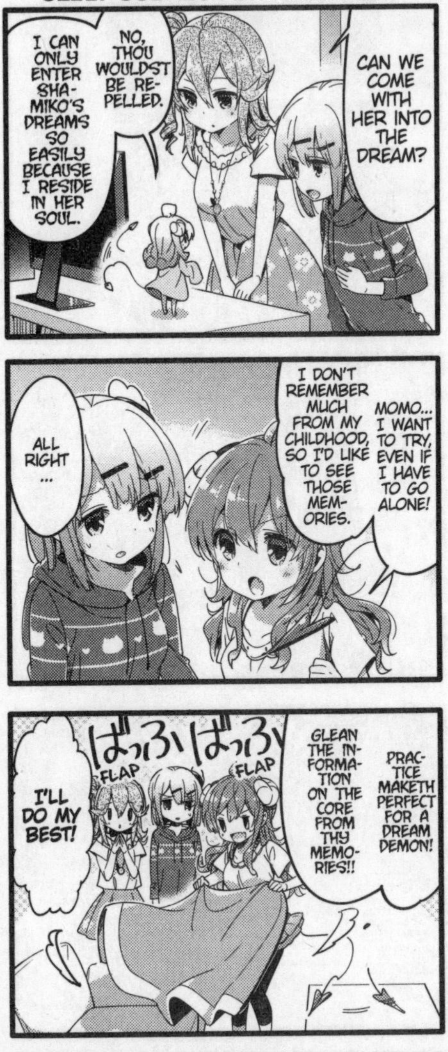
CAN WE COME WITH HER INTO THE DREAM?
NO, THOU WOULDST BE REPELLED.
I CAN ONLY ENTER SHAMIKO'S DREAMS SO EASILY BECAUSE I RESIDE IN HER SOUL.
MOMO... I WANT TO TRY, EVEN IF I HAVE TO GO ALONE!
I DON'T REMEMBER MUCH FROM MY CHILDHOOD, SO I'D LIKE TO SEE THOSE MEMORIES.
ALL RIGHT ...
PRACTICE MAKETH PERFECT FOR A DREAM DEMON!
GLEAN THE INFORMATION ON THE CORE FROM THY MEMORIES!!
FLAP
FLAP
I'LL DO MY BEST!
PREPARE TO BE AMAZED!!
GOOD NIGHT!!
SHAMIKO... YOU JUST LOOK LIKE YOU'RE ABOUT TO TAKE A NAP!
FWIP

OVERCOME IT WITH SPIRIT

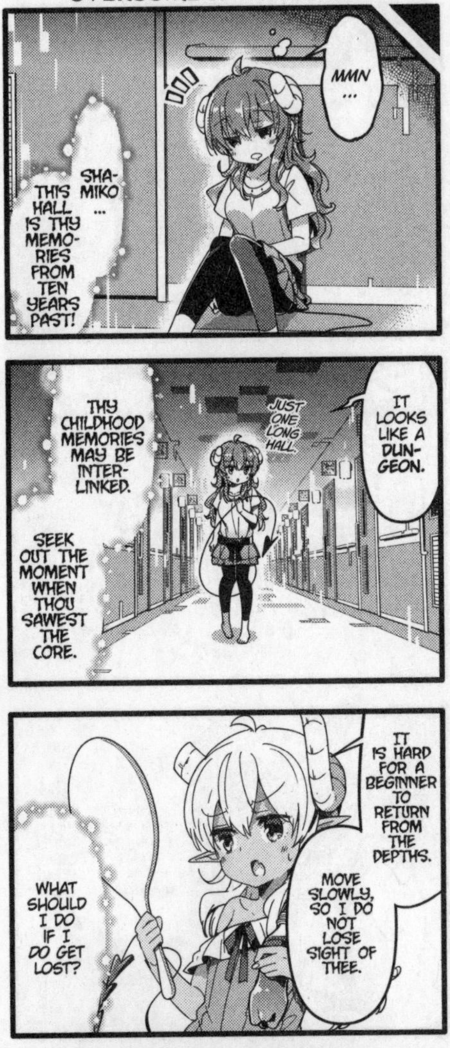
MMN ...
SHAMIKO ...
THIS HALL IS THY MEMORIES FROM TEN YEARS PAST!
IT LOOKS LIKE A DUNGEON.
JUST ONE LONG HALL.
THY CHILDHOOD MEMORIES MAY BE INTERLINKED.
SEEK OUT THE MOMENT WHEN THOU SAWEST THE CORE.
IT IS HARD FOR A BEGINNER TO RETURN FROM THE DEPTHS.
MOVE SLOWLY, SO I DO NOT LOSE SIGHT OF THEE.
WHAT SHOULD I DO IF I DO GET LOST?
DEMONS GROW STRONGER WITH EACH TEAR THEY SHED.
RETURN BY USING THY GUTS AND GUMPTION!
I SEE. SO I'LL JUST HAVE TO FIGURE IT OUT.
VWOOOOSH...

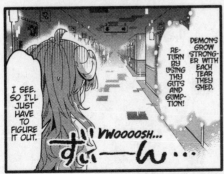

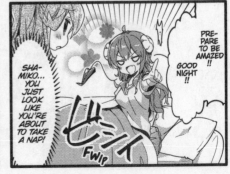

A STRONG-MINDED CLAN

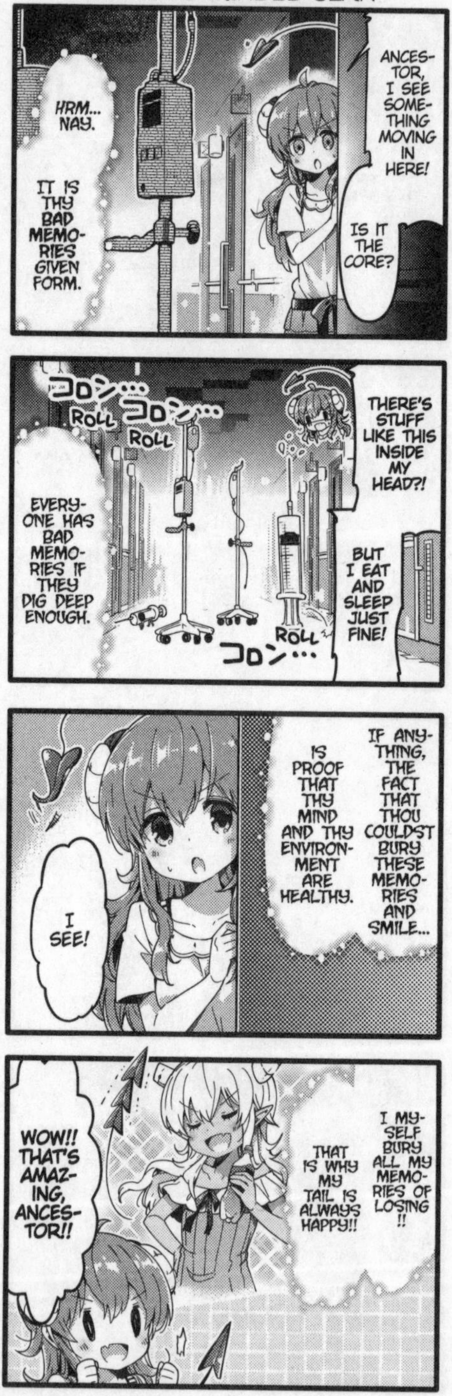
ANCESTOR, I SEE SOMETHING MOVING IN HERE!
IS IT THE CORE?
HRM... NAY.
IT IS THY BAD MEMORIES GIVEN FORM.
THERE'S STUFF LIKE THIS INSIDE MY HEAD?!
BUT I EAT AND SLEEP JUST FINE!
コロン… ROLL コロン… ROLL
ROLL コロン…
EVERYONE HAS BAD MEMORIES IF THEY DIG DEEP ENOUGH.
IF ANYTHING, THE FACT THAT THOU COULDST BURY THESE MEMORIES AND SMILE...
IS PROOF THAT THY MIND AND THY ENVIRONMENT ARE HEALTHY.
I SEE!
I MYSELF BURY ALL MY MEMORIES OF LOSING!!
THAT IS WHY MY TAIL IS ALWAYS HAPPY!!
WOW!! THAT'S AMAZING, ANCESTOR!!

PLAN OF ATTACK! ACTION DEMON!

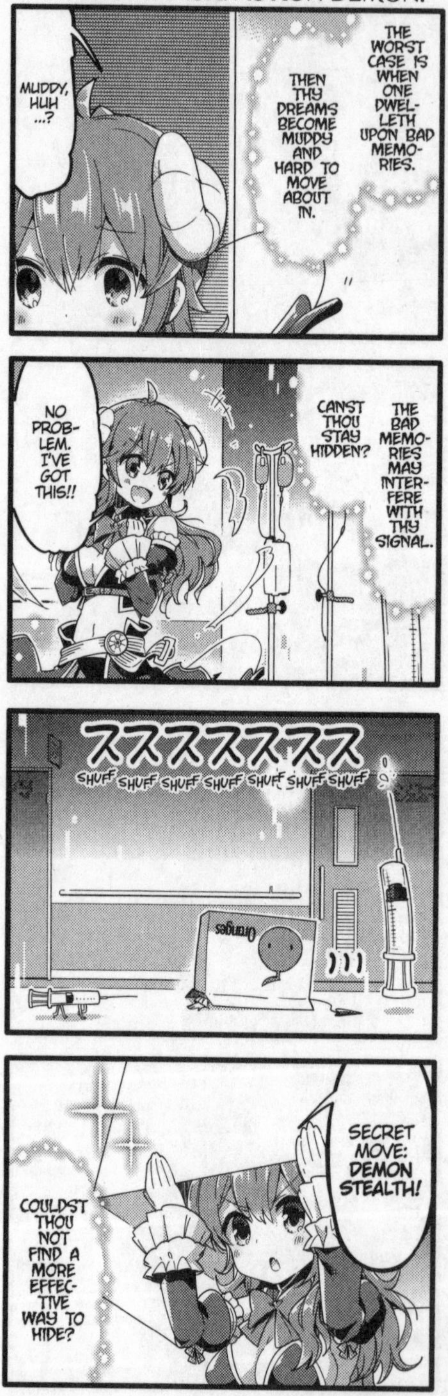
THE WORST CASE IS WHEN ONE DWELLETH UPON BAD MEMORIES.
THEN THY DREAMS BECOME MUDDY AND HARD TO MOVE ABOUT IN.
MUDDY, HUH ...?
THE BAD MEMORIES MAY INTERFERE WITH THY SIGNAL.
CANST THOU STAY HIDDEN?
NO PROBLEM. I'VE GOT THIS!!
ススススススス
SHUFF SHUFF SHUFF SHUFF SHUFF SHUFF SHUFF
SECRET MOVE: DEMON STEALTH!
COULDST THOU NOT FIND A MORE EFFECTIVE WAY TO HIDE?

I'M AN ANCESTOR, NOT AN IMPROVISER

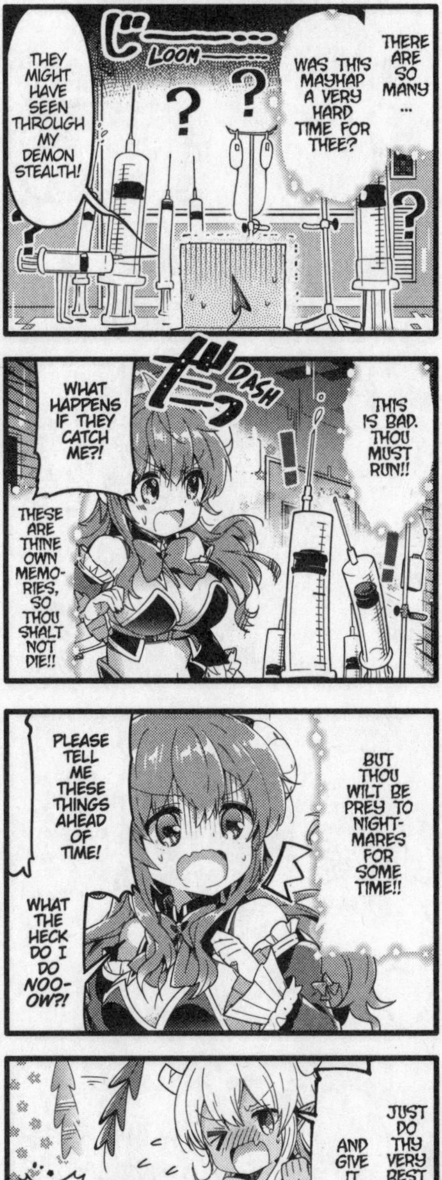
THERE ARE SO MANY ...
WAS THIS MAYHAP A VERY HARD TIME FOR THEE?
THEY MIGHT HAVE SEEN THROUGH MY DEMON STEALTH!
LOOM
THIS IS BAD. THOU MUST RUN!!
DASH
WHAT HAPPENS IF THEY CATCH ME?!
THESE ARE THINE OWN MEMORIES, SO THOU SHALT NOT DIE!!
BUT THOU WILT BE PREY TO NIGHTMARES FOR SOME TIME!!
PLEASE TELL ME THESE THINGS AHEAD OF TIME!
WHAT THE HECK DO I DO NOOO-OW?!
JUST DO THY VERY BEST!!
AND GIVE IT THY ALL!!
I GUESS I'LL FIGURE IT OUT!

IT'S A HAUNTED HOUSE!!

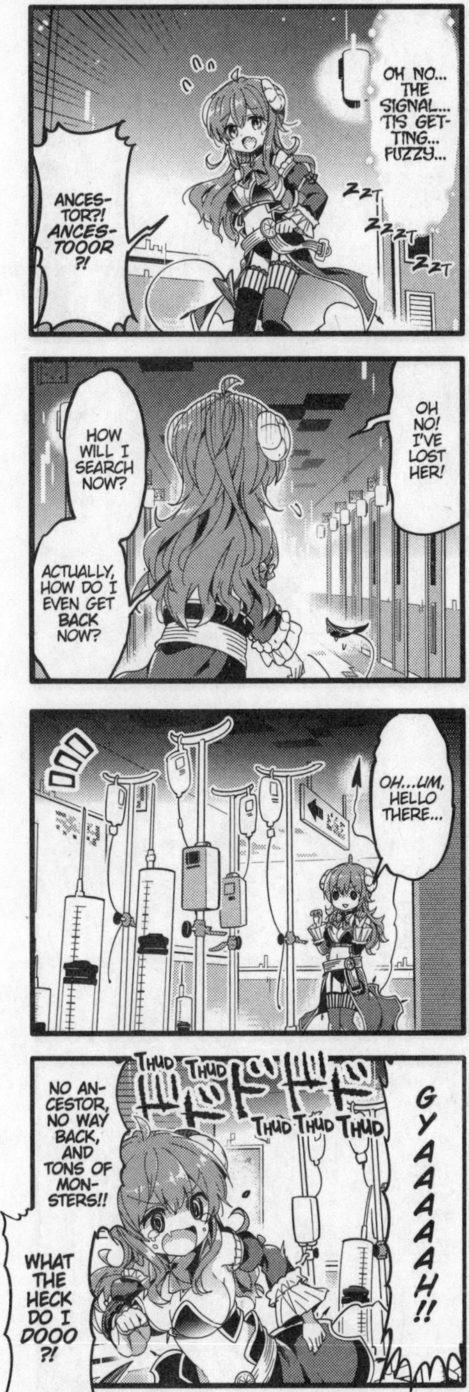
OH NO... THE SIGNAL... 'TIS GETTING... FUZZY...
ZZT ZZZT ZZT
ANCESTOR?! ANCESTOOOR?!
OH NO! I'VE LOST HER!
HOW WILL I SEARCH NOW?
ACTUALLY, HOW DO I EVEN GET BACK NOW?
OH...UM, HELLO THERE...
GYAAAAAAH!!
THUD THUD
THUD THUD THUD
NO ANCESTOR, NO WAY BACK, AND TONS OF MONSTERS!!
WHAT THE HECK DO I DOOO?!

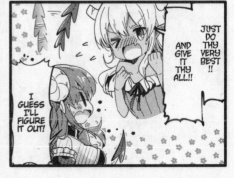

LEMON LAMENT

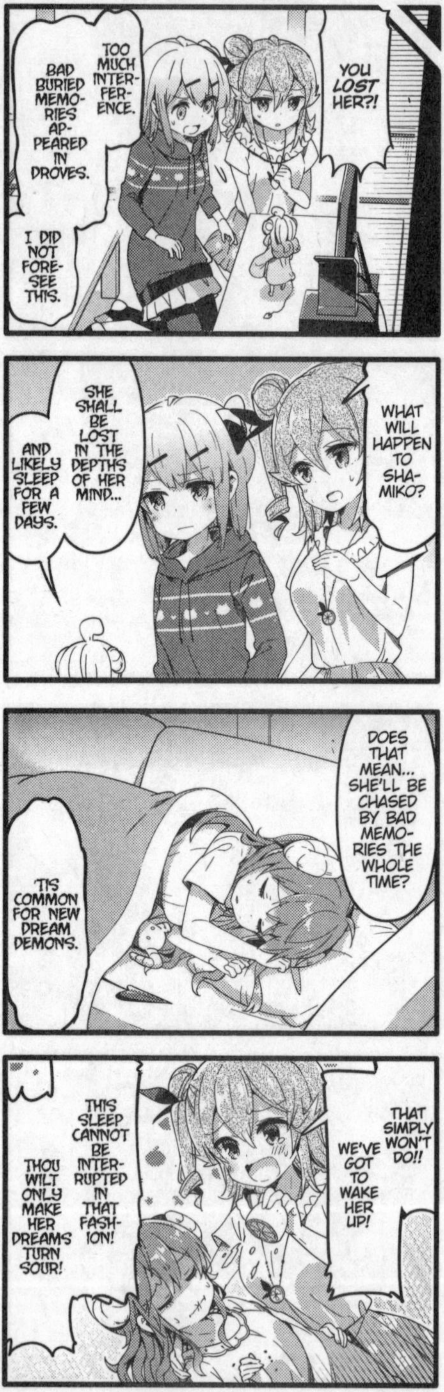
YOU LOST HER?!
TOO MUCH INTERFERENCE.
BAD BURIED MEMORIES APPEARED IN DROVES.
I DID NOT FORESEE THIS.
WHAT WILL HAPPEN TO SHAMIKO?
SHE SHALL BE LOST IN THE DEPTHS OF HER MIND...
AND LIKELY SLEEP FOR A FEW DAYS.
DOES THAT MEAN... SHE'LL BE CHASED BY BAD MEMORIES THE WHOLE TIME?
'TIS COMMON FOR NEW DREAM DEMONS.
THAT SIMPLY WON'T DO!!
WE'VE GOT TO WAKE HER UP!
THIS SLEEP CANNOT BE INTERRUPTED IN THAT FASHION!
THOU WILT ONLY MAKE HER DREAMS TURN SOUR!

BECOME A MAGICAL GIRL WHO ACTS ON HER FEELINGS

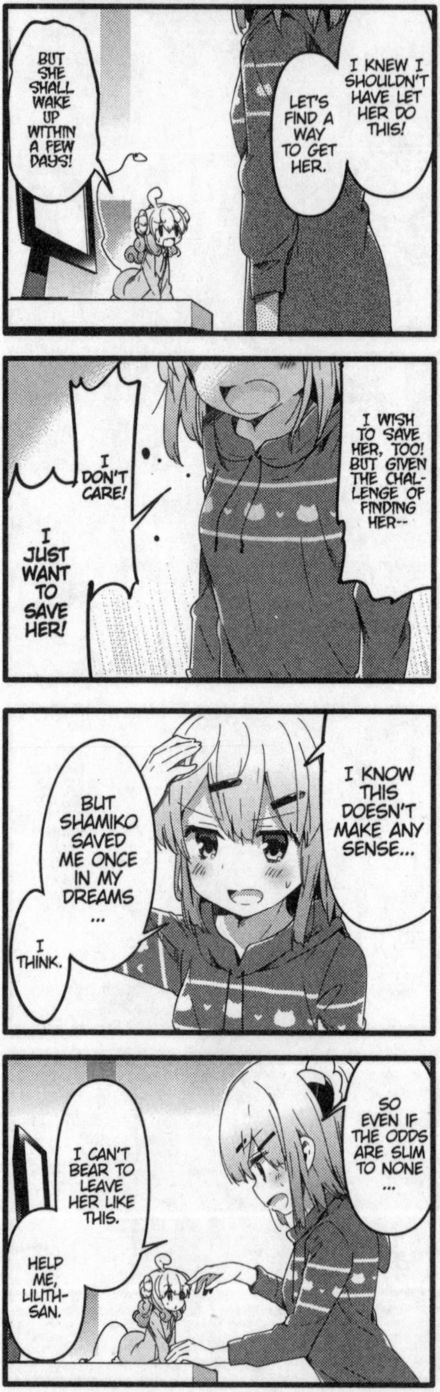
I KNEW I SHOULDN'T HAVE LET HER DO THIS!
LET'S FIND A WAY TO GET HER.
BUT SHE SHALL WAKE UP WITHIN A FEW DAYS!
I WISH TO SAVE HER, TOO! BUT GIVEN THE CHALLENGE OF FINDING HER--
I DON'T CARE!
I JUST WANT TO SAVE HER!
I KNOW THIS DOESN'T MAKE ANY SENSE...
BUT SHAMIKO SAVED ME ONCE IN MY DREAMS...
I THINK.
SO EVEN IF THE ODDS ARE SLIM TO NONE...
I CAN'T BEAR TO LEAVE HER LIKE THIS.
HELP ME, LILITH-SAN.

OP WEAPON

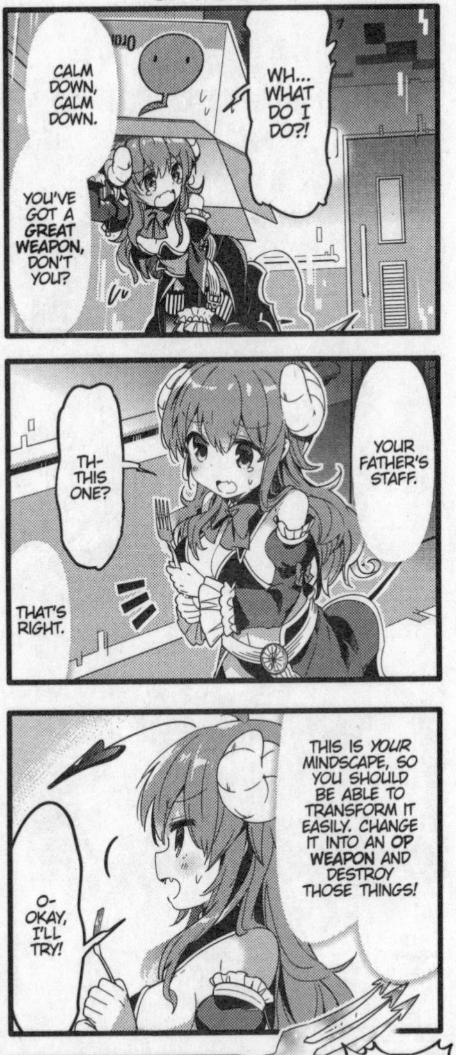
WH... WHAT DO I DO?!
CALM DOWN, CALM DOWN.
YOU'VE GOT A GREAT WEAPON, DON'T YOU?
YOUR FATHER'S STAFF.
TH- THIS ONE?
THAT'S RIGHT.
THIS IS *YOUR* MINDSCAPE, SO YOU SHOULD BE ABLE TO TRANSFORM IT EASILY. CHANGE IT INTO AN OP WEAPON AND DESTROY THOSE THINGS!
O-OKAY, I'LL TRY!
OP WEA-POOON !!
ALLOW US TO EXPLAIN!
AN "OP WEAPON," OR OVER-POWERED WEAPON, CAN DEFEAT ANYTHING, BUT ONLY IN THE DREAM WORLD!!

EGG WHITES WHISKED WITH SUGAR

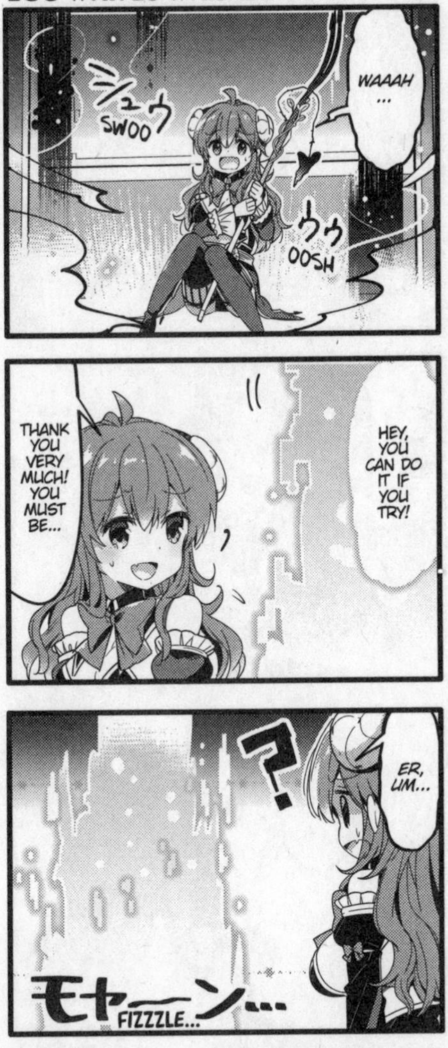
WAAAH ...
シュウ
SWOO
ウゥ
OOSH
HEY, YOU CAN DO IT IF YOU TRY!
THANK YOU VERY MUCH! YOU MUST BE...
ER, UM...
モヤーン...
FIZZZLE...
LET ME GUESS.
THE MEMORY OF A MERINGUE!
NO, NO! I'M NOT A MEMORY AT ALL!!
AND I'M NOT A MERINGUE, EITHER !!

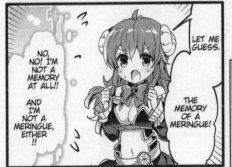

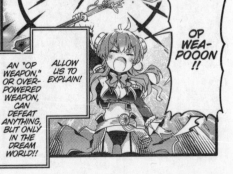

MERINGUE-SAN'S REQUEST

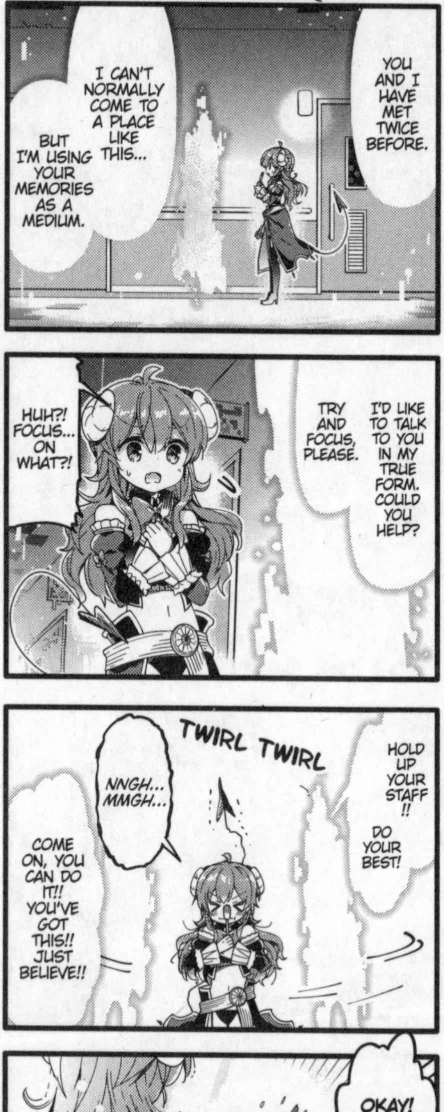
YOU AND I HAVE MET TWICE BEFORE.
I CAN'T NORMALLY COME TO A PLACE LIKE THIS...
BUT I'M USING YOUR MEMORIES AS A MEDIUM.
I'D LIKE TO TALK TO YOU IN MY TRUE FORM. COULD YOU HELP?
TRY AND FOCUS, PLEASE.
HUH?! FOCUS... ON WHAT?!
HOLD UP YOUR STAFF!!
DO YOUR BEST!
TWIRL TWIRL
NNGH... MMGH...
COME ON, YOU CAN DO IT!! YOU'VE GOT THIS!! JUST BELIEVE!!
OKAY! FORMATION COMPLETE!!
?!
FLASH

SAKURA COMEBACK

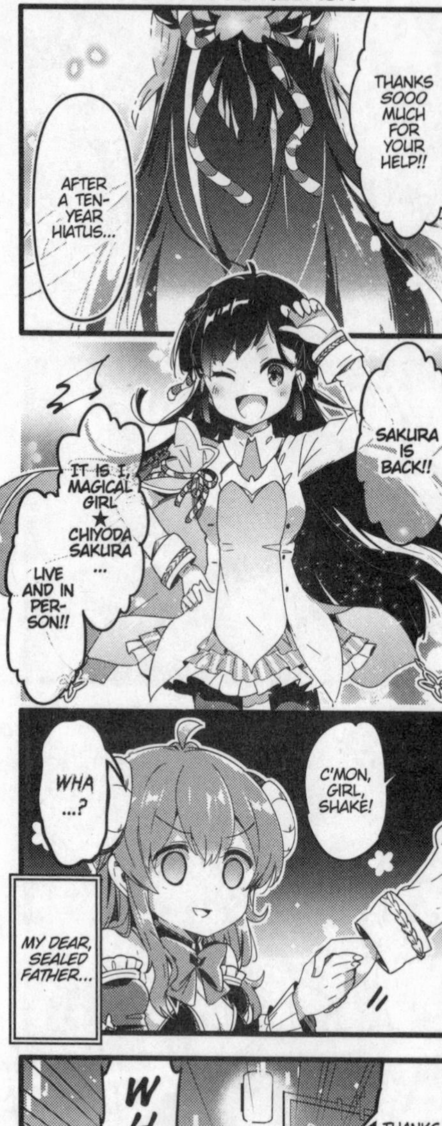
THANKS SOOO MUCH FOR YOUR HELP!!
AFTER A TEN-YEAR HIATUS...
SAKURA IS BACK!!
IT IS I, MAGICAL GIRL ★ CHIYODA SAKURA ...
LIVE AND IN PERSON!!
C'MON, GIRL, SHAKE!
WHA ...?
MY DEAR, SEALED FATHER...
THANKS FOR LOOKING AFTER MOMO-CHAN!!
WHAAAAAAA?!
I THINK... SOMEONE REALLY IMPORTANT JUST SAVED ME.

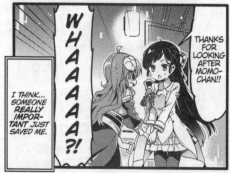

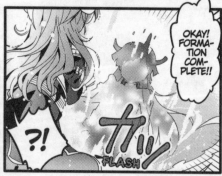

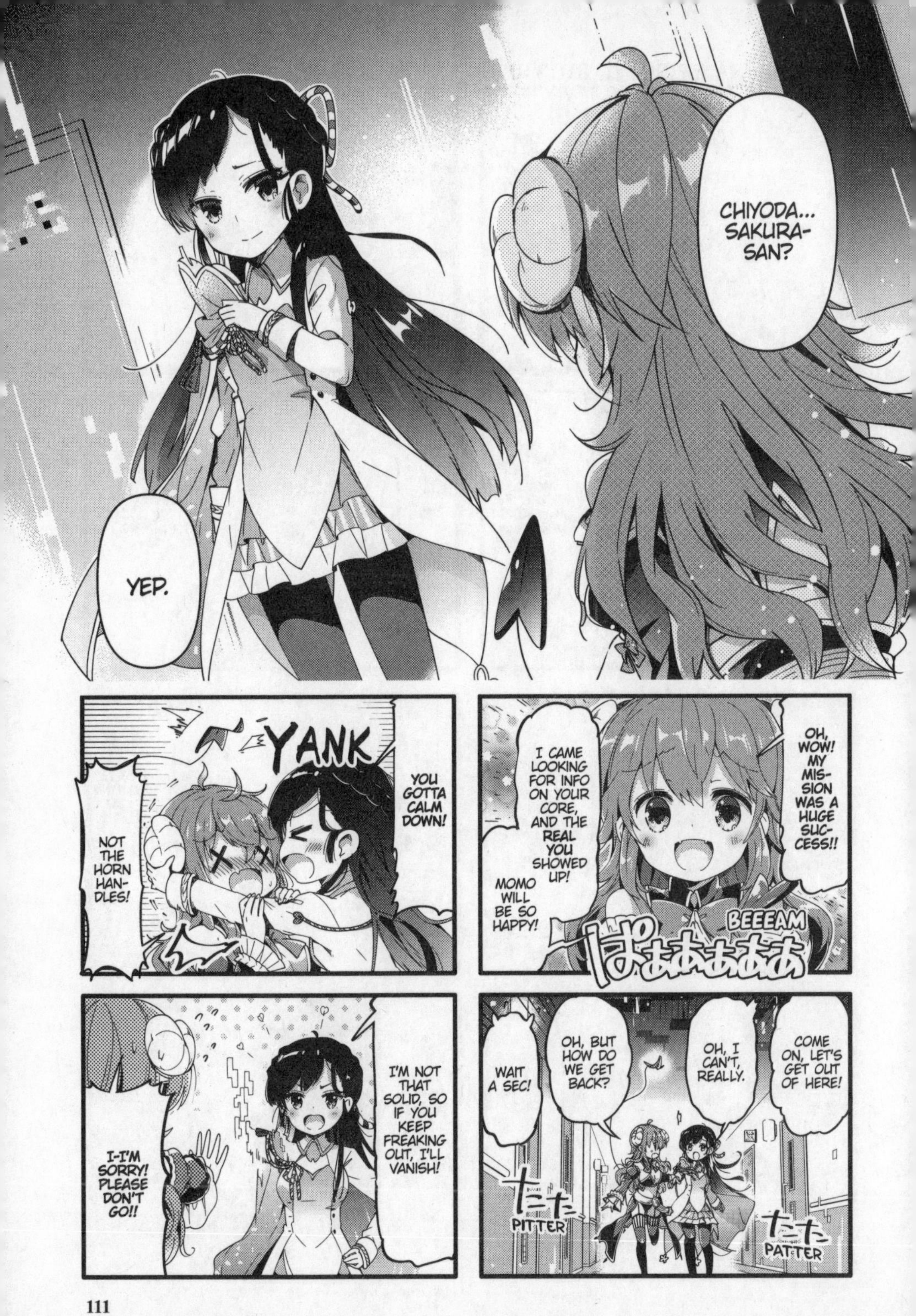
CHIYODA... SAKURA-SAN?
YEP.
OH, WOW! MY MIS-SION WAS A HUGE SUC-CESS!!
I CAME LOOKING FOR INFO ON YOUR CORE, AND THE REAL YOU SHOWED UP!
MOMO WILL BE SO HAPPY!
BEEEAM
YANK
YOU GOTTA CALM DOWN!
NOT THE HORN HAN-DLES!
COME ON, LET'S GET OUT OF HERE!
OH, I CAN'T, REALLY.
OH, BUT HOW DO WE GET BACK?
WAIT A SEC!
PATTER
PITTER
I'M NOT THAT SOLID, SO IF YOU KEEP FREAKING OUT, I'LL VANISH!
I-I'M SORRY! PLEASE DON'T GO!!

FRESH PEACH BLOOD SHOWER

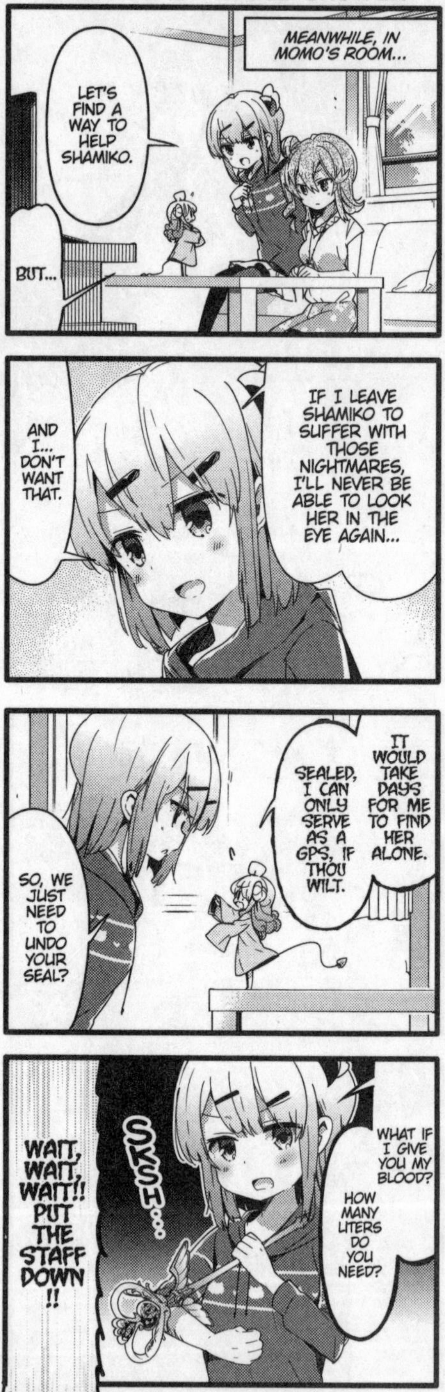
MEANWHILE, IN MOMO'S ROOM...
LET'S FIND A WAY TO HELP SHAMIKO.
BUT...
IF I LEAVE SHAMIKO TO SUFFER WITH THOSE NIGHTMARES, I'LL NEVER BE ABLE TO LOOK HER IN THE EYE AGAIN...
AND I... DON'T WANT THAT.
IT WOULD TAKE DAYS FOR ME TO FIND HER ALONE.
SEALED, I CAN ONLY SERVE AS A GPS, IF THOU WILT.
SO, WE JUST NEED TO UNDO YOUR SEAL?
WHAT IF I GIVE YOU MY BLOOD?
HOW MANY LITERS DO YOU NEED?
SKSH...
WAIT, WAIT, WAIT!! PUT THE STAFF DOWN!!

HAD TO TRANSFORM TO STOP HER

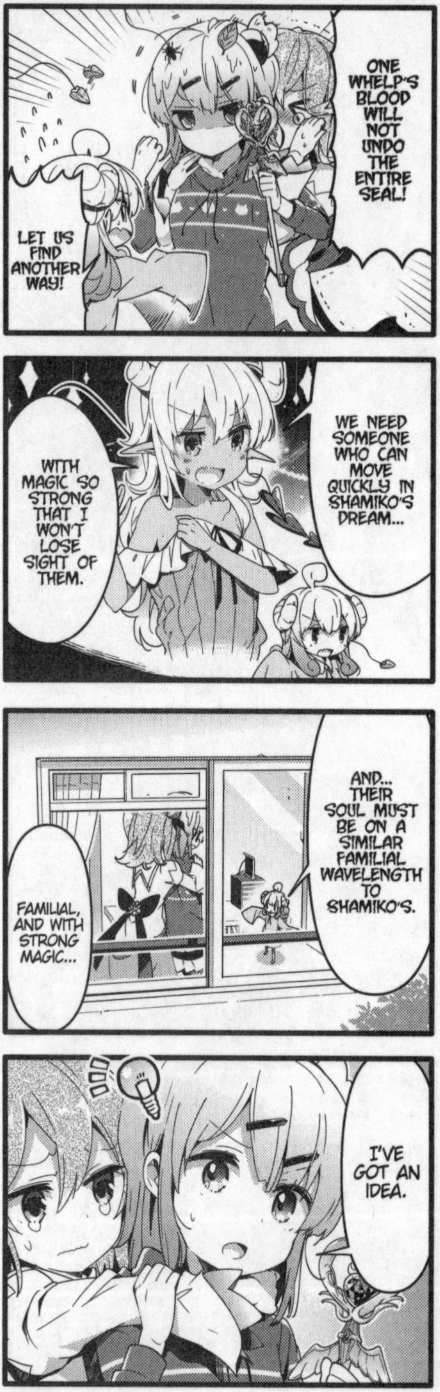
ONE WHELP'S BLOOD WILL NOT UNDO THE ENTIRE SEAL!
LET US FIND ANOTHER WAY!
WE NEED SOMEONE WHO CAN MOVE QUICKLY IN SHAMIKO'S DREAM...
WITH MAGIC SO STRONG THAT I WON'T LOSE SIGHT OF THEM.
AND... THEIR SOUL MUST BE ON A SIMILAR FAMILIAL WAVELENGTH TO SHAMIKO'S.
FAMILIAL, AND WITH STRONG MAGIC...
I'VE GOT AN IDEA.

THE SHOCKING TRUTH, REVEALED!

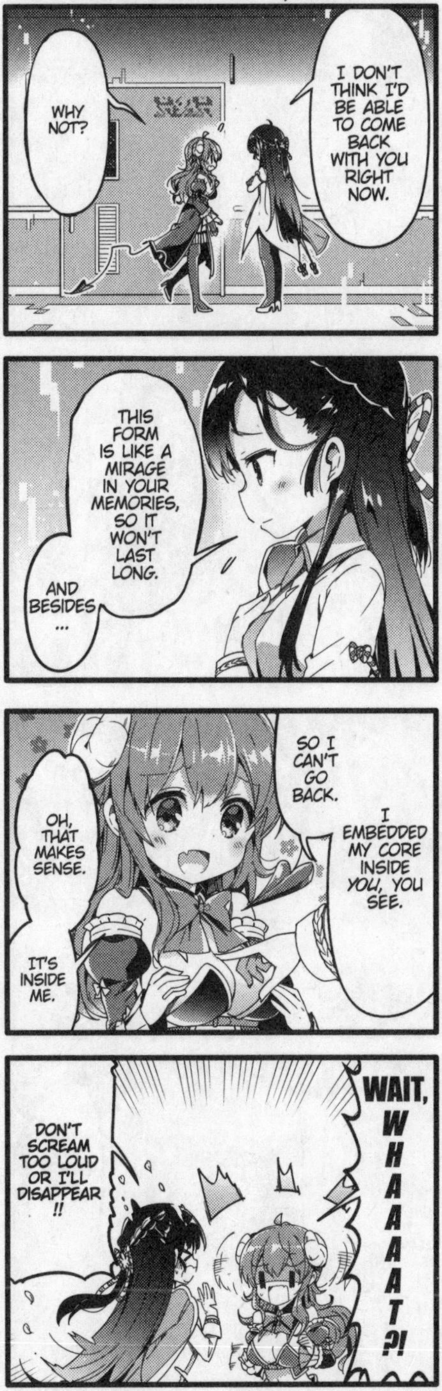
I DON'T THINK I'D BE ABLE TO COME BACK WITH YOU RIGHT NOW.
WHY NOT?
THIS FORM IS LIKE A MIRAGE IN YOUR MEMORIES, SO IT WON'T LAST LONG.
AND BESIDES...
SO I CAN'T GO BACK.
I EMBEDDED MY CORE INSIDE *YOU*, YOU SEE.
OH, THAT MAKES SENSE.
IT'S INSIDE ME.
WAIT, WHAAAAAT?!
DON'T SCREAM TOO LOUD OR I'LL DISAPPEAR!!

SECRETLY DISSING A DEMON'S BRAIN

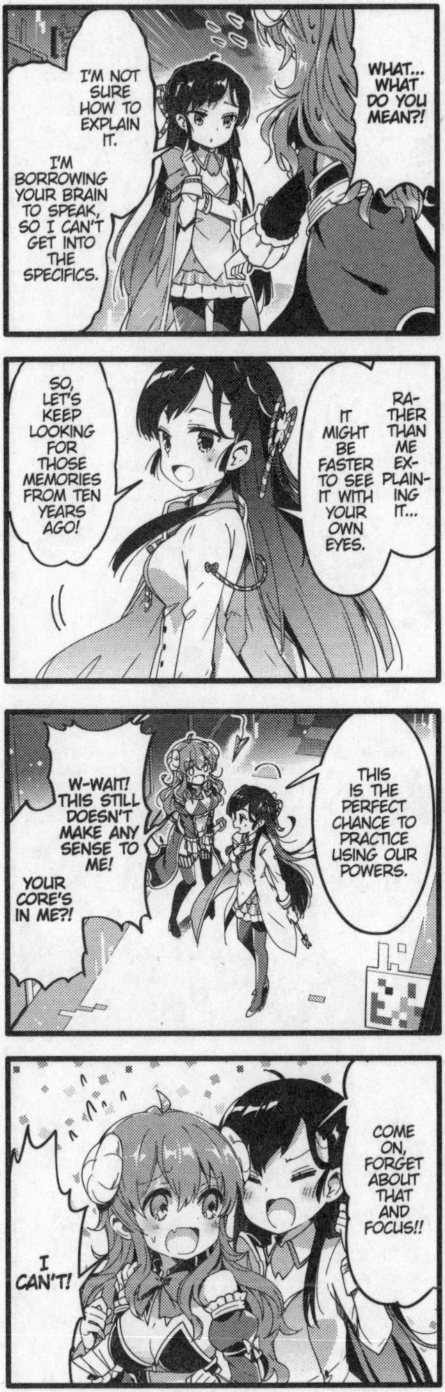
WHAT... WHAT DO YOU MEAN?!
I'M NOT SURE HOW TO EXPLAIN IT.
I'M BORROWING YOUR BRAIN TO SPEAK, SO I CAN'T GET INTO THE SPECIFICS.
RATHER THAN ME EXPLAINING IT...
IT MIGHT BE FASTER TO SEE IT WITH YOUR OWN EYES.
SO, LET'S KEEP LOOKING FOR THOSE MEMORIES FROM TEN YEARS AGO!
THIS IS THE PERFECT CHANCE TO PRACTICE USING OUR POWERS.
W-WAIT! THIS STILL DOESN'T MAKE ANY SENSE TO ME!
YOUR CORE'S IN ME?!
COME ON, FORGET ABOUT THAT AND FOCUS!!
I CAN'T!

TEACHINGS OF THE GIFTED

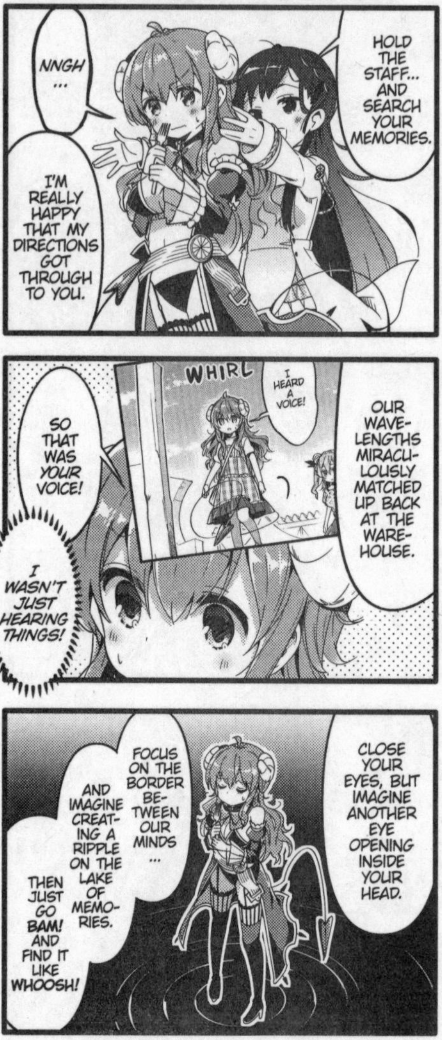
HOLD THE STAFF... AND SEARCH YOUR MEMORIES.
NNGH...
I'M REALLY HAPPY THAT MY DIRECTIONS GOT THROUGH TO YOU.
OUR WAVELENGTHS MIRACULOUSLY MATCHED UP BACK AT THE WAREHOUSE.
I HEARD A VOICE!
WHIRL
SO THAT WAS *YOUR* VOICE!
I WASN'T JUST HEARING THINGS!
CLOSE YOUR EYES, BUT IMAGINE ANOTHER EYE OPENING INSIDE YOUR HEAD.
FOCUS ON THE BORDER BETWEEN OUR MINDS...
AND IMAGINE CREATING A RIPPLE ON THE LAKE OF MEMORIES.
THEN JUST GO **BAM!** AND FIND IT LIKE **WHOOSH!**
I DON'T THINK I GOT THAT LAST PART.
?
WAIT FOR THE **SPLASH**, THEN GO **BAM**, THEN **WHOOSH!!**

WENT BAM AND THEN WHOOSH

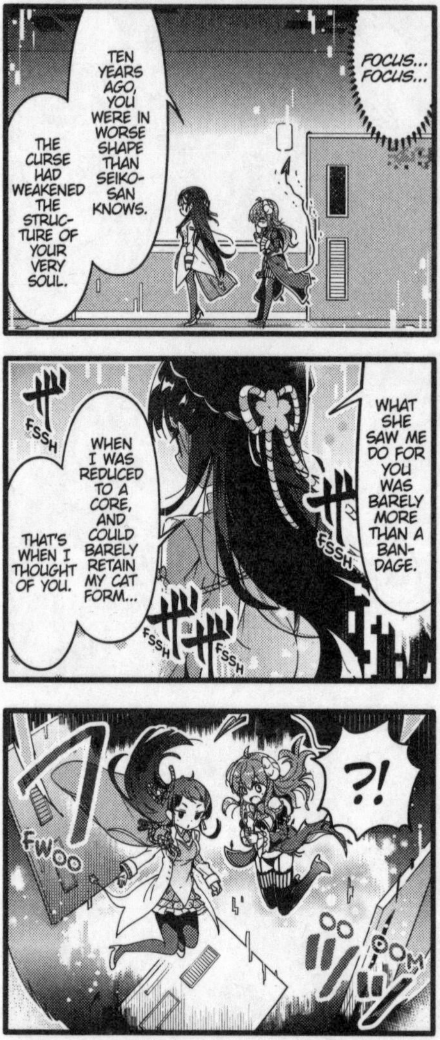
FOCUS... FOCUS...
TEN YEARS AGO, YOU WERE IN WORSE SHAPE THAN SEIKO-SAN KNOWS.
THE CURSE HAD WEAKENED THE STRUCTURE OF YOUR VERY SOUL.
WHAT SHE SAW ME DO FOR YOU WAS BARELY MORE THAN A BANDAGE.
FSSH
WHEN I WAS REDUCED TO A CORE, AND COULD BARELY RETAIN MY CAT FORM...
THAT'S WHEN I THOUGHT OF YOU.
FSSH
FSSH
?!
FWOO
WH-WHERE ARE WE...?!
I THINK YOU GOT IT!!
SEE? YOU CAN DO IT IF YOU TRY!

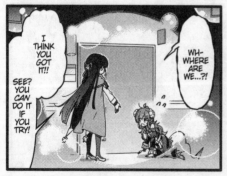

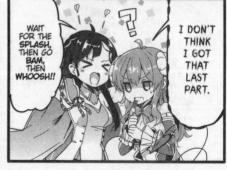

THE CORE'S WHEREABOUTS, REVEALED!

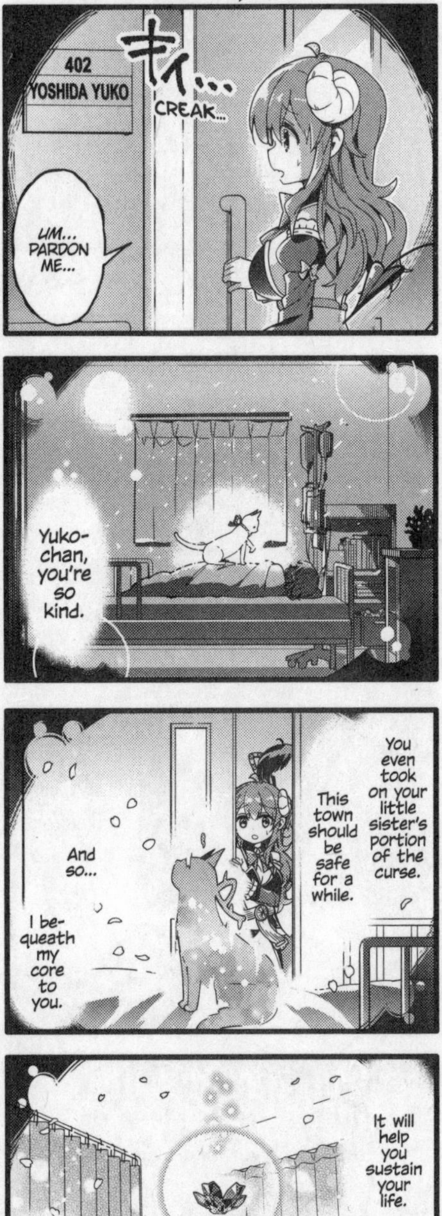
402
YOSHIDA YUKO
キィ…
CREAK...
UM... PARDON ME...
Yuko-chan, you're so kind.
You even took on your little sister's portion of the curse.
This town should be safe for a while.
And so...
I bequeath my core to you.
It will help you sustain your life.
So please... grow up healthy.

MORTAL ENEMY

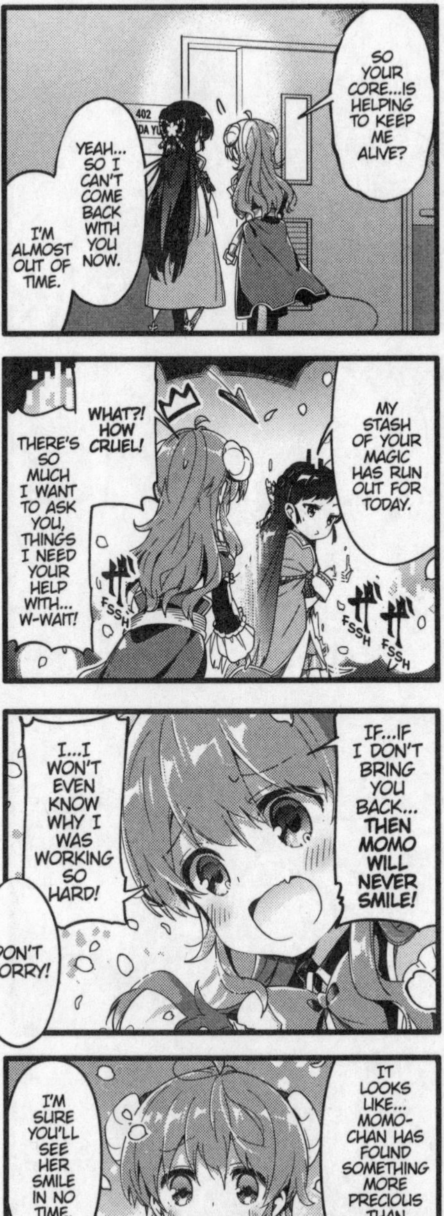
SO YOUR CORE...IS HELPING TO KEEP ME ALIVE?
YEAH... SO I CAN'T COME BACK WITH YOU NOW.
I'M ALMOST OUT OF TIME.
MY STASH OF YOUR MAGIC HAS RUN OUT FOR TODAY.
WHAT?! HOW CRUEL!
THERE'S SO MUCH I WANT TO ASK YOU, THINGS I NEED YOUR HELP WITH... W-WAIT!
FSSH
FSSH
FSSH
IF...IF I DON'T BRING YOU BACK... THEN MOMO WILL NEVER SMILE!
I...I WON'T EVEN KNOW WHY I WAS WORKING SO HARD!
DON'T WORRY!
IT LOOKS LIKE... MOMO-CHAN HAS FOUND SOMETHING MORE PRECIOUS THAN ME, THE TOWN, OR HERSELF.
I'M SURE YOU'LL SEE HER SMILE IN NO TIME.
......??

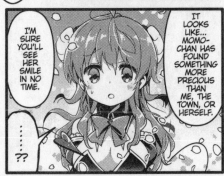

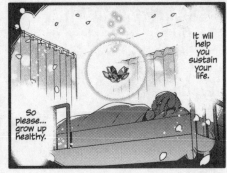

A WELL-SLEPT DEMON IS A WELL-KEPT DEMON

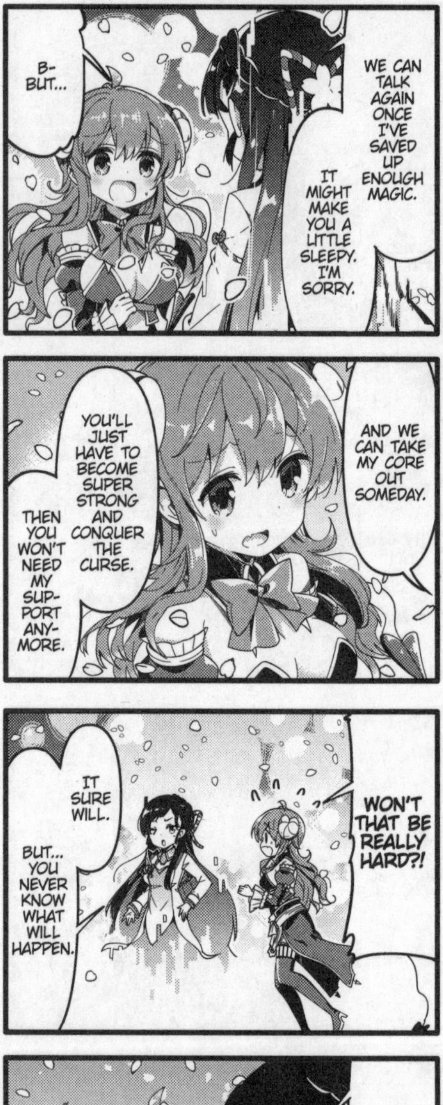
WE CAN TALK AGAIN ONCE I'VE SAVED UP ENOUGH MAGIC.
IT MIGHT MAKE YOU A LITTLE SLEEPY. I'M SORRY.
B-BUT...
AND WE CAN TAKE MY CORE OUT SOMEDAY.
YOU'LL JUST HAVE TO BECOME SUPER STRONG AND CONQUER THE CURSE.
THEN YOU WON'T NEED MY SUPPORT ANYMORE.
WON'T THAT BE REALLY HARD?!
IT SURE WILL.
BUT... YOU NEVER KNOW WHAT WILL HAPPEN.
AND I HAVE ONE LAST REQUEST FOR YOU...
......

TWO-PANEL BATTLE FAIL

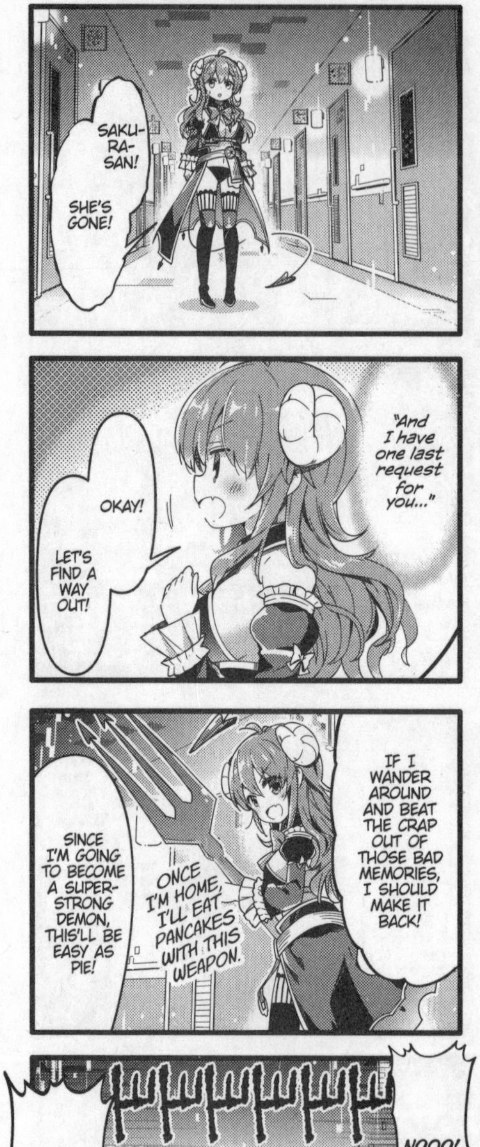
SAKURA-SAN!
SHE'S GONE!
"And I have one last request for you..."
OKAY!
LET'S FIND A WAY OUT!
IF I WANDER AROUND AND BEAT THE CRAP OUT OF THOSE BAD MEMORIES, I SHOULD MAKE IT BACK!
ONCE I'M HOME, I'LL EAT PANCAKES WITH THIS WEAPON.
SINCE I'M GOING TO BECOME A SUPER-STRONG DEMON, THIS'LL BE EASY AS PIE!
NOOO! I WAS WRONG!!
THUD THUD THUD THUD THUD THUD
THIS IS MUCH, MUCH HARDER THAN PIE!!

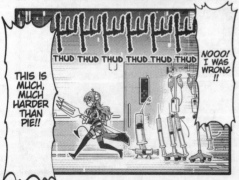

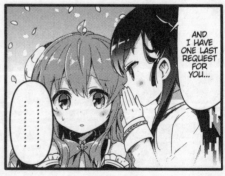

MORTAL ENEMY APPEARS

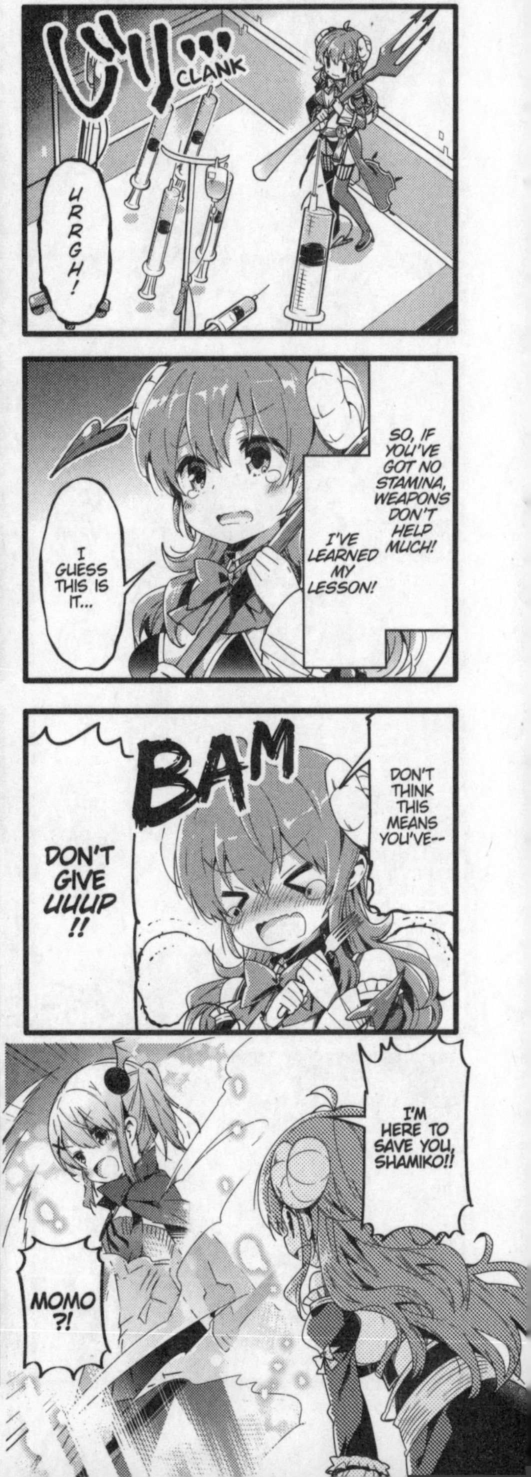
じり...
CLANK
URRGH!
SO, IF YOU'VE GOT NO STAMINA, WEAPONS DON'T HELP MUCH!
I'VE LEARNED MY LESSON!
I GUESS THIS IS IT...
BAM
DON'T THINK THIS MEANS YOU'VE--
DON'T GIVE UUUP!!
I'M HERE TO SAVE YOU, SHAMIKO!!
MOMO ?!

LIKE "I RODE MY BIKE HERE"

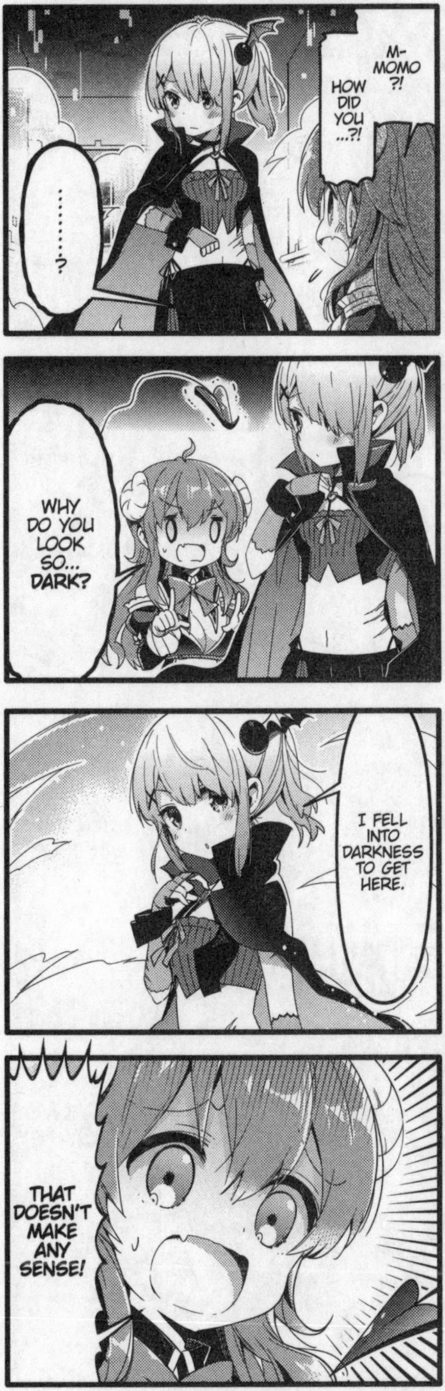
M-MOMO ?! HOW DID YOU ...?!
.........?
WHY DO YOU LOOK SO... DARK?
I FELL INTO DARKNESS TO GET HERE.
THAT DOESN'T MAKE ANY SENSE!

A PROPER ONE-ARMED SHOULDER THROW DOESN'T HURT

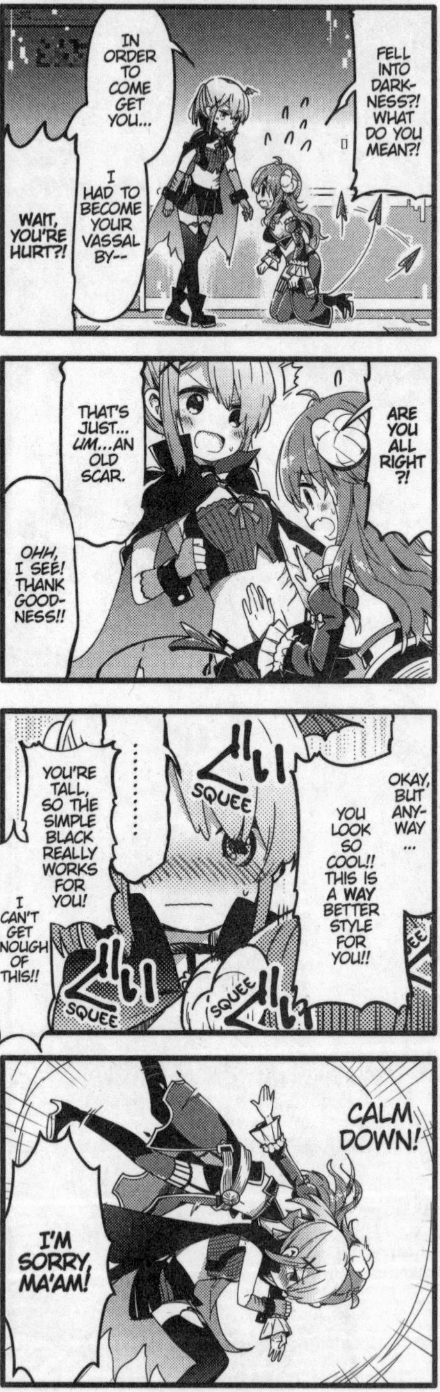
FELL INTO DARK-NESS?! WHAT DO YOU MEAN?!
IN ORDER TO COME GET YOU...
I HAD TO BECOME YOUR VASSAL BY--
WAIT, YOU'RE HURT?!
ARE YOU ALL RIGHT?!
THAT'S JUST... *UM*...AN OLD SCAR.
OHH, I SEE! THANK GOOD-NESS!!
OKAY, BUT ANY-WAY ...
YOU LOOK SO COOL!! THIS IS A WAY BETTER STYLE FOR YOU!!
SQUEE
YOU'RE TALL, SO THE SIMPLE BLACK REALLY WORKS FOR YOU!
I CAN'T GET ENOUGH OF THIS!!
SQUEE
SQUEE
CALM DOWN!
I'M SORRY, MA'AM!

EVIL PINK CODENAME

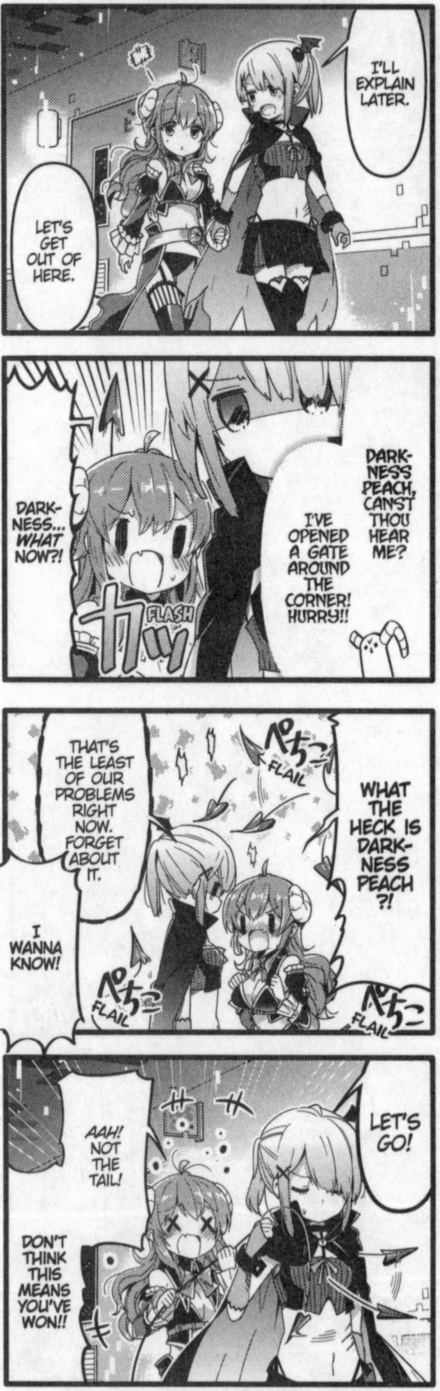
I'LL EXPLAIN LATER.
LET'S GET OUT OF HERE.
DARK-NESS PEACH, CANST THOU HEAR ME?
I'VE OPENED A GATE AROUND THE CORNER! HURRY!!
DARK-NESS... *WHAT* NOW?!
FLASH
WHAT THE HECK IS DARK-NESS PEACH ?!
FLAIL
THAT'S THE LEAST OF OUR PROBLEMS RIGHT NOW. FORGET ABOUT IT.
I WANNA KNOW!
FLAIL
FLAIL
LET'S GO!
AAH! NOT THE TAIL!
DON'T THINK THIS MEANS YOU'VE WON!!

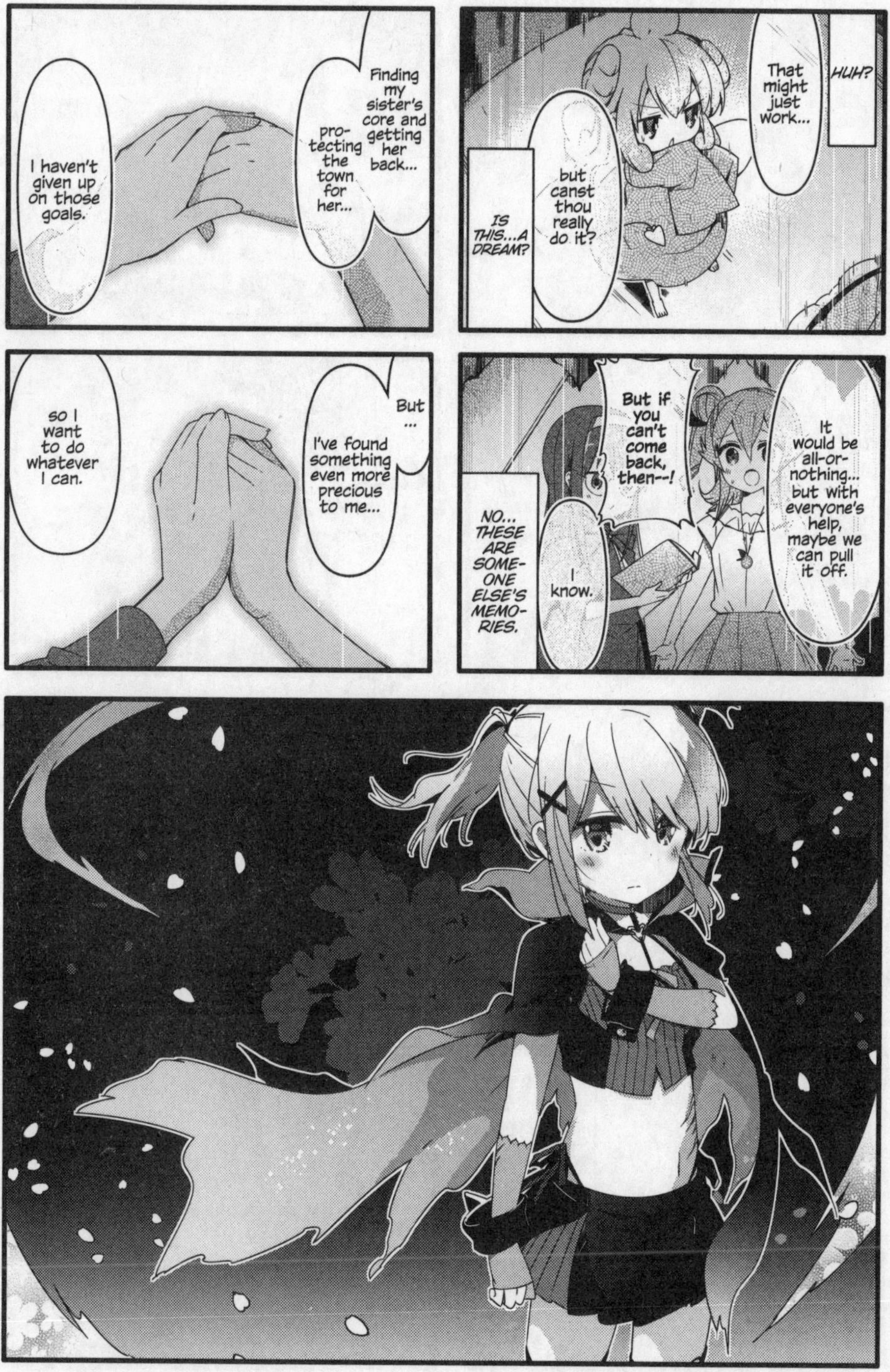
HUH?
That might just work...
but canst thou really do it?
IS THIS...A DREAM?
Finding my sister's core and getting her back... protecting the town for her...
I haven't given up on those goals.
It would be all-or-nothing... but with everyone's help, maybe we can pull it off.
But if you can't come back, then--!
I know.
NO... THESE ARE SOME-ONE ELSE'S MEMO-RIES.
But ... I've found something even more precious to me...
so I want to do whatever I can.

THERE ARE HERBS AND STUFF IN THE BEAK

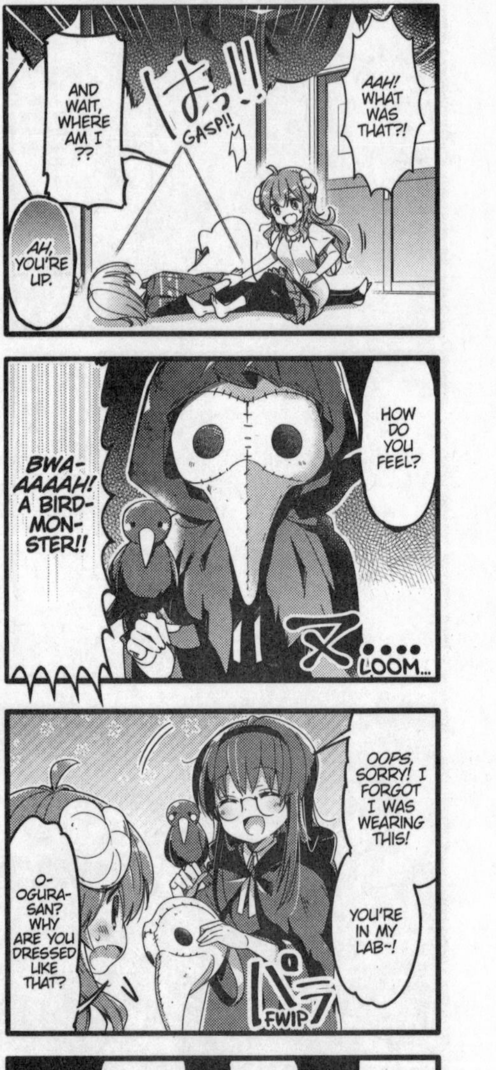
AAH! WHAT WAS THAT?!
はっ!!
GASP!!
AND WAIT, WHERE AM I ??
AH, YOU'RE UP.
HOW DO YOU FEEL?
BWAAAAAH! A BIRD-MONSTER!!
ヌ....
LOOM...
OOPS, SORRY! I FORGOT I WAS WEARING THIS!
YOU'RE IN MY LAB~!
パラ
FWIP
O-OGURA-SAN? WHY ARE YOU DRESSED LIKE THAT?
I'M COSPLAYING AS A DOCTOR FROM THE MIDDLE AGES.
WHY?
I... WAS... A BIRD...
'CAUSE IT MAKES THINGS MORE FUN!!
IF... YOU SAY SO...

LIKE A MANGA PROTAGONIST!!

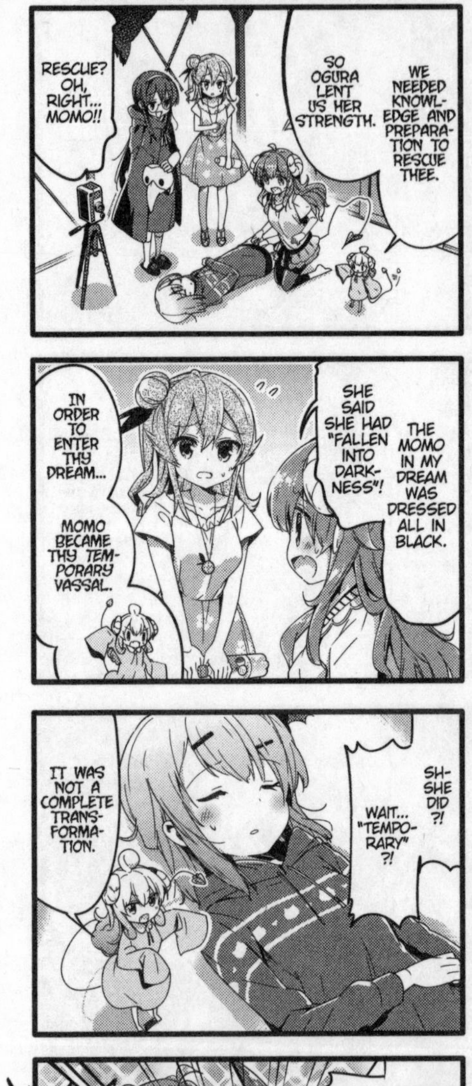
WE NEEDED KNOWLEDGE AND PREPARATION TO RESCUE THEE.
SO OGURA LENT US HER STRENGTH.
RESCUE? OH, RIGHT... MOMO!!
THE MOMO IN MY DREAM WAS DRESSED ALL IN BLACK.
SHE SAID SHE HAD "FALLEN INTO DARKNESS"!
IN ORDER TO ENTER THY DREAM...
MOMO BECAME THY *TEMPORARY* VASSAL.
SH-SHE DID ?!
WAIT... "TEMPORARY" ?!
IT WAS NOT A COMPLETE TRANSFORMATION.
MOMO'S SPIRIT IS DARK, BUT HER BODY IS LIGHT.
SHE IS A "DOUBLE-TYPE" MOMOOO!!
WH... WHAT... WHAT THE HECK?! THAT'S SOOO COOL!!

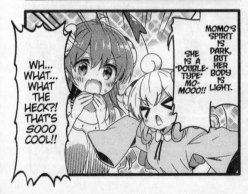

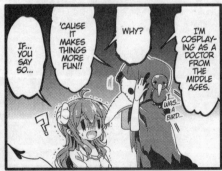

PEACH REMOTE CONTROL

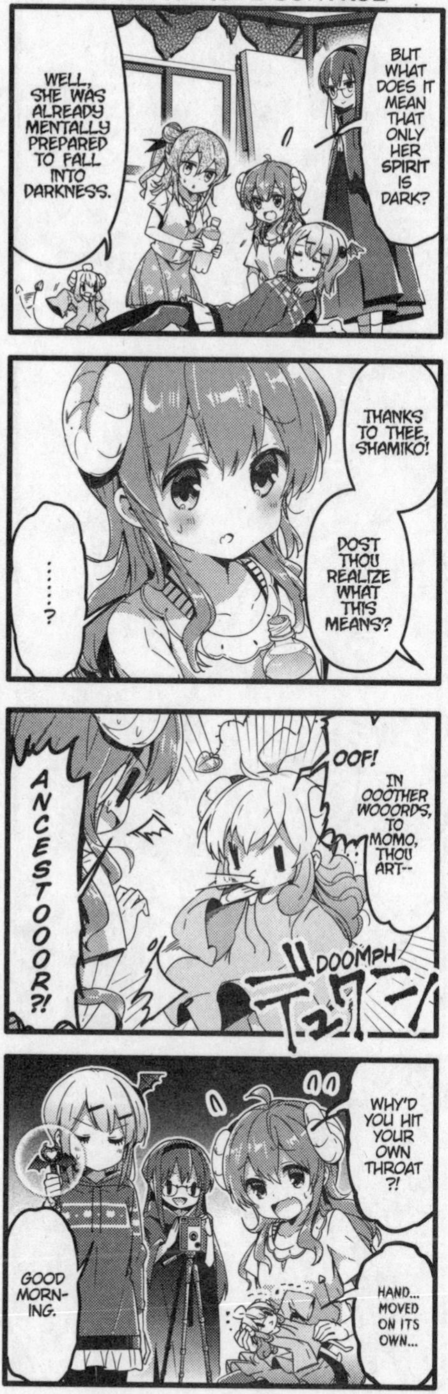
BUT WHAT DOES IT MEAN THAT ONLY HER SPIRIT IS DARK?
WELL, SHE WAS ALREADY MENTALLY PREPARED TO FALL INTO DARKNESS.
THANKS TO THEE, SHAMIKO!
DOST THOU REALIZE WHAT THIS MEANS?
......?
IN OOOTHER WOOORDS, TO MOMO, THOU ART--
OOF!
ANCESTOOOOR?!
DOOMPH
WHY'D YOU HIT YOUR OWN THROAT?!
HAND... MOVED ON ITS OWN...
GOOD MORNING.

DARK RESEARCH REPORT

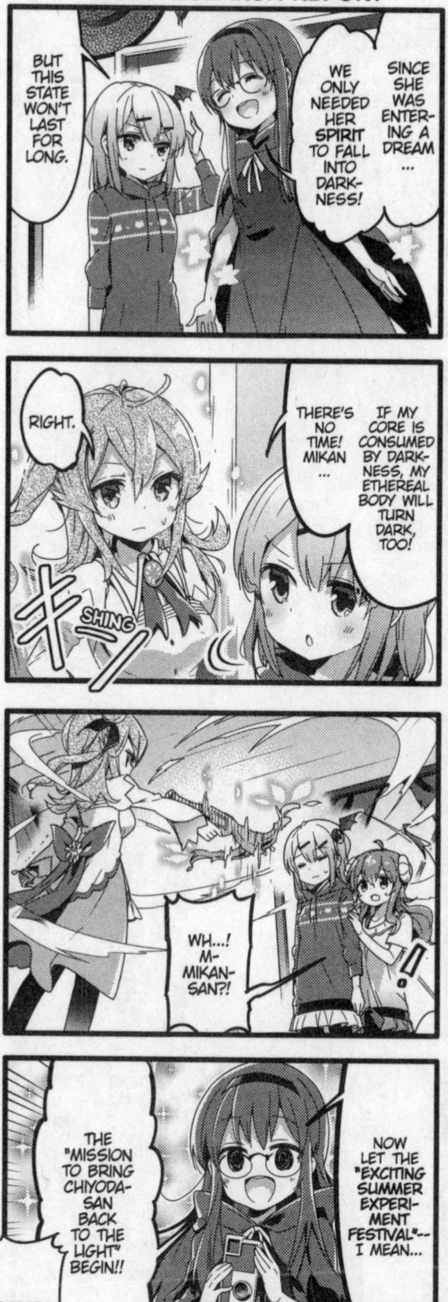
SINCE SHE WAS ENTERING A DREAM...
WE ONLY NEEDED HER SPIRIT TO FALL INTO DARKNESS!
BUT THIS STATE WON'T LAST FOR LONG.
IF MY CORE IS CONSUMED BY DARKNESS, MY ETHEREAL BODY WILL TURN DARK, TOO!
THERE'S NO TIME! MIKAN...
RIGHT.
SHING
WH...! M-MIKAN-SAN?!
NOW LET THE "EXCITING SUMMER EXPERIMENT FESTIVAL"-- I MEAN...
THE "MISSION TO BRING CHIYODA-SAN BACK TO THE LIGHT" BEGIN!!
EXPERIMENT?!

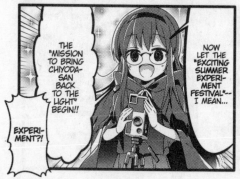

BECOME A RESOURCEFUL DEMON

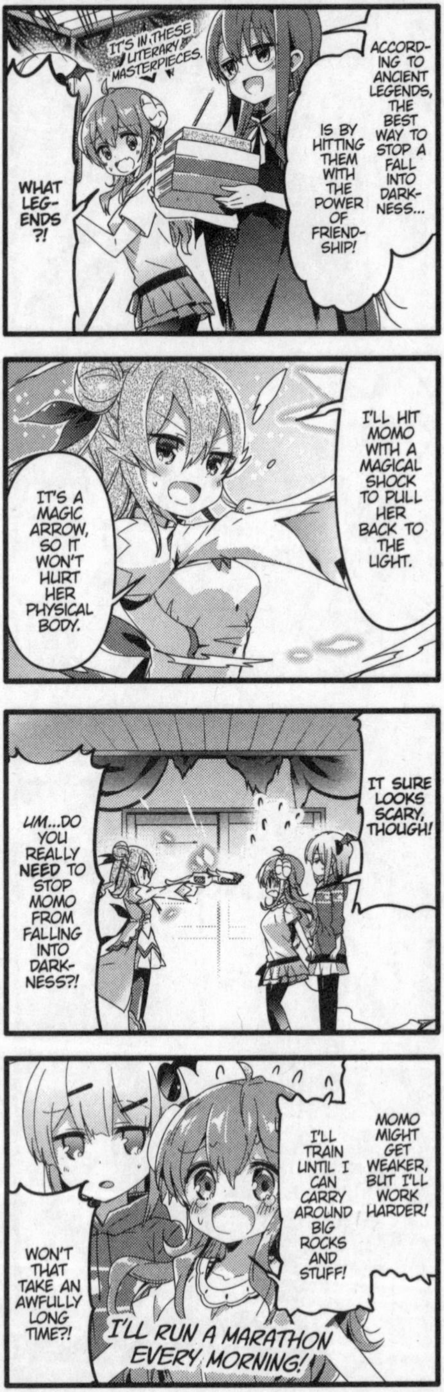
ACCORDING TO ANCIENT LEGENDS, THE BEST WAY TO STOP A FALL INTO DARKNESS...
IS BY HITTING THEM WITH THE POWER OF FRIENDSHIP!
IT'S IN THESE LITERARY MASTERPIECES.
WHAT LEGENDS?!
I'LL HIT MOMO WITH A MAGICAL SHOCK TO PULL HER BACK TO THE LIGHT.
IT'S A MAGIC ARROW, SO IT WON'T HURT HER PHYSICAL BODY.
IT SURE LOOKS SCARY, THOUGH!
UM...DO YOU REALLY NEED TO STOP MOMO FROM FALLING INTO DARKNESS?!
MOMO MIGHT GET WEAKER, BUT I'LL WORK HARDER!
I'LL TRAIN UNTIL I CAN CARRY AROUND BIG ROCKS AND STUFF!
I'LL RUN A MARATHON EVERY MORNING!
WON'T THAT TAKE AN AWFULLY LONG TIME?!

ARROW PEACH

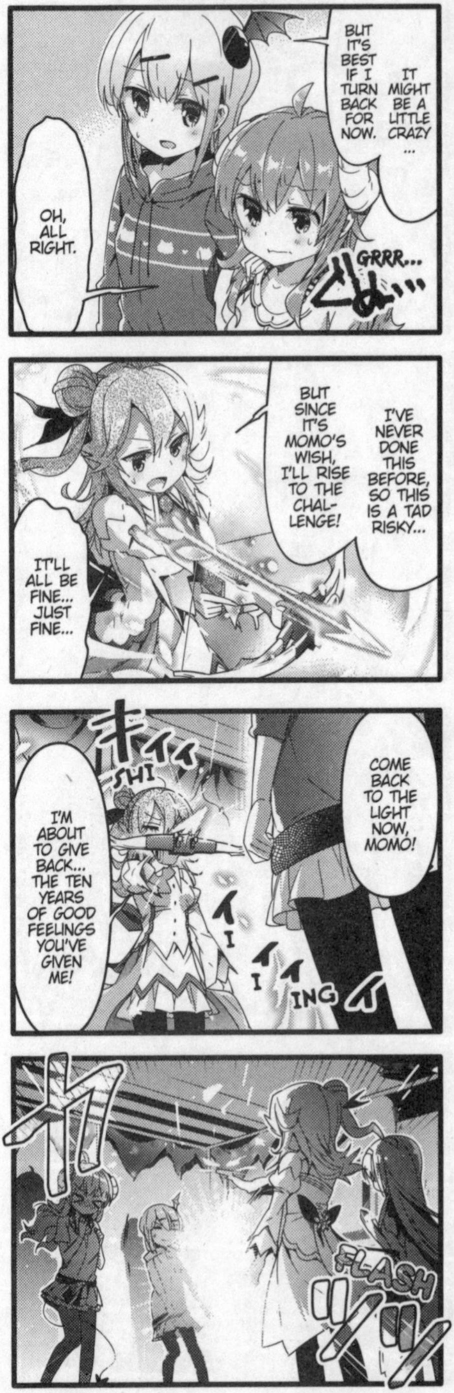
IT MIGHT BE A LITTLE CRAZY...
BUT IT'S BEST IF I TURN BACK FOR NOW.
OH, ALL RIGHT.
GRRR...
I'VE NEVER DONE THIS BEFORE, SO THIS IS A TAD RISKY...
BUT SINCE IT'S MOMO'S WISH, I'LL RISE TO THE CHALLENGE!
IT'LL ALL BE FINE... JUST FINE...
COME BACK TO THE LIGHT NOW, MOMO!
I'M ABOUT TO GIVE BACK... THE TEN YEARS OF GOOD FEELINGS YOU'VE GIVEN ME!
SHI
I
I
ING
FLASH

ANCESTOR'S EXTRA LIFE, LOGGED OUT

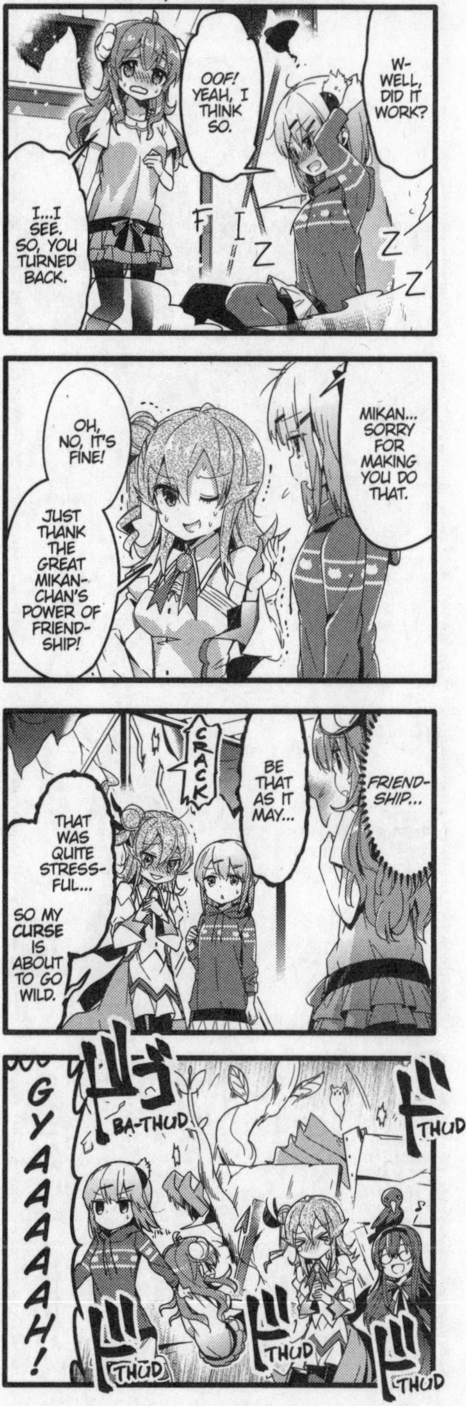
W-WELL, DID IT WORK?
OOF! YEAH, I THINK SO.
FIZZ
I...I SEE. SO, YOU TURNED BACK.
ZZ
MIKAN... SORRY FOR MAKING YOU DO THAT.
OH, NO, IT'S FINE!
JUST THANK THE GREAT MIKAN-CHAN'S POWER OF FRIENDSHIP!
FRIENDSHIP...
BE THAT AS IT MAY...
CRACK
THAT WAS QUITE STRESSFUL...
SO MY CURSE IS ABOUT TO GO WILD.
THUD
BA-THUD
GYAAAAAAH!
THUD
THUD
THUD

THE MAGICAL GIRL PAID FOR THE BUILDING

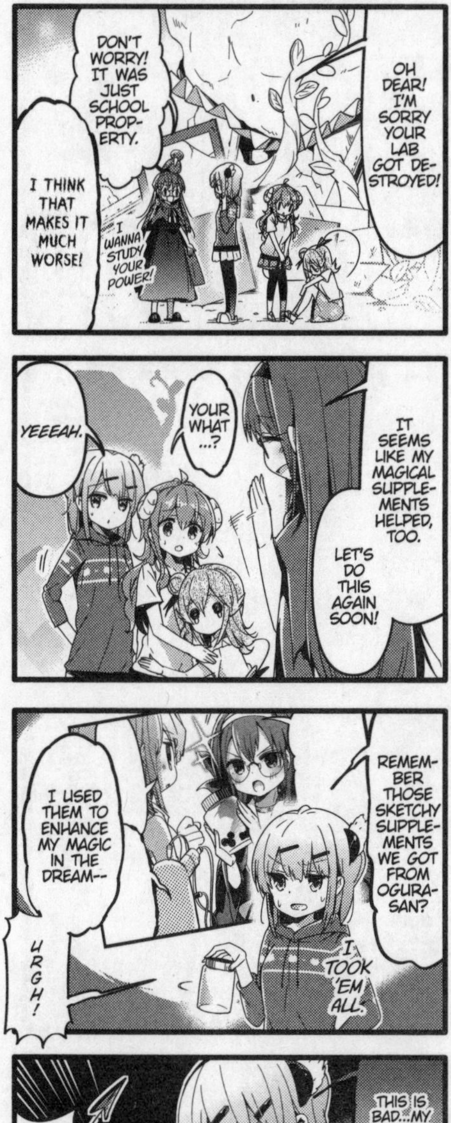
OH DEAR! I'M SORRY YOUR LAB GOT DESTROYED!
DON'T WORRY! IT WAS JUST SCHOOL PROPERTY.
I WANNA STUDY YOUR POWER!
I THINK THAT MAKES IT MUCH WORSE!
IT SEEMS LIKE MY MAGICAL SUPPLEMENTS HELPED, TOO.
YOUR WHAT ...?
YEEEAH.
LET'S DO THIS AGAIN SOON!
REMEMBER THOSE SKETCHY SUPPLEMENTS WE GOT FROM OGURA-SAN?
I USED THEM TO ENHANCE MY MAGIC IN THE DREAM--
I TOOK 'EM ALL.
URGH!
THIS IS BAD... MY ETHEREAL BODY AND STOMACH ARE REBELLING!
THOSE THINGS AREN'T SAFE FOR HUMAN CONSUMPTION!
MMMGH!
MOMOOOOOOO!!

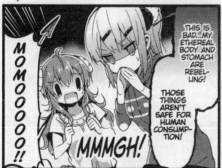

WEAPONIZED FISH, NUMBER ONE

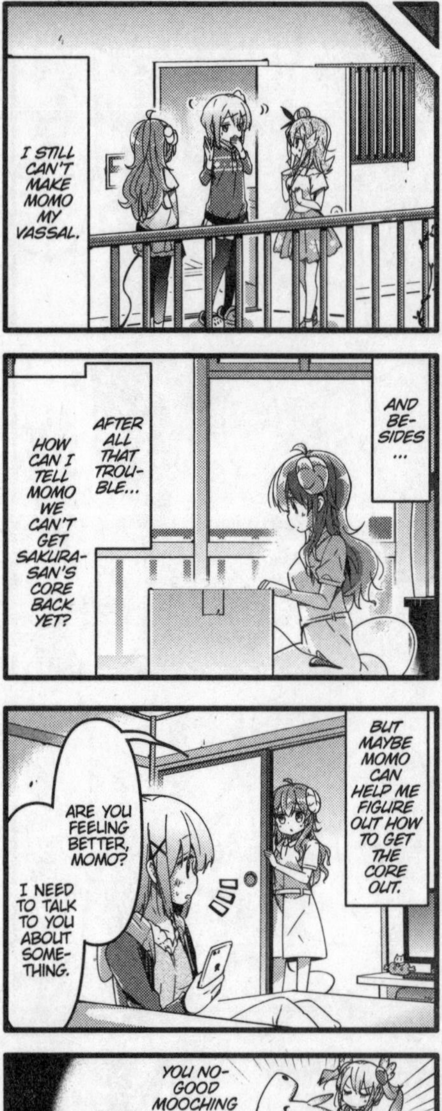
I STILL CAN'T MAKE MOMO MY VASSAL.
AND BESIDES...
AFTER ALL THAT TROUBLE...
HOW CAN I TELL MOMO WE CAN'T GET SAKURA-SAN'S CORE BACK YET?
BUT MAYBE MOMO CAN HELP ME FIGURE OUT HOW TO GET THE CORE OUT.
ARE YOU FEELING BETTER, MOMO?
I NEED TO TALK TO YOU ABOUT SOMETHING.
YOU NO-GOOD MOOCHING DEMON!
FRESH PEACH HAMMERHEAD SHARK!!
I KNOOOW!
GULP...
UMM... WHY ARE YOU SO PALE? ARE YOU ALL RIGHT?

THE STAFF BECOMES A HOUSEHOLD TOOL

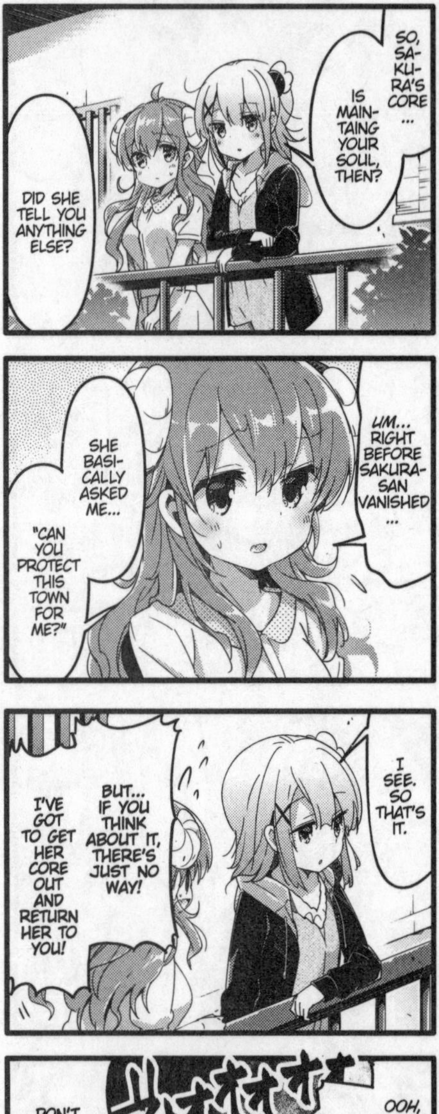
SO, SAKURA'S CORE...
IS MAINTAING YOUR SOUL, THEN?
DID SHE TELL YOU ANYTHING ELSE?
UM... RIGHT BEFORE SAKURA-SAN VANISHED...
SHE BASICALLY ASKED ME...
"CAN YOU PROTECT THIS TOWN FOR ME?"
I SEE. SO THAT'S IT.
BUT... IF YOU THINK ABOUT IT, THERE'S JUST NO WAY!
I'VE GOT TO GET HER CORE OUT AND RETURN HER TO YOU!
VWOOOOOOOOOO
OOH, MAYBE WE CAN VACUUM IT OUT!
OR YOU COULD SMACK MY BACK UNTIL IT POPS OUT?!
DON'T EVEN THINK ABOUT IT!! IT'S NOT FOOD STUCK IN YOUR THROAT!

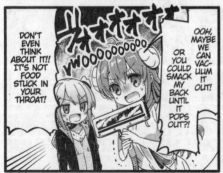

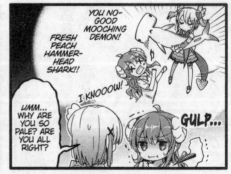

SUPER BIG GOAL

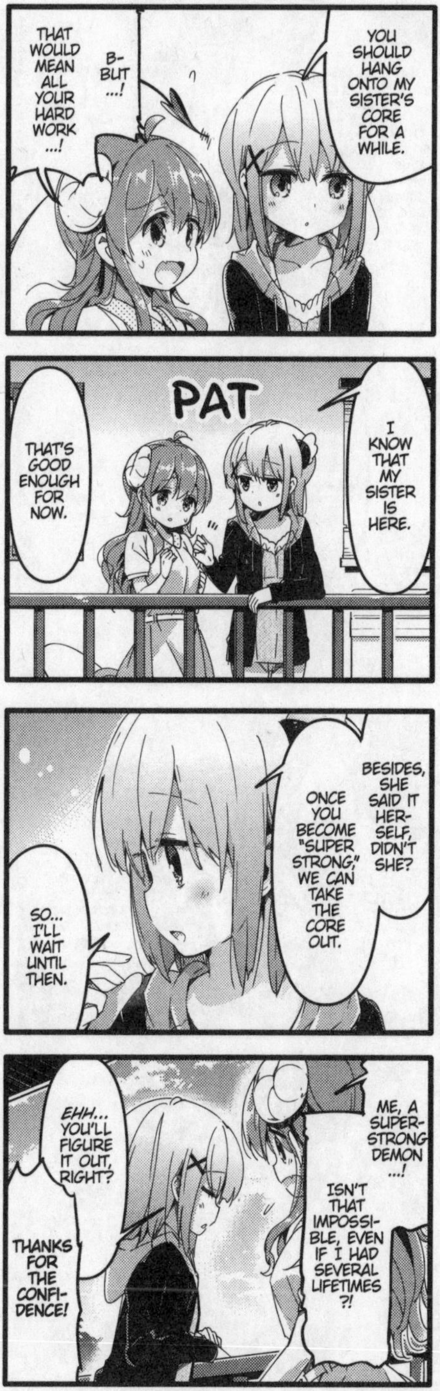
YOU SHOULD HANG ONTO MY SISTER'S CORE FOR A WHILE.
B-BUT...!
THAT WOULD MEAN ALL YOUR HARD WORK...!
I KNOW THAT MY SISTER IS HERE.
PAT
THAT'S GOOD ENOUGH FOR NOW.
BESIDES, SHE SAID IT HERSELF, DIDN'T SHE?
ONCE YOU BECOME "SUPER STRONG," WE CAN TAKE THE CORE OUT.
SO... I'LL WAIT UNTIL THEN.
ME, A SUPER-STRONG DEMON...!
ISN'T THAT IMPOSSIBLE, EVEN IF I HAD SEVERAL LIFETIMES?!
EHH... YOU'LL FIGURE IT OUT, RIGHT?
THANKS FOR THE CONFIDENCE!

IN THIS BIG, MIRACULOUS TOWN

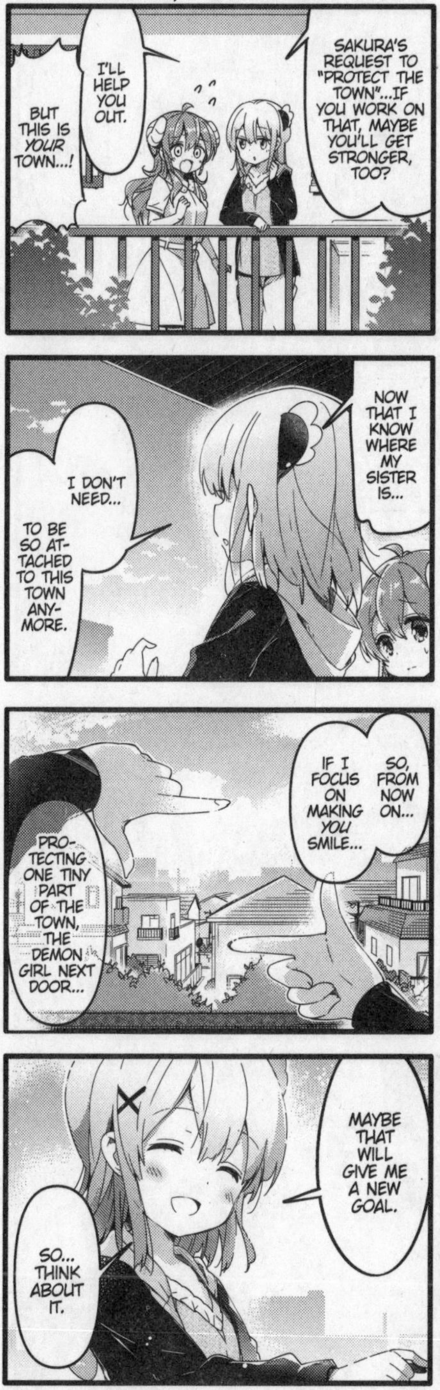
SAKURA'S REQUEST TO "PROTECT THE TOWN"...IF YOU WORK ON THAT, MAYBE YOU'LL GET STRONGER, TOO?
I'LL HELP YOU OUT.
BUT THIS IS *YOUR* TOWN...!
NOW THAT I KNOW WHERE MY SISTER IS...
I DON'T NEED...
TO BE SO ATTACHED TO THIS TOWN ANYMORE.
SO, FROM NOW ON...
IF I FOCUS ON MAKING *YOU* SMILE...
PROTECTING ONE TINY PART OF THE TOWN, THE DEMON GIRL NEXT DOOR...
MAYBE THAT WILL GIVE ME A NEW GOAL.
SO... THINK ABOUT IT.

A MAGICAL GIRL MAKES A DEMON CRY

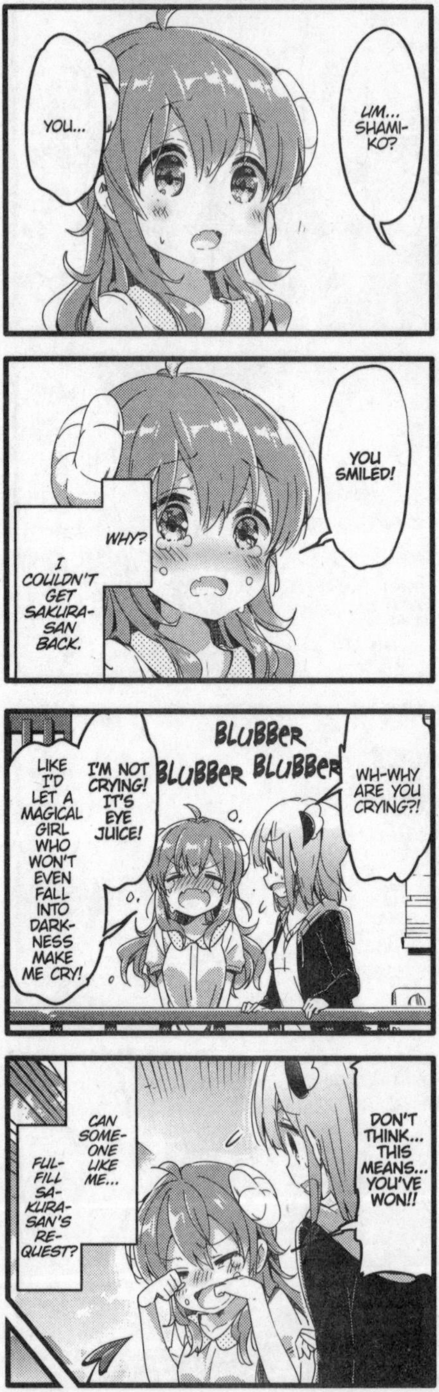
UM... SHAMIKO?
YOU...
YOU SMILED!
WHY?
I COULDN'T GET SAKURA-SAN BACK.
WH-WHY ARE YOU CRYING?!
BLUBBER BLUBBER BLUBBER
I'M NOT CRYING! IT'S EYE JUICE!
LIKE I'D LET A MAGICAL GIRL WHO WON'T EVEN FALL INTO DARKNESS MAKE ME CRY!
DON'T THINK... THIS MEANS... YOU'VE WON!!
CAN SOMEONE LIKE ME...
FULFILL SAKURA-SAN'S REQUEST?

A DEMON ENTRUSTED WITH AN EXTRA MISSION

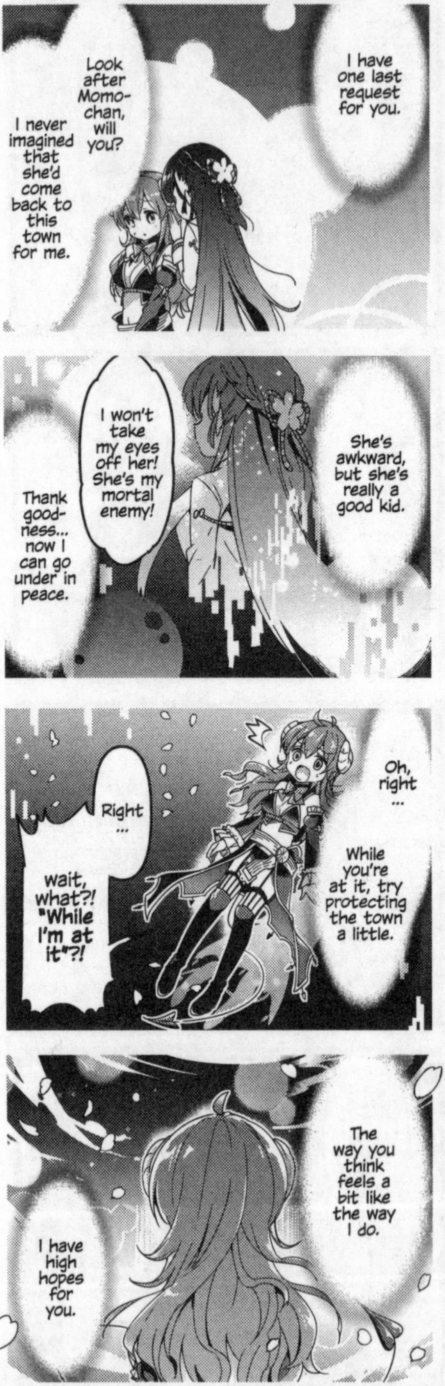
I have one last request for you.
Look after Momo-chan, will you?
I never imagined that she'd come back to this town for me.
She's awkward, but she's really a good kid.
I won't take my eyes off her! She's my mortal enemy!
Thank goodness... now I can go under in peace.
Oh, right ...
While you're at it, try protecting the town a little.
Right ...
wait, what?! "While I'm at it"?!
The way you think feels a bit like the way I do.
I have high hopes for you.

SHADOW MISTRESS, READY TO STRIKE!

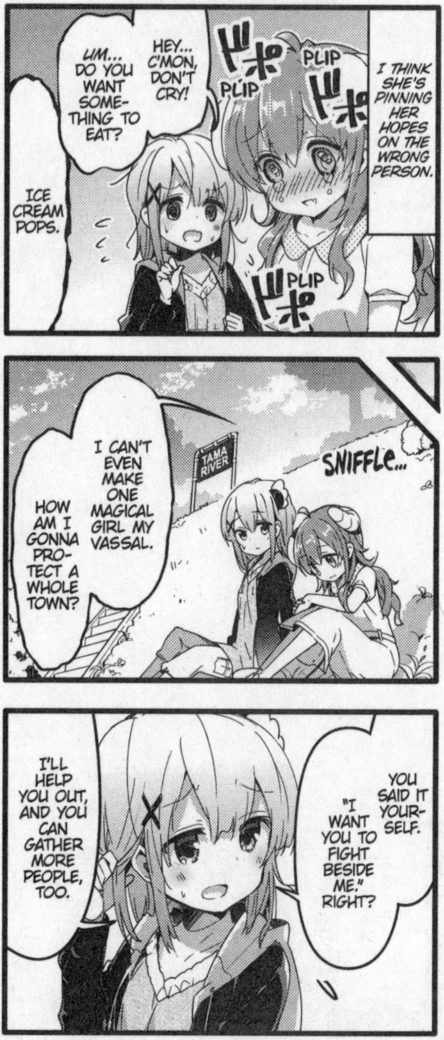
I THINK SHE'S PINNING HER HOPES ON THE WRONG PERSON.
ドポ PLIP
ドポ PLIP
HEY... C'MON, DON'T CRY!
UM... DO YOU WANT SOMETHING TO EAT?
ICE CREAM POPS.
ドポ PLIP
SNIFFLE...
TAMA RIVER
I CAN'T EVEN MAKE ONE MAGICAL GIRL MY VASSAL.
HOW AM I GONNA PROTECT A WHOLE TOWN?
YOU SAID IT YOURSELF.
"I WANT YOU TO FIGHT BESIDE ME." RIGHT?
I'LL HELP YOU OUT, AND YOU CAN GATHER MORE PEOPLE, TOO.
!
YOU ARE A "SHADOW MISTRESS," AFTER ALL.
IT WOULD BE WEIRD IF YOU FOUGHT ALONE!
AH...I THINK MY TEACHER TOLD ME THAT, TOO!
CLENCHH

A PEACHY PROMISE

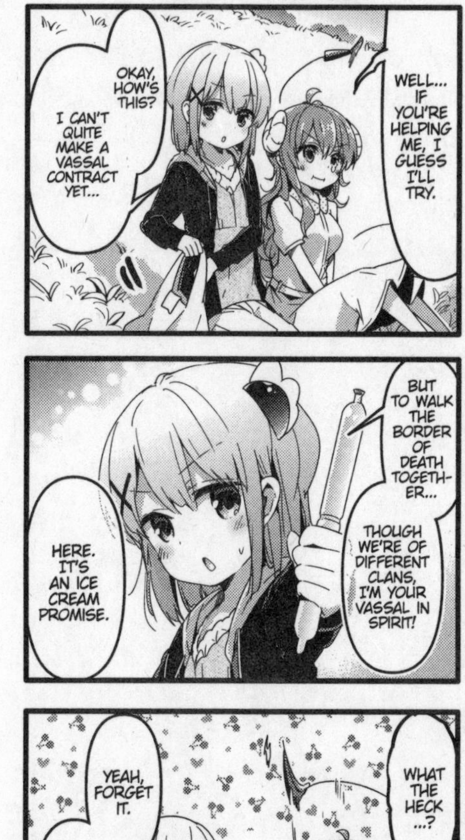
WELL... IF YOU'RE HELPING ME, I GUESS I'LL TRY.
OKAY, HOW'S THIS?
I CAN'T QUITE MAKE A VASSAL CONTRACT YET...
BUT TO WALK THE BORDER OF DEATH TOGETHER...
THOUGH WE'RE OF DIFFERENT CLANS, I'M YOUR VASSAL IN SPIRIT!
HERE. IT'S AN ICE CREAM PROMISE.
WHAT THE HECK...?
YEAH, FORGET IT.
JUST TAKE THE ICE CREAM.
NO, NO! SAY THAT AGAIN!
EAT YOUR ICE CREAM BEFORE IT MELTS ALREADY!!
DON'T GIVE UP, DEMONS! WORK HARD WITH YOUR FRIENDS AND GET STRONGER TOGETHER!!

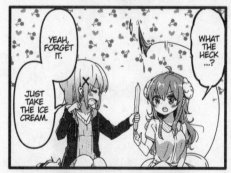

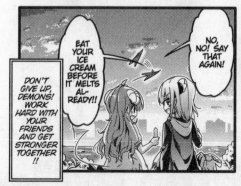

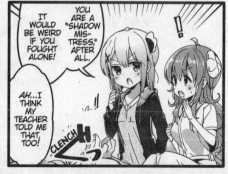

KIRARA MENU 1375

03

Seven Seas

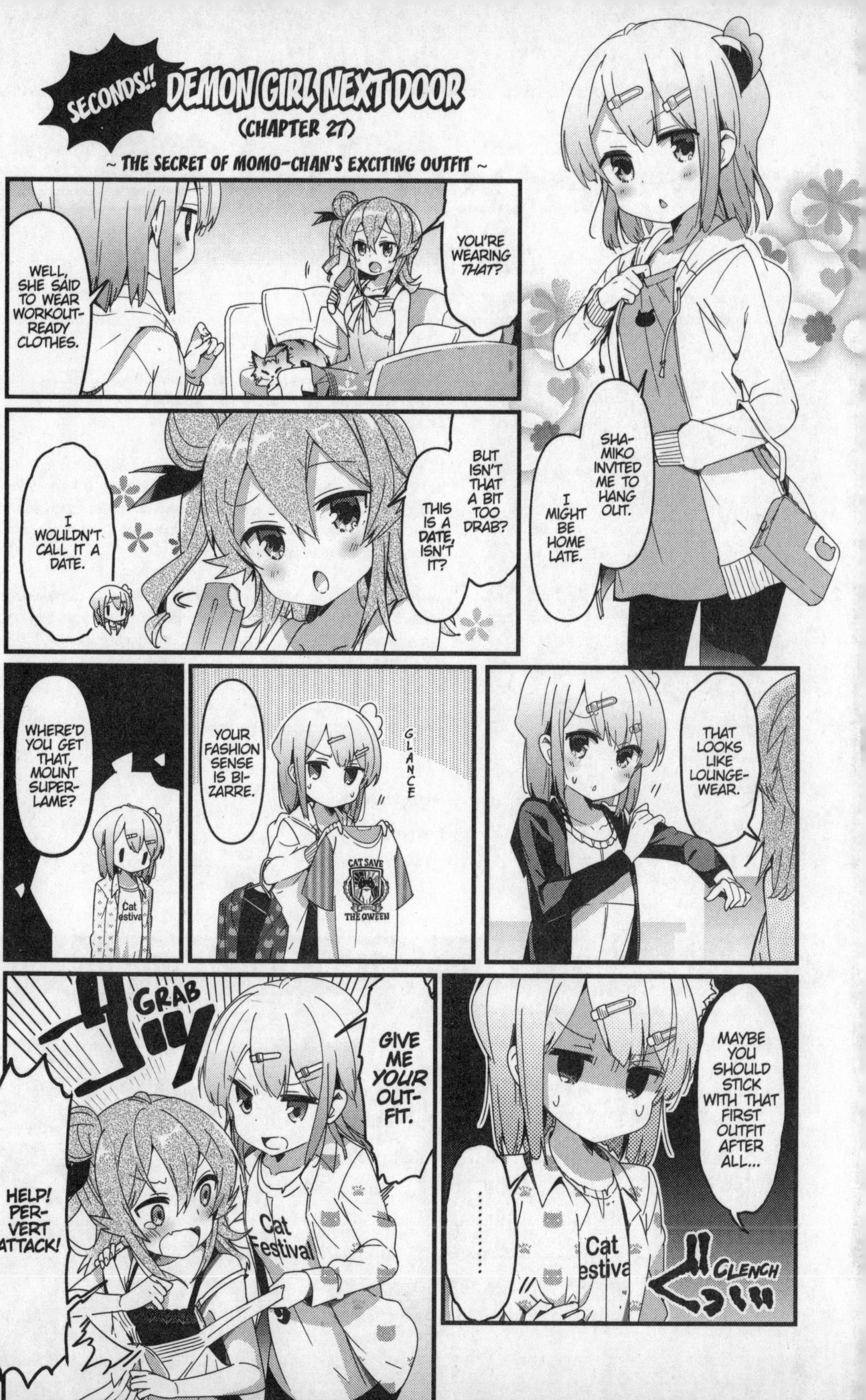
SECONDS!!
DEMON GIRL NEXT DOOR
(CHAPTER 27)
~ THE SECRET OF MOMO-CHAN'S EXCITING OUTFIT ~
SHAMIKO INVITED ME TO HANG OUT.
I MIGHT BE HOME LATE.
YOU'RE WEARING *THAT*?
WELL, SHE SAID TO WEAR WORKOUT-READY CLOTHES.
BUT ISN'T THAT A BIT TOO DRAB?
THIS IS A DATE, ISN'T IT?
I WOULDN'T CALL IT A DATE.
THAT LOOKS LIKE LOUNGE-WEAR.
GLANCE
YOUR FASHION SENSE IS BI-ZARRE.
CAT SAVE
THE QWEEN
WHERE'D YOU GET THAT, MOUNT SUPER-LAME?
MAYBE YOU SHOULD STICK WITH THAT FIRST OUTFIT AFTER ALL...
......
CLENCH
GRAB
GIVE ME *YOUR* OUT-FIT.
Cat Festival
HELP! PER-VERT ATTACK!

SEVEN SEAS ENTERTAINMENT PRESENTS

The Demon Girl Next Door

story and art by IZUMO ITO

VOLUME 3

TRANSLATION
Jenny McKeon

ADAPTATION
Kim Kindya

LETTERING AND RETOUCH
Rai Enril

COVER DESIGN
Hanase Qi

PROOFREADER
Danielle King, Dawn Davis

EDITOR
Shanti Whitesides

PREPRESS TECHNICIAN
Rhiannon Rasmussen-Silverstein

PRODUCTION MANAGER
Lissa Pattillo

MANAGING EDITOR
Julie Davis

ASSOCIATE PUBLISHER
Adam Arnold

PUBLISHER
Jason DeAngelis

Machikado Mazoku Volume 3
© IZUMO ITO 2017
Originally published in Japan in 2017 by HOUBUNSHA CO., LTD., Tokyo.
English translation rights arranged with HOUBUNSHA CO., LTD., Tokyo,
through TOHAN CORPORATION, Tokyo.

Seven Seas press and purchase enquiries can be sent to Marketing Manager
Lianne Sentar at press@gomanga.com. Information regarding the distribution
and purchase of digital editions is available from Digital Manager CK Russell
at digital@gomanga.com.

Seven Seas and the Seven Seas logo are trademarks of
Seven Seas Entertainment. All rights reserved.

ISBN: 978-1-64827-269-1

Printed in Canada

First Printing: July 2021

10 9 8 7 6 5 4 3 2 1

FOLLOW US ONLINE: www.sevenseasentertainment.com

READING DIRECTIONS

This book reads from *right to left*, Japanese style.
If this is your first time reading manga, you start
reading from the top right panel on each page and
take it from there. If you get lost, just follow the
numbered diagram here. It may seem backwards at
first, but you'll get the hang of it! Have fun!!

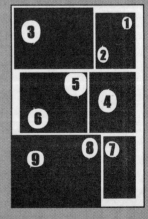